Refiguring
ENGLISH
STUDIES

Refiguring English
scholarship on Engli
fession, and a vocati
lishes historical woi
which English Studie

objects of study; investigations of the ....ips among its constituent parts as conceived in both disciplinary and institutional terms; and examinations of the role the discipline has played or should play in the larger society and public policy. In addition, the series seeks to feature studies that, by their form or focus, challenge our notions about how the written "work" of English can or should be done and to feature writings that represent the professional lives of the discipline's members in both traditional and nontraditional settings. The series also includes scholarship that considers the discipline's possible futures or that draws upon work in other disciplines to shed light on developments in English Studies.

Volumes in the Series

David B. Downing, editor, *Changing Classroom Practices: Resources for Literary and Cultural Studies* (1994)

Jed Rasula, *The American Poetry Wax Museum: Reality Effects, 1940–1990* (1995)

James A. Berlin, *Rhetorics, Poetics, and Cultures: Refiguring College English Studies* (1996)

Robin Varnum, *Fencing with Words: A History of Writing Instruction at Amherst College during the Era of Theodore Baird, 1938–1966* (1996)

Jane Maher, *Mina P. Shaughnessy: Her Life and Work* (1997)

Michael Blitz and C. Mark Hurlbert, *Letters for the Living: Teaching Writing in a Violent Age* (1998)

Bruce Horner and Min-Zhan Lu, *Representing the "Other": Basic Writers and the Teaching of Basic Writing* (1999)

Stephen M. North, with Barbara A. Chepaitis, David Coogan, Lâle Davidson, Ron MacLean, Cindy L. Parrish, Jonathan Post, and Beth Weatherby, *Refiguring the Ph.D. in English Studies: Writing, Doctoral Education, and the Fusion-Based Curriculum* (2000)

Stephen Parks, *Class Politics: The Movement for the Students' Right to Their Own Language* (2000)

Charles M. Anderson and Marian M. MacCurdy, *Writing and Healing: Toward an Informed Practice* (2000)

Persons in Process

Four Stories of Writing and Personal Development in College

ANNE J. HERRINGTON
University of Massachusetts Amherst

MARCIA CURTIS
University of Massachusetts Amherst

National Council of Teachers of English
1111 W. Kenyon Road, Urbana, Illinois 61801-1096

Manuscript and Production Editor: Thomas C. Tiller
Interior Design: Jenny Jensen Greenleaf
Cover Design: Evelyn C. Shapiro

NCTE Stock Number: 35129-3050

Library of Congress Cataloging-in-Publication Data

Herrington, Anne, 1948–
      Persons in process: four stories of writing and personal development
in college / Anne J. Herrington, Marcia Curtis.
            p. cm.—(Refiguring English studies)
      "NCTE stock number: 35129"—T.p. verso.
      Includes bibliographical references and index.
      ISBN 0-8141-3512-9
      1. English language—Rhetoric—Study and teaching—Psychological
aspects. 2. Report writing—Study and teaching (Higher)—Psychological
aspects. 3. College students—Psychology. 4. Maturation (Psychology) I.
Curtis, Marcia Smith. II. Title. III. Series.

PE1404.H45 2000
808'.042'07—dc21
                                                                    99-056816

To Nam, Steven, Rachel, and Francois, with thanks

CONTENTS

ACKNOWLEDGMENTS

We are tempted to say that, for a project that has extended over nine years, those we should acknowledge are too numerous to mention, and be done with it. While that is true, it is also too glib. So, knowing that we will inevitably neglect to name some whose contributions we would wish to name, we will attempt to put into words our thanks to many who supported us, put up with us, and contributed in very real ways to the substance of our study:

The National Council of Teachers of English Research Foundation, for a grant-in-aid that helped us launch this project in 1989.

Elizabeth Bachrach Tan, our graduate research assistant during the first year of the study, for her professionalism, levelheadedness, and patience with us as we scrambled to follow eighteen students scattered across nearly ten classes and then began trying to refocus our study.

The teachers and students who allowed us into their classrooms, participated in interviews, and shared their writing with us, for their generosity and good spirits.

The University of Massachusetts Writing Program for the lively and supportive environment created for teaching, experimentation, and the study of teaching.

The teachers and staff in the Writing Program who create that extraordinary environment and enable the teaching enterprise to move forward, and, who, for us, acted as if our study really mattered—reading and offering feedback on drafts, helping to duplicate and collect research materials, and encouraging us to keep on with the study. Those people include Christine Hoekstra, Emily Isaacs, Wendy Matys, Charles Moran, Irene Price, Sara Stelzner, and Heidi Terault. And, they include many graduate students with whom we have taught, shared ideas, and discussed problems of teaching.

In addition to these collective acknowledgments, Anne wishes to acknowledge her loving partner and toughest and best reader, Tina Plette. Marcia wishes to acknowledge Asheley Griffith for always knowing when to praise and how to critique.

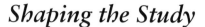

CHAPTER ONE

Shaping the Study

The choices children make every day about literacy have deeper personal and social significance than we usually imagine. For in their choices, children are defining who they are and who they are becoming.

JUDITH W. SOLSKEN, *Literacy, Gender, and Work: In Families and in School*

It may seem odd to open our study of college students with a quotation describing the literacy choices made by young children. However, in our own work with the four young people who are the focus of this book, we have found that what Judith Solsken says about children is valid as well for young adults, and perhaps for adults of all ages: they actively use writing—including the sorts of public writing often required of them in college—for the ongoing development of their personal identities, including their sense of themselves in relation to others. Through our study, we have come to understand that this is more the case than we had previously imagined. We have come to realize, too, the significant and inescapable role we teachers have in our students' ongoing self-definition.

In the chapters that follow, we relate stories of these four students—Nam, Lawrence/Steven, Rachel, and Francois—during their college years, using extensive interviews and the writing they did for their courses as the focal points for exploring their development as writers and as people, their interactions with specific teachers, and the nature of the discourses they encountered. In the concluding chapter, we discuss more fully what we learned from these students about teaching and learning as they are carried out through the writing that students are asked to do at a large university. In this introduction, we introduce key themes, tell the story of our research, and provide our own individual narratives as well as our shared narrative in order to explain the theoretical perspectives that shape our work and how we each came to the understandings we present.

Writing as a Self-Constituting, Relational Act

As Solsken describes the difficult course that student writers negotiate through their learning and growing processes, Nancy Sommers both highlights and problematizes our involvement in those processes, as she describes the equally difficult course we instructors negotiate throughout our teaching:

> Some colleagues fear that if we don't . . . teach [students] to write as scholars write, we aren't doing our job. . . . [I]t is one of those either/or propositions: either we teach students to write academic essays or we teach them to write personal essays— and then who knows what might happen? The world might become uncontrollable: Students might start writing about their grandmother's death in an essay for a sociology course. Or even worse, something more uncontrollable, they might just write essays and publish them in professional journals claiming the authority to tell stories about their families and their colleagues. The uncontrollable world of ambiguity and uncertainty opens up, my colleagues imagine, as soon as the academic embraces the personal. (30)

In setting the terms of public debate between those of us who teach students to write "academic essays" and those who admit "personal" essays into our curricula, Sommers's statement suggests the poles between which a good many of us privately navigate our own self-definition as writing instructors. For even though, like Sommers, we may decry the polarity of either/or propositions, that is, of "academic"/"personal" definitions, believing full well that the academic can embrace the personal— believing that, indeed, all writing inescapably *does* contain filters of subjectivity, whether those filtering lenses are formally and intentionally evidenced or not—it is still only a very few of us who never harbor doubts, who have managed to silence completely the authoritative voices from our own schooling that associate "process-based," "student-centered" pedagogies not only with notions of uncontrollable student chaos but also, in some dark recess of our minds, with suspicions of teacher—of our own—laxity and ineptitude. The result of this private struggle is not infrequently some measure of defensiveness in the public debate.

Sommers's comments resonate not only with current dialogues about the roles of writing teachers but also with historical discussions regarding the role of education generally. We need not be familiar with nor even particularly appreciative of Freud's entire oeuvre to hear his remarks echoed in Sommers's; here, for example, is Freud discussing education:

> The child must learn to control his instincts. It is impossible to give him liberty to carry out all his impulses without restriction. . . . Accordingly, education must inhibit, forbid and suppress, and this is abundantly seen in all periods of history. But we have learnt from analysis that precisely this suppression of instincts involves the risk of neurotic illness. . . . Thus education has to find its way between the Scylla of non-interference and the Charybdis of frustration . . . which will enable education to achieve the most and damage the least. . . . [H]itherto education has fulfilled its task very badly and has done children great damage. (613)

That we seldom think of Freud as a teacher matters little. His gift was to express, with great clarity and to lasting effect, the sentiments of our modern age, including the sentiments that have prevailed among educators for the last half century. Hence the statement central to his remarks quoted here—that "education has to find its way between the Scylla of non-interference and the Charybdis of frustration"—both reverberates with the "either/ or propositions" to which Sommers refers and underscores the inescapableness of our current debate as its terms are defined. That is, if in speaking of education's necessary "suppression of instincts" among its school children Freud implicitly justifies the Victorian repudiation of Romanticism, so do we. We do so both when, as Sommers says, we worry that our students' personal essays might erupt in an "uncontrollable world of ambiguity and uncertainty" and when we hope they do.

Such is the paradox in which process-based writing teachers find themselves, and such are the "either/or propositions" in which we are caught, whether the debate they define be public, private, or internal. The Victorian era has come and gone but with the enduring effect of having established its predecessors as "Romantics." So we are called by some whenever we choose Scylla over Charybdis, however we phrase it, whether we opt for a "student-centered classroom" of nonjudgmental peer response or otherwise leave our students writing without a teacher's repressive force; so are we called by others whenever we give students license to define for themselves, in Solsken's words, "who they are and who they are becoming" (2). Over and over we find ourselves made to take a "Romantic" position in a debate of binary oppositions, the terms of which have been defined by our "Victorian" colleagues, including the central term and subject at stake, the student "self." Viewed from either side, that "self" remains seen as a font of irrepressible drives toward self-expression to be or not to be checked by the counterforces of audience and outside authority, and by the durable defenses of academic discourse—in the case of us process-based teachers, not to be checked. But having left the polarities intact, we also leave the impression that, left to their own devices, our students would indeed write only naively "personal" pieces about family and self. Worse, we leave ourselves, as their instructors, with the single unsatisfying (and, again, often doubt-ridden) choice of withdrawing from rather than frustrating those we mean to instruct.

Our work with the students whose stories are contained in this book tells us something quite different. Though they all, in their own diverse ways, speak of the desire for "self-expression," for a voice expressive of their "selves," they are not what we might call "self-content." They do write most easily *of* personal experience, in the same way that most young writers seem more easily to compose narrative rather than analytical pieces. They do write most confidently *from* personal experience, as that seems to be where not just their principal interests but also their primary stores of knowledge, and therefore authority, lie. Nor is the personal wholly absent from even their most apparently public, academic writing: For each of these four writers, a single impulse born of personal experience seems to motivate writing done for the most apparently distant and disparate assignments. In looking down through the drafts of a single essay or across each student's full oeuvre and in listening to their reflections on the composing process, we discovered that deeply private impulse, often articulated in their "personal essays," suspended like the tenor of some obscure metaphor beneath the academic: beneath, for instance, Nam's writings for his Psychology Methods course, his sense of alienation as a Vietnamese speaker in an English-speaking world and as a devout Catholic in an adamantly humanist culture, or, for another example, beneath Lawrence's analysis of the biblical book of Job, his sometimes suicidal and sometimes death-defying will to construct a viable gay self through writing and therefore in ongoing relation to a volatile, essentially untrustworthy audience and world.

But if the personal is seldom absent from their public writing, neither is a more public concern ever truly absent from their most private composing. All four students speak of the wish, the tendency, to write from personal experience toward something more public, toward essays addressed to an audience capable of understanding and for a kindred group capable of identifying with them. Nor are these young writers—even "basic" writers—so naively "self expressive" as student writers are often assumed to be. A desire, need, or, in Francois's terms, "struggle" to make themselves understood in their writing and, quite literally, to remake themselves through the understanding achieved—to communicate and, through that act of communicating, to construct coherent selves acceptable to others—links the four individual themes. That variously phrased wish to compose a coherent, intelligible self intimates to us a discomfiting awareness these students share with deconstructionists and poststructuralists alike: a perhaps not quite articulated, yet no less real, knowledge that in the absence of any intrinsic, fully formed "self" ready to be communicated, writing becomes less a self-expressive performance than a self-constituting, relational act. Meeting their wish implies for us, in our relationship to them as teachers and as readers, a different role that is neither Scylla nor Charybdis.

Our Story of the Research: Methods, Encounters, and Evolving Perspectives

Like most research projects, this one is as much a story of the "researchers"—Anne Herrington and Marcia Curtis—as it is a story of our "subjects"—Nam, Lawrence, Rachel, and Francois. And so we begin with a brief history of our work together at the University of Massachusetts.

The collaboration that led to this project began in 1988. That year, Anne received a Lilly Fellowship—a University teaching fellowship sponsored by the Lilly Foundation—that gave her two courses of release time for the 1988–89 school year to study some topic related to her teaching. At the time, Anne's teaching responsibilities included teaching in our College Writing program and supervising ten graduate instructors of College Writing. Marcia was then assistant director of the Writing Program and director of its prerequirement Basic Writing component, serving some eight percent of the entering first-year class, many of them from nonmainstream social and academic backgrounds, and all of whom were required to take an extra semester of writing as a result of their performance on the Writing Program Placement Test. She was also supervising graduate instructors of Basic Writing and teaching one class each semester herself. Given our shared sense that the Basic Writing curriculum needed to be revised, as well as our shared interest in that project, we agreed Anne would use her teaching fellowship to join with Marcia to that end. We worked during the summer months to revise the course curriculum, influenced in large part by David Bartholomae and Anthony Petrosky's *Facts, Artifacts, and Counterfacts*. During fall semester, Anne sat in on Marcia's class and observed its implementation; during spring semester, Anne taught a section of Basic Writing as well. From this project grew our interest in understanding more about the writing experiences of Basic Writing students when they went on to other courses, including College Writing. In learning more about their experiences, we hoped as well to learn more about our curricula, for both Basic Writing and College Writing. To that end, we applied for and received a grant from the National Council of Teachers of English for the 1989–90 school year. The product of that second, extended study, begun nearly a decade ago, you are about to read here.

While our initial interest in the experiences of basic writers persisted throughout our years of work on the project, our ways of conceptualizing the study and our particular focus changed as we changed and learned from the students participating in the study. Perhaps it was fortunate that our lives as teachers and administrators kept us from finishing the study as soon as—and in the way that—we first anticipated. Time, which always seemed against us because it was in too-short supply, also worked for us in that it both forced and allowed us to stay longer with the four students we write about here, learning more from them as we followed their experiences in various settings in the University, watched their growth and personal self-definition, read their writings, and talked with them throughout it all.

Initial Phase and Changes in Direction

We did not begin with the intention of studying a small number of students over time or studying their self-composition. Our initial focus is evident in the questions we posed in the proposal submitted to the National Council of Teachers of English to request funding for our project. Interested in learning from the students themselves, we intended these questions to give us entry into their experiences and perspectives:

1. What is entailed for basic writers in learning to write in college? What type of writing is asked of them?

2. What is the nature of this discourse as perceived by basic writers and demonstrated in their writing? How do they perceive themselves as writers and learners? How do these perceptions compare to those of students who were not judged to be "basic writers" when they entered the University?

3. How are individuals in both groups and their writing perceived by their writing instructors and other instructors?

4. How do the basic writers change in their writing and in their perceptions of themselves as writers during their initial three semesters at the University?

Our aim was to learn more about the experiences and writing of students placed into basic writing by studying a number of them in relation to a number of students who, on entering the University, were judged as not needing basic writing. To that end, during the first year, we surveyed a large number of students in both groups (a total of 1630 students)[1] and followed closely a case study group of nine basic writing students and nine nonbasic writing students. During the first year, the research team included Marcia, Anne, and Elizabeth Bachrach Tan, a doctoral student in English who was serving as our research assistant.

We began in the fall by focusing on Marcia's section of Basic Writing. On the first day of class, Anne and Elizabeth were introduced, and Anne explained the study and asked for volunteers, stressing that the aim was "to learn how teachers can teach better and make writing experiences more positive for students." She asked for volunteers, saying, "You need not perceive yourself as a good writer to volunteer; you need only to be willing to help and talk about your experiences writing." And she stressed that participation in the study was not at all tied to performance in the class: that she and Elizabeth would not be talking with Marcia about what was said in interviews until long after the course had ended. Here are Anne's notes on how she concluded:

> What's in it for you? Not a lot.
> —$5.00 per interview—a small token to recognize the time you'll give us
> —a chance to reflect on your writing
> —knowing that you're contributing to a study that aims to help others.

Essentially, we were asking students to be "expert witnesses": to help us understand how they experienced our instruction and what they were trying to do as writers. Also, given the way we presented the reward for them, it was clear that we planned little by way of external compensation for those who volunteered. We say that to stress our belief that those who volunteered did so more out of internal than external motivations—to have some attention paid to their writing and their experiences, and to have a chance to help others by having their views passed on.

All nine volunteers passed Basic Writing and during second semester entered sections of College Writing, with each student enrolling in a different section. Among the original nine, Nam elected to take a section taught on computers, Lawrence enrolled in the section Anne was teaching, and Francois chose a section offered in his residence hall. In each section, we asked for an additional volunteer, someone who had entered College Writing directly without taking Basic Writing. Rachel was one of these students—although not from a section that Nam, Lawrence, or Francois was in.

During this first year, we collected information from various sources: interviews with students, two per semester; interviews with the teachers of their writing classes, two per semester; single interviews with teachers of a few of the students' other classes; observations of the writing classes students were in; documents from these classes; all of the students' essays for their writing classes—with drafts and any preliminary notes and written peer reviews—and any writings from their other classes the students gave us. All eighteen students signed releases allowing us to use their writings and interviews for our project.

During the first semester, when we focused on Marcia's Basic Writing class, Elizabeth and Anne did all of the classroom observations, sitting in on nearly all class sessions, and conducted all of the interviews, with Anne interviewing Nam and Lawrence twice and Elizabeth interviewing Francois and Marcia twice. During the second semester, the three of us divided the responsibility for following the original nine students plus the additional nine who volunteered from the sections of College Writing. We interviewed all eighteen students and their teachers twice, and observed classes for two three-day periods (one early and one toward the middle of the semester) for a total of six observations.

We did not plan to follow these students' experiences any further than their first year. Indeed, from following the nine students for two semesters and the other nine for one semester—covering ten writing classes—we felt we had more than enough information to work from and more than enough of a challenge to determine how to proceed. During that first summer, we began organizing the information as we also attended to our usual summer administrative responsibilities. We—Elizabeth included—were looking to identify categories that we could use to analyze and interpret the experiences of each student in ways that would allow us to generalize about connections and differences among them: their prior experiences as writers, their experiences in their writing classes at the University, their perceptions of themselves as writers, and their writing and its change over time. We were hoping to use these categories to code the interviews in such a way that we could use a commercial research software program to help us sort through all the interviews. To that end, we began reading through our folders of interviews with and writings by a few specific students, focusing initially on a handful of them, trying to describe what we found and, as we talked together, to identify categories.

Time pressure crystallized our focus on that first selection of students even as it pushed us forward in our research. With a new school year beginning, our assistant Elizabeth was engaged in other projects for her doctoral studies and no longer available to work on ours; the two of us each had teaching and administrative responsibilities. The only way that we were able to keep working on the study was by proposing conference papers that served to set deadlines for each bit of interpretive work to be accomplished. Essentially, the conference papers kept us working through our individual student folders, shaping and testing our interpretive view. When in the fall of 1991 we were invited to do a presentation of our research project at the June 1992 Association of Departments of English (ADE) Conference in Waterloo, Ontario, we selected three of the four students you will read about here. We used the presentation as an occasion to focus more intensively on Nam, Lawrence, and Rachel, choosing them because they interested us and were quite different from one another, and because Anne had learned, quite by happenstance, that Rachel and Nam had taken the same Psychology Methods course. Having recently presented a conference paper using Nam's experiences in that course, Anne found the intersection of his and Rachel's experiences potentially intriguing. Marcia chose to present a brief sketch of the portrait of Lawrence elaborated here, believing his nascent awareness of the possibility of "re-storying" himself through writing would interest ADE members.

Marcia's predictions proved right—and wrong. In the question-and-answer period following our presentations, group members, almost to the one, riveted their attention on Lawrence and, with unabashed hostility, attacked his effort to compose himself as a publicly gay person in his writings. Some termed it "expressivism" and "naive Romanticism"; others, the sort of "confessionalism" that results from "watching too much Oprah." The words they spoke effectively reenacted Sommers's warning. Though by and large the language of academic theory, its intensity signaled, to us at any rate, something akin to the more deeply private fear of an "uncontrollable world of ambiguity" Sommers describes as opening up when, quite literally, the academic meets the personal.

En route home from what we came to call "our Waterloo," we talked about the ways in which our audience's preoccupation with Lawrence not only demeaned his efforts but, by ignoring Rachel (a woman) and Nam (a second-language English speaker), silenced them both beneath the weight of so much theory. And we asked each other, in our own fumbling words, the question so many writers, especially women writers, find themselves asking: as Nancy Hartsock, for one, phrased it, "Why is it that just at the moment when so many of us who have been silenced begin to demand the right to name ourselves, to act as subjects rather than objects of history, that just then the concept of subjecthood becomes problematic?" (163). We did not have an answer, but we did have new resolve to pursue the telling of Nam's, Lawrence's, and Rachel's stories and make them the center of this book. To these three, we later added a fourth, the story of Francois, who faithfully maintained an interest in our project and a desire to be included in its publication, yet who also remained, throughout the years of our study, in large measure elusive, and perhaps determinedly so. By then, we had implicitly given up trying or wanting to write about all eighteen students. We had stumbled—or been pushed—instead into what could be called a "longitudinal" study of four students, though perhaps not the kind of purposive longitudinal study done by Marilyn

Sternglass in *A Time to Know Them* or by Richard Haswell in *Gaining Ground in College*.

Later Phase

Even in the first phases of our research, sorting through students' folders for ways to categorize them and their experiences, we found that aside from the most general terms—e.g., prior experience, perceived purpose for writing—we could not distinguish categories that were useful without being overwhelming. More important, differentiating categories for sorting was leading us toward a kind of atomistic analytic approach that failed to capture the meaning of a given statement for a particular student because it took it out of the context of that student's experiences and perceptions. Generalizing to groups, we were losing what seemed most significant about how each individual was using writing. As Shane Phelan argues in reference to classification based on race, class, gender, and sexual orientation, to understand social identities in other than totalizing ways we need to get specific, "both to specify, through categorical reference, our location in various systems of power, and to insist that there is more to us than the categories, that we have an integrity that cannot be captured in those terms. . . . Specificity demands the simultaneous exploration of categories of social marks and orders and attention to the unique or the individual" (8). And the more we attended individually to Nam, Lawrence, Rachel, and Francois, the more we found that Phelan's skepticism regarding social categories applied to our own initial grouping of basic and nonbasic writers and to distinctions among discourse communities generally.

Certainly the social and linguistic marks these students each carried with them were, to varying degrees, palpable and distinct: Nam, a Vietnamese speaker who immigrated to the United States at age eight; Lawrence, a native-born English speaker, white, male, and quite apparently gay; Rachel, a woman of Anglo-Irish descent, a native English speaker, and from a working-class community; and Francois, a black male who immigrated to the United States at an unspecified age, and a second-language English speaker (though fluent in spoken English). And just as certainly, commonalities among Nam's, Lawrence's, and Francois's writing performances—which no doubt would have marked them as "basic writers" in most any academic situation—distinguished them from the nonbasic writer Rachel. But the evident cultural, linguistic, and academic distinctions among them were transcended by similarities in the ways all four students regarded writing and themselves as writers, the ways in which they came to claim writing for themselves even as it was required of them by others, and, above all else, the ways in which they saw themselves using writing at once for participation in the University world (i.e., as a mediator between self and others) and for self-reflection and self-fashioning (i.e., as a mediator between self and other selves). Thus the more alike they became for us, the more each emerged as unique.

When we began following the students' work, all four of them were first-year students, and, as a result, they were all persons in transition—and their private as well as shared struggles to find some stability as they moved from past circumstances to University contexts were also clear in their essays and conversations. Writing was part of each individual's personal struggle, and each individual's struggle with writing was part of that larger effort to find a comfortable place in this new, often discomforting world. At a time of change, they were all developing new writing skills as they were recomposing themselves as human beings in response to other human beings, and, according to their testimony and the content of their papers, what they experienced as student writers had much less to do with any particular sequence of writing tasks or teaching methods than with how they felt they were expressing themselves and being responded to as people. Writing was not a purely academic matter for any of the four.

This is not to say they were careless of their performance as writers, of the formal aspects of writing, or of the forms their writing took. All four cared about writing, worried about writing, and attributed to writing an almost anthropomorphized power to expose them to shame: "my essay was alone," my writing "had trouble displaying its purpose," my paper "came out dissatisfied." Nam worried that at the University he would be identified and excluded by others on linguistic grounds: "If I write, I'm going to mess up." He also characterized himself as "stupid in English, but intelligence in native language." Lawrence, who "hated" to write as a high school student, said in an interview, "I still have a lot of shame about who I am when I write." Though admitted directly into College Writing, Rachel indicated that, despite the positive reception her writing enjoyed among teachers, she "almost never" felt it was as good as other students' writing and "often" believed it fell short of the standard: she could recall just one essay she'd "been happy writing" in high school. And Francois, who of the three young men most adamantly resisted identification as a basic writer, yet whose writings perhaps most clearly identified him as such, worried that, if he gave free rein to his writing, he would be taken as "crazy."

The four also saw, however, even in its failure, language's potential to reveal them to themselves. Francois, for instance, recalled his confusion after moving to the United States (from an unnamed country of origin, perhaps in the Caribbean) and its English-language culture in childhood; not only did others misunderstand him, but "sometimes I could not even understand myself." Similarly Nam, feeling constrained by his limited grasp of both Vietnamese and English, expressed how essential language is to self-understanding: "Emotion cannot be truly understood if there is no language to express it." Similarly, Lawrence, commenting specifically about written language, observed that sometimes he did not realize what he was thinking or feeling until he wrote. And Rachel returned often, in various essays for various courses, to the related topics of adult alcoholism and child abuse in order to understand, through writing, her own family history and, by reflecting on it, to move beyond her high school identity as an abused, self-contemptuous adolescent.

Listening closely to these four young people, we began to sense that it was indeed the very real personal importance writing held for them that occasioned moments of what we might before have identified as simple *resistance*, especially to the sorts of depersonalized "academic" writing that some courses required. Throughout Basic and College Writing, Nam, for instance, used writing to work out private decisions about behavior and about religion: how to acquire self-discipline, for example, and whether to withdraw from secular life to the more meditative setting of a seminary. He also, however, valued writing's ability to link him to other human beings and recalled in particular an instance of praise and recognition that Marcia had given one of his essays because it "meant people got what I was trying to say." Simultaneously freed and bewildered by the encouragement he received from her to move beyond the bounds of the five-paragraph essay learned in high school—an essay structure particularly suited to the sorts of homiletic pieces he customarily read and wrote—he attended Anne's composition class during the spring semester and read various books on writing, including Peter Elbow's *Writing Without Teachers*, in an effort to discover new forms to replace the old, and to move beyond what seem to have been for him the comforting limitations supplied by the old forms' structures. Yet he quite consciously disengaged himself from his Psychology Methods course where, in his estimation, form was all—and therefore empty. And while Lawrence, as you will see, presented an apparently willful determination to compose all personal, self-revelatory essays, we learned in our interviews with him that what might have seemed on the surface mere willfulness was, in truth, an almost obsessive need literally to contain and compose himself by writing, a need at times worrisome to him as well. So, too, for Francois, who seemed of the four most "resistant" to formal instruction, only to reveal in talking with us that his "resistance" was born not only of real confusion but also of an equally real fear that in taking on the style required by others he might lose himself. Even Rachel, who adapted to the impersonal academic mode so readily that she appeared almost to take refuge in it, expressed in her own way similar concerns about ultimately developing a style that would not be "cold writing" but would reflect "who I am as a person."

Reading the four students' early essays brought challenges to old definitions as well. In particular, their use of various forms challenged any easy delineations we might have made between "academic" and "personal" writing. An example is Nam's essay "The Lord is My Shepherd," written for College Writing and based on his reading of Thomas à Kempis's *The Imitation of Christ*. Like so many of Nam's essays, this one may have been a deeply personal and highly personalized exploration of how he might become a better Christian, but it also fell squarely within a long tradition of meditative essays by Catholic scholars and thinkers, in whose shadows Nam intended to walk. Similarly, the final draft of Rachel's research paper on child abuse, her "documented essay" for College Writing, may have marshaled material from a variety of professional psychology journals to analyze the case study of an abused acquaintance. But in her first draft, the "case study" was not of an acquaintance but of Rachel herself, suggesting that the more objective, less personalized research paper was also a private, self-referential exploration. Her substitutive, metaphoric use of an acquaintance indeed suggested a purposeful technique not altogether different from one Lawrence employed in "Breaking Traditions." Unlike Rachel's "The Psychological Effects of Child Abuse," Lawrence's piece could only be called a "personal essay." Yet, seen in its full context of drafts as well as companion essays, "Breaking Traditions" appears a mirror image of Rachel's documented essay, as in it Lawrence, much in the same way Rachel used her acquaintance's childhood abuse, used his own "coming out" as a vegetarian as both a means and a pretext for widening his discussion to encompass the public health and ethical benefits of vegetarianism—and simultaneously, as we knew and he acknowledged, as a metaphor for his own more profound coming out as gay.

In that first year of our study, Nam, Lawrence, Rachel, and Francois—as writers and as people, as a group and individually—met their various writing tasks with varying degrees of comfort as well as success. And the tasks required of them were various indeed. They faced assignments in courses outside their writing courses that ran the gamut from strictly "academic" to highly "personal": critiques and reports demanding that, in adherence to traditional "academic discourse" conventions, they avoid first-person references, directly stated opinions, and overt connections to individual experiences altogether (for courses in psychology, sociology, and comparative literature); research analyses requiring that they situate themselves explicitly in relation to their subject (for courses in anthropology and education); and unabashedly personalized essays asking that they make themselves the explicit subject of reflection (again for courses in education and comparative literature). Time and again, we were struck by the contrasting and sometimes conflicting demands that these four first-year students were called upon to negotiate (and by the truly slippery nature of "academic" writing, if it is to be defined by what is actually written in today's academy).

Yet as tricky as the route through his or her courses was for each of them to navigate, equally tricky was the use to which each student put the writing that he or she was required to do. In their own ways, each seemed intent upon making her- or himself the "subject" of the composing processes in the full sense of the word. However "personal" or subjective their essays may have seemed, each sought a sense of agency through the writing, a sense of both speaking for and speaking to others whose thinking, if not behavior, they might in some way affect. And they used what they knew best, as any of us would, to demonstrate their truths—in the case of these entering first-year students, the experiences they brought with them from home. But they all sought as well to make themselves subjects of change through writing, choosing and sometimes creating new ways to present themselves to others, new ways to represent themselves in the presence of others, new ways to be in the future without losing the thread of who they were and had been. In short, each expressed through writing, and at times articulated in an interview, an impulse to act upon the world even while being formed by it. They were, indeed, not just writers but persons in process.

As we followed Nam, Lawrence, Rachel, and Francois closely throughout their singular and collective struggles during that first transitional year, one truth emerged as clear: Their experiences along with our experiences of them exceeded our own preliminary expectations and previously established categories, including the polarities of basic/nonbasic writers as well as personal/academic writing within the larger academic setting. Therefore, we chose to alter the set of questions originally guiding our study. Though we would continue to address characteristics that led these four students to be identified as basic or not, we would neither compare them according to these categories nor, by comparing them, risk constructing them within the framework these categories established. We would focus our research and its interpretation on two broader, more encompassing and, we hoped, more revealing questions:

- ◆ How are these students developing as writers and people? Specifically, how are they using writing and what are their projects as writers?

- ◆ What specific kinds of writing are they asked to do by instructors across the curriculum, and what sorts of relationships between student-writer and teacher-reader are established within and through the writing process?

We further determined that in order to be true to our originally stated aim of learning from the students "how teachers can teach better and make writing experiences more positive for students," we would have to continue studying them—studying with and learning from them—not only through their first year but through their entire time at the University. Nam left the University at the end of his first year to enter a seminary in California, but with Lawrence, Rachel, and Francois we did just that, continuing to amass essays written both inside and outside their majors, interviewing each student annually, and speaking with their instructors when we could. We would also have to let Nam, Lawrence, Rachel, and Francois each step forward as the "expert witnesses" we had originally promised they would be. By devoting a chapter to each of these four persons and by allowing each one, through extensive interview as well as essay transcriptions, to speak directly to you, we hope we have kept that pledge.

Composing the Narrative—and Its Composers

We two narrators are not altogether unlike the four students we present to you here: we know that even as we try to let them show themselves, as well as us and their other teachers, through their particular lenses, we also show them through particular lenses of our own. They are not "Nam," "Lawrence," "Rachel," and "Francois"; each has another, "real" name—or, in "Lawrence's" case, as you will see, another set of given and self-claimed names. "Nam," "Lawrence," "Rachel," and "Francois" are pseudonyms, protecting the students along with their families and teachers— and no doubt us, too—from exposure but also highlighting the inescapable fact that the images you receive of them will bear our own idiosyncratic tints and colorations. As Judith Solsken writes of the learning biographies she composed from her extensive study of children's literacy acquisition, so too for the stories we have composed of Nam, Lawrence, Rachel, and Francois: they "are more like an artist's sketches than a photographer's snapshots; they represent the vision of particular adults who had particular relationships with the [students] (and with each other) under particular circumstances" (222).

As the particular adults who composed these stories, we believe our interests and histories as people and as teachers of writing, more than anything else, have motivated us throughout our study, from its original design through composing the interpretive stories that follow. And in composing this section, we discussed what aspects of our identities and histories we should make known to you to help you understand how we have approached this study and these four students. That we are both Anglo-American Protestants, of middle-class families, and lesbians certainly contributes to the interpretations we share of the world and of our own as well as others' positions in it. Our color, class, religions, and families marked us for the "mainstream." At the same time, each of us in our own ways experienced disjunctions with the predominately male, heterosexual world in which we grew up. These awarenesses of both disjunction and relative advantage influence how we understand our students. As teachers, we each developed, over time, a particular interest in students who, for reasons of class or race or other factors, are not "schooled" to succeed in college and are treated as "other" by many students and faculty. Between us, by choice, we have devoted significant parts of our careers to teaching and developing curricula for writing courses, including courses identified as "developmental" or "basic": Marcia for fifteen years at the University of Massachusetts at Amherst, working consistently with basic writing; Anne, having a more checkered career, including eight years teaching in a developmental writing and reading program at Johnson State College in Johnson, Vermont, and ten years at the University of Massachusetts. We both have an interest in the expectations and purposes students encounter for writing in all their courses in various disciplines. As teachers, we believe in the validity of and seek to understand students' perspectives on their writing experiences in order to learn more about our own work with them, about the nature of the academic world, and about the discourses students navigate.

We are thus alike in many ways—physically, philosophically, and professionally—enough ways that students and colleagues occasionally mistake one of us for the other. Still, these identifiers of our apparent similarities—like the classification identifiers of which Phelan writes—do not account for our distinct ways of seeing and speaking. Anne tends to foreground context—viewing the actions of individuals as situated in and influenced by social and discursive forces. Marcia tends to foreground each person's inner life—viewing their texts and interactions with others in relation to their psychological life. We began this study less aware of our differences than we are now. But as it was in our work with the four students, so it was in our work together: the more closely we listened to each other, the more our differences emerged—only to blend again as complements rather than contradictions.

We have tried to leave sufficient tracings throughout this introduction for you to perceive both our shared and our distinct interpretive standpoints and our positions in relation to each student. The distinctions will become more apparent, we believe, as you read the following chapters, since the two on Nam and Rachel have been composed by Anne, and those on Lawrence and Francois by Marcia. These chapters are distinct not only in stylistic ways but also in what we foreground in the interpretations we shape and in the ways we have been trained (in theory and in practice) to shape those interpretations. In order not to impede the students' four narratives, we have consciously left most theoretical references out of our chapters, choosing instead to outline briefly here, each in her own voice, some of the influences—the other voices—behind our teaching and our descriptions of our students' learning.

Marcia's Narrative

Both Lawrence and Francois were members of my Basic Writing class in the fall of 1989, and so, as their teacher, I am very much a part of each young man's classroom experience and of the narrative I have composed about their experiences. No doubt my presence in Lawrence's and Francois's stories is equally a result of my own style and inclinations, too. Though I have been teaching basic writing for the past fifteen years, my original training was not in composition studies but in literary criticism, with special emphasis on contemporary critical theory and, aptly or ironically, British Romanticism. My doctoral dissertation on the poetry and letters of John Keats drew heavily upon the work of Margaret Mahler and other object relations psychologists of the time. Since completing my degree work in the late 1970s, I have maintained an interest in the field, attending local and national psychoanalytic conferences, lectures, and seminars; participating in psychoanalytic supervision groups; and taking occasional courses at our neighboring Smith College School of Social Work.

I began teaching basic writing quite by happenstance—and, as I see now, quite unprepared. Having finished a three-hundred-page thesis on Keats, I doubted I had another word in me to say about him and could hardly imagine a lifetime ahead trying to discover one. Moreover, job opportunities in the field were slim at the time, and, like many others who come to the Pioneer Valley for school and develop deep ties here, I preferred to find work locally rather than seek a faculty post wherever it might take me. Happily, I was hired on as a teacher and administrator by what was then the University of Massachusetts Freshman Rhetoric Program, just as it was being dissolved and replaced by the current Writing Program with its new and directorless Basic Writing component. With little more preparation than a few semesters of teaching The Rhetoric of the Social Sciences as a largely untrained lecturer, along with some previous experience as a graduate student teaching literature, I volunteered for the task.

A "student-centered" curriculum and "process-based" method provided the foundation of the evolving Freshman Writing Program, and while today its approach might be called "untheorized," its emphases on writing from personal experience and on drafting offered real practical help. Developing topics out of their own interests and knowledge bases gave students a sense of ownership over their own composing processes and, with that, a feeling of authorship as well; revising relieved them of the anxiety of "getting it right" the first time as early drafts afforded them private places out of which to construct more public—and publicly acceptable—forms; and student-centered classes removed, or at least lightened, the strictures of "teacher authority" and provided the wider, often more receptive audience of peers. But for all the virtues of the process approach, there remained a singular fault, or, more accurately, default: it left any positive teacher role undefined. I was to retreat from the center of my classroom, but to where? I was to abdicate authority to the students, but what was my responsibility to them? Many of them still perceived me not only as the authority in the classroom but also as the authority on exactly the sorts of writing matters they wanted to learn. I was the one who knew what they wanted to know. My retreat frustrated some students and made others more anxious than they already had been. I often found myself frustrated and anxious, too. The drafting process opened a space for learning and teaching to take place: for the students to learn about their subject and their own conscious relationship to it, and for me to teach them ways to communicate that relationship to others. But how was I to enter? In the strictly student-centered classroom of those early days, a colleague and I often joked that, after a seemingly endless line of nondirective questioning and subtle prodding, when we and our students had reached the end of our mutual tethers, we would finally point at their essays and say, "Do this and this and this!"

Despite our joking, I remained uneasy, and, despite their evident desire for more pointed instruction, my students were frequently unsettled when they got it. I have never believed that even so sensitive a writer as Keats could be killed, as Lord Byron claimed, by a harsh review; nonetheless, like most writing teachers, I occasionally discovered myself, to my surprise, embroiled in struggles with students whose rage or reticence suggested they had been deeply wounded by what seemed to me only the slightest, most reasonable critique of their writing—even the hint that their meaning or its phrasing was unclear. Talking with other teachers about such "resistant" students, along with reading in composition and teaching journals about ways to help them—insist that they—recognize their audience's needs along with their own responsibility to make themselves more easily understood, seemed only to separate me further from them: They were the students, and I was the teacher; they were the writers, and I was their audience; their job was to communicate, mine to indicate where they succeeded and often where they failed; they were resistant, and I was reasonable; they were sometimes rageful, and I was now as frustrated by my action as by my inaction.

The old, traditional notions of the student-teacher relationship that were still in the air, and in my own consciousness, clearly proved an inappropriate substitute for the amorphous model that "student-centered" teaching provided me. My students were not writing out of any willful solipsism: they were struggling to build their own bridges between private thought and public expression, between their own concrete experiences and the shared world of abstract issues. And they were in little need of a more corrective audience to compel greater clarity and coherence, a sturdy "academic" style. Most of the students, in fact, wrote under overwhelming, even silencing, pressure from an audience they perceived all too acutely to be not just "corrective" but potentially punishing: teachers who judged them "deficient"; English-speakers who judged them "stupid"; the Anglo, middle-class majority who judged them "inarticulate" and whose accepted language system misrepresented and denigrated their experience; and a whole host of figures from the adult world, even family members, who had implied by action or word that they were not worth listening to. As I continued to read their papers and hear them describe their efforts at writing, what seemed to me to distinguish these "basic writers" from more effective writers was not the presence or absence of an intended audience but the character of the audience intended, and the effect it had on them as they wrote. And what they needed, perhaps what all of us need, seemed to be not a "corrective" audience but a receptive and therefore "constructive" audience that they could imaginatively carry with them long after their writing course had ended. According to that need I perceived in my students, I determined to design my role as their teacher.

Over the succeeding years, as I became more immersed in my work with basic writers and in reading the literature on basic writing and composition generally, I found the various strands of my life intertwining in strange, sometimes confounding ways. By the mid and late 1980s, strains of the French post-Freudian

Jacques Lacan and the social historian Michel Foucault, along with echoes of bygone poststructuralist deconstructionists and intimations of social constructivists to follow, were being sounded in various psychoanalytic conferences, lectures, and articles. These same formulations that had gripped graduate studies in critical theory when I was a graduate student in the mid 1970s were beginning simultaneously to take hold of composition theory and to set the base for a series of now "postmodern" theories to come: the derivatives of Foucault, social constructivism, cultural studies, and critical pedagogy. What struck me as most interesting, however, was the split these theories effected between the professional psychologists, whose work was with people, and the psychoanalytic academics, whose work was with theory. Moreover, the rift I witnessed then between psychoanalytic practitioners and theorists was nearly identical to what Kurt Spellmeyer recently identified as "the real split in our profession . . . not between practice and theory *per se*, but between two different versions of professional authority" ("Out of the Fashion Industry" 427), that is, between the experience-based knowledge of writing teachers and the text-based authority of composition theorists. The psychoanalytic theorists seemed not just to describe but insistently to prescribe ways of being in the world that the practicing therapists sought daily to help their clients overcome: ways that took the form and feeling of desperate fragmentation, isolation, alienation, helplessness, and anger. And those therapists' arguments, with only the slightest changes in terminology, might have been summarized again by Spellmeyer when he elsewhere asked of cultural studies and other "post-theory" theorists whether, "at a moment in our history when many observers have commented on the accelerating breakdown of communities and the spreading mood of cynicism . . . , learning as we now imagine it helps to strengthen our students' sense of agency and self-worth while replenishing the fragile sources of compassion and mutual aid. Or have our 'projects' actually served to discredit local ways of life on behalf of the knowledge society?" ("After Theory" 904).

Despite my own penchant for theory, my own private need to find some larger thought system in which to locate myself generally and my identity as a teacher specifically, I stood then with the professional psychologists, as I would stand with

Spellmeyer now, on the other side of a widening divide from most theorists. This is not to say I saw myself as my students' therapist. A client's way of "being in the world" is the psychotherapist's domain; a student's way of "being in writing" is mine. Yet teachers and therapists alike are both educators as well as interpreters of sorts, and the separate contexts in which we work seemed to me parallel, if not entwined. In the essays of basic writers with whom I worked, I often saw expressed—either implicitly through form or explicitly through content—much of the same fragmentation, isolation, alienation, helplessness, and anger that therapists reported their clients were bringing with them to their sessions. Like Nam, Lawrence, Rachel, and Francois, many other students wrote of the dispiriting or enraging alienation brought by racism and homophobia, the profound helplessness enforced by adult assault and childhood abuse; they spoke of isolation and fear that their ideas, not "good enough" or well-expressed enough, would be dismissed or misunderstood; and the same halting diffidence came through in their writing as a lack of structural coherence, truncated development, fragmented sentences, sheer brevity or plain silence altogether. And as the therapists I listened to at various conferences and meetings were seeking ways to be with their clients in therapy in order to help those clients be in turn less fragmented, more whole and resourceful in the world, I was searching for ways to be with my students in their learning that would help them exhibit greater coherence, agency, and understanding both of and for their subjects in their written expressions.

The array of composition theories then just beginning to challenge process-based teaching seemed particularly inappropriate to my needs and the needs of my students. Straddling cultures and classes, speaking a variety of languages and grappling with their various discourse demands, struggling to locate themselves among often-conflicting familial, social, and academic worlds, these young people were intensely aware of the contingency of their own identities and hardly needed their sense of "self" challenged by me. Theirs were already the very same alternate stories Foucault himself claimed should be told—the "buried" truths to be unearthed, the "local" knowledges to be resurrected, not "interrogated" and replaced by my own. More to the point, sitting beside them in our computer classroom as they labored to compose, revise, and edit, I felt increasing responsibility for the intimate, inescapable connection inevitably occurring between us. It was a humbling experience for me, and I had no desire to take a position as elitist and, it seemed to me, fundamentally vicious as many of the new theorists proposed.

Then, in the summer of 1990, as a break from my administrative chores at the University, I enrolled in Heinz Kohut and the Principles of Self Psychology, a course offered through the Smith School of Social Work. Conducted by an extraordinary teacher and therapist, Mildred Moskowitz, it left an indelible imprint on my perceptions and teaching practices. It was not that Kohut's views differed radically from the psychological theories of earlier as well as contemporary object relationists; in fact, though Kohut himself seldom acknowledged his connections with others in the field, the bridges are apparent. Nor did his principles contradict the prevailing climate of opinion outside psychology's domain; Kohut's concept of a "self" inextricable from the "selfobjects" surrounding it suggests numerous parallels with recent poststructuralist and social-constructivist thought. But in these terms, as used by Kohut and his successors, I found a theoretical vocabulary with which to speak and think about my students' "self-expressions" (at a time when "selfhood" was quickly falling out of fashion), and, in the conceptual framework this vocabulary defined, a metaphor for the kind of constructive audience I hoped to provide.

Kohut first distanced himself from and then challenged Freudian drive theory, rejecting what he perceived to be its mechanistic foundation, its bulwark notion of a primary, all-determining conflict between instinct and reality. In the place of Freud's ego-id-superego triad, he proposed instead the self-in-relationship-to-its-selfobjects as the core of individual personhood. With this substitution, Kohut simultaneously replaced Freud's notion of instinctual aggressive and sexual drives, and their critical suppression, with the more hopeful vision of a "self" flourishing from birth onward amid, to borrow from D. W. Winnicott's "good enough mothering," a world of good enough selfobjects. Distinct from the "person," "individual," or "subject" *per se*, the "self" can be defined as a mutable yet enduring psychological structure experienced by the subject as a center of unity and initiative, evoked and maintained throughout life by its harmonious relations to selfobjects. In *How Does Analysis Cure?* Kohut describes the three-part involvement of the felt self and its selfobjects:

> Throughout his life a person will experience himself as a cohesive, harmonious, firm unit in time and space, connected with his past and pointing meaningfully into a creative-productive future, only as long as, at each stage in his life, he experiences certain representatives of his human surroundings as joyfully responding to him, as available to him as sources of idealized strength and calmness, as being silently present but in essence like him, and, at any rate, able to grasp his inner life more or less accurately so that their responses are attuned to his needs and allow him to grasp their inner life when his is in need of such sustenance. (52)

In turn, Kohut defined the "selfobject" not as an "object" per se but as an object in a particular functional relationship with the self: in simplest terms, an object is a "selfobject" when experienced by the individual as contributing to his or her sense of self. Though the nurturing parent is almost always the first selfobject, she or he is by no means the last. Kohut insisted, over and again, that the need for selfobjects is normal, humanly natural, and lifelong. And the host of potential selfobjects is limitless. Restricted to neither the familial nor even the human realm, it may include such persons as one's parents, peers, mentors, sexual partners, and personal heroes, or such abstract entities as religious or political symbols, pictures, philosophies, texts, and even self-sustaining discourse most often encountered, Kohut observed, in the "reassuring magic of hearing one's mother tongue on returning from foreign language excursions" (200). Indeed, any and all of these objects may function as *selfobjects* so long as they enhance one's sense of a cohesive, enduring *self* by providing a "mirroring" responsiveness to the person's presence, a source of "idealized" strength in their own presence, or a felt sense of "twinship," what Kohut elsewhere called the all-important affirmation of one's existence as a "human among humans."

"Twinship" selfobject relationships involve people or their symbolic representatives who, by their likeness, affirm one's sense of belonging—to a family, to a group, to a society, to the world as a whole. The presence of such selfobjects—most often conveyed via the multiplicity of familiar cultural constructs such as religious, political, and linguistic systems and signs—results in a sense of competence and confidence in the social world. Their absence, Kohut hypothesized—resulting from the absence of *"human* humans" from the home environment of children (*How Does Analysis Cure?* 200) and the subsequent absence of kindred humans from the social environment of adults—leads to something far more dire than a lack of competence. It leads to what Kohut envisaged as the central problem and personality distortion of the Western world today: not, that is, to the guilty and hysterical symptoms of Freud's oppressive Victorian society, but to the "crumbling, decomposing, fragmenting . . . empty self"—the not-quite- and sometimes far-from-human self—epitomized in Kafka's *Metamorphosis*, inscribed in almost every great art work since, and alternately described and demanded by many poststructuralist theorists:

> The musician of disordered sound, the poet of decomposed language, the painter and sculptor of the fragmented visual and tactile world: they all portray the breakup of the self and, through the reassemblage and rearrangement of the fragments, try to create new structures that possess wholeness, perfection, new meaning. (*The Restoration of the Self* 286)

With his emphasis on the essential continuity of selfobjects through each stage of life, Kohut also redefined the course of "normal" development: Maturity is marked neither by the suppression of infantile instincts, as in Freud's paradigm, nor by a repudiation of self or selfobjects. Rather, Kohut concludes, as "we must have a healthy biological apparatus in order to utilize the oxygen that surrounds us, but we cannot live without oxygen," so the healthy progress of a self does not diminish but instead increases its natural capability to use, freely choose, and, when necessary, even envisage or create selfobjects for its own sustenance (*How Does Analysis Cure?* 77). "Conflicts in the realm of object love and hate," he observed, are not, as they are in traditional Freudian theory, "the primary cause of psychopathology but its result" (52). Depression, fragmentation, rage, and the like all arise, that is, when present selfobject failures threaten to repeat deeply felt selfobject failures of the past.

The shifts Kohut's theories produced in psychoanalytic inquiry replaced the essentially adversarial model of classical analysis with another model and shifted the position of analysts themselves from outside to inside the psychoanalytic process. Fully implicated in the analysis, self psychologists have come to see the analytic process as a fully intersubjective experience between analyst and patient. No longer charged with leading the patient from merger to independence or, in more classical Freudian terms, from infantile narcissism to mature altruism, they no longer see themselves as "interrogators" of their client's various "defenses" and "resistances." Their role, instead, is to remain interpreters of their client's observations, but always to interpret empathically, that is, from the client's point of view. Resurrecting Freud's own earliest injunction to *listen afresh* to the patient, Kohut emphasized "sustained empathic inquiry" and what he called "vicarious introspection" as the primary therapeutic technique. This mode of understanding requires that analysts be, as clinician E. A. Schwaber put it, "tuned more sharply to how it feels to be the subject rather than the target of the patient's needs and demands" (qtd. in Bacal and Newman 247) and more ready to acknowledge that confusion, incoherence, and fragmentation of the client's self might well be protective reactions to the analyst's own actions, to his own present failure to fulfill the selfobject functions essential to fruitful analysis and growth. For when empathy is sustained, the act of interpreting becomes as therapeutically significant as the material content of interpretation. Responding empathically, the analyst comes to function as a selfobject to the patient's self—*mirroring* the patient's unique capacities and needs and thereby affirming the self's inherent worth; providing the trust-evoking, soothing experience of an *idealizing* relationship; affording a sense of *twinship* from which the patient might gain a feeling of being a competent and skilled presence among kindred presences—thereby restoring to the patient, through the internalization of these functions, the enduring and resourceful structure of a healthy self.

The impact of Kohut's principles on therapeutic practice was profound. As Robert Stolorow *et al.* have written:

> Once an analyst has grasped the idea that his responsiveness can be experienced subjectively as a vital, functional component of a patient's self-organization, he will never listen to analytic material in quite the same way. (*The Intersubjective Perspective* 17)

Nor do I read or respond to student writing in quite the same way since applying Kohut's concept of the self-selfobject relationship—not as a model perhaps, but certainly as a metaphor for the teacher-student and writer-audience relationship I enter every day that I enter a writing classroom. Even the very phrasings of Kohut's theory seem to lend themselves as metaphors for teachers, especially teachers of writing, and to suggest new meanings for common phrases of our own. For when Kohut defines the healthy felt self as "a cohesive, harmonious, firm unit in time and space, connected with his past and pointing meaningfully into a creative-productive future" (*How Does Analysis Cure?* 52), it takes but a small stretch to recognize a structural likeness not only in what most of us would want for our student writers but also in what we want for the writing they produce. It also suggests redefining our notion of "self-expression," including self-expression manifested in writing, not as solitary act of Romantic self-revelation or even discovery, but as the sort of self-constituting act intimated in the "struggles" carried on by the four young writers of our study, carried on always in a relationship—in a readership—with others. Hence the step to seeing the likeness of a potential selfobject in the audience addressed, whether an audience present or imagined, becomes equally short. And in accepting my place within my students' audience, often as the representative member of that audience, I acknowledge my responsiveness as vital to their written expressions. Again I want to emphasize that I do not see myself *as* an analyst. But *like* an analyst, I am, by my position as a teacher, among each student's limitless host of potential selfobjects. The analyst's role is to be a successful selfobject where others have failed; the analyst's job is to restore to her patient, through her own effective responsiveness and the patient's resultant internalization of effective selfobject functions, an equally successful self structure. Whether I succeed or fail in my role may well depend upon how effectively I help cultivate in my students similarly enduring and resourceful structures capable of recognizing, seeking out, and even imaginatively re-creating for themselves as writers successful *and* success-producing selfobject audiences (audiences for whom they can write purposefully, coherently, and gladly) in and beyond my classroom. To do so, again like (not as) the analyst, I make every effort to employ "sustained empathic inquiry"—more than either "non-interference" or suppressive instruction—as my primary pedagogical technique, "reading afresh" students' writings, standing alongside them in their quest for coherence and "self-expression," tuning in more sharply to "how it feels to be the subject rather than the target" of their communicative efforts, and generally following the advice Mina Shaughnessy gave basic writing teachers twenty years ago: searching "in what students write and say for clues to their reasoning and their purposes, and in what [I do] for gaps and misjudgments" (*Errors* 292). In doing so, I often discover that the resistance I meet in students is really my own.

Recognizing the fully relational self behind every act of written or spoken expression does not mean unflagging approval and endless nods of comprehension. Kohut was at pains throughout his career to separate "empathy" from any sort of "I'm-okay-you're-okay" empty agreement. Teachers should be, too. Empathy requires the more complex, honest act of truly listening for the meanings behind our students' written and oral expressions in order to convey a sense of true understanding—an understanding that recognizes when to mirror their successes along with their struggles, when to offer the idealizing force explicit instruction can supply, when to acknowledge the alienating as well as sustaining powers held by new and old discourses and discourse communities. It requires, in essence, modulating our instructional responses according to our students' personal and educational needs rather than according to our own personal, theoretical, or institutional desires. But while empathy requires all this of us, it may well present in return a place for students and teachers together beyond Freud's Scylla and Charybdis.

Anne's Narrative

I am drawn to studies of writing in contexts, studies that observe how texts are used and that seek writers' and readers' understandings of those texts and their interactions around them. I am drawn to such studies both as a teacher-reader and as an educational researcher seeking to answer questions about teaching and learning, in my own and others' classrooms. As a charge to myself, I often return to Mina Shaughnessy's injunction that to understand the challenges facing students as they learn to write, we need to turn to "the careful observation not only of [our] own students and their writing, but of [ourselves] as writers and teachers" ("Diving" 236). My research interests have also been influenced by Janet Emig's general claim that "writing represents a unique mode of learning . . . active, engaged, personal . . . in nature" ("Writing" 122, 124), and by Lee Odell's more specific questions about the relation between writing and learning: "What does it mean to learn history? What does one have to do in order to think and write like a biologist?" ("Process" 49).

I was drawn to such studies, in part, because of my formative teaching experience in a developmental program at Johnson State College in the 1970s. With an M.A. in literature and my own life's background, I was not prepared for the students I met in my classes. Like them, I was the first generation in my family to attend college; unlike them, I was from a middle-class family and had been "schooled" fairly well for college. In contrast, many of my students were from low-income families; many had received a poor education, some dropping out and completing GEDs; and many were not familiar with essay forms and felicities of grammar, let alone accustomed to reading college-level textbooks and doing research papers. While I was searching for where and how to begin teaching in our writing and reading classes, I and other colleagues were simultaneously seeking ways to reinforce and extend students' development as readers and writers beyond our classes. As we talked with colleagues from other departments, we became interested in writing across the curriculum (WAC) theory and practice because of the promise it seemed to offer for helping our students develop as thinkers and writers. Looking at assignments from courses in such disciplines as economics, geology, and history underscored for me the variety of kinds of thinking and writing that students are asked for across disciplines, and also the variation in conventions. From students, I learned of the value they felt writing contributed to their learning in some (but not all) courses and of how influential teachers were in shaping their perceptions of the relative value of writing in both positive and negative ways.

The more I observed and heard from teachers and students, the more I wanted to know: What kind of learning was occurring for students in their courses across the college? How were they experiencing that learning? How did our interactions with our students shape their learning experiences? With those questions in mind, I went back to school for a Ph.D. in composition and rhetoric.

Reading the work of James Britton, with his dual focus on social and psychological perspectives, had a formative influence on me. His conception of writing in terms of the personal, developmental functions it can serve for writers, as well as its public functions, guides my thinking as a teacher and researcher. Further, I continue to find validity in his notion of the spectator stance for writing. Drawing on the work of psychologist D. W. Harding, Britton theorizes that the spectator stance is that stance in which we attempt to make sense of our lives by stepping back, contemplating experiences and the feelings associated with those experiences, and even *reconstructing* them. The personal function of such writing is, he writes, "to preserve our view of the world from fragmentation and disharmony, to maintain it as something we can continue to live with . . ." (117). While Britton links this stance and function only to children's make-believe stories, gossip, poetry, and fiction, it is evident in other genres as well, notably personal essays and journal writing. Kohut's theory offers a fuller articulation of this psychological need to quite literally *make* sense of our lives by creating coherence and continuity, a function that writing can sometimes further. This conception of writing has played an important role in my teaching although it did not figure in my earlier studies. Its presence is more evident in this study, including as it does our own writing classes and, more important, considering these students' experiences over time.

In earlier studies and this one, I have also found social perspectives particularly valuable for understanding what students are being asked to learn through the writing they do and how that learning is shaped in specific courses. Sociolinguistic theory (e.g., Halliday, Hymes) offers a lens for viewing contexts for learning from two perspectives: (1) the disciplines and institutions from which derive many of the values and genres that students are asked to learn; and (2) specific classrooms where those values and genres are articulated by teachers and learned by students. From my earlier studies, drawing also on rhetorical theory (Bazerman, *What Written Knowledge Does;* Bizzell, "Cognition"; Toulmin), I have seen how, through the writing they do, students are learning ways of thinking (e.g., formulating issues and making and justifying claims) as well as ways of presenting themselves (e.g., social roles and purposes for writing).

My interviews with students—including those in a class where revising was stressed (see Herrington, "Composing"; Herrington and Cadman)—underscore that for some students, more than for others, this learning was not a passive acculturation process, but a negotiation where they were actively considering how they would position themselves in relation to teacher and disciplinary expectations. These expectations are experienced with varying degrees of force, depending not only on the learner but also on the teacher. Drawing on Foucault, poststructuralist and critical linguistic theories of language stress these questions of power in relation to language. For these theories, the key term is discourse, instead of speech communities. I find this a useful term for thinking about writing in college because it focuses on how beliefs, ways of thinking, and social subjectivities are embedded in language and maintained and learned through language. As we inhabit discourses, we take on "particular orientations to the world" (Luke 15). A discourse could be a general social perspective—e.g., conservative Republicanism or feminism— or a more specialized one associated with academic pursuits— e.g., poststructuralism or student-centered process theory. Further, and I realize I am simplifying here, we can consciously intermingle these orientations (e.g., a feminist poststructuralism), and we can contribute to changing discourses as we use language.

To say that these theories stress the constitutive power of discourse is to say that the link between identity and learning to write a given genre involves much more than just learning neutral intellectual and writing strategies, and is much more intimate than learning to take on a particular persona or mask that is somehow easily separated from identity. When we read and compose specific texts and use particular kinds of language repeatedly—particularly those associated with an established genre—we inhabit particular ways of making sense of things and thus we inhabit a particular subjectivity, a particular position. As Allan Luke writes, "through texts, social identities are constructed and remade. . . . It is through texts that one learns how to recognize, represent and 'be,' for instance, a 'rapper,' a 'learning disabled,' a 'loyal American'" (14)—or, I would add, a certain kind of composition teacher-scholar, biologist, anthropologist, or student. Taking on this orientation as a teacher has made me more reflective about essay projects I assign, particularly the discourses that may only be implicit in those projects. In turn, I now also try to teach students ways to be more aware of the discourses that shape their own thinking and better able to identify discourses they are asked to learn.

When we attempt to learn a new discourse, particularly as writers, we are entering a subjectivity, and how we experience that subjectivity depends on how it fits with our private/personal sense of identity and values. When the fit seems quite natural, we may take on a particular orientation without critical awareness that we are doing so. At the other extreme, if we are asked to take on an orientation that violates our basic sense of self, then we may feel assaulted. For instance, if I were asked to take on, through writing, the language and orientation—the social subjectivity—of a homophobic person, I would resist aggressively. Far from feeling a compatibility or shared identity, I would feel an extreme disjunction, an assault on my identity. In the writing we ask students to do in our courses, they face similar situations, situations where trying to do a particular writing assignment is far from a detached activity and where questions of personal identity can be at stake. As the experiences of all four students illustrate, they negotiate these situations with a good deal of awareness of what is happening: they are not shaped in deterministic ways by disciplinary discourses, although they definitely feel the force of those discourses. (See Thesen for a related critique of deterministic views of discourse forces.)

Awareness of this link between personal identity and the social subjectivity created and maintained through writing requires us, as teachers, to be more reflective about the nature of the genres we assign, how they position writers, and the ways in which we present them. More powerfully than the rhetorical and sociolinguistic theory I had read in graduate school, critical discourse theory and what Brodkey calls critical literacy offer a frame for this reflection. Arguing that the force of discourse is defined by how it is presented in specific situations, and, particularly, by the power dynamics associated with that language use, Norman Fairclough writes,

> Language use is . . . constitutive in both conventional, socially reproductive ways, and creative, socially transformative ways, with the emphasis upon the one or the other in particular cases depending upon their social circumstances (e.g., whether they are generated within broadly stable and rigid, or flexible and open, power relations). (131)

The social circumstances we focus on here are college classrooms, including the power relations between students and teachers and, linked to that, the implicit power relations between students and the genres/discourses they are asked to inhabit. In Fairclough's continuum, at one end, the teacher holds all the power, and genres are presented with determinative force to be reproduced rigidly by students; at the other end of the continuum, students also hold some power and genres are presented as more flexible and open to creative reworking by students.

In *Textual Orientations: Lesbian and Gay Students and the Making of Discourse Communities*, Harriet Malinowitz critiques scholarship in composition that views the learning of academic discourses in socially reproductive ways, posing these questions that parallel Fairclough's concerns:

> What are our students learning when they learn to mimic a discourse, a posture, a stance? What aren't they learning? Might

they learn something very different if they were to examine the ways in which the privileged discourse of the university repre- sents particular agendas, perspectives, and principles and con- trasted these with the ways other discourses—in which they play a part—represent particular agendas, perspectives, and principles? (83)

Malinowitz, with others, is stressing the importance of naming discourses for the socially and institutionally powerful constructs that they are and making room for students to question privi- leged discourses and consider alternatives.

Lisa Delpit makes a related point, stressing the connection between discourses and how speakers/writers experience the worldviews and social subjectivities those discourses may ask them to take on. Speaking specifically of the importance of teaching African American students to speak and write in the language of "the culture of power," she implicitly distinguishes between learn- ing to use the "superficial features"—i.e., the grammar and locu- tions—of the dialect that is called Standard English, and using that dialect and associated genres in transformative ways. As examples of those who do the latter, she cites Frederick Douglass, Ida B. Wells, Martin Luther King Jr., and bell hooks. As Delpit argues, the alternatives are not solely to resist and remain on the outside or capitulate and be colonized. Resistance can also be coupled with efforts to acquire and reshape the dominant dis- course.

Delpit recognizes as well, however, that, in some instances, trying to take on a certain language and/or discourse may pose too great a conflict with or violation of one's personally felt iden- tity. In this situation:

> [Teachers] must understand that students who appear to be unable to learn are in many instances choosing to 'not-learn' as Kohl puts it, choosing to maintain their sense of identity in the face of what they perceive as a painful choice between alle- giance to 'them' or 'us'. The teacher, however, can reduce this sense of choice by transforming the new discourse so that it contains within it a place for the students' selves. (*Other People's Children* 163–64)

Here, and throughout her work, Delpit stresses the important role of the teacher at the point of articulation of a discourse: in a classroom working with specific students. In some instances, the degree of transformation may be limited: for example, for Nam, I doubt any teacher could have transformed the research paradigm taught in the Psychology Methods course so that it would have provided a place for his sense of himself as a devoted humanitarian and deeply introspective Christian. In this instance, as in others, a choice has to be made between discourses that may be experienced as incompatible. Still, that choice can be represented by teachers as a viable choice, and room can be made for respectful discussion about the differing alternatives, particularly their basic orientations and epistemologies. Further, when students seem to be choosing to "not-learn," we should recognize that the choice may be related to their sense of personal/social identity, and may even be a defense against an assault on that identity, as was the case for Francois when asked to represent a racist discourse in a writing assignment for a sociology course.

Discourses can also be felt to enhance oneself. Here, I find Kohut's notion of the selfobject particularly powerful in explaining why any one of us finds a particular worldview or discourse attractive: it offers a feeling of identity, a fit with who we feel ourselves to be. Drawing on poststructuralist theories of discourse instead of psychological theories, Linda Brodkey writes, "a discourse is attractive because its worldview and subject positions defend us against our experience of being at odds with ourselves, others, and the world" (18–19). Eli Goldblatt makes a similar point. In 'Round My Way: Authority and Double-Consciousness in Three Urban High School Writers, Goldblatt theorizes that we all need a sense of a sponsoring institution from which to speak, an institution to *authorize* our speaking. As I interpret him, I believe he is using *institution* as analogous to *discourse*, i.e., to indicate a cluster of beliefs and ways of seeing. Referring to the situation facing anyone who seeks to write, Goldblatt explains:

> As authors, they must feel a sense of identity with the sponsoring institution itself, so that to elaborate institutional categories is a satisfying and personal goal for the writing. To function as an author, the writer must become more and more fused

with the life of the institution itself and feel her or his "work" contributes in some way to the "body of knowledge"—the institutional substance—in the field. Writers need to feel a stake in their writing project. . . . (46)

In a comment that refers specifically to students identified as "basic" writers but that pertains, I believe, to all, Goldblatt argues:

What is "basic" about basic writers is that writing for them involves a fundamental power negotiation with the institutions that live by and for writing. They hold the tickets that admit them to classes and reserve rooms for them in the dorms, but the crucial question of their entrance into the discourses of college life revolves around whether or not they can see themselves, or be seen by others, as representing the institutions they are required to serve as authors-in-training. It is one thing to buy the sweatshirt of your school; it is quite another to be asked to think of yourself as a sociologist, an astronomer, or a literary critic. (45)

Whether they will be able to find or create this "institution" that provides them with a sense of responsiveness and that they can imagine themselves a part of is a crucial question for all college students. Goldblatt points to the integral role teachers play as gatekeepers and to the question of whether they are able to see students for their potential rather than solely for their initial skills and command of the surface features of written language. From Kohut, we see the important role teachers can play as mentors, as ones to imagine oneself joining with. Another determining factor will be whether students can imagine that "institution," that discourse, as helping them further important personal goals—in other words, whether that discourse offers a way of joining with others and linking private with public interests.

Saying that we composition scholars need to reconceive how we think of the relation of *personal* to *academic* writing, Malinowitz argues that the question is not whether references to personal experience are present in a text, but whether the writer feels the text serves as a way "to relocate the articulation of this experience from private to public realms" (*Textual Orientations* 172). Students—as were Nam, Lawrence, Rachel, and Francois—

are seeking to make this move as they learn and create for themselves ways of thinking and writing, as well as social subjectivities,
that will enable them to accomplish personally important projects
in public forums. In so doing, they are, as Solsken writes, "defining who they are and who they are becoming" (2). To understand this becoming and our implications in it as teachers, Marcia
and I have come to believe—as we aim to demonstrate in this
book—that it is important to view our students' learning and
our work with them from dual psychological and social perspectives.

Common Ground

We began this study without being so conscious of these differences in theoretical perspective and discourses. Indeed, we began
because of our sense of shared values in teaching and a shared
interest in learning more about students' experiences from their
own perspectives. That common ground remains and has broadened. Along the way, as we began to interpret interviews and
texts, discuss possible key themes, and compose drafts, we became more conscious of our distinct perspectives, and we have
worked since to understand their relationship. Most often, we
have been struck by how our approaches often lead us to the
same conclusions—certainly to the key themes that trace through
our chapters—yet each with insights not brought forth by the
other. At a few points, when we discussed something one of us
questioned or did not understand, we came up against the anxiety that perhaps our views were incompatible. We no longer have
that anxiety. Through talking and listening, trying to think
through the language and gaze of the other, translating into our
own language and saying back, questioning, we have come to a
fuller understanding of what we had felt in the beginning: the
compatibility of our social and psychological perspectives. Most
important, we have learned from each other in ways that have
shaped and enriched each of our interpretative approaches, so
that what is foregrounded in one chapter is also present as a
harmonic counterpoint in the next. Because we honor each other's
approach and voice, we have chosen not to try to write each
chapter in a merged voice, although each of us has contributed

to the chapters authored by the other. For each case study, regardless of who was the primary author, both of us have read through all interview transcripts and the students' writings and collaborated in shaping emerging interpretations. Further, for each case study, we have also read and given feedback on draft after draft, revising interpretations through the give and take of discussion and reading drafts of other chapters. In short, while we divided up responsibilities for primary authorship of the chapters, we collaborated throughout.

A common stance that has guided both of us in composing our interpretations has been to read each student's work with the same respect that we would accord established authors. While we were already personally inclined to this approach as teachers and researchers, it became more imperative to us after the chummy laughter from some of the ADE audience that greeted the comment from the man who introduced us by saying, "All of us enter this profession loving the world's greatest literature, but some of us end up reading the world's worst—freshman essays." As we drove the many miles home from Waterloo, Ontario, to Amherst, Massachusetts, we wondered what produced for them such an irreducible division not just between "real literature" and "freshman essays," but also between the sorts of personal pieces they enjoyed—the essays and stories of, for instance, Martin Amis or bell hooks or Raymond Carver or Amy Tan or Henry Louis Gates—and the "confessional" pieces of Nam, Lawrence, and Rachel that they disparaged. We wondered what it was that prevented them not just from regarding these student efforts as literature, but from treating them as they would literature. Was it something in the style? The content? The person within the personal? Or was it something in our audience that refused to accept these first-year writers as saying anything worth hearing, writing anything worth reading, thinking or feeling anything felt in ourselves?

We write against this attitude, conscious that what was spoken and assented to at that conference is also manifest in the attitude and practices of too many teachers in too many classrooms. We write to those not entrenched in that attitude, teachers of literature, writing, and other subjects who enter the profession for a love of their students as well as their subject. We aim to show what we can learn from students when we accord them the same respect and the same authority we would established authors. We share Steve North's view, as articulated in his 1986 study of writing in a philosophy class, that such an approach is as generative for researchers and participants in their studies as it is for teachers and students. In practice, in this study, it has meant that we have made the students' writings our primary sources, viewing their texts, as we would a writer's collected works, as an oeuvre. Further, we have tried to read this oeuvre—in-process drafts and final drafts—to reconstruct each writer's self-understandings, particularly as they relate to central issues and themes that recurred throughout each writer's work. In this way, we have wanted our project to be the kind of hermeneutic project characterized by North and, more recently, Kurt Spellmeyer. We tried, that is, to make our study

> [a] project of reconstructing, always admittedly from an outsider's perspective, the self-understanding of its subjects, but instead of doing so for the purposes of therapy, it would seek to promote unobstructed communication between reader and texts, writers and writers, writers and teachers. (Spellmeyer, "Being Philosophical" 27)

While our project was not therapy, our approach shares with therapy the technique of empathic listening, trying to mirror what we read in order to reconstruct it as faithfully as possible and interpret it in the light of each student's intention and understanding. Through such a reading, much as through a hermeneutic reading of Andrew Marvell or Emily Dickinson, we are able to see how these students are using writing—over time and across their various courses—to pursue personally important projects and seek ways to authorize their views through a socially shared discourse.

We aimed to be empathic listeners not only as readers, but also as interviewers, our goal in the interviews being primarily to further the students' self-understandings and their reflections about themselves as writers and thinkers, about their writings, and about the contexts out of which their writings arose. From these interviews, we gained something of the writers' perspectives on their texts, and we used these interviews, as fully and faithfully as we could, to shape our own interpretations. Still, our interpretation and a writer's are not always the same. For this reason, in the chapters, we quote extensively from the interviews in order to present both our own understandings and the writer's self-understandings of her or his texts. With Spellmeyer, we believe:

> While the self-understanding of novice writers is no more definitive than anyone else's, their voices, heard in counterpoint to ours, can challenge methods, assumptions, and hidden agendas that have hitherto authorized profoundly disabling—and profoundly dishonest—"constructions" of the student and the student's language. ("Being Philosophical" 27)

As our ADE introducer reminded us without intending to do so, those who voice disabling and dishonest constructions have all-too-easy access to public forums, while students have too-limited access.

Our role has not been solely that of empathic listeners. While striving to honor that role, as reader-interpreters with particular interests, we have also stepped back to interpret students' experiences in relation to the questions that guide our inquiry, questions about these students' individual development as writers and persons and questions about the academic culture they experienced. To answer these questions, we have drawn not only on our primary sources—the students' writings and interviews—but also on secondary, contextual sources where available: interviews with teachers, notes from class observations, teachers' written responses and peer responses, and other students' writings and interviews. Our aim has been to create textured stories that situate students' actions and perceptions in their immediate classroom contexts. (See Appendix A for a fuller explanation of our interview methods and interpretive approaches.)

While Solsken calls her case studies "artist's sketches," we have chosen to call ours "stories," connoting that they are interpretations in words, composed by a teller. They are also narratives told in time. Calling them stories or artist's sketches does not mean that they were not rigorously thought out and com-

posed: we have tried to be thorough and fair in our interpretation of the piles of interviews, writings, and observation notes,
testing out our interpretations against alternatives with one another and with others (i.e., listeners to our conference papers and
readers of our drafts). It does mean, though, that we recognize
that we cannot represent the students' experiences and views in
an unmediated way (Herrington, "Reflections"). Further, we do
not choose to do so: in our roles as researchers and tellers of
these stories, just as in our roles as teachers, we have particular
aims that shape our interpretations and interactions with those
participating in a study or working with us in our classes.

Having recognized this shaping role as interpreters, we turn
to the question that Jacqueline Jones Royster posed in her Chair's
address at the 1995 Conference on College Composition and
Communication: "How do we negotiate the privilege of interpretation?" ("When the First Voice" 36). Royster, an African
American woman, was speaking of the anger and violation she
feels when others appropriate black experience and presume to
speak for it: "when the subject is me and the voice is not mine"
(31).

We recognize that to have been able to conduct this research
study is a privilege granted to us by Nam, Lawrence, Rachel, and
Francois. Each has given us a good deal actually, sharing with us
their writings, their views, and their time. We feel privileged to
have read their work and gotten to know them as writers and as
people. For all of that, we are very grateful.

We hope that the giving has not been totally one way. We
hope that our interview conversations have served some function for each of the students as well, offering occasions to reflect
on experiences, to shape understandings by articulating them,
and to receive some validation. We have also tried to give something back to them, as we would have anyway in our relationships with them as teachers—reading drafts of papers for other
classes when requested, writing recommendations when requested,
and advising informally. We also enjoyed their company—enjoyed seeing them and chatting, even when not ostensibly "interviewing."

As the ones conducting a study—as "researchers"—we have
tried foremost to listen, to listen with respect and as believers, as

Royster calls us to do, "treating the loved people and places of Others with care" (33). We are aware that we cannot fully know or speak for another individual's perspective, and particularly not for others whose experiences of the world are quite different from ours for reasons of culture, race, class, childhood abuse, or different childhood experience. In "Geography Lessons for Researchers," Kaitlin Briggs offers the metaphor of "border crossers" for conceiving of how to negotiate this privilege. Drawing on the work of Gloria Anzaldua, Renato Rosaldo, and Hannah Arendt, Briggs examines the research relationship, considering extremes of the overidentification that masks differences, particularly ones of class, gender, race, and power, as well as the extreme of the overdistancing that positions a researcher at too great a distance to cross over a border to understanding. She calls instead for an approach that aims to respect our own and our subjects' humanity, with researchers being aware of both the possibilities for identification across a border and, given the presence of differences, the limits. As she writes, "much depends on the consciousness of these border crosser researchers, their ability to consider and to empathize with their border crosser participants, and their commitment not to dismiss difficulties" (20). Out of that consciousness and respect—treating the loved places of others with care—can arise not only an ethical research practice, but also a fuller understanding of ourselves and others. We do not claim to speak *for* Nam, Lawrence, Rachel, and Francois, but we do aim to speak *with* them: it is to this end that we include long passages from their writings and their interviews along with our interpretations. We hope that each would say, "The subject is me, and the voices are mine and Anne's and Marcia's."

In writing about these four students, we are writing about some of their teachers, including a few Writing Program graduate teaching associates. We recognize that we present a partial view of them—in comparison to the students—and offer only a limited glimpse of their perspectives, given our focus on the students' writing and their perspectives. Having acknowledged this choice, we want to stress that with few exceptions—which we believe you will recognize from our representations—we found the teachers we write about to be conscientious, caring, and helpful to students. Still, even with some of these teachers, we point to some ways in which their practices may not have been perceived as helpful or may not have been understood by a student. We include ourselves amongst this group and admit that seeing our own limitations has been painful. For this reason, we want to stress that in noting a difficulty in another teacher's practice as experienced by a given student, we are not implying any more of a judgment than we would apply to ourselves: that we need to keep learning from and working on our teaching. We feel this particularly strongly in relation to the graduate teaching associates who figure in these case studies. They were still developing as teachers, and, for ones teaching in the Writing Program, we were in positions of authority over them. For these reasons, we appreciate all the more their openness to us. All were thoughtful about their teaching and respectful of their students' intelligences and capabilities. By having the opportunity to look in on their interactions with these four students, we learned things we could not learn about our interactions with students in our own classes. Finally, as ones implicated in the training program for teaching associates in the Writing Program, we accept partial responsibility for the preparation these teachers had.

The stories follow. For each, we begin with a brief background narrative as we learned it from each student, focusing on their experiences of learning English and of writing in high school, and then move to their experiences of writing for their college courses, beginning with their first-year writing courses. We recognize that the curricula of these courses contributed—just as the curricula of their other courses did—to what they wrote and to the genres they used. For that reason, in the first chapter, on Nam, we introduce the Basic and College Writing courses to give readers a sense of their curricula and pedagogy. Course syllabi are contained in Appendix B. We have chosen to keep both the syllabi and the courses they represent in the background because our purpose has not been to make a case for these particular curricula. Indeed, both have changed since this study, Basic Writing most notably (see Curtis *et al.*). More particularly, as we will discuss in our closing chapter, our own views and teaching practices have changed since this study began—and in ways informed by it.

The Stories

Claiming the Essay for Himself: Nam

With Anne's story of Nam, our group narrative begins. A refugee with his family from Vietnam and now an American citizen, Nam stayed at the University for only one year before entering a Catholic seminary and fulfilling a wish he had had even before arriving in Amherst. An original member of our study group, Nam was enrolled in Marcia's fall 1989 Basic Writing class, which Anne observed. Anne conducted most of the interviews with Nam throughout both the fall 1989 and spring 1990 semesters, and, though she was never his teacher, it is clear that he became quite attached to her as a sort of de facto mentor: during his second term, he sought her out, not just for his regularly scheduled interviews but for bits of academic advice; often, as you will see, feeling quite lost and alone in his own College Writing class, he occasionally sat in on Anne's; and some months after completing Marcia's course (and much to her chagrin), it was to Anne he went with his confounding question, "What is an essay?" His story speaks persuasively of the power of language as experienced by a person in a new culture, with a language and race setting him apart from that culture. His writings provide a window into his thoughts: his struggles with feelings of being apart from others because of language and culture; his struggles to reconcile his own desire to be in the world with others and his belief that God called him to retreat from that world; his struggles to transmute feelings of powerlessness and selfishness and, at times, a desire for revenge into some "better way." For him, Biblical tenets and language seemed to offer this better way, to speak with and for those who, like him, were the objects of others' prejudices; in addition, the essay, as he would come to understand it, offered a means "to make what I experience helpful for others." In his Basic and College Writing classes, Nam experienced two different classroom worlds: one where he felt part of a learning community, as one among others of different races and languages, and the other where he felt apart from others, as *the* one with a different language and color. A final section in this chapter focuses on Nam's negotiations with his teacher in a psychology course, Methods of Inquiry in Psychology. His experience shows the challenge—one often unrecognized by teachers —that students face when a discourse they are asked to learn conflicts with their basic values; for Nam, the conflict was between the positivist epistemology of the course and the epistemology of Catholicism, his faith, and between the laboratory report genre and the essay genre of his writing classes. As his other writing makes clear, Nam understood the nature of the challenge far better than his teacher did. Although he passed the course, he rejected this discourse and used other writing, including his journal and essays in College Writing, as vehicles for expressing these conflicts.

Composing a Self He Can Live With: Lawrence/Steven

Lawrence was enrolled in Marcia's Basic Writing class during the fall of 1989, and, beginning in the spring of 1990, she conducted our interviews with him throughout his remaining four and a half years at the University, including interviews with Lawrence when he was a member of Anne's College Writing section. In this chapter, Marcia presents a student who, among those we have met, could be characterized as most likely to antagonize the colleagues Nancy Sommers described as fearing an "uncontrollable world of ambiguity and uncertainty" opening up "as soon as the academic embraces the personal." At the least we can say that Marcia's story of Lawrence's own self-storying, barely outlined in 1991 and more fully narrated here, most antagonized those attending the ADE conference in Waterloo with its tales of Lawrence's intractable insistence on writing for and about himself, and his unflagging drive to compose a viable gay identity by every means of signification—every discourse—available to him. Throughout nearly all his writings for both Basic and College Writing, Lawrence revisited the scenes of his preadolescent and adolescent years, scenes fraught with abuse, homophobia, and his own suicidal impulses. But he did so always in the effort to convince himself as well as his readers that "gay is good" and thus to create both a self he could live with and a sympathetic audience he could live among. His efforts met with varying degrees of success, as shown by the responses he received from fellow students in these two classes and from instructors in courses he took at the five system campuses including the University as well as Amherst, Hampshire, Mount Holyoke, and Smith colleges. This is not to say Lawrence was altogether comfortable with his own self-preoccupation. As he sought to compose not just a private but also a public gay identity, he struggled as hard as most students—perhaps harder than many—to compose in a less personal, more public "academic" style. And, paradoxically, of the four students we followed, Lawrence, whose writing was demeaned by the majority of ADE members as "expressivist" and "confessional," finally found what seems the happiest niche in the academy's "discourse community"—or at least a segment of it. Designing his own interdepartmental, Five-College major in gender studies, he surrounded himself with kindred gay students and teachers and immersed himself in the language of social constructivism; following what was truly his own curriculum vitae, he peopled his world with audiences willing to believe that gay is, indeed, good, and speaking a language that accommodated easily the full complexity of homosexuality and the irony of drag.

Understanding Personal/Academic Connections: Rachel

Having tested directly into the required College Writing course, Rachel did not take Basic Writing her first semester but volunteered to join our study during the spring of 1990, when she was enrolled in the College Writing class Anne observed. Consequently, Anne, who wrote this chapter, conducted our interviews with Rachel and chose to focus on her because, as we have mentioned, Rachel happened to be enrolled in a class Nam was taking that spring, Methods of Inquiry in Psychology. In contrast to Lawrence's writing, Rachel's is, for the most part, the sort that would be welcomed by those who want to maintain the illusory divide between academic and personal. The tensions (in her writing and in her mind) around this division (as maintained and bridged in specific courses) are the focus of this chapter. Rachel was born and grew up in the United States, speaking English as her primary language. Yet, like Nam (and like many women students, both first- and second-language English speakers, whom we surveyed), she entered the University lacking confidence in herself as a writer. During her college years, however, she grew in confidence and in her sense of herself as a woman, a writer, and potentially, a clinical psychologist, completing her degree with an honors thesis in psychology. Throughout her studies, Rachel found ways to pursue questions and topics that allowed her to keep composing herself—reflecting on her past and present, working to contain past hurts and create a healthy self-image, and acquiring a discourse from which she could speak with authority—attempting to speak of past pains, not as an individual victim, but as a spokesperson for those who might be victimized. That discourse was the discourse of behavioral psychology, one which allowed her to write about past pains, while also veiling her own involvement. Though Rachel, unlike Nam, took on this discourse, she would, by her senior year, critique conventions that could "depersonalize" subjects, and she would speak insightfully about how personal involvements can contribute to and shape knowing. While the discourse of the detached knower predominated Rachel's academic experience, two of Rachel's elective courses called for self-reflective and empathic knowing where one's personal involvement in knowing is acknowledged. The separation, interaction, and tension between these two stances for knowing are a focus of this chapter.

"A BILINGUAL AND SOCIAL STRUGGLE": Francois

This chapter introduces Francois and concludes our group narrative. In his first interview for our study, conducted by our research assistant, Elizabeth Bachrach Tan, Francois expressed the intentions behind his writing and, wittingly or unwittingly, set the tone of his relationship with Marcia, both in her work with him in Basic Writing and in her rendering of him in this chapter:

> Just because I'm a student, you might want to read something, and not understand it, and then comment on it, and then come back the next day, and tell me, "I didn't understand this, I didn't do that." Well, if you read a piece of literature, then you would

just break it down. I want people to do that to my writing. . . .
You might have to read a paper of mine more than once to
understand it, not because it's not clear, but because you just
need to do a little more than that.

With these words, Francois asked, perhaps demanded, that he be
read like a book, that he be fully understood but not in the way
one of those easily accessible popular pieces is so readily and
immediately comprehended. Francois set himself before Marcia
and other instructors as a "piece of literature," a literary work
with all the hidden meanings that students and teachers alike
struggle to understand—and appreciate. "A BILINGUAL AND
SOCIAL STRUGGLE" is, therefore, equally about Francois's
struggle in the academy and about Marcia's struggle with Francois,
not in combat with him but in an effort to accede to his wishes,
in the classroom and in this chapter. Here, as in Basic Writing,
the effort to understand Francois has truly been a "struggle" of
comprehension: a struggle for Marcia as his teacher to make a
comprehensible writer of him, and now for Marcia as writer to
make something comprehensible of him for herself and for you
reading about him, and a struggle for Francois to make himself
intelligible to others without forfeiting his own intentions to his
readers' interpretations. The arena of struggle has at times seemed
boundless, extending far beyond the classroom and written page.
When asked where he was born, Francois replied, "It's kind of
hard for me to say." When asked where he lived as a child, he
responded, "I was at a distance, a long way." And when asked
whether English was the only language spoken in his home, he
answered that he heard spoken a combination of French and
Spanish but considered English his own language "because I'm
Americanized, that's why. That's why I consider it, because that's
the place that I'm at." Yet following Francois through his courses
in writing, education, and sociology, one sees what had originally been cast as a personal struggle with his reader over meaning making and self-definition evolve into a broader, social struggle
shared with other minorities and women for the power of self-
determination—the struggle to inscribe, over and over, their own
stories on what Francois himself called the ever-erasing "governing palimpsest" of a society which "unlike my last takes notice

of your skin color." By his final interview, conducted just prior to his graduation, the terms of struggle had changed from literary to social, from personal to universal:

> I do talk about struggles a lot. Maybe because I'm personally experiencing struggles in my life, . . . but I think everyone is experiencing struggles. I mean, struggles on the street: you turn on the TV, you see struggles. You go into a new family, you open up the door, you take a look, and you see struggle. . . . You see problems everywhere. . . . I mean, everyone is not living in La-La Land.

Note

The survey was administered to students in ten sections of Basic Writing and seventy-five sections of College Writing. The survey asked a series of closed-ended questions about students' perceptions of themselves as writers (e.g., confidence, attributes, attitudes) and three open-ended questions:

1. What are you most confident of or pleased with about your own writing?

2. What are you least confident of or pleased with about your own writing?

3. Please list what you believe are two or three of the most important characteristics of good writing in college.

In order to follow possible changes in perceptions, we administered this questionnaire at the beginning of the first semester in Basic Writing sections and at the beginning of the second semester in College Writing sections. The case-study group completed the open-ended section again at the end of second semester.

The questionnaire yielded statistically significant information that confirmed some of our hunches and other research findings: e.g., females were less confident of their writing than were males; students for whom English is a second language were less confident than were native English speakers; students placed in Basic Writing (as compared to those placed directly into College Writing) and females (as compared to males) reported having more trouble writing on issues that have many interpretations. Most striking to us, the majority of students—with no statistically significant difference among groups—indicated that they liked to express their ideas in writing. The questionnaire offered no further insight into this attitude and, given what we were learning from individual students, we felt it failed to do justice to the impulses that draw students to writing. For these reasons, we have chosen not to make the survey results a major part of this book.

CHAPTER TWO

Claiming the Essay
for Himself: Nam

I have not seen Nam for over five years, although we have corresponded, and the Nam of his college writings and of our long talks is vivid in my mind. He is now finishing school at a Catholic seminary. When I try to picture him to describe him for you, I see him sitting at the word processor in Basic Writing, looking intently at the screen, typing occasionally at the keyboard, as I do now. I recall him as soft-featured, with dark eyes and dark hair. Quiet, soft-spoken, reflective to the point of being philosophical, he also had a hearty laugh.

I hear his voice more strongly in his writings. Here is the opening to an essay he wrote midway through College Writing, his second semester in college:

ONE OF THOSE DAYS

"Merge!" A MERGE command? How the heck do I use it to merge my programs? The teacher just briefly demonstrated how to do "merging" on the blackboard and advised the class to use it whenever we needed to. Unlike a computer memory, I could not recall her presentation and turned to the nearest classmate for help. At first he refused, but I thought he was just joking. Then, when I asked him the second time, he showed no sign of attention as though I was speaking to a wall.

To most people, young and old, being a minority or being different from a large group of people who strongly oppose certain people, class, age, or sex, is a terrible experience. The feeling of being loneliness at the time when we really need a friend, but no one would want to associate with us. A silent cry uttered repeatedly when a verbal remark smacks our face hard for we are not good enough to be around. Our stomach turns and grinds its enzymes, wanting to digest every bone who has just spoken offensively to us. Every harsh word must pay! Every immoral deed must be counted! Soon our innocent mind would turn to hatred, and everything would get ugly. There must be a better way to ease this horrible confirmation of being prejudice, different, or minority than just by expecting a fair treatment from the majority group.

Nam writes in other voices as well. I chose to open with this one because in this essay Nam expresses something of the social experiences and internal struggles out of which he writes. In it, he speaks both of the silent wall and harsh words of rejection that he has experienced because of being treated as "different," and of the loneliness and anger he has felt and feels. Implicitly, Nam is also writing of being misrepresented and misunderstood. Working to resist his anger, he writes that "there must be a better way . . . than just expecting fair treatment from the majority group," and he conveys the urgency he feels to find an alternative that will avoid the consequence he understands of remaining passive and internalizing all the anger: "Soon our innocent mind would turn to hatred."

Despite the opening command of the essay ("Merge!"), I do not interpret Nam as saying that the answer lay in some simple merger and erasure of differences. For him, it lay in trying to turn from anger and hatred to efforts to understand and accept one another—that is, as he wrote in a later passage of "One of Those Days," the answer lay in efforts "to correlate our differences." Through his year in college, Nam came to see that writing could be an instrument of that effort, one of the "better ways."

As a person who had been born into another language (Vietnamese) and who began to learn English only when his family came to the United States in his childhood, Nam understood through experience the multiplicity of languages and their power to define him—"stupid in English, but intelligence in native language"—as well as their power to shape how he could relate to others, for instance isolating him when he knew little English: "I was isolated. It's just like sounds, no meaning. I can't say anything." He understood that language and words could be used to hurt others: "a verbal remark smacks our face hard." He also believed that language could potentially be used as a means of creating community with others—by using a "family language," a language of openness, even in public—and a means of helping others, that is, "making what I experience helpful to others." Being able to use written language for these positive purposes— to be an agent and not a subject or victim because of lack of knowledge of language—became a central writing project for Nam.

Most fundamentally, he wanted to be able to explain himself and his beliefs to others and be understood and not feel as if he were "speaking to a wall." He would say repeatedly that being understood was what was most important for his writing: being understood by others for who he felt himself to be, and also being understood for the message of love and understanding that he wanted others to follow. In a way, he was trying on a role he had chosen for his future, that of a Catholic priest, using writing to shape homilies for others. As someone who aspired to a contemplative life serving his Lord, he also came to use writing for meditation and self-reflection.

When Nam entered UMass, he still felt isolated because of his difficulties with English and far from being able to use language to explain himself or create community with others. At that time, in answer to a question about what he was least confident of as a writer, he had written, "My least confident about my writing are how to make my writing clear enough to be understandable, how to use appropriated word. . . ." While I believe this is an instance of Nam not finding quite the *appropriate* word, the double meaning—appropriated, appropriate—still suggests the tension in Nam's relation to language.

Growing up having to acquire a second language through total immersion, Nam had relied on imitation as one way to learn appropriate words by "appropriating" what he read and heard. He continued to do so while in college: his essays showed traces of language—words and whole phrases—that he appropriated from conversations and other texts and that in some instances represented whole discourses (e.g., a discourse of empirical psychology, or a discourse of Catholicism). Whether he was conscious of doing so, I cannot say. But it does seem that he was selective in how he took on the discourses he encountered in his college courses. He internalized—"appropriated"—only the discourse that matched or seemed to speak for what he wanted to say and the subjectivity he wished to inhabit, that is, the discourse that seemed to offer the appropriate forms and words. On the other hand, when he encountered a discourse—as you will see, with the empirical laboratory report as taught in a psychology course he took—that conflicted with ways of writing and knowing that he valued, he distanced himself from that discourse, mimicking it in order to pass the course, but separating it from "his way."

Nam also felt that in order to appropriate the English language as a speaker and writer, he had to learn its rules. He felt that previous teachers had failed him by not explaining grammatical rules and *how* to apply them in writing, and he wanted his college teachers to help him. On the other hand, it appeared that he would distance himself from teachers who foregrounded rules and grammatical correctness without also and first conveying that they were listening to what he was saying, listening with him in order to "understand" what he was trying to get at.

Nam was also working to try to understand a genre, the essay, as he was being asked to write it in our writing classes. As he developed his understanding of this genre, he also developed a more flexible understanding of "rules" for writing, particularly ones relating to structures of texts. That the nature of "essay" was a question for Nam was something we were not aware of until midway through his second writing course. Indeed, I was quite taken aback when in April—a month after Nam had written "One of Those Days" in College Writing—he asked me in passing, "What is an essay?" I had stopped by his class to set up an appointment with him. As usual, he was sitting on the edge of the class, working away at his computer workstation. Here are the notes I scribbled down right after we talked:

> Says he's behind. He's having trouble again with stopping when he tries to write. Gets hung up over getting the right word and can't get stuff out. Says he finds it helps to meditate some before beginning.
>
> Also wants to know what's an essay? Can it be a story or an argument? Any other kinds?
>
> I answer saying everything he's written so far in his writing classes is an essay.

N: Then what isn't an essay?

A: Well, a lab report, a news article. Essay more "I's" view or reflections.

[Good question. Bad answer—it's a catchall term. Who knows what it is.]

This exchange between us is telling, reflecting both my own fuzzy conceptions at that time and Nam's experiences writing in his Psychology Methods class while also being in College Writing. This genre had become so taken for granted that I and other colleagues in the Writing Program had failed to articulate adequately to our students what we assumed it entailed beyond talking perhaps about ranges of purposes and writer/audience relationships. Further, we assumed our students already knew the genre from their prior schooling. Now, here was Nam making me painfully aware of these assumptions. His question also helped me realize that while through my practices I was leading students to compose essays of certain kinds, I was not being explicit in naming what these certain kinds were, nor was I providing an adequate framework for understanding this genre called "essay" in relation to others that students might be called on to write in college.

Nam had learned well and was writing "essays," at least what seemed like essays to me and to his writing teachers. Along the way, he had also been formulating his own definition of the genre, a definition that reflected the values of his teachers and our Writing Program. I now believe he came to wonder about his evolving understanding of the essay because the notion of "essay" that he had been forming through his writing classes conflicted with the kind of writing he was being asked to do in one of his other college classes, a psychology class where students were asked to write laboratory reports following the most traditional conventions of empirical research reports. In asking me, Nam was trying to figure out how to understand these differences.

Now, as I have looked back through our interviews, I realize that the nature of an essay had been a centrally important question for Nam in Basic Writing as well. In our final interview, he said that when he began Basic Writing,

> I don't have much idea what is essay. When people say essay, I was kinda stuck. What should I do because most—in high school, I'd usually do a report paper, like book report or history report or something like that. But come up with something that I think that nobody ever think, say what I think it is, I do not have much practice, so I have no idea what is essay.

Nam finished Basic Writing having decided that it was a genre for expressing personally meaningful ideas: "a topic that is meaningful to me . . . it's not have to be a certain form." Integrally connected to developing this notion of an essay was accepting more flexible strategies for writing and recognizing that form evolved with meaning. Equally important, this conception of the essay also allowed him to appropriate writing for his own purposes. It offered him a medium and genre for using writing to counter damaging constructions of himself from external voices and to maintain a positive self-identity, to try to reconcile conflicts between experiences and his Christian beliefs, and to compose himself in preparation for a future as a Catholic priest. To compose a role for a future self meant also bridging private and public purposes for writing and developing a sense of speaking with and for others.

Background

During our first interviews, I asked Nam a bit about his background. He told me that he came to the United States in 1979, when he was about eight. He and his family came as refugees from Vietnam. Before the war, his family had been relatively comfortable financially; after, they were reduced to having little. Nam did not write or speak of his experience during the war, save to say that his father was in the army—South Vietnamese, I presume—and at some point, the family entered a refugee camp. From there they came to the United States.

Nam also did not speak much of his family. Until he went away to school, he lived with his parents and some siblings. In his comments and writings, he conveyed respect for his parents, noting that they worked long hours to earn a basic income but still made time for the family to do things together. He also separated himself from some of their values. In one essay, where he develops the point that we should reach out to others, he writes that they are too distrustful and closed off from others. In another, where he criticizes grades as an invalid sign of one's intelligence, he characterizes his parents as placing too much importance on grades. This was a standard by which he would have had to be judged as inferior, given that his grades were not outstanding, primarily because of his difficulty with English. Nam would reject these external and, to him, invalid means of judgment and assert for himself his own self-worth and intelligence. In a journal entry on the autobiography *Hunger of Memory: The Education of Richard Rodriguez*, Nam identified himself with Rodriguez, saying, "Same with me, stupid in English, but intelligence in native language."[1]

Nam had little continuity of place after his family came to the United States. Indeed, his family moved at least five times in ten years, so, as Nam said, "I never stay in one school for two years. I was always moving." His family finally settled in a small city near the University, although Nam spent his last two years of high school in Wisconsin under the auspices of A Better Chance (ABC), a program that offers urban minority students a chance to attend a school in a less urban and more affluent setting while living with other ABC students. Although he spoke positively of his education during his ABC years, it was also at this school that he experienced the wall of silent rejection and verbal taunting he wrote of in "One of Those Days."

He entered UMass directly after completing high school. Not until our third interview, in January, did I learn that he had hoped to enter a seminary instead but had not been accepted. Much to his disappointment, Nam found that most seminaries, like his parents, valued grades as a measure of one's potential:

> They look at my grades, my SAT scores, and I am not too high on those scores. . . . They judge me, based on grades, and I

didn't like that too well because I want to be priest. I want to learn, I want to study. But, grades seem to them is a big thing.

Finally, just before entering UMass, he was accepted at another seminary, one he planned to enter after a first year at UMass. He said of this seminary:

> They accept me as me, not my grade. . . . They just accept me because I want to go there and pray and worship, you know, be a holy Christian or something. Anyway, they accept me the way I like it, so I felt this is good.

To be understood, to be accepted for who he perceives himself to be, not on the basis of external and invalid signs such as grades, or dress, or race, or language—this was his desire.

Nam's recollections of his schooling center on language, telling a moving and vivid story of the difficulties, isolation, and ridicule experienced by a child who knew little English. For me and for others who entered school having English as our native language—to be more precise, the English of the dominant culture—it is a story to be understood by trying to put ourselves in Nam's place, entering elementary school, not able to understand his teachers. As he recalled in an interview, "When the teacher speaks, it's just like sounds, no meaning." And, more generally, "When I couldn't speak English or hear the language, I was isolated, just hoping people would come up to you and start talking, say something, but I just keep quiet. I can't say anything. So, I was kind of like the guy Richard Rodriguez. When I read his essay, he remind me so much of my life."

He gradually did learn English, although he did not feel that his language and writing instruction in elementary school was very helpful. He recalled it mostly as workbook drills in grammar and vocabulary, with fill-in-the-blank exercises. To illustrate, he talked about exercises with verb tense, pointing to the limitations of repetitive, decontextualized, and isolated exercises:

> Like they list out a sentence and drew a blank and you try to fill in the blank what tense. And I was good doing that, because it's easy. It's like a pattern. If one sentence say something and I have a choice—"was" or "were"—it's so easy. But writ-

ing a paragraph, I have no idea how the words like "was" or
"were" or "is," like how they would fit, you know? So it was
hard. I was never encounter how to write a full paragraph correctly, just words in individual sentences.

In this comment, Nam is also pointing to his desire to learn ways
of composing, not just ways of doing exercises. His confusion
over verb tenses surfaced again in College Writing.

Nam also felt that he did not receive enough individual instruction from his teachers. He felt that he was different from the
English-speaking students: "I need more help than just 'what's
this word mean?', you know. Other first grade students are learning, but I need more than that because when the teacher speak,
they understand." And he did not.

Nam reported more positive experiences with writing and
his teacher in his English class for his senior year: "Senior year, I
guess the whole year I do a lot of writing and I like that. I love it.
I love it when I start to write." He also felt that his teacher gave
him more help with trying to learn the rules of grammar, working with him individually, going over his grammar with him, and
trying to answer his questions. Still, though, he spoke of his teacher
not being able to tell him all the rules he felt he needed to know
about grammar:

> You know, there's a lot of question on grammar. I guess some
> rule, he just didn't know the rule. But if I know what the rule
> is, then I'll stick to the rule and that will be correct, every time.
> But if I don't know that rule, then chances are I'm gonna make
> the same mistake over again.

Nam's desire to learn the rules that would be correct every time
fit with his feeling that there was some piece of knowledge that,
if he could find it out, would enable him to write: "There's something, some material or some technique, something that I miss in
the class, that I know I'm missing, but I don't know what it is."

It was also from his senior class teacher that Nam would
learn a structure for writing essays, one that many American students learn: the five-paragraph essay format—what Janet Emig
characterized as "so indigenously American that it might be called
the Fifty-Star Theme" (97). Given his desire to learn the rules of

English, particularly rules for composing, it is not surprising that he spoke positively about learning a structure for writing essays. In an interview, he recalled: "Then I start to learn five-paragraph and sentence structure, getting to do more writing." As he explained in a later interview, this five-paragraph model was presented as the 1-3-1 model: introduction stating the thesis, three points of support, and a conclusion restating the thesis. He also learned to compose following a sequence that began with deciding on a thesis, outlining, writing a draft, and then revising. These two interrelated models—one for structuring and one for composing—were helpful to Nam in demystifying writing and offering him at least one way to begin to write; they also proved to be limiting.

Nam's quest for rules to guide him would continue through his first year in college; it was a quest that Nam quietly pursued on his own by listening to his teachers, reading his peers' writings, and seeking out other books on writing. At times, his need for rules would conflict with his growing desire to use writing to express personally important matters. By the time he finished Basic Writing, he had moved to understanding that "rules" for structuring may not be "right every time" and that having only one preset structure can be constraining. He was beginning to move from seeking preset rules for structuring to developing flexible strategies for composing. Most important, he was using those strategies to serve his ends as a writer, drawing on his own knowledge and experiences to position himself to speak to readers of his essays.

Basic Writing

> "I guess the course taught me that the essay is write what come out, but make sure that it's very important . . . . It's not to have a certain structure." (Nam, at the conclusion of Basic Writing)

As I have indicated, although I was not aware of it at the time, Nam entered Basic Writing feeling that he did not have an adequate understanding of what an essay was, other than the 1-3-1 model that he had learned his senior year. While Marcia did not address that question directly at the beginning, her initial assignments and classroom approaches problematized that model and asked Nam and the other students to try a new model of composing that included a different vision of an essay, one shared by many of us in the Writing Program: exploring their ideas through writing before settling on a thesis, using the guided writings as a way to "make meaning," to think widely and speculatively, *before* and in order to shape a thesis that was important to the writer. By the end of the semester, Nam could articulate his provisional understanding of that new model. In his first writing, he followed the composing process and the basic format he had learned his senior year: "When I write I have to make a general outline of what it is I want to say, and then do a rough draft, and then read over for correction and then the final draft." This procedure fit with his conception of an essay, which was essentially that one selected some thesis and then wrote to demonstrate it: "Make a thesis, . . . try to explain it, and make a conclusion."

The themes of the messages Nam wanted to convey, as well as his structuring strategies, were evident with his first writing for Basic Writing. Marcia designed the first writing unit, Reading Images, to introduce the dominant paradigm for the course: observation and interpretation, or, as she explained in the syllabus, both "making meaning for one's self and discovering a meaning for others." She introduced the unit by having everyone work together on generating observations and interpretations of a reprint of Grant Wood's *American Gothic.* Then she handed out copies of photos from a series, "A Day in the Life of America" (*Newsweek,* Oct. 27, 1986). The photos included, among others, an elderly woman in bed with her grieving husband by her bedside, a scene of homeless people in a city, a man playing a saxophone, and a group of college students splashing around in a park fountain.

Out of all the options, Nam selected a symbol of prejudice and hatred, a woman dressed in Ku Klux Klan robes, but this symbolic message is complicated because she is giving a kiss to her young granddaughter whom she holds in her arms. As he composed this essay, he tried to deal with the tension between hatred and love that he saw in the photograph, a personal tension he would return to many times. He also tried to fold the observation-interpretation model that Marcia introduced into the basic paragraph model he had learned in high school.

In class, Marcia had asked that students use the observation and interpretation guide as a way of brainstorming and had encouraged them to write "anything that comes to you": "Don't edit. That can come later." Nam followed her guide, although he wrote very little:

> Observation:
> the baby does not seemed to please the kissing, having her right hand protect her chess and turning away as the KKK kisses her.
>
> Interpretation:
> hiding its true self by showing love to an innocent child;
> a child would not hide his feeling nor the truth;
> good and evil do not work together;
> if the KKK is evil, then their offspring would be evil;
> prejustice starts from youth;

At the next class meeting, Marcia had students use another heuristic—the particle, wave, field heuristic of Young, Becker, and Pike (1970)—in order to generate more observations and interpretations about the photo. She encouraged them to explore their ideas widely: "Just let your mind go as far as it will." At this point in the semester, Nam seemed not to engage in this kind of exploration. Instead, he drew on the procedure he knew, returning to the 1-3-1 model he had learned, writing out his thesis first and then his basic essay frame, although without substantive points:

> People molded their young to be the person whom they want to be.
> 1) say what you want to say.
> 2) give supportions to what you've said.
> 3) say what you have said.

This thesis seems to be taken from the final two comments in Nam's initial interpretation. He then composed a draft, writing atop the draft a new version of his thesis and his title:

Thesis: Children learn from their families who have been taught by their families.
Title: Family traditions live!

This first draft was substantively similar to Nam's final draft (shown below), except that it began with a sentence not included in the final draft, one that suggests that Nam's own cultural knowledge may have contributed to his interpretation of the photo: "Asians, especially Vietnamese, pay highly respect to their families and friends."

Even though Nam wrote a two-paragraph essay in this instance, traces of the basic 1-3-1 model are evident in his final version, which includes an introductory thesis, three "reasons," and a concluding restatement of his thesis (the underlining is mine):

FAMILY TRADITIONS LIVE!

Looking at the photograph of Gerrit Fokkem in "A Day in the Life of America", *Newsweek*, 27 October 1986, I feel there is an uniqueness of love between a woman and her granddaughter. Unfortunately, she is a member of the Ku Klux Klan, an American group believing themselves as a "supreme" who would dare to demonstrate violence in order to fulfill their supremeness. Though she may be nasty to Blacks, Asians, and Whites who are opposing her Klan, we cannot assume her love to the child is a fake because love and hate to do not mix. For one reason, if we accept her love as a deception, we are no less evil than her, prejudging before seeking for a deeper meaning. For another reason, she loves her grandchild as much as we love ours. Love is one of the most beautiful gift a human could every receive; therefore, we must respect her for she has love even though it is a limited one.

Another prospect that comes to my mind, while observing the photo, is that children learn from their families who are taught by their families. . . . Therefore, my hunch for the photographer's main message is that the Ku Klux Klan will continue to exist from one generation to the next as we understand our parents learn from their parents and our children will learn from us.

I interpret the lead-in words that I have underlined ("For one reason," "For another reason," "Another prospect," and "Therefore") as Nam's attempts to follow the 1-3-1 model, having three points as supports for the thesis, although the points he is trying to get across do not really fit into that additive "one, then another, then another" structure. Although not aware of the 1-3-1 model Nam had learned, Marcia, in her written response to him, pointed to the limitation of the additive frame for conveying the more complex logical relationships that Nam seemed to be getting at in his essay. Focusing on the relation between the ideas in the first and second paragraphs, she wrote:

> I think the two are really intertwined: elders love their children because they see themselves reflected in their offspring, and children, wanting to maintain their love, mirror their elders. This is the complex relationship you suggest in your last paragraph. Why suggest to your readers you've made two separate, simple interpretations? Let them know the full complexity of your thoughts right from the start!

In this comment, Marcia implicitly directed Nam away from the additive structure cued by the lead to paragraph two ("Another prospect . . ."), and she did so in a way that conveyed that she valued his ideas.

She conveyed that same sense in the beginning of her response:

> Nam: I am impressed by the logical and forceful way in which you present your interpretations. Your writing is clear and precise and so, as a reader, I feel that I can really trust you, as a writer, to lead me through a path of interesting ideas. My trust develops in part too, I believe, from the fine way you interweave observations of the photograph with your own interpretations of its meaning.

Marcia's full response was two pages long and included a comment showing how some of Nam's noun forms could be replaced with adjectives (e.g., "uniqueness" by "unique") to "make the English more colloquial."

Marcia's response was important for Nam for two reasons. One, it offered him substantive suggestions that he could apply in future writings. Even more important, it conveyed to him that he was being understood, which was what he felt least confident of and felt was most important. Here is how he recalled her response: "It meant people got what I was trying to say. It was helpful to me to see, you know, for me writing a quality essay, instead of a useless essay with no meaning."

In this "quality essay," his first in college, Nam introduced his understanding of the world in which he lives, writing from his own experiences and his strongly felt beliefs about who he wants to be for himself and for others. Nam also included himself, indirectly, amongst those who have been misjudged and wrongly persecuted by others (including "Asians" amongst the groups that the Klan targets). He wants to be understood by others for his "deeper meaning," and he understands that he will become a lesser self if he follows the way of prejudgment and hate ("if we accept her love as a deception, we are no less evil than her, prejudging before seeking for a deeper meaning"). It is this message of love and understanding that he would keep returning to, fashioning it as a way of being for himself and preaching it to others as a way he asks them to be toward him and one another.

For the second essay, Nam would focus again on this tension between love and hate (or cruelty), but he moved to reflecting on an experience from his own life, one about which he had not resolved his conflicting feelings. It was because of this, I believe, that he again came up against the inadequacy of his old process model of selecting a thesis in advance and then writing an essay to demonstrate it. For this essay, his thesis was a Biblical maxim, as forecast by the title he chose, "Love Your Neighbors As I Have Love You," and summed up in the final paragraph of the essay:

> This experience has taught me a lesson which I give my advise is this: "the only way to change a person from 'bad' to 'good' is to show him the true love God has given us. Only true love can win over 'evil'." I guess being "bad" is like the way Huy have treated me, and being "good" is like I have continued to be nice to him.

Nam's problem with the essay was that the story he chose to tell did not fit with this message. In the essay, he writes about Huy, his roommate his senior year of high school, and how Huy mistreated him. As Nam tells of their relations, despite his repeated attempts to befriend and help Huy, Huy continued to mistreat

Nam, taunting him with cruel words and even shoving and kicking him. In her comment, Marcia pointed to the disjunction between this story and Nam's thesis. Her response began, "This is a truly humane and compassionate essay, Nam, all the more impressive because you demonstrate such humanity in the face of such inhumane treatment." She closed with a suggestion and a question:

> I think that if you had balanced a picture of his hurtfulness against a picture of your kindness, you would also have ended with a different lesson. As you state it in your last paragraph, your lesson is this: "the only way to change a person from 'bad' to 'good' is to show him the true love God has given us." But, as your reader, I need to ask you: Did you *change* Huy? Maybe you did, but we don't see that change in your essay. I also think you told me in class that your claim would be different: sometimes you must treat people with respect even though they treat you disrespectfully.

In an interview, Nam said he recognized the disjunction that Marcia pointed to. In that interview, he struggled again to try to articulate what he had learned from the experience, saying again that it was not that we should love one another—because he already knew that, he said—and trying to put into words the coda he had learned about trying to follow this maxim in everyday life:

> But I guess my purpose is saying even though I don't know whether he's gonna change or not, I just keep on doing what's right, and let him see what's right, what's the appropriate way.

As his tentativeness suggests, he was still not clear as to his purpose. In composing the essay, he had difficulty in part because he was still hurt over Huy's treatment of him and still conflicted as to his own feelings toward Huy: both wanting to expose Huy for his meanness and feeling that he should love him without expecting love in return. He also had difficulty because his process of composing—pick thesis and add examples—was still too mechanical, lacking the crucial step of thinking through his ideas and questioning himself as to what he was trying to say.

For the third essay, Nam experienced much less difficulty. Indeed, even though he wrote more and longer drafts for this essay than for his first and second essays, he recalled this writing as "fun." I think that a primary reason that he found this writing less difficult was that he was dealing with a topic that seemed clearer to him and about which he did not have conflicting feelings. It was also with this writing that Nam began to use writing to explore his ideas before settling on a thesis and that he began to take more authority over structure by shaping it to fit the message he wanted to get across. The resulting essay was more fully contextualized and developed than his previous two. As he explained in an interview, "I like that one. I guess I learn a little bit more . . . how to write what I really want to say, try to bring my point across through the essay. I guess I learn a lot. I have more idea, more technique, more appropriate way to do it."

In class, Marcia introduced this unit by saying that the focus would be on "making meaning of another kind of experience, a reading." This was a major unit that the class worked on for three weeks, spending time in class reading, annotating, and discussing two stories; doing two different guided writings; selecting a focus; and drafting and revising their essays. When they began the unit, Marcia had said to me that she was concerned that many of them were too concerned with "getting the right answer." Consequently, she devoted even more time to exploratory work and to explaining its purpose to the class.

They began the unit by reading a short fictionalized memoir, "So Tsi-fai" by Sophronia Liu. In the story, Liu recalls the suicide of a sixth-grade classmate, So Tsi-fai, and describes the social, institutional, economic, and personal factors that pressured him to kill himself. Using techniques adopted from Bartholomae and Petrosky, Marcia asked students to read the story, checkmarking anything that struck them as significant or puzzling, and then to reread it and begin writing speculatively on why they made the checks. She stressed the exploratory purpose of the writing: "What we're doing now is helping you explore your own thoughts to find out what's interesting to you. Anything you write is right, okay? You're not writing your essay now. You're exploring your thoughts." Nam made the check marks and wrote marginal notes, the first being, "a sign of suicide. Why a child has such a thought?"

At the end of the story, he wrote a note to himself: "Write—explore my ideas—writing what really interesting to me. Anything."

In the next two class sessions, Marcia introduced two guided writings as heuristics for exploring ideas. One, entitled Exploring Perspectives, continued the observation-interpretation paradigm of the previous writings, but also asked students to try looking at the story from different perspectives. In the introductory instructions, Marcia urged them to press themselves: "Just keep writing your thoughts and try not to stop. . . . Keep pushing yourself to discover more ideas."

Students were first to take on the role of someone in the essay and tell that character's story—"that is, give your *observations*." Nam chose So Tsi-fai. Next, they were to tell their *interpretations* of So Tsi-fai's story. In response to these two prompts, Nam generated three pages, beginning, "I am So Tsi-fai." In the persona of So Tsi-fai, he wrote about the unreasonably high expectations from his parents, their continual scolding of him, all the work he had to do at home, hating homework and having no time to do it, not doing well in school, and his teacher's meanness toward him. In an interview, asked if he knew why he happened to write so much, he explained, "I see his problem, I mean, it was kinda similar to my problem, but his problems was—I could see it, like I could see it clearly."

After students had completed both of these guided writings, Marcia asked them to read through all they had written and "start developing an idea or question of interest to you and a way to present it that you believe will interest someone." After talking with them in small groups about their provisional ideas, she asked each student to write in "very rough form your guiding question or lesson and overall plans."

Nam had no difficulty writing out what he wanted to focus on, drawing very much on the themes that he wrote out in his long guided writing:

> One of the topics is the death of So Tsi-fai; pattern of ill thoughts; a compilation of depression and lack of love in his environment: parent, teacher, grades. That is the main idea which shows up often during my exploring for a wider range

topic. Nun under name of love (the teacher) lacks love; parent lacks love + tools (their hope but no supportion).

Though this story is in the past, I concern a great deal that this example may also happen in today's families. If parents are lack of knowledge and tools for their children, then their children will be disadvanged in their life until is help around them. Those who have an experience of observing misfortune while they are fortunate may learn and try to improve other people lives. I feel sorry for So Tsi-fai. His parents sure do not support him. . . . And surely the nun do not help him much; and worst she gives him negative re-inforcement—"filthy, dirty, you" which I disapprove of such words come from the nun.

These notes show how Nam moved to connect the themes that interested him in the story to issues he saw for children in contemporary society. In his final sentence, he also introduces what will evolve into a major point of the essay and other essays: the pain inflicted by cruel words.

While in retrospect these two paragraphs seem to offer a structural plan for the final version of the essay (talking first about Sister Marie and then about So Tsi-fai's parents), Nam did not immediately select this structure embedded in his own ideas. Instead, he tried to fit his ideas into preexisting structures. He tried first to use a shorthand form of the Exploring Perspectives guided writing heuristic, as if to use it as his outline (something Marcia had not intended): "1. Story's character— observation. 2. Interpretation. 3. Someone else would interpret differently. 4. 23 yrs. later, author is teacher." In interview, he said one of the reasons he thought that guided writing was "helpful" was because "it was like an outline. I like outline when I write things."

Apparently Nam then changed his mind and returned to an elaborated version of the 1-3-1 technique:

Theme (thesis)
(focus) significant information—explanation—backups
(focus) different but equal information—. . .
(focus) different but equal information—. . .
conclusion (claim)

On a new page, he outlined his essay following that format:

Topic: teenage suicide
Thesis:
What are some problems that may lead to suicide?
2. Educational System. . .
1. Classroom (Sister Marie. . .
3. Family. . .
Thesis: [In the story of So Tsi-fai by Sophronia Lui]
teenage suicide.

The blank spaces next to "Thesis" suggest that Nam had not yet articulated his thesis. From this outline, Nam then wrote his first draft—the first of six he would write before he finished! He would also choose this essay as one of the two he revised again at the end of the semester. Through those drafts, he gradually shaped his interpretation and worked himself out of the 1-3-1 structure and into a structure that evolved from his interpretation.

His successive drafts also show how Nam monitored himself as he wrote, prompting himself with questions and commands. For instance, toward the end of this first draft, as he tries to work out his interpretation, he prompts himself as follows:

> Something about people don't want to help or don't let themselves help others or offer to help others who are less fortunated than them or just don't know how—don't carry out the act of supportion. Something like that. What is it that I cannot make it out from my mind- - - - what is it- - - - People (negative) about (support-action) to the less fortunated than them.

He is trying to express the broader point he wants to get across about our failure to help those who are less fortunate than we are. Here, more than in any previous writings, he is using the activity of writing to try to clarify and find words for his message. In an interview, I asked him about these prompts to himself. He explained, "If I don't have it organized, or if don't have nothing in my head, or if I can't think, then I'll write that and say, 'Okay, what do I want to say.' So that will come gradually."

In his third draft (three typed pages), he moves to an overall problem-solution format that he outlines as follows: "Overall: Show problems—interpretations of their existences—some possible answers (solutions)—final best solution." For his final point (what he notes as the "primary answer?")—he returns—for the first time in this essay—to the importance of language:

> People should be careful with words (why—sometime we believe who we are by what other people have said. If you often hear people calling you a no-good-for-nothing, you would feel that you are no-good-for-nothing."

Here, Nam writes out of his awareness of the power of language to shape our self-images as we internalize others' judgments of us. Throughout his writings, we can see traces of his efforts to resist what others have said of him (e.g., "stupid in English").

From this draft on to the final draft, Nam's essay stays focused on the power of dismissive language and on children's need for positive support from adults. The sixth and, for then, final draft of the essay consisted of four paragraphs that developed this overall thesis. In this final draft, Nam also moves to position himself to address us as ones who judge others, calling on us to be understanding and not put onto others *our* understanding of them, but to accept them *as they want to be accepted*:

> People should accept one another as they are and should be more careful with word choices. We all need to be accepted in our societies, having a sense of belonging security, or trust. If people often say what they see in us, we would accept it as true. However, life would be hopeless and miserable without the acceptance and encouragement from other people. In school his teacher, Sister Maria, treats him no less than a worthless animal! . . .

This is Nam's message—don't accept me as represented by my grades or my still-awkward use of English. Accept me as I know myself to be or want to be: intelligent and loving.

Through successive drafts and outlines, Nam had shaped the structure to fit the message he wanted to get across. In an interview, I asked him if he thought his final draft still had a 1-3-1 pattern. He laughed and said, "I have no idea. I have no idea." In working out what he wanted to say, he had lost track of that pattern and moved on to create his own.

Marcia responded very positively to this essay, seeing it as a "big step" for Nam. Her response began:

> In this essay, Nam, you have kept your eye—and your reader's eye—directly on your subject, So Tsi-fai and the people who essentially failed to love and to help him. The result is a clear claim—young people need help, not just criticism—and a well-ordered, well-developed essay. This represents a big step, a true improvement, since your second writing. Good for you.

For Nam, this response was another validation that he was getting closer to his goal of being understood by others. In an interview, asked about how he reacted to Marcia's response, he explained:

> I know I spent a lot of time doing this, a lot of time, trying to be clear in my essay, and it was—what do you call it, not really a surprise, but it's like, I guess like I'm going in the right direction, and at least I have people response that this is, that I'm doing—it meant people got what I was trying to say.

This was exactly what came across to him as important about Marcia's response to his first essay: "it meant people got what I was trying to say."

Despite this positive response and the feeling that he had been understood, Nam did not feel that he had fully expressed what he wanted to say. For this reason, he chose to revise this essay one more time at the end of the semester. His main change was to add another paragraph at the end of the essay:

> In So Tsi-fai's time, his parents and teacher give him no supportion, recognition, nor compassion which every child needs it for an emotional strength. Without that strength, the child will become ill and even not fit to live. Furthermore, the sharp tongue of the adults can strike a child dead or at least a deep wound. So Tsi-fai needs love and compassion from the adults, but instead he receives the tongue, the sharp one.

Here, he restates forcefully the power of language to hurt, of language as a weapon, and a "sharp one." In an interview, when

I asked him why he wanted to revise this essay, he explained: "The conclusion, when I read it over, I didn't find my conclusion here. I didn't see what I'm trying to say." In this essay, Nam had succeeded in making *his* meaning, using his interpretation of the story to bring to the fore for readers his personally felt belief about the power of language to hurt others and to shape others.

Marcia published everyone's third essays in a class anthology that she titled "Meditations from a Writing Workshop." The day after handing out copies for all to read, Marcia asked each student to complete a guided writing on an essay that he or she found "particularly intriguing." Nam chose "It Was Years Ago," a fictional story by a classmate, Chris, where the narrator, a married man, reflects on his youth, remembering his father's drinking and his abuse of his mother and separation from the family, and resolves to spend more time with his own family. Although the story is framed with an introduction and conclusion where the narrator is an adult, most of it is told through the voice of the man as a young boy, overhearing the fights and not knowing what to do.

In the guided writing, Nam wrote that he chose this essay because "it has a good essay structure." In an interview at the end of Basic Writing, he recalled how this essay helped him revise his notion of an essay:

> First of all I went, "Wow, is this an essay?" But then, it's like this is writing as long as it make sense, as long as it have some purpose or as long as it has some meaning, I guess. Reading his essay, I felt like you can do something like that instead of make a thesis, try to explain it, and make a conclusion. I felt now, I guess I felt essay is just writing what people think. It's not to have to be a certain form. Before I try to do that but then what I'm trying to say is not really there at all.

Reading Chris's essay helped Nam see that he could use writing—through the genre of the essay—to try to express his beliefs, and that what he wanted to say could shape the form, not vice versa. Still, working out alternative forms was not so easy. His experiments with alternatives are evident in the fourth essay. The beginning reading for this essay ("Aria," from Richard Rodriguez's memoir) also encouraged him to continue to develop his view on language. Nam here develops his view about the potential for language to be a way of overcoming isolation and creating a community.

For the essay, students were again free to decide on their focus, after first doing the reading and then doing guided writings. Nam began with some brainstorming notes, titling them "As Rough As It Is." After having written about a page and a half of notes, he wasn't sure how to proceed. At about this time—when most others already had a full draft completed—Marcia gave them a guide titled Self-Assessment. Although Nam didn't have a draft to assess, the guide proved particularly helpful for him in articulating a point he wanted to focus on: the isolation caused by people who close themselves off from others (the italicized questions were the prompts):

> 1. *What question or issue am I exploring in this paper?* we tend to be isolated from our public world, but those who feel that they are open get along with the world well.
> 2. *Why does this particular question or issue interest me?* I see my family, friends, other people and even myself fall into this isolation in public. I don't think it is a healthy attitude when everybody are keeping away from everyone else.
> 3. *What am I saying to my reader about this question or issue?* we can grow and become mature only we are willing to be open in the world other than our own private world.

Nam then sketched a skeletal plan for his essay and worked through three drafts. His final draft is a four-paragraph essay that opens with a quote from Rodriguez that focuses on "bilingual education" and the impossibility of using "family language" in school: "not to understand this is to misunderstand the public uses of schooling and to trivialize the nature of intimate life" (523). In the first full paragraph, Nam presents his interpretation of the passage. Interestingly, instead of focusing on issues of bilingualism in the U.S., as Rodriguez does, Nam uses "family language" as a metaphor for a way of being open and in community with people. He develops this thesis in his final three paragraphs, setting up a contrast between two ways of being in the public world:

Most people tend to be isolated in their public or external world. For examples, my parent does not want any guest, whether he is a friend or relative, to be invited into the house when they are out; KEEP OUT or NO TRESPASSING signs hang on my neighbors' fences and in a class or auditorium, we often sit at least a chair away from a stranger who is sitting there in the same role. Perhaps, we are used to these surroundings and are not concerned much about them. But these aspects are form of isolation, which proof that we are unconsciously isolated people, separating ourselves in the public.

In contrast, some people, using "family language," do fairly well in their external world. They keep themselves open. Consider the people who volunteer to work in the Peace Corps; people who donate their time and effort helping the poor, the homeless, and the abused; and people who work with other people who have different background, culture, and ethnic, such as councilor or a priest. Language that they speak in public is no longer "public language" but as "family language," for they are a part of the people whom they work with.

We can be a part of each other, only if we are willing to be open. In general, we are open more to our families at home than to the people in public. If we close our mind and withdraw from the people, public separateness will increase its tension and shall probably create a unhealthy community since everybody is keeping away from everyone's else business, like we live to survive rather than appreciate life. Henceforth, being open would help us to cope other people with ease and would keep things running smooth in our community as well as our lives.

The students' fourth essays were also published as a class anthology, titled "Tales From the Melting Pot." The guided writing about this anthology also asked students to comment on what they learned about themselves in reading through the essays. In his response, Nam reflected a growing confidence in himself as a writer and also his developing understanding of an essay. He wrote, "There are more techniques and styles of writings. Mine is one of them. About myself, I learn that writing comes from within, true and honest. I am not sure about claritiness of my writing, but other essays do help me how to be cleared in writing." Here he expresses a sense that he has a "style," and an additional understanding about an essay, one that confirmed his own sense of what he was most confident of in his own writing—that it was "honest" and that it came from "within."

Nam's statement that "writing comes from within, true and honest" echoes the opening to Langston Hughes's poem, "Theme for English B," which the students had just read in class:

> The instructor said:
>> Go home and write
>> a page tonight.
>> And let that page come out of you—
>> Then, it will be true.
> I wonder if it's that simple?

In class, after Francois had read the poem aloud and they'd discussed it, they had written their own impromptu "theme" poems. As a number of students read their poems, I was struck by one telling line from Nam's: "If you know me, then you are part of me." Perhaps for Nam, Hughes's lines had resonated as true— if not as simple to achieve—and they had remained in his mind. Could Nam's writing then be said to come from "within"? I think yes. If indeed Nam was appropriating language from Hughes, it was because he was reading those lines and using that language in the way that was consonant with his beliefs and with his emerging view of how he could use writing for his own purposes.

Nam's title and thesis for his final essay consisted of another maxim phrased in the manner of the Ten Commandments from the Bible: "Thou Shall Not Judge." At the time this essay was introduced, he was feeling overwhelmed by the work in his other classes and behind in all. In an interview, he said that he wrote the essay on the day that it was due and that, as a consequence, "it didn't come out too well." Actually, his composing process was more extensive than that. Following Marcia's instructions, he began by talking over his ideas with a classmate. He then jotted down some ideas, composed a draft, and revised it. His final essay is, as Marcia wrote in her response to him, "clearer than ever before. You've 'unpacked' your ideas, not tried to express more in one sentence than any single sentence could hold. Good for you!" It may have come out more fluently and clearly because he didn't worry over his words so much and because he was writing about what was for him a heartfelt belief. As he said in an interview, pointing to his heart, "It come from here."

As with other essays, this one explores the tensions between isolation and connection, between misunderstanding and understanding:

THOU SHALL NOT JUDGE

To seek understanding is wiser than to judge our neighbors. Sometimes we do not have enough knowledge about a person to judge him. And sometimes we misjudge the person from his appearance. Whereas, by seeking knowledge about the individual, we can understand why he is acting as he is. As long as we understand the individual's actions, we can never be mistaken about him.

Not everyone is the same because the backgrounds are different from one another. We are raised in a different family, different environment with different disciplines, role models, and customs even in the same circumstance. In Japan, a formal way of greeting a person is by bowing the upper part of the body, whereas, in America, a simple hand shake, a hug or kiss would do just fine. But for Vietnamese, kissing or hugging in public can never be a sign of greeting but a sign of having an affair. Because we have different experiences and different views on a certain matter, we are different from one another. Therefore, we cannot judge one another by our own tradition for other behaviors are similar to our undesirable ones, which may be acceptable for them in their tradition.

By judging someone we make a conclusion from what we already know about him. This action is no less than stereotyping a person. My parents always advise me to make friend with those who are "A" average students and keep away from those who are out-going (party-wise) too much. According to them, the scholar friends can help you achieve better in school. My parents care for me, I understand. But at least one thing they overlook is that some scholar students can do me more harm than support me with my academic years.

Furthermore, we can be mistaken for judging from the outside instead of from the inside where the heart lies. Unlike my parents, those "A" students may not be a true scholar students. Some students who cheat on their homework and exams receive a high average grade, but they are not scholar students. Therefore, judging people, we tend to stop from exploring more about them, and we could be wrong from judging their appearances, like judging a book from its cover.

No one knows who we are because we are all different from one another. We cannot say that two or more Vietnamese boys having their arms on shoulder to shoulder are gay even they probably are. In order for us, Americans, not to misunderstand their "arms on shoulder to shoulder" could be meant in their culture. (In this case, it means "best friend.") So, it is important not to judge what represents the appearance but to understand its meaning.

We often approach people with judgment and seldom seek to understand them. And because of it, we fall into misunderstanding people with our own fashion, mode, or fad that exists in our society. Finally, sometimes we just don't have access to understand the person; in this case, we can only be aware and keep away from that undesirable behaviors.

As I look back through Nam's essays, I see this one as a continuation of themes in earlier ones, even as a response to the first essay. In that first essay, "FAMILY TRADITIONS LIVE!," Nam speaks to the social processes that present barriers to transcending family and group identities and prejudices. In his fourth essay, he speaks to the corresponding personal tendencies to isolate ourselves from the "public"—that which is not intimate to us. In this final essay, he speaks of the need to transcend those barriers—to try to work against the potential of family and group to lead us into viewing others only one way ("we cannot judge one another from our own tradition") and to try, rather, to understand others from their own perspectives. Although he does not speak explicitly about language, the essay is all about signs and interpreting them, demonstrating how the meaning of signs varies by our culturally shaped interpretive lenses, how language can be the instrument for speaking misjudgments and creating separations, and how writing—specifically, for Nam, through the essay genre—can be used in service of community and understanding.

Nam finished Basic Writing, then, with a new understanding of what an essay is and a basic notion of a new composing process. Most significant for him, he had moved from viewing the essay as something dissociated from himself and his beliefs to viewing it as a medium to express personally meaningful beliefs—to express something that "is meaningful to me"—to others. Trying to use writing for this purpose and to communicate with a supportive yet questioning audience led him also—particularly with his essays on Huy, "So Tsi-fai," and Rodriguez—beyond merely expressing beliefs and into encountering questions and previously unreconciled tensions in his thinking; it led him, in other words, to facing the challenge of trying to recompose his beliefs. Further, to view and use the essay in this way entailed learning new ways of composing as well as shifting from using a preset form to using the process to shape a form as he shaped his meaning.

Accomplishing that aim was something Nam felt he had to keep working on, as he indicated in an interview as he concluded Basic Writing:

> Brainstorming—I have this idea from Marcia, 'cause she said, "Just write down whatever come to mind. . . . Then write your essay after you have enough information that you can write on. . . ." But it's very hard to write out what's coming inside. It's very hard for me to do that. But I need the outline to see what it is to reflect on. Sometime that guide me, that I can write. And then for the essay, I learn from this course, doing that outline is very tough. And you actually make things harder than it is. I guess—I'm not sure. [He laughs.] But, uh, I guess this semester, this course taught me that the essay is write what come out, but make sure that it's very important—why is it important that you're doing that. And write what come out. And I learn that, but it's kind of hard for me to follow.

He would keep working on that—primarily on his own—throughout College Writing.

College Writing

> "I felt worried about my essay, try to get it done— the essay was alone."

> "Choose topics that are meaningful"
> (NAM, *at the conclusion of College Writing*)

Nam entered a different world in his section of College Writing, one where he felt different from the other students more than he felt he was a participant with them in their work as writers. Just looking at the class, it was apparent that he was different in that he appeared to be the only one who was not Anglo- or European American; he was also the only one who was not a native English speaker.

The language difference was what he said he felt most acutely, especially at the beginning of the course. In an interview just after completing College Writing, Nam recalled being in a small group discussion about drafts of their first essays. He had a two-page draft and another student had five pages:

> How can he have that much paper? At first I feel, this is a challenge course. I can't write that fast. I felt like the whole class write more, or can write easier than I can. I felt I needed to do more work in order to keep up with the class.
>
> But then later, I felt that I guess we kind of the same. The only problem I have was writing [fast enough] and other than that, I felt like we're the same. Like no one is better, no one is worse.

That comment reflects, I think, Nam's underlying sense of his own self-worth in relation to others and also his growing confidence in himself as a writer.

Still, Nam was apart from the class. It was as if he were doing his own independent study while sitting on the fringe of another class. It was easy for this to happen, without any apparent intention on anyone's part: the other students had more in common with one another, given their generally similar ethnicity, culture, and language. And given that Nam was quiet and unassertive, it was easy not to see him. Further, it took him so much more time to write that he was thus often behind, rarely having a draft ready in order to participate in peer review sessions, and often being late with final drafts so that he had no essays printed in the class publications.[2] In a final interview, Nam explained, "Since my essay wasn't done in class, I don't have advice from classmates, and I don't have a chance to see what they see." When he was in Basic Writing, Nam said that while peer review of drafts was not as helpful as teacher response ("they like me, they don't know much about writing"), he still valued it: "to see what other people see in your essay, instead of this is the way I see it." And he valued brainstorming ideas for his essays with a peer: "To listen to other people, the purpose of their writing, I felt more idea coming from it." In contrast, in College Writing, he felt a double pressure: the pressure of not being able to keep up with the pace of the writing assignments, and the pressure of having to work on his own without the "help of classmates."

Nam also felt a more distanced relationship with his teacher, Eleanor, than he had with Marcia. This distance may have been in part attributable to the structure of the class: where Basic Writing met for five classroom hours in order to allow for more in-class writing and consultation, College Writing met for only three classroom hours. Perhaps related to this structural difference was the fact that Marcia's and Eleanor's manners in approaching the students differed as well: Marcia regularly sought to maintain a one-to-one relationship with each student. In Nam's Basic Writing class, she regularly moved about the room during in-class writing time, checking in with each student. When I asked Nam about that, he said, "I think it's nice because the teacher is communicating to everybody, spend a little time talking to that person. I think she make herself acquaint with everybody doing that." In contrast, in Nam's College Writing section—which also had in-class writing time—Eleanor usually sat at her desk, inviting students to feel free to come up to her. Nam did not. Perhaps he declined to do so out of a reluctance to approach authorities, although Nam said it was because of the time pressures he felt. Contrasting his experience in College Writing with that in Basic Writing, Nam explained:

> Uh, in 111, I guess it's both discussion with the class and able to speak with Marcia alone. Like I talk to you about a problem. Just come up to you. I was also do that with Marcia a lot. This semester, I felt like I don't have time to do that—instead just concentrate on my work, meet the class requirement. I do talk with her individually, but not too much. I don't have time to do that.

During class time, then, it seems that neither sought the other out. Nam also felt some distance from Eleanor because of misunderstandings that arose over the first two essays, misunderstandings in which one or the other misinterpreted the intentions of the other: whereas Eleanor seemed to misread Nam's intentions for his first essay, Nam misinterpreted Eleanor's intentions for

the second essay assignment, and they misunderstood one another regarding a verb tense instruction for this second essay.
Had they had more interactions while Nam was working on drafts
for these essays, some of these misunderstandings might have
been averted.

Fortunately, in her midsemester conference with Nam, Eleanor
was able to clarify some of these misunderstandings. More important, she conveyed to him that she saw him in one important
way that he wanted to be seen: as a conscientious student. As he
explained, "I just do my best. I know she understand that I just
write. Don't worry about grade when I write. And not to worry
about getting it done." Given Nam's belief that grades are not
valid indicators of a person's intelligence or character, it is significant that he felt Eleanor saw him as working from an internal, not an external, motivation. In his comment, Nam also
alluded to her understanding of his difficulty in keeping up with
the pace of the class and to her willingness to adjust due dates for
him. Further, although her written responses to his papers did
not convey this directly, she conveyed in conference that she believed he was writing worthwhile essays and improving. "She
mention that I have good topics to talk about. I am improving in
my writing. She say it right there in the conference."

Nam's Essays for College Writing

In contrast with Basic Writing, where specific readings were often the prompts for writings, the prompts Eleanor used in her
College Writing section were in the nature of general places to
look for subjects to write about: for example, a memory of a
childhood experience, an object that has some personal value, a
contemporary social value or practice the writer takes issue with,
or a meaningful reading. All were presented as having public
purposes, and Eleanor, like other teachers, worked to help students be more conscious of their imagined relationship with an
audience and of the purpose they were trying to achieve. Reflecting the general practices of the Writing Program at that time, the
prompts were purposely open for students to form their own
topics, and many invited drawing on personal experience and
observations with "I" as the knower.

This sort of writing fit with what Eleanor explained in an interview as one of her goals for students: "I want them to be confident about themselves as somebody with experiences, and because they've had experiences, they are authorities on what they want to write about." Eleanor's belief in her students' authority and the validity of their experiences was compatible with Nam's own evolving conception that an essay should be written about personally important matters, and he seemed to make the most of these invitations to reflect on his own experiences and values.

Indeed, he used this writing in personally constructive ways at a time of considerable personal confusion and turmoil. Although I came to know this only after the fact, Nam had considered not returning to UMass for the second semester. He wanted to be in a seminary, not at UMass, but could not enter the seminary until the following fall. Also, during intersession, he had read Thomas à Kempis's *The Imitation of Christ*, which had been given to him by his sister. Reading this meditation, which begins with a chapter headed "Of the imitation or following of Christ and of the despising of all vanities of the world," seemed to focus Nam's thoughts all the more intently on his own position as one who would follow Christ while existing in a world filled with material temptations and false teachings that would draw one away from God. One of the messages of the book is the danger of secular learning, that is, of "knowledge that bringeth but little profit or fruit to the soul" (5). As Nam wrote in his exploratory writing for a later essay in College Writing, this warning was in his mind when he started the semester:

> When school started, I had been thinking about the book and what à Kempis said about knowledge. I was afraid to learn knowledge from people, basically professors and teachers, because their knowledge may be limited and may be deceitful, both of which I may be mislead. I did not want to go to school. However, I had no choice but to go.

Having returned to school, Nam seemed to use the essays he wrote in College Writing as a sort of venue—within a place of secular learning—to affirm the Christian truths he valued. He used them also as a vehicle for thinking—not just to convey preselected maxims, but to try to fashion some coherence in the moment as well as over time. Indeed, three of the essays seem addressed to himself with no move to address another audience, although God or Christ may have been an imagined listener or even partner in dialogue. All—including those addressed more obviously to others—contribute to his effort to know himself better and become a better follower of Christ: self-examinations of formative influences and temptations he had fallen prey to and rededication to the precepts of Christ; homilies on the false, superficial values of many people and on the cruelty of one person to another; and a meditation on his search to find his way as a follower of God in this world. In these essays, Nam seems also to be using language as "the better way," the alternative to hate, that is, using language to speak out against those who may have wronged him (e.g., Huy, and high school students who mocked him and other Asians) or misjudged him because of misplaced values while simultaneously advocating Christian precepts.

Some of these essays convey a sense of closure, of Nam explaining beliefs that he has arrived at; others have a feeling of immediacy and lack of containment, of the writing being the immediate vehicle of his thinking and his efforts to compose himself, including trying to reconcile past and present actions with his goal to be a priest. As he advised other students to do, he was going into "more meaningful writing."

The first assignment in College Writing was open for students to write about whatever they chose. Nam's initial brainstorming (below) shows his line of thinking, beginning, as instructed by Eleanor, with what first came to his mind:

> I am confused . . . what I am confused about it not important to anyone but me.
> let not talk about what I am confused about because that would make me even more confused.
> let talk about my day, it would be easier than talking bout my confuseness.
> my day. how was my day? it was alright, I guess. I get up in the morning at seven thirty, but did not want to get up. . . . I get up from a help of an encouragement from a book, Imitation of Christ. it was to discipline yourself if you want to overcome your laziness. I certainly didn't want to be lazy; hearing the word "lazy" makes me chill.
> self-discipline will probable be my topic for the next essay.

Whenever I read this passage, I am struck by the apparent ease and fluency with which Nam "talked" with himself, in contrast with his first notes in September in Basic Writing. In this dialogue with himself, I think Nam was not simply saying he was confused about the assignment. He was referring to much weightier confusions about returning to school and about the nature of secular knowledge. And, as he writes in these notes, the only way he can deal with that confusion is by not dealing with it—acknowledging it and then trying to push it aside. He decides instead to write in a more oblique way about this book that has caused him this confusion. He will write about a lesson from the book that he can deal with: his realization that he needs to exercise self-discipline and avoid the temptation of laziness.

He focuses on being slothful about cleaning up his room, and once again he talks about Huy, his roommate during his senior year in high school and the subject of his second essay in Basic Writing, "Love Your Neighbors As I Have Love You." In an interview, when I asked Nam how he happened to write about Huy again, he said, "I don't know. I guess Huy is still there in my mind." Given that he had written in the earlier essay that Huy had "led me into a darkest experience I have ever encountered," it is not surprising that Nam would return to including him in a writing, and again in a way that seems to serve to work out the hurt that Nam felt. He does so by again casting Huy in an unfavorable light, in this instance as a slothful person lacking self-discipline.

This essay seems considerably more coherent than "Love Your Neighbors," reflecting both Nam's growth as a writer since he entered Basic Writing and, I believe, the difference in the specific issues Nam was dealing with in each essay: this second essay was easier to contain. The final version is interesting also for its form. It is not a 1-3-1 essay. Instead, like his classmate's essay that he liked in Basic Writing, Nam begins with a scene in the present as he stretches out in his room to relax from a long day. As he surveys his room, his thoughts flash back to memories of the previous year and Huy in his room. That section is striking also for its lighthearted tone:

SELF-DISCIPLINE
After a day work of attending college courses and forty-five minutes coming home, I threw my backpack on the bed as

I entered my room. I was tier and exhausted; those commuting were killing me. Kicking those shows off my feet to one corner, I hung my overcoat over the chair and threw myself to the bed. Those steaming socks had to go! I quickly pulled them out and launched them to another corner. Slowly I leaned back. Ah, how relaxing it was! At a moment I felt sweaty under my shirt but I did not bother it; it would spoil my mood.

I stared at the far ceiling and emptied my mind; but not very long before a vision appeared in my mind. It was a year ago when I had a roommate Huy in high school, We had a mini-couch, old but it was still in a good condition. We used to read some old comics, relaxed, or napped from it. But as time passed, we never sat or used the old thing again; simply because he had his books and sketchy notepapers stacked on top of it until there was not a space left for its purpose.

I remembered his clothes and socks were hardly picked up from the flour. You might walk on top of them and probably could not tell them apart from the trash. I had always asked him to pick up his socks from the flour and store them in appropriated places like the drawers, or if they were dirty, the laundry basket. And in a countless time I advised him to throw his crumpled papers in the trash can and not on the floor. "Perfectionism," he mocked me but did it any way; somehow, he could not break his old habit a hour later. Neatness was just not his characteristic . . .

Eleanor's response to this essay and Nam's interpretation of it reflect a misunderstanding—or difference, at the least —between Nam's intentions and Eleanor's reading. In her summary comment, Eleanor focuses on the form of the essay, beginning with praise: "Nam— I like the relaxed tone of this essay, and the way you 'ease' into your topic. The essay is so smooth and effortless, which is nice!" In the next sentence, she takes away the praise she has just offered with a comment that seems to contradict that praise: "On the other hand, I think you needed to bring your topic into focus a little more quickly. I just needed to know where you were going with this. I wasn't sure what the 'drift' of the essay was for quite awhile." When I asked Nam about Eleanor's response, he said that he liked how he had begun the essay. As he said, "I don't want people to know what I'm going to write yet." He had consciously tried to "ease into" the topic and felt that he had succeeded.

Hearing his response, I could not help but think of how my students and I may be working at cross-purposes at times and not realizing it either. In this instance, it seems that as Eleanor read the essay, she had in mind a more expository structure, wherein the writer states the purpose and topic directly, while Nam had in mind a more indirect structure, one where he would begin by setting the scene and tone before announcing his topic explicitly. A conversation over a draft, or as a follow-up to Eleanor's response, might have brought these differing perspectives out for discussion in ways instructive for both parties: for Eleanor to understand that Nam was writing with a conscious purpose and structure in mind, and for Nam to understand how one reader experienced his text, given her expectations.

Nam and Eleanor also had a misunderstanding about the second essay. For this writing, she asked students to begin with some meaningful object as their starting point—a familiar prompt in some composition classes and not one that would seem to present value conflicts for students. It did for Nam. At first, Nam interpreted her as asking them to write about the object. His difficulty was that he did not value material possessions. "I don't like any objects." In class, Eleanor was able to clarify that they were invited to write on anything that a given object prompted. Still, in writing his essay, Nam decided to write something that would resist his initial perception of Eleanor's explanation of the assignment. As he said, he decided to write to show that "the object itself is not important, but the way that people give it." He developed this point by writing about an older man, Joe, whom he respected greatly, and the story of Joe giving his rosary to Nam.

As with the first essay, Nam worked on the essay outside of class. He said that he freewrote a number of pages and used about one-third of them in the first draft that he brought to class. In moving from this draft to his final one, Nam made only a few formal changes—notably, changing many past tense verbs to present tense. For example, in a section describing projects he and his brothers did for Joe, he changed the following sentence in the first draft—"We did not work much but we did a lot of resting."—to this sentence in the final: "We do not work much but we do a lot of resting." Here is the final draft:

MEMORABLE OBJECT

There are a few objects that are meaningful to me, but asking for one of them, I would choice the rosary which my friend Joe has given to me. What's special about it is that it reminds me of Joe and my devotion to God. Joe is a special friend to me. Although he is old, old enough to be my grandfather, we treat each other as a friend; perhaps, a best friend would be more appropriated to our relationship. The rosary also reminds me to pray and workshop God and be faithful to Him as He is to me. Somehow Joe enables and encourages me to have a better relationship with God through the rosary.

I know Joe not too long ago, over the last summer working for him with my two older brothers whom he has hired to build his new shed on his five-acre backyard. We work from morning to late evening, but we are [not] complaining because he very nice to us. . . .

. . . .

As we are invited in his house, he shows us his processions as the way many of us do when our processions are meaningful and have some great pride to be shown. He has his own workshop equipments from nails to bulldozer, and shows us his woodwork from small table to boat. As it is his hobby, he loves to make or fix household appliances. . . .

At one time Joe takes me into his room to the old oak desk and shows me his family albums and personal belongings. Pictures of his family and friends are collected neatly in a stack of albums but no dust seems to appear on any of its cover. . . .

Many personal objects he displays on the desk and keeps them cleaned. Finally, he picks up a wooden rosary that is kept in a wooden treasure box inside the drawer and informs me that his mother has given him at the time of her death. It is made up of wooden beans connected together by a fine thread and attached to a dried wooden cross with a sandy-like body of Jesus Christ. Then he looks at me and hands it over, saying, "I want you to have it because I trust that you will take care of it."

Joe knows my vocation of priesthood through my father and has asked me earlier whether or not it is so. He is interested to know, because he, too, has gone to a seminary with his older brother. Although he did not stay long enough to become a priest, he encourages me and every young men should go to seminary at least a year in our lives to get a feeling of being religious. Thus, because it is true of my intention of going into St. John Seminary, he trusts me to use and keep the rosary safe.

At this moment, it is not that he would twist my arm if I refuse, but I look at the rosary and know not what to say. How could I accept it that is more value than silver or gold? Things that belong or relate to God are always valuable to me, and since this rosary has no purpose but to guide a person in worshipping God, I consider it a priceless treasure. Because I use a rosary of my own in prayer usually on sacred day and on some special or personal occasions, I know its purpose well. How could I reject it when he trusts me and no one else even his grandchildren to keep it safe? . . . For me, it is too honorable duty to be its keeper. Finally, it is not long for him to convince me to take the rosary; either it will be saved in my hand or it will be lost when he is gone. For the sake of its safety, I accept his gift and promise to keep him in mind when I use it to pray.

When school starts, we hardly see each other, but he is always with me daily in prayer. Sometimes I take the rosary out and use it to pray. And sometimes I stop to reflect on the cross seeing how much it reminds me of Joe. Joe is old and his body no longer wealthy as most young people, it is worn, beaten, and dried just as Christ on that cross. His request of me which are to pray for him and to keep the rosary safe resemble Christ's, asking me and His followers to have Him in our mind else our hearts. Like Joe, Christ Jesus is important to me. He wants me to be His friend, to love and be faithful to Him. According to my Catholic belief, He is my Savior and my Salvation and King of all kings. How could I not carry out their requests of me when I am a part of them and they are a part of me? However, a simple prayer of the rosary and keep them in mind each day is not much to ask, but I tend to forget and need something to remind me; and the rosary is just the right one to do the job.

In her response, Eleanor opens by praising the essay, commenting on its effect: "This is a very touching, eloquently described, story." She then moves on to focus on formal features, praising Nam for his use of detail and the "flow" of the essay. Throughout the text of the essay, she also "corrected" Nam's verb revisions, changing them back to past tense—I believe not noticing the systematic changes Nam had made from his first to final draft. She closed her summary comment to him with this comment: "Please look over my corrections, and speak to me about them. Also, I think it might be beneficial to you if you got some extra help from a tutor (for grammar). We'll talk about this."

When I asked him how he interpreted Eleanor's comments, Nam expressed his frustration. To his mind, he had created these tense errors not because he didn't know the rules, but because Eleanor had confused him by something she had said in class. According to Nam, Eleanor had talked in class about how telling a story in present tense can, in Nam's words, "capture people." I can imagine many teachers—myself included—giving that sort of advice about creating dramatic immediacy. For Nam, though, "it was confusing because what I'm saying is past. It was difficult for me to go back and change it, and then I say, 'Well, okay, if she want present tense, I put present tense.' I'm not sure why I'm doing it." So, he followed her advice—her authority—without asking her about his confusion, and then was judged again as deficient, as needing a tutor. In an interview, Nam named this as another instance of the problem of a teacher giving general advice to the class—something that often served to confuse him—instead of particular advice in response to each individual's needs. At best, their exchanges represent a misunderstanding created by lack of communication between them while Nam was drafting the essay. Nam did not seek out a tutor:

> ANNE: Are you going to work with a tutor? Do you think that seems like a good idea?
>
> NAM: I not sure. I don't have any tutor yet. I think I working alone and try to do what I think it is corrected for, and see what happen. I have an idea of like how to write.

While Eleanor's formal correction frustrated Nam, I believe it is equally important—given Nam's wariness of the secular world of college—that she did not in any way question his expressions of religious faith. In this more quietly serious and reflective essay (in contrast with the more playful voice of his first essay), Nam connects his past experience with his present and future, reaffirming his respect and love for Joe and God, both of whom are represented to him by the rosary, and announcing his vocation of priesthood. And, as Eleanor wrote to Nam, it is "eloquently described," reflecting Nam's sensitive eye for detail and his ear for the rhythms of language. The language of the final paragraph also echoes the language and meanings he incorporates from other voices—the Bible, Catholicism, and Langston Hughes ("when I am a part of them and they are a part of me")—to voice his beliefs.

It was about this time, after completing this second essay, that Nam asked me if he could sit in on my class. (I didn't know then that Eleanor had suggested he see a tutor.) He did so a couple of times. In an interview, he explained why:

You're doing this research. I guess, I hope you have more—I felt like you have more area of teaching students. That's why I check in, to try to learn something.

So, he came looking for an "authority." He went on to offer another reason, one related to the pressure he felt in "graded" classes in general:

> I felt kind of like at ease in your class. It's not like you have to be there to get grades. It's just I go there and see if I can get techniques. So, it's like a relaxed study.

A "relaxed study" because Name did not feel the pressure of grades while sitting in my class or while talking with me at other times when we would meet. (As you will see in Chapter Three— and for quite different reasons—Lawrence experienced the class-room climate in my section as much less comfortable.)

In his next three essays in College Writing, Nam continued to focus on important personal views that were rooted in his own experience and consistent with his Christian beliefs. Reflecting the prompts introduced by Eleanor in class, these writings focused more on public issues and informative or persuasive purposes. For all of them, Nam moved to connect private with public concerns and to position himself as a part of a group, writing as a spokesperson either to others in the group or for the group to ones outside the group. In his end-of-the-semester portfolio review, Nam explained his purposes and his own imagined role in relation to his imagined audience:

> Essay #3: "Money Is Not Everything"—I was explaining that money is not that important to everybody. As I explained, I was a skeptical figure who was taking a look at money which was damaging society. I could imagine my cousin reading this writing and wondering about what changes he, too, had on the same topic. The thing I liked the most in this piece was part which I "grew up as young money-lover."

> Essay #4: "One of Those Days:"—I wrote this piece to the minority of which I was a part, explaining the rough times we had gone through. As I explained, I was an authority figure

like a leader that spoke for peace between the two groups and a model that spoke for itself.

Essay #5: "A Fraud in GPA"—I wrote this piece to the people who cared for better education. As I explained, I was not an authority figure but just a student asking for a reform of the important of the GPA or some logical senses of understanding the purpose of GPA. The thing I felt most successful was the evidences from both my own experiences and the articles that supported my argument.

For both the third and fifth essays, Nam develops his point through a narrative of his own wandering and return: for "Money Is Not Everything," being a "young money-lover" who comes to realize that love is more important than money; for "A Fraud in GPA," turning to cheating to get good grades and then realizing how cheating was dishonest and that honest efforts to learn are more important. For this essay, he drew also on two research sources.

The fourth essay, "One of Those Days," was written in response to what Eleanor called "my try at the diversity agenda." Her comment refers to a perceived University and Writing Program "agenda" at that time for faculty to do something in their courses to heighten awareness of prejudice and increase appreciation of diversity. That agenda had been foregrounded since a 1986 brawl at a campus residential complex—ostensibly over the defeat of the Boston Red Sox by the New York Mets in the World Series—had brought to the surface concern over racial divisions that had been, until then, ignored or covered over at our university. In 1986–87, the Writing Program had initiated its own self-examination and conducted a series of workshops, including an intensive one for all Program teachers, to attempt to uncover our own racism and identify ways to counter it through curriculum, teaching approaches, hiring, and program structures (Curtis and Herrington; Herrington and Curtis). One of the University's visible symbolic responses was to designate an annual Civility Week during which public lectures and other social and cultural events were scheduled to discuss issues of discrimination and racism and to celebrate diversity. Also for this week, teachers were asked to do something in their classes related to the goals of the week. Some faculty and staff were critical of having such a week because, counter to the intended aim, it seemed to ghettoize the aims of multiculturalism within a distinct week and program. Still, most also felt pressure to do something in their classes that week in order not to be seen as resisting this effort. Eleanor's difficulties reflect those of many teachers, particularly graduate teaching assistants who did not have the classroom authority of faculty yet were put in the position of feeling expected by the institution to take on socially and personally difficult issues. While we, as faculty and administrators in the Writing Program, tried to lessen this feeling of expectation for our graduate teaching assistants and focus our efforts instead on more comprehensive changes, we were still complicit in circulating single assignments that teachers could use in their classes if they chose.

In an interview, Eleanor explained that she did not present the assignment as she had intended, and, as a result, she saw a "mean side" to some of her students that she did not know how to deal with. She said that she asked students

> to write about a time when they perceived themselves to be a member of a minority, how they were affected and what they thought about. Or, to write about perceiving someone different from them in a way that bothers them. But I didn't totally articulate that one, and I'm really disappointed about what happened with that one. Some of them are using it to rant about their stereotypes, saying incredibly negative things. What I should have done—and what I did last semester—it should be that their attitude changed for some reason. [This semester] I didn't stress the change; I didn't even mention the change.
>
> So, now I have to deal with these papers. Some of them are just terrible, just horrible, just every teacher's nightmare—"why I hate Puerto Ricans," you know. I'm not sure what I'm going to do about that.

Note that Eleanor had used a similar assignment during the previous semester and felt it had been more productive. That time, she asked students to focus on a "change in attitude," and this time she did not. It seems also that Eleanor framed the assignment from/for the perspective of ones used to feeling that they are in the majority, asking them to write about "a time when they perceived themselves to be a member of a minority." As Nam explained to me, identifying this essay as "the most diffi-cult" one to write, he had too many things to write about: "I had a variety of experiences of being a minority, and I couldn't choose which one."

Tellingly, another student I interviewed in that class found this essay difficult for exactly the opposite reason: she had too little to write about. A white Anglo-American, she wrote in her portfolio review:

> I haven't had much experience with prejudiced feelings. The only way I felt I could write about prejudices was to explain why I didn't have any. I don't know if I don't have any because I've lived in a small sheltered town all my life, where no one is noticeably different, or if I just don't think very much about the way people are different.

At least she seemed open to thinking about the nature of differ-ence and prejudice, and perhaps she would have been a receptive reader of Nam's essay had it been published in the class.

She and others of the racial "majority," however, were not Nam's primary intended audience, and this is understandable given what he wanted to say. Instead, as he indicated in his port-folio review comments, he directed his essay to "the minority of which I was a part. . . . I was an authority figure like a leader that spoke for peace between the two groups and a model that spoke for itself." In contrast with his first two essays, this one is more transactional, aimed toward an audience in order to reinforce their self-concept and feeling of solidarity and to influence their actions. Here is the essay:

ONE OF THOSE DAYS

"Merge!" A MERGE command? How the heck do I use it to merge my programs? A teacher just briefly demonstrated how to do "merging" on the blackboard and advised the class to use it whenever we needed to. Unlike computer memory, I could not recall her presentation and turned to the nearest class-mate for help. At first he refused, but I thought he was just joking. Then, when I asked him the second time, he showed no sign of attention as though I was speaking to a wall.

To most people, young and old, being a minority or being different from a large group of people who strongly oppose certain people, class, age or sex, is a terrible experience. The feeling of being loneliness at the time when we really need a friend, but no one would want to associate with us. A silent cry uttered repeatedly when a verbal remark smacks our face hard for we are not good enough to be around. Our stomach turns and grinds its enzymes, wanting to digest every bone whose has just spoken offensively of us. Every harsh word must pay! Every immoral deed must be counted! Soon our innocent mind would turn to hatred, and everything would get ugly. There must be a better way to ease this horrible confirmation of being prejudiced, different, or minority than just by expecting a fair treatment from the majority group.

The high school was dominated by white native American students, and most of them were raised from a rich environment where the colors of their outfits matched the season and their hairs were neatly cut in style. They walked around in school like models and fashion shows like that shown on television and magazine. . . .

As for me and three other Asian classmates, we were the low-class students, and the blue and white were our colors. . . . Our low price, high school sweater, a white dressed shirt with a button missing or with the ripping arm-pit, and any non-jean pant were good enough for us and barely satisfied the school dressed-code requirement. We were the only students wearing that way; anyone would recognize us at a distance once he recognized the blue-and-white. We, obviously, did not have adequate clothings like our schoolmates, but we managed.

. . . .

We were four party-poopers forming a small group. We talked and hung around ourselves more than we associated with the Americans. We hardly participated in most school activities such as sports' fan, school dance, prom, and other social events. Almost everyone one talked about so and so looked beautiful on prom night. How tragedy it was for the girls basketball team to loose a title-match to the all-time-championship-team by a single point away at a second to end. And many other exciting and emotional events occurred, and it would be a great loss to miss all the fun. While all these things were happening, we were at home, studying, or went out shopping for a descent dressed shirt so we would not be laughed at if someone in school discovered what we were wearing. The missing button. The ripping arm-pit. Maybe we did not know too many people who would at the event, nor did we have any interest in most of these activities. We migth be afriad to meet new people, or perhaps we just wanted to be kept alone.

We were the wimps before most students in our school. When food-fight start from one side of the dining hall to the other, we used our food trays for shields. Foods were sometimes thrown at us, but we pretended that they were just a few accidents. We simply pushed the mess off our table and continued with our business. Maintaining neutral, we kept ourselves at peace.

In academic, it was difficult for us to get any higher than an average grade. We flunk a few quizzes and texts and usually handed in our homeworks late. How embarrassing it was for us when we passed in our homework, thinking two to three pages long than enough, while our classmates handed in a stack of papers of the same homework assignments. And we did not participate much in a class discussion, but we did allots of watching, listening, and trying to figure out what the incarnation was the class talking about. But, hey, is there a person have not had one-of-those-days? Furthermore, English is not our native language. Translation was a hassle for us. Some informations were lost when translating from one language to another. How could we know when we were misinterpreting? And yet, only a few English-speaking people could explain the syntax of the standard English; therefore, it was difficult for us to learn and understand the language. Thus, if we wanted to keep up with the class, we must study at least twice as hard as a normal American student would.

Many tears had dropped because we are Asian and foreign. Many upsetting situations were kept in silence, sometimes biting our teeth in vain to release the overload. And numbers of times of disappointment were letting go for they were not worth the energy to grieve about. Because our American classmates and we were significantly different, they were new to us as much as we were to them. Things were shaky at first, but in time both parties would gradually adapt each other differences and the relationship would gradually be improved. Thus, our tears must be wiped away by mean of giving them and ourselves enough time to correlate the differences and by mean of making peace with each other, so that their lives and ours may continue with a lighter burden.

In this essay, Nam expresses both his anger and his conviction that he and other minorities have to find a better way than anger. Throughout his drafts for the essay, he struggles to contain his anger, and not altogether successfully. In early notes he wrote, "Soon our mind would turn to hatred and everything would get ugly. Savage is savage but we are not it and must not become it. All we ever want is to be treated fairly and not to get even." In this final draft, he refers to the still-present hurt out of which he writes—"the verbal remark [that] smacks our face"— while also trying to advocate that he and those he addresses "correlate the differences and . . . make peace with each other." He has experienced the ridicule and unfair treatment of those who mocked him because of race and class—just as Eleanor read it in the "nightmare essays" she received—but he struggles to resist becoming the "savage" he perceives the mockers to be. He struggles also to believe in a future of peace although the experiences of which he writes seem to belie that hope. This tension is evident in his final paragraph, where Nam leaves ambiguous whether things did or would improve. Whether this ambiguity reflects his confusion over verb tense or his own effort to believe what may feel unbelievable, I cannot say.

Certainly, though, the essay demonstrates the difficulty of believing in understanding across race and class differences—especially in the face of collective feelings of prejudice from dominant groups. Nam is aware of the endless passing-on of organized hatred from one generation to another: "KKK will continue to exist from one generation to the next. . . ." He feels his own anger and struggles to contain it. He could retreat into silent submission. He could choose the path of violent action against those who mistreat him and others because of race or class. Or, he could choose the path of loving action, the path he chooses as he aspires to be a priest. For him, this is a path that allows him to feel positive about himself as a "good person" while also hoping for understanding and peace. It is a position in which he will use language—as he is trying to do in this essay—as a means of action, trying to convince himself as he tries to assure and convince the "minority of which I was a part."

His fifth essay was the persuasive critique of the undue importance placed on grade point averages. Then, for his final two essays, Nam turned to himself again. In the sixth essay, for which Eleanor asked students to focus on a passage of their choice that struck them in some way, Nam focused on *The Imitation of Christ* and the profound effect it had on him. For this writing, Nam gave me copies of all of his drafts: a 3½-page handwritten first draft, a 2-page handwritten revised opening, a 4½-page typed third draft, a 5-page fourth draft, and a 4-page fifth and final draft substantially like the previous one. Just the amount of writing he did for this essay is a sign of its importance to Nam, given all the time pressures he felt trying to keep up with his studies. As he wrote in his portfolio review of this essay, "The Lord Is My Shepherd":

> I was thinking about how *The Imitation of Christ* affected me, changing my views about God and people. I began the writing discussing how I was with God in my childhood and how I was alone and without worldly concerns. Then the big change came as I involved with my peers and took interest in worldly affairs, forgetting that I could seek God for a companion, knowledge and wisdom, and His affairs. As I wrote, I was reviewing my past experiences from my childhood to the present.

As with his drafts for "One of Those Days," Nam's successive drafts for this essay demonstrate how drafting and revising can be a dynamic process for reflexive thinking, motivated in Nam's case by an impulse to reconcile internal conflicts he felt in his present life and to shape a self for his future. Note that because he was behind in his writing, Nam did not receive any in-process responses to his drafts from Eleanor. Still, he seemed to have audiences in mind. While some of his revisions indicate an awareness of a public audience as readers for a final draft, I believe a primary imagined audience as he composed the essay was his God, who—as Nam writes—"would not let any of His sons be lost in the wilderness." Throughout this essay, Nam conveys the feeling of affirmation and restorative presence he feels from his God and also his aspiration to follow the ways of God and Christ. It is this feeling of a listening audience coupled with his motivation to make sense for himself that drove Nam's drafting for this essay as he worked—not altogether successfully—to put aside his interests in the world in order to turn to a monastic life with God.

The first draft opens with an epigraph from Thomas à Kempis: "He who seeks anything but God alone and the salvation of his soul will find only trouble and grief." In this draft, Nam recalls his state of mind during winter break when he started reading the book, and how he read it with "passion," for it seemed to answer his questions about how to be a disciple of God. He quotes the book's statement that, "Indeed it is not learning that makes a man holy and just, but a virtuous life makes him pleasing to God," and interprets it to mean that "in order to become holy and just I must live out or apply what I had learned"—as he seemed to have been trying to do in his College Writing essays. It is also in this draft that he writes of how the book made him distrustful of secular knowledge and fearful of the potentially "limited and deceitful knowledge" that might sway him at the University.

The second draft—two handwritten pages—is a substantially different reflection on the book, this time focusing on the book itself and its meaning to Nam. In this draft, much as in a private journal entry, he goes on to try to work out for himself his understanding of passages from the book. He devotes the full second page to reflecting on one quote, and, in doing so, seems to be using a strategy introduced in Basic Writing. He selects a passage that strikes him: "One of the many things I find most interesting is that about 'being secluded from the world and avoiding public affairs for the sake of peace and good conscience.'" He then tries out possible interpretations: "This probably means . . . Perhaps this may also mean that. . . . " Finally, he states one of the reasons it is difficult for him to turn from worldly affairs: "Still, it is hard to get away from the public or worldly affairs when lives are at stake, especilly those who are close to you are involved in issues like birth control, AIDS, abortion, homocide, rape and so on." Nam interprets à Kempis as saying that he should do so: "However, if I want to devote myself to God, I have to leave these situations aside and follow God." He accepts this interpretation, attributing his difficulty in understanding it to God's unfathomable wisdom: "Perhaps here is something greater than what the eye can see and that the ear can hear, that God wants his people not to worry but be at peace."

In his third draft, a 4½-page typed draft, Nam continues to explore his personal quandary: to enter the world's dialogue or to step aside to meditate with God. In this draft, he explores the question indirectly, returning to focusing on himself and his own prior belief that being alone and solitary is a negative, lonely experience instead of being positive. While he seems still to be exploring his own thinking, his editorial remarks in the draft suggest that he was thinking also of composing a text for readers. He titles the draft and begins it as follows:

BACK TO MEDITATION

the topic is silence and solitude can be a profitable progress of spiritual exercise. but I did not know it so when I came across a book The Imitation of Christ sitting on a bookshelf and collecting a year worth of dust. . . . I thought if a person withdrawn from the society is crazy and very unhealthy. The person is probably afraid to meet people like the way I used to.

In this opening, with his reference to a hypothetical situation for "a person," Nam moves to connect others with the quandary he is experiencing. In the draft, he goes on to recount his early experience of feeling isolated and lonely because he did not know English well and "felt out of place." He concludes that section by writing, "The loneliness I had experience was not a nice one." He then tells a story of wandering and return, of learning to socialize and letting himself be distracted from God by the ways of the world: "Anyway, I was saying that being in the crowd and watching TV in order to be in a group or to be with peers caused me to withdraw away from God." Here he reminds himself to add text from his initial draft: "insert here the writing about the winter break I got the book." He then returns to the dilemma he continues to see between being in the world and being with God, and he tries to work out a resolution:

So, in the last two weeks of the winter break I began to recollected myself, locked out from the world, basically from the TV and spent my times meditating. It also make me wonder about going back to the crowd, to the world, to the university where temptation were everywhere. This was the second time I was ever afraid of the world: one was from my youth in elementry schools, and the other is in college. Perhaps, I was afraid to lose God again. Also, I wanted to spend time with God more than with the people. However, although it is tougher to be faithful to God in the world than in my room, something tells me that I should not be afraid to be in the world. I have learned many things from the book and one thing I have learned facing the world is that we are all imperfect human beings, but we do not have to choose imperfect actions, for we have a choice to do what is right and fitting to God and to ourselves.

Here Nam moves from his understanding in his second draft that he should avoid the world to what seems to me a more complex understanding that we can accept that we are "imperfect beings"—by nature—yet also be agents in the world, that is, we can choose and can make choices to be faithful to God and "do what is right and fitting to God and to ourselves."

His fourth and fifth drafts are very similar. (Unless I note otherwise, I will talk of them in the singular, using excerpts from the fifth.) In this draft, Nam seems even more conscious of composing for an audience and more selective about what he presents of his life and how he shapes that presentation. This final version, entitled "The Lord Is My Shepherd," is a moving meditation on his wandering and return from God, closing with the conflict he still feels about wanting to be in the world and wanting to serve Christ:

THE LORD IS MY SHEPHERD

God would not let any of His sons to be lost in the wilderness. The Bible has mentioned that God is like a shepherd who watch over his sheep. If one of his hundred sheep is lost, He would leave His ninety-nine sheep and go out to seek for the lost sheep. And I was lost and He brought me back to His side.

One night in January winter, I was in my room, breathed heavily, and was bored to death. It was a big break for me or any college student to have fun, relax and take it easy before the second semester began. Surely, there would be many things to do for recreation, but I did not do anything much. It was too cold to do anything outside. And everyone I knew was working. A few things I could do were to clear up my room and things in the house and watch TV. However, when the house ran out of things to be clearn up, and old movies were shown over and over, I was bore again. I wanted to do something, anything but to sit here and do nothing.

So I went to my bookshelf to see if there any interesting book to read. I found one, *The Imitation of Christ*, which my little sister gave me a year ago, and it had been sitting there in the shelf ever since then. I was curious about the book and half was judging from its cover. I did not want to imitate someone's life; I wanted to be me. Besides, everyone is a unique individual. However, at the same time, I felt that it would be alright to imitate Christ because He is Holy and the Son of God. Little did I remember that Christ is my Lord and God. A little voice in the back of my head encouraged me to read it and decide later whether or not imitating Christ would be a good idea. So I settled down comfortably on a couch and began to explore it.

As I was read each word and line slowly, I felt as if there was a great cloud in my head with thunders flashing and a great voice called out to me, saying every word I was reading. My heart beat a little faster as I continued reading, and I dared not to set the book down. The book was not brainwashing me or anything the like, but I felt very tense as though my heart, my mind, and my soul were melting. Perhaps, I had been so far away from God and was afraid to see Him. I felt I had displeased Him in many ways: I was deaf to His voice, ignored His Words, and more.

Ever since when I was young, I liked to be a part with a group, to fit in with my classmates, to have the same talent as my peers'. I liked to fit in with everybody and to be a part of the group, but I could not. Despite that my language barrier had a part of it, I had no interest in the things that my peers desired such as in sports: basketball and baseball. These two sports are popular and everyone had something to talk about them. I had no interest in "sex talk" or perhaps "dirty talk" that my peers loved to talk about too. Perhaps, I was lack in many interests. Thus, it was hard for me to fit in with a conversation. But again, I did not like to have conversation as a group. Therefore, it was almost impossible for me to be a part with the group, to be like my peers, or to fit in with them.

Consequently, I was alone and lonely. No friend. No one that I could share my life with. During the time of loneliness, I found God at my side, Who comforted me as a father to his son. He listened to me all my troubles and grieves and helped me through this depressing time. At a time when my older brother like to pick on me, ordering me to do things around the house which were helpful but I was the only one who was working while he disappeared or sitting around watching me working. When the chore was done, he ordered me to another task. And when he was told to do a chore by our parents, he passed it over to me and his chore became mine. Sometimes I felt like Cinderella.

My brother also like to call me name, usually "Hey, stupid" or "Cho Hang" which means, in a way similar to "white trash" in English. I did not know why he treated me in such a manner. Was it the way I looked, the way I acted, or was it just his way of being an older brother? But God was there all the times, advising me to be patience and forgive him for he knew not what he was saying. I felt almost like a saint. Although there were a few times I wanted to take vengeance on him, but very soon I would feel horribly wrong for having such a thought. For it was written, one who loves all his brothers truly loves God, but he is a liar to say he loves God but hates one of his least brothers.

Happily-ever-after lasted for a few years. My relationship with God began to fade away when I became involved with the world around me. I started to listen to my peers and did things which they considered fun. At the same time I wanted to be in a part of the group, but not too an extreme. My peers advised me to watch television shows and movies, and to be involved with school activities like sports and clubs. I took their advises and involved with the world. As I began to spend time with my peers and with the things existed in the world, my time with God was shorter and shorter until a short moment with God was a routine not a meaningful time as before.

Many years later I got used to the world, the crowd, and to what the people have to say about themselves, about what they were thinking or feeling. I was interested more in how people behaved the world around them. I was also interested in the knowledge the scholars had recently discovered something about the people. And what about my fairy father? Well, I still prayed and offered my troubles and problems to Him, perhaps like the way my brother left his problems to me, but I was not give Him enough time to hear His teachings or guidance for me; I did not seek Him for knowledge or want to be comforted in His arm; thus, I became a worldly person.

After reading *The Imitation of Christ*, it was time for me to turn back to Him like I once was, for me to spend more time in meditation on Him, and for me to avoid the company of men whenever I could. For it has written, "Avoid public gatherings as much as possible, for the discussing of worldly affairs becomes a great hindrance, even though it be with the best of intentions, for we are quickly corrupted and ensnared by vanity." That means politic, news, social gatherings in public, movies, and so on would be given up and put them aside for God's sake, and because they are considered distractions for spiritual devotion.

Ever since I finished the book, I re-read it a few more times as a way of meditation. And ever since I have attempt to withdraw from the world, but I found it very difficult to do so, because I am very interested about people and their affairs, and because I am in college where I have to involve with the crowd in order to learn something. But the fact that I love God and dare not to go against His will for me. Thus it is wise for me to imitate Christ for He was set a great example to all man kind to be the children of God.

Nam opens focusing not on the book itself, but on the message of God's promise to watch over his sheep, drawing those who wander away back into His fold. In this first paragraph, using language of the Bible, he again states his feeling that God has given him the sense of belonging that he so needs.

He then recalls his discovery of the book *The Imitation of Christ*, placing himself in a narrative scene and dramatizing his experience reading it, with the intention, I believe, of drawing us into the experience through the sensory imagery he uses. He evokes a vivid sense of a moment of salvation, but while he tells us that his heart, mind, and soul "were melting," he is also careful to add that he had his wits about him: "the book was not brainwashing me."[3]

Midway through the essay, in telling about his brother's mistreatment of him, he casts himself as the long-suffering, unjustly treated one. And, in characteristic fashion for Nam, he mixes secular and religious images and language, casting himself as both "Cinderella" and "saint." Casting himself in those roles, he counters the roles his brother was trying to put him into with his harsh words, "Hey, stupid" or "Cho Hang."

He then recounts how he wandered again from God, starting to make friends and spend time with them, and attending to worldly matters while forgetting God. In the third to last paragraph, note the opposition he sets up between secular knowledge ("knowledge the scholars had recently discovered") and spiritual knowledge ("His teachings . . . I did not seek Him for knowledge").

In the closing two paragraphs, Nam returns to the book and how it has recalled him to Christ and heightened his awareness of the tension he feels between his difficulty in "withdraw[ing] from the world" and his resolve to "spend more time in meditation." These paragraphs convey as well the unresolved struggle Nam feels between, on the one hand, trying to reconcile the message of the book to his own impulse to be in the world ("ever since I have attempt to withdraw from the world, I have found it very difficult to do so") and, on the other hand, acquiescing fully to this discourse that promises him total acceptance when he puts himself within it ("Thus it is wise for me to imitate Christ. . . .").

Nam's seventh and final essay, "A Helping Hand," continues the inner debate begun and left unresolved in "The Lord Is My Shepherd." In this essay, though, he seems to have moved from trying to convince himself to live a monastic life to focusing on the difficulty of being in the world and serving God there. This focus seems more consistent with his ultimate goal of serving a pastoral role as a counselor to others. The genre shifts as well, from meditation to homily. In the essay, he pursues a theme he introduced in the fall in one draft of his essay on "So Tsi-fai": "People don't let themselves help others or offer to help others who are less fortunate than them or just don't know how." In this final essay for College Writing, Nam shows how he experienced that tension in his everyday life when in a situation where acting for others may have meant acting against his own self-interests. In the essay, Nam focuses on two scenes that took place when he worked at a large bakery, loading delivery trucks, and a hungry man named Roy approached him at the loading dock and begged for bread: one when Nam was alone and gave the man bread, and a second when his manager, Bill, was present and thus he did not. As he concludes in his final paragraph:

> It is hard to do good deeds for other people in public, especially the poor or homeless. I was afraid to help Roy, because Bill was there. He might scold me for giving something away that did not belong to me and would probably ask me to pay for it. This would be most embarrassing. Like most people, I did not want to be scolding by anybody. And if I got fire, how would I get another job with only a few weeks before the summer ended? But when I was alone, I decided to help and cared less about the consequences that I might receive. Nevertheless, to help a person is like to save a fire, because a second opinion may be too late.

Characteristically, Nam ends with a maxim, but not a Biblical one. It is a more everyday adage, one that seems apt, even if perhaps unexpected in context.

In an interview, Nam said this was one of the two essays he liked the most: "I had fun writing it. . . . The information's here, as much as possible. It's a real clear picture." Providing a "clear picture" was important to Nam, and learning to do that was what he considered his main accomplishment over the whole year from Basic Writing to College Writing:

> ANNE: If you think about the whole year and you as a writer, what would you say you have accomplished the most?
>
> NAM: I guess, explaining my thesis. I like that I'm able to come up with these things and explain them. Before I just say what it is, like a quick sentence, and then try to explain it. I learn to do a lot of explaining—that's the key—and let the reader see what I was seeing. That's my accomplishment.

Another accomplishment was following for himself the advice he told me he would offer to other students entering College Writing: "Choose topics that are meaningful." His essay assignments and teachers in both courses—while distinct from one course to the other—were similar in encouraging him to make this choice: all essay prompts were open enough for students to decide their own approach, and both teachers respected Nam's interests and his writing. Nam's experience shows why this advice is important beyond merely making the course more interesting for students. By following his own advice both in Basic Writing and College Writing, Nam did not always arrive at final drafts that were fully contained or resolved, but he did encounter the challenge of trying to make sense for himself, as well as for others, of real issues concerning his place in the world and his position on private and social issues. Facing that challenge repeatedly created a situation conducive to his development as a *writer* also—a situation where a "quick sentence" and simple explanation were insufficient, and where elaboration, consideration of multiple perspectives, and revising to shape ideas and self-presentation were essential.

Writing in Philosophy and Psychology

"It's quicker to write their way, than my own." (Nam, on writing for his psychology course)

During his two semesters at UMass, Nam reported having to write for three other courses: Introduction to Philosophy, Human Development, and Methods of Inquiry in Psychology. (Since I don't have copies of his writings for Human Development—for which he received a final grade of B—I will comment only on the philosophy and psychology courses.) The writing he did for these two courses demonstrates clearly that academic writing is not all of a kind and that the differences are linked to the ways of thinking of a discipline and, more particularly, to how those ways of thinking are articulated by specific teachers for whom students write. This, however, is not the primary point I want to develop here. I will stay focused on Nam's experience in writing for these courses. In the first two courses, Nam had little difficulty with the writing, save for the time it took; in Methods of Inquiry in Psychology, however, he encountered more difficulty. I believe the reason that the first two courses posed less difficulty is that, in both, the writing he was asked to do was more like the genre of essay writing that he was learning in Basic Writing and College Writing. For Methods of Inquiry in Psychology, the genre for writing was quite different. The problems Nam had with this psychology course, however, derived not only from the fact that he was being asked to write in a new genre; they also hinged on the way that this genre was presented and on a conflict he experienced between the way of knowing valued in the course and his personal values.

Nam took Introduction to Philosophy, a course that fulfilled general education requirements, concurrently with Basic Writing. He told me that his major difficulty with the course was the time it took him to complete the assigned essays. His teacher was understanding about his needing more time and granted it without penalty. Indeed, he allowed Nam to take an Incomplete in order to finish the final essay during intersession. (Nam subsequently received a B for the course.) There were three major essays required, each asking students to explain how specific philosophers dealt with a particular philosophical problem; for example, for the second essay, they were to discuss how both Descartes and Hume dealt with the question of the foundation of knowledge. These essays differed from essays in Basic Writing only in that they were framed in terms of the discourse of philosophy. Otherwise, they were similar to the essay as presented in Basic Writing: the writer was positioned as the knower, and reference to "I" as the knower/writer was acceptable, as was reference to one's own personal knowledge and observations (although such references were not required).

From Nam's explanation of the assignments, I infer that students were asked primarily to demonstrate their knowledge of the readings and lectures by restating them. (As we will discuss in later chapters, Rachel and Francois report a similarly limited "display" purpose for writing in an Introduction to Sociology course.) To Nam, this limited purpose was boring—both for him and potentially for his teacher-reader:

> When I write something, it has to be me. It has to be something new, something that people haven't explored before. And when I do that I feel great. But when I have all these note of what the teacher say, it's like I rewrote it again. . . . If you know the material already, it seems like this is boring. It's simple you know. . . . He's not going to learn anything by what I'm writing.
>
> I guess I want to . . . make it more than what they expect.

Nam's nine-page essay for the second assignment reflects his perception of the task. The opening two paragraphs and an excerpt from the section on Descartes follow:

FOUNDATIONALISM

Some people process their knowledge from personal self; some gain knowledge from the world. Whichever internal or external sources that people absorb knowledge from, the knowledge had to derive from some foundations of all knowledge. Looking for the foundation of knowledge from personal prospective, Rene Descartes has his own technique. While David Hume builds his knowledge from the world. Both, however, seek the foundation of all knowledge in order to build true knowledge.

Foundationalism is a theory about the structure of knowledge that all propositions that are knowable can ultimately be justified by an appeal to a set of basic proposition. These propositions are basic because they cannot be justified by an appeal to any other proposition. They are self-evidences. This set of basic propositions is the foundation of all our knowledge. . . .

Now we know that "I" necessarily exists, but who is this "I" as we look into ourselves. Some believe that we human beings are rational animals. In order for us to know whether or not we are rational animals, we would have to inquire what is an "animal" and what "rational" means. From solving this one problem, we will fall into many more difficult ones. As for Descrates, he rejects this rational business for the "I" that exists, and he simply claims that the "I" has a body which has shape and location, and takes up space. Also this "I" has a soul which feels, thinks and is resistant to other beliefs. However, we can be deceived about the existing of our bodies but not doubt the existence of our selves, the souls or "I's". The body might not exist but the "I" would still exist. Therefore, the "I" that exists cannot be a body. Furthermore, to Descartes, the "I exist" is a thinking being. By thinking, we are doubting, understanding, firming, denying, willing, sensing, and imagining. Thought is one thing that cannot be detached from us. As long as we think, we exist.

Notice that Nam's text shows his awareness of writing in a different context and for a different purpose from his Basic Writing class. He begins the essay in more direct, expository fashion and sets it up in terms of issues in philosophy. The rest of the essay is, for the most part, a detached recitation of Descartes' and Hume's views, relying a good deal, I think, on the language of the teacher and the course readings. Still, the text shows Nam engaging in the kind of questioning and testing out of ideas and careful use of language that this philosophy teacher valued. Further, Nam works to weave this language into the conversational, reflective style he had used in Basic Writing, and he does add some of his own examples in a way appropriate for thinking as a philosopher. For instance, to define "propositional knowledge," he includes his own example: "I know that the Tower Library is closed on Saturday." Notice here that he does not mark *I* with quotations, indicating that he is distinguishing this use of *I* from the *I* marked as the object of philosophical reflection in other parts of his text. Later in the essay, he refers again to the library to illustrate how Descartes reasons that our senses can deceive us:

When we sight people down from the 20th floor of UMass Tower Library, we picture them very small. In general, the sense can deceive us about very big, very small, or very distant things such as the size and distance of the Sun cannot be sense accurately by our own naked eyes.

I read these examples as one attempt to make the essay "more than what they expect." I cite them also to indicate that such in-text references to "I" and "we" and examples from personal observation were fine in this essay for Philosophy. For the essay, Nam received an A. While the teacher marked a few corrections of Nam's wording and grammar, he did not indicate in his written response to Nam or in an interview with me any difficulty in understanding Nam's written English.

In an interview with Nam, I asked if he could apply anything he learned in Basic Writing to the writing he did in Philosophy:

NAM: Oh yeah.

ANNE: What, do you think?

NAM: I guess try to make clear or use examples. Even though I have what he said already, even though there's notes already there, I guess I use from English that make clear what you know. So I try to make it clear by showing examples.

Thus Nam experienced no apparent disjunction between the ways of writing valued in Basic Writing and those valued in his Introduction to Philosophy class. More important, I think, he also experienced no disjunction between the ways of thinking that were valued in Introduction to Philosophy and his own interest in questions of self and soul or his inclination toward introspection with "I" as the discursively present knower. That fit is reflected in the seeming ease with which he talks through Descartes' line of thinking: "Now we know that 'I' necessarily exists, but who is this 'I' as we look into ourselves . . . "—a question Nam was pondering for himself as well.

Second semester, when he entered Psych 241, Methods of Inquiry in Psychology, Nam experienced more of a disjunction—with both the kind of writing he valued and his way of knowing. As described in the University catalogue, Psych 241 (often called Psych Methods) teaches "research methods in psychology . . . [with] emphasis on hands-on experience in labs and on lab reports." An important foundation course for all psychology majors, it introduces students to basic empirical research methods and to the genre of research articles. Although the catalogue description does not specify this, the course also stresses methods for quantitative research in the tradition of scientific discourse, specifically behavioral research. Students are introduced to a basic research paradigm (formulating hypotheses and obtaining and analyzing data using quantitative methods) and a genre consistent with it. The central part of Nam's course consisted of four laboratory experiments that students completed and wrote up. It was taught as a large, multisection course with one lecture per week given by the supervising teacher and smaller lab sections taught by graduate teaching assistants (TAs). The TAs also responded to and graded the lab reports.

For this course, Nam was asked to write in a genre at odds with the kind of writing that he had come to value and that had been privileged in the Writing Program courses. For this genre, as presented by Nam's lab teacher, the researcher/writer is positioned as distanced and is not to appear in the text at all; personal knowledge is not to be drawn on. The discourse is that of experimental, quantitative research, where the objective procedures of the experiment and statistical tests are the instrument of knowing. In discussing this course and this genre, my intention is not to critique the genre in general. While, admittedly, I do not practice this type of research or write in this genre, I read and value some research done in this way. Further, I believe that students should have the occasion to try out various ways of seeing and the genres associated with them. Not all of those ways will feel like a fit for each student. Having made these disclaimers, I admit still to having a critique to make about Nam's experience with this course. That critique involves the way in which the genre seemed to have been presented to him by his lab teacher, even though her approach was well-intentioned. Specifically, the lab teacher who read and graded Nam's reports seemed to have presented the genre much more rigidly than did the supervising teacher or the *Publication Manual of the American Psychological Association*. As with College Writing, Nam's difficulties with this course may also reflect misunderstandings that arose between Nam and his lab teacher.

The lack of fit that Nam experienced also related, I believe, to a conflict with his personal values, one that was perhaps inevitable. He refers to this conflict in his exploratory drafts for "The Lord Is My Shepherd," written in College Writing toward the end of that semester. As he wrote in these drafts, after reading *The Imitation of Christ* he was wary of the secular knowledge disseminated by professors in college:

> Why should I go to classes when I was afraid to learn from what would be teaching. In statistics class, the professor was teaching the class to use mathematics to show the truth of nature, especially human behavior. By taking a small porporsion of the population, statistics would test and draw a conclusion. In statistics class, the students were taught to believe what was said by testing or seeing. [Here, Nam drew an arrow pointing to the previous sentence.] In Methods of Psychology class, students are taught to study human behavior by [The sentence stops here.]

Although Nam doesn't finish that sentence, I think it is fair to infer that he was as wary of Psych Methods as he was of statistics, and wary specifically of using statistics and "testing" to understand "the truth of nature" as if these methods were the means to foundational knowledge. These are the courses that he names explicitly when reflecting on his fear that he might be influenced by the kind of knowledge taught by professors, "knowledge that may be limited and may be deceitful, both of which I may be mislead."

After reading a draft of this chapter, the supervising teacher told me that in lecture she tried to convey that statistics is just one way of making claims, that it was a "kind of game." This view seems not to have come through to Nam. That may have been due to his wariness, his need to distance himself out of his fear that he might be drawn in. I suspect that he got through both of these classes by doing what was expected of him but keeping himself distanced from it so as not to be "misled." I do not mean to imply that all students experienced the course this way. As I will show in Rachel's chapter, she felt no such conflict and apprenticed herself willingly to psychology and to quantitative, empirical research methods as a way to pursue personally important questions.

Writing his first lab report underscored for Nam how different the world of Psych Methods was from what he knew and valued. He initially misread what was expected of him. For this experiment, students were asked to frame and test a hypothesis through observation of others' behavior. The focus was not on the substance of the study or on the findings but on correctly following research procedures and conventions of laboratory reports. In writing it up, since they had not yet been introduced to doing literature reviews, the students were told to introduce the study drawing on their own knowledge. The introduction to Nam's first report is presented in Figure 1.

Nam received a C for that report from the TA of his lab section. The grade was arrived at based on ratings using a detailed analytic rating guide with categories for each section of the report and one for style. For the introduction, Nam received specific ratings of "Fair" (the third ranking on a scale of 1 to 7 where the seventh rank represented "Excellent") for each of three subcategories: broad, general description of the area; statement of purpose and brief summary of what was done; and overall logical justification for the study. He received a "marginal" rating (second ranking with seventh excellent) for style (clarity of expression and grammar). In her final written comments, the teaching assistant was encouraging in tone while foregrounding Nam's difficulty with English:

> Nam, I can see that you put a lot of effort into this, and you have most of the correct information. However, there are some fundamental problems in your writing that keep recurring. I strongly advise that you seek some assistance at the University Writing Center in Bartlett Hall. Once you master them, you'll have some great papers.

The TA reported to me that after reading Nam's first paper, she was concerned that he could not write well enough to stay in the class. I can imagine that she might have felt overwhelmed by his difficulties with English and his more conversational style. She consulted with the department's undergraduate advisor about

> Naturalistic Observation of Door Holding
>
> Mother always told me to be a gentleman whenever encountering with the opposite sexes; young girls and ladies alike. A manhood is a big deal in my family. A manhood is to "hit the sack" early and wake up when the rooster cries, to work hard for any purpose and endure from any hardship, to have patience as well as kindness, and so on. And when he interacts with the opposite sex (female), he always gives her his most respect as would a knight in the Middle Age respect his lady.
>
> Upon hearing my classmates who were going to do a ~~study of~~ naturalistic observation of door holding in order to determine which gender (male or female) would hold for whom, I was for sure that this study would not be much of a study, and believed that the males would ~~appear most after~~ the findings. In contrast, most of the female classmates strongly believed that there would be no difference between both genders, claiming that female population does hold door for the opposite sex as well as male. Thus, this report is based on ~~the study of~~ naturalistic observation of door holding in order to determine whether or not holding door for the ladies is the men's job.
>
> Note: The handwritten markings were made by the teacher.

FIGURE 1. *Introduction to Nam's first lab report for Psych Methods.*

making him withdraw from the class. The undergraduate advisor did not support such a move: Nam was allowed to stay, and they resolved that the TA would focus only on, as she said, "content and not the style": "If I had commented on style, then he wouldn't have passed." Here, in contrast with his philosophy class, language was the barrier because in this case—at least on the basis of the evaluation of the first report—there was no reason to judge that Nam could not handle the intellectual demands of the class. Writing of a survey of faculty concerns regarding non-native speakers of English, Zamel reports that some of her respondents evidenced a similar difficulty in seeing beyond surface errors. Once the decision was made that Nam would remain in the course, the TA did focus on "content and not the style," and her written comments on his reports appeared to be both fair and supportive.

The TA's suggestion that Nam "seek assistance" with his writing came at about the same time that Eleanor suggested he seek a tutor. Nam did not seek assistance, nor did he mention his difficulty to me, although he did consult with me about similar concerns of clarity and grammar in relation to his writing for College Writing. However, he did seek out the TA to find out what was lacking in this paper. Here is how he explained what he learned from her:

> First, I wrote it in my own style. I talked of my own experience that males should open doors for females, tradition, something like that. And you're not supposed to say that. You're not supposed to say this is my experience. . . . My past experience wasn't good enough because there's a lot of people may do the same experience and my own experience may not be significant because it just happen by chance. Or, it must not be too much sophisticated. . . . It's supposed to be other people experience. Like other people did research on it. And, it's not necessary what I experience.

Nam's comment reflects his understanding of style as including how one positions oneself as the knower. What he says about not referring to one's own experience pertains more to the expectation for subsequent reports, since students were allowed to draw on personal knowledge for the first "hybrid" report.

Still, the TA's gloss, in an interview with me, of his first report introduction indicates that she felt it was problematic even there. Her comment also reflects how what is first represented as a stylistic convention is closely connected with her perception of the researcher's authority:

> Starting with this anecdotal information about what his mother told him is fine. . . . It's just the way of saying it and the way he was presenting it. The voice he was using, using the first person and talking about the class . . .

She pointed to a sentence in paragraph two: "In contrast, most of my female classmates strongly believed that there would be no difference between both genders." The TA commented:

> This sentence is inappropriate because he's talking about—what you should be doing when you present your hypothesis is "the experimenter believes" or "based on past literature." This is

akin to saying that, "Well, my one friend believes this, and my other friend believes this and . . ." or, "I think this but someone will disagree with me." It's just—it's not done . . .

She went on to comment,

> TA: It's just not acceptable by APA standards—unfortunately. [Here she is referring to the *Publication Manual of the American Psychological Association*.]
>
> ANNE: Unfortunately?
>
> TA: Well, unfortunately, because it's nice that [the style is] standardized, but the APA format is extremely—it's a big pain in the butt. It can be restrictive.

These comments reflect the teacher's difficulty in figuring out how to respond to Nam's writing, which to some may have looked, to use a term from Bizzell, quite "outlandish" ("What Happens" 164). In the first comment, she says that reference to "anecdotal information" is acceptable for the first writing and in the next comment she says no. In that second comment, she seems to conflate her judgment about acceptable warrants with a judgment about style, implying, I believe, that "the experimenter believes" would have represented a stronger warrant than "I believe." Indeed, had Nam positioned himself as "the experimenter" and used more of the language of empirical research ("data," "test," "hypothesis"), he might have created more discursive authority for himself.

While the TA reacts against the "first person voice," she also calls the APA format that proscribes it "a big pain in the butt." That feeling—along with the seemingly contradictory effort to enforce the rules she finds "too restrictive"—is based, I believe, on her own experience with a manuscript she submitted to a journal. In an interview, she said she recalled having submitted a manuscript—in which she used some first person references—to a journal and had it returned with editorial comments to the effect of, "You can't say this." She said "that was years ago," and acknowledged that "APA has changed about this also. They will now accept it, but discourage it heavily, and depending on the journal." The TA is most likely referring to a shift from the second to the third edition of the APA's publication manual. Still, my reading of the third edition of the *Manual* suggests that it does not "discourage" first person usage as strongly as she suggests. For example, it addresses the use of first person pronouns in a section on clarity, advising as follows:

> Inappropriately or illogically attributing action in the name of objectivity can be misleading. For example, writing "The experimenter instructed the subjects" when "the experimenter" refers to yourself is at best ambiguous and may even give the impression that you disavow your own study. (33)

In the sample paper included in the *Manual*, "I" is used not only in the introduction, but also in the methods section. (For further discussion of these style conventions see Bazerman ["Codifying"].)

Further, and perhaps more important, the supervising teacher also seemed more flexible in how she presented the genre. In an interview with me, she said that the assigned readings for the course included various genres, including review and research articles. She also indicated that, in lectures, she encouraged students to consider differences in the genres as they read them, although these differences were not presented in relation to the writing that students themselves were doing. She also said that she encouraged the lab teachers to point out differences in style.

I question whether Nam's lab teacher followed this suggestion, given her response to his reports and her comments to me. She had experienced a force that was real and powerful, the proscription issued by a journal editor who, like many, still found first person unacceptable. In the face of this experience and as a graduate student with limited professional authority herself, she presented the first person proscription as an invariant rule. Her rationale:

> I find it easier just to tell them, "Don't use it." . . . It's consistency more than anything. And the more consistent the rules you give them, the easier, I think, they find the writing.

Nam only needed the one meeting with her to understand the rules and what she wanted. In his second lab report, he showed himself sufficiently adept at adapting to expectations. See Figure 2 for Nam's introduction to this lab report.

Mnemonic Methods: Loci and Rote in Noise ⎰ a bit awkward

The point of the study is to find out which mnemonic method, loci or rote, performs better result in

noise and in quiet. Current study found that high imagery concepts were generally attained easier than low

imagery concepts (Ketz and Paivio, 1975). Thus, since rote memorization has a low to none image coding, and

since method of loci has high image coding, concrete words recalled would be higher for method of loci and

lower for rote memorization.

The experiment also tests the noise effect in memory performance by stimulating the half of the subjects

with mid-rock music as a noise condition. According to Gisselbrecht-Simon's (1988) study, noise effect appears

only through the unexpected recognition test, and not through the unexpected recall test; thus, the present

study, which is based on the recall test, would likely have no noise effect on memory performances.

Note: The handwritten markings were made by the teacher.

FIGURE 2. *Introduction to Nam's second lab report for Psych Methods.*

This time, as you can see, Nam relies solely on other research to introduce the study he conducted, and he writes in a distanced voice. He also takes on some of the language of the genre (e.g., "the experiment" and "tests"), and he seems to have relied heavily on appropriation of language and phrases from his research sources, although this is not commented upon by the TA. The teacher's analytic rating of the introduction indicated her judgment that he had improved in statement of purpose ("Very Good" rating); failed to provide a broad, general description of the area ("Failing" rating) and done a "Fair" job of reviewing of the literature and providing an overall logical justification. She rated Style as "Very Good" (grade of A/B). This rating may reflect her decision to focus only "on content and not the style." The overall grade is first represented as a B, with the comment, "N, a great improvement;" 20 points are deducted for lateness, making the grade finally a D.

When I asked Nam how he felt about writing as he did in the second report, he focused not on the epistemological issue, but on the style of the writing, referring to what seemed to him to be the unnecessary repetition that it asked for—especially in the results section—and the emphasis on "just the facts."

ANNE: How do you feel about those differences in the writing?

NAM: First I felt awkward. They're asking me to do something that I don't want to learn. I had learned a better way, like the English-writing way, and now they ask me to do something that I—I felt kind of awkward. . . . A couple of labs later, I thought, okay, if this is what they need, just give it to them. [He chuckles.]

ANNE: Does it make sense to you that it would be different or it's just because it's what they want?

NAM: I guess this is what they want. Just give it to them.

Elsewhere in the interview, he commented, "Okay, this is what she wants. It's quicker to write their way than my own."

After his first lab report, Nam proved able to adapt to this new genre and understand what was happening. As he explained to me, "I wrote it my way and she felt awkward, because she didn't want it that way." So, Nam wrote it their way—but without accepting that style or, I believe, its accompanying epistemology. Essentially, he submerged his questions and proceeded in a rather mechanical fashion to do the chores of the course.

I think it is a testament to Nam's will that he persisted. Early on, he had to resist the teacher's efforts to have him dropped from the course. Why did he not take the chance offered to get out of the course? He may have needed the course in order to maintain his standing as a full-time student, an important distinction for financial aid purposes. He may also have wanted the credits for transfer, especially since it was a psychology course, his planned major at that time. It may have been a matter of pride for him to resist what he saw as a false judgment of him as "stupid in English." In any case, he did complete the course, receiving a C/D grade. This low grade reflects points the lab teacher deducted for lateness on all except the first report. (Nam received a B/C for Psych 240: Statistics.)

Aside from going to his lab teacher for an explanation of his grade on the first lab report, Nam did not seek her out for additional assistance. The reason he did not do so may have been wariness because of the efforts to have him drop the course or the pressures of time. In an interview with me, the lab teacher indicated that she was available to comment on drafts and that she would not have penalized Nam for late papers had he contacted her in advance each time. He did not.

Nam's experience in this course could be read as illustrating the difficulties of a student for whom English was not his native language: when he moved into a new writing situation with new language to learn, his writing became less coherent. Certainly, his difficulties with English were the reason the lab teacher wanted him removed from the course. They were also why he had difficulty completing the reports on time. Nam's experience in the course could also be read as a success story: through his persistence and with some guidance, including detailed evaluation rubrics from the teacher, he passed the course.

It is also a story of a conflict between discourses, and it was this submerged conflict, I believe, that caused Nam to detach himself from the course, going through the motions but resisting taking in the discourse. The style of that discourse would remain "their way," in contrast to "my way." Given Nam's skepticism about the discourse of science in contrast with the discourse of religion, any intermingling of these discourses may have been impossible for him. Certainly, it can be a valuable experience to try out different ways, if only to help clarify the ways one wants to claim. As I look in from the outside, though, it seems that the experience of writing for the lab section would have been more of a productive occasion for learning if there had been some way of bringing the differences out in the open for discussion—to discuss, for example, beliefs about the place of one's own thinking and observations in empirical research and how those beliefs are embedded in stylistic conventions. The lab teacher could also have discussed her own experience and shown examples of variations in journal practices. Such discussions may have created a more positive environment for learning—not just for compliance with conventions taught as rules without reasons, but for further understanding of the ways of a given genre and their link to disciplinary practices and values—whether one ultimately accepted them or not. I take this as a lesson for my own writing courses as well, where I now strive to do more to present a rhetorical framework by which students can read and reflect on the various genres they may encounter as they write for their college courses. In my work with graduate students who are teaching our writing courses,

I also try to bring these issues to the fore for them, as they encounter them as teachers and writers.

Although the questions that Psych Methods raised for Nam were not addressed in that course, they surfaced in other places. As I wrote in the opening, I now believe that his April question of me, "What is an essay?" reflected his effort to understand the different ways of writing asked of him in this class in relation to "the English-style way." And his late April drafts of "The Lord is My Shepherd" reflect his sorting through of the authority of various sources of knowledge. In that essay he resolved:

> I was not give Him enough time to hear His teachings or guidance for me; I did not seek Him for knowledge. . . .
>   After reading <u>The Imitation of Christ,</u> it was time for me to turn back to Him like I once was, for me to spend more time in meditation on Him, and for me to avoid the company of men whenever I could.

Nam was writing his way out of college and into seminary.

Closing Reflections

Readers of an earlier version of this chapter said they wanted more of my interpretations of the implications for teaching. I think perhaps that I resisted jumping to possible teaching implications because I felt a primary point of Nam's first-year experience in college has to do with how his personal history, goals, and interests were so closely implicated in his learning. In this, Nam is not exceptional, even though the particulars of his experience are his alone.

For Nam and many other young people, the first year of college is a time of instability and turmoil as they move into a totally new academic and social environment and begin to think about preparing for their futures in a more immediate and pressing way than they had before. For Nam, the turmoil was so great that in a draft for "The Lord is My Shepherd," he identifies this year as the "second time I was ever afraid of the world: one was from my youth in elementary school, and the other is in college. Perhaps, I was afraid to lose God again." While not all students may be this afraid and not all may view the different ways of learning they are encountering in their classes as earthly temptations, all are encountering alternative ways of thinking and alternative paths for a future—for example, thinking as a philosopher, or thinking as a research psychologist. They are looking for sponsoring frameworks—disciplinary approaches—through which they can pursue their interests. Also like Nam, they are reflecting on their families and pasts, sorting through and trying to shape how that past fits with their present and future.

It is with these questions and interests that Nam approached his courses. Indeed, they were the means by which he could become engaged in a course, and Nam was looking to be engaged. When he shut down and distanced himself was when it seemed there was no place for consideration of his background and interests, even to discuss differences. Nam's story—and the ones that follow—remind me to approach all students as if this were so for them: they are looking to make something of the learning opportunity of a course; they are looking to be engaged in their learning as they seek to discover and prepare for a future and make sense of their past and their place in the world.

For Nam, the essay, as he learned it in his Basic Writing class, was an important vehicle for his self-reflections and his development as a writer. When he entered Basic Writing, he said he had already started to love to write during his senior year in high school: "Senior year, I guess the whole year I do a lot of writing. And I like that. I love it when I start to write." During his Basic Writing course, he learned further that writing an essay, in contrast to the "report" form he had learned, could be a way of developing his own thoughts about something and doing so in ways that encouraged him to engage in various kinds of dialogues in his mind. I am thinking here of Marcia's emphasis on writing as a process of "making meaning," and of the heuristics that she introduced asking writers to explore multiple possibilities and points of view. Following this process for composing, Nam learned that form followed meaning, not the reverse.

As I summarize the definition of essay that Nam pieced together through his Basic and College Writing courses, I'm developing a better answer to his question, "What is an essay?" than I offered him. I am also making a case for the value of this genre—

not as a privileged genre above all others—but as one genre that is of value for engaging personal with public interests, for dialogic and reflective thinking that serves the writer as well as readers, and for developing as a writer. Here also, I'm thinking of the essay genre quite broadly, to include writing in dialogue with texts (e.g., Nam's essay drawing on Richard Rodriguez's *Hunger of Memory* and his essay focusing on *The Imitation of Christ*); writing to make sense of some past experience; and writing to develop a position on a public concern to convince readers (e.g., "Thou Shall Not Judge," "One of Those Days"). In all these types of essay writing, "I" is the instrument of knowing. And while reading many of them, I have the feeling that an "I" is being made in the writing.

In a response to a critique of his essay "A Common Ground: The Essay in the Academy," Kurt Spellmeyer writes to defend the essay as a genre for dialogic, exploratory "conversation" with others:

> We exist as "human beings," as "societies" by virtue of our ability to constitute ourselves in language. . . . [Students] must learn, as we have, to constitute a self which actively resists its own appropriation by appropriating the language of others, through a process of conversation. . . . ("Response" 337–38)

The "process of conversation" Spellmeyer refers to is a process of encouraging students to use "writing as a way of thinking dialogically" ("Common" 271) as prompted by readings of other texts. While that approach was used for two essays in Basic Writing and only one in College Writing, Spellmeyer's comment explains well what was happening in many of Nam's essays. Through the essays, Nam was constituting a self, and, through many of them, he was writing to resist appropriation—indeed, resist the construction of himself through the language of others, such as "the verbal remark that smacks our face hard," or false judgments of him by others, or the language of secular sciences—and to constitute a worthy self drawing on the voice he had internalized from the Bible: intelligent, godly, and one with others. Further, he was using the essay as a vehicle for sorting through and trying to make sense of his own conflicting emotions, his conflicting "selves": a self who was angry and sought revenge for wrongs suffered, in conflict with a self who aimed to turn the other cheek, as well as a self who yearned to be in the world, in conflict with a self who yearned to turn from the world to God.

While I want to stress what I believe is a personally valuable function this writing served, Nam saw his accomplishment as learning to use writing to connect with others. In our last interview, when I asked Nam what he felt he had accomplished most in his writing courses, his response focused on making a connection with readers: "Try to make the event clear and let the reader see that event as I would see it. That's my accomplishment. . . ." In another portion of that same interview, he stated more pointedly the value he attached to connecting with readers:

> ANNE: Can you see yourself continuing by choice to do writing, any writing?
>
> NAM: I'm going into an area that involves helping people. I guess I'll be counseling people. And I need writing skills to make what I experience helpful to others. If they read it, they have to understand what I'm saying. I have to have clear evidence or explanation for what I'm saying so that people would understand or take my suggestion.

For Nam, the essay seemed to be the vehicle that would help him bridge private concerns with public ones. In his writing in both Basic and College Writing, he had tried to use essays for that purpose, writing to imagined public audiences—for example, "the minority group of which I was a part," "people who cared for better education," and people who may place too much value on money. Nam was using the essay as a "family language" for the public world, as he described in the essay in which he disagreed with Richard Rodriguez's view that family language cannot be used in public. For Nam, a public "family language" is one of "openness," one used by people who work with others, such as "a councilor or a priest." As he writes, "language that they speak in public is no longer a 'public language' [what Nam termed "a language of separateness"] for they are a part of the people whom they work with." This group of priests was the group with whom Nam wanted to stand, and the discourse of religion was the one he sought as his sponsoring base. While the essay as he learned it in Basic Writing seemed a suitable genre, neither his writing courses nor his other courses provided the specialized discourse or potential collegial group for Nam to be a part of. For this, he moved to a seminary.

Still, I hear readers asking, what more specifically can you say, based on Nam's story, about learning and teaching writing? In telling of his first year, I have backgrounded his difficulties with English. I have done so primarily because I do not mean to generalize from one student's experience about the experiences of others for whom English is a second language. Still, Nam's experience does accord with what some other studies have shown, and these correspondences are worth noting. According to him, in elementary school, he had been taught English through decontextualized exercises and found them lacking when it came to actually writing something: "But writing a paragraph, I have no idea how the words like 'was' or 'were' or 'is' fit." Danling Fu, in *My Trouble Is My English: Asian Students and the American Dream*, reports similarly on the frustration that the students she studied experienced over decontextualized approaches and tracking in lower level courses where they were "taught" through work sheets and tests (195).

Most obviously, in college, Nam felt the pressure of time. In contrast with native speakers of English, it took him more time to write, and, given all of the expectations weighing on him, he would get behind. In "Coping Strategies of ESL Students in Writing Tasks across the Curriculum," Ilona Leki comments on this same pressure felt by other ESL students. As one student told her, "Everything so rush; I feel the pressure; I feel rush" (254). Nam's writing teachers and philosophy teacher recognized this pressure and gave him more time to complete his work without penalty.

Nam also used some of the same strategies for succeeding that Leki identified in the five college students she studied. As Leki writes, "they consistently showed themselves to be resourceful, attentive to their environment, and creative and flexible in their response to new demands" (253). I see the same in Nam, who showed himself to be a perceptive rhetorician, working to interpret the kinds of writing being asked of him in his writing, philosophy, and psychology courses. While he may have misread the psychology genre for the first writing, he sought out the teacher and learned from her what was expected. As with the students Leki studied, he also used a coping strategy of accommodating to the teachers' demands. Whether he did that for cultural reasons—submitting to authority, although only in a superficial way—or because, as he said, "it was easier," he did accommodate and did pass the course.

Also as with the students in Leki's study, Nam sought out models as a way of learning new genres. In contrast to decontextualized drills, such models were functional when doing purposive writing in specific contexts. One way that he grew as a learner and writer was to move from relying too much on rigid models and structures to looking at models as flexible guides. In Basic Writing, he used the class publications to look for models from his peers' essays. He also looked to the heuristic prompts Marcia introduced as models and guides for drafting. In Psych Methods, he tried to follow the model expected of students, checking in with the teacher to ascertain her specific expectations. His experiences underscore the value of presenting genre conventions rhetorically, naming them as conventions, and trying to present the epistemological and social-rhetorical bases for these conventions. Leki concludes that students "did ferret out their own paths" (255). While each student does have to make her or his own path, we can help students understand the various paths we are asking them to try out; we can and should do that in our writing classes as well as in literature and other classes across the curriculum.

Clearly, it was also important to Nam to be perceived as being intelligent and not "stupid in English," and to be understood. For Nam, in Basic Writing, having the experience of a teacher who conveyed that she respected his intelligence and listened *with* him served that purpose. More fundamentally, the responses he received conveyed that he was being understood. Further, by aiming to be present as a reader who could mirror his thoughts back to him, Marcia could both validate his thinking as well as help him extend his thoughts. He did not experience the frustration of writing against someone as he strove to make himself understood.

Nam, in turn, looked to her as a teacher he could respect, an external audience he would consider as he wrote, and someone whose responses he would take seriously when revising. Here is what another student told Vivian Zamel in a study she conducted of ESL students' experiences across the curriculum:

> "We are learning English as well as the major of our choice. It is very hard sometimes and we don't need professors who claimed that they don't understand us. The effort is double. We are very intelligent people." (512)

In her study, Leki makes a strong call for teachers to do more to learn of their students' experiences in order to understand how students are experiencing the assignments they are asked to do in their courses. Commenting on the experiences of the students she studied, Leki writes:

> We might, as teachers, be left somewhat uncomfortable with the realization of how little faculty across the curriculum are aware of what really takes place among their/our students. . . . In these cases as well, the professors gave no indication of anything amiss, and yet from the students' point of view the experiences varied from meaningless and a waste of time to actively destructive." (254)

She concludes her article as follows:

> What does seem reasonable is to consult with students to learn what strategies they already consciously use, help them bring to consciousness others that they may use and not be aware of using, and perhaps suggest others that they had not thought of before. (259)

To consult with students implies aiming to engage in a dialogue with them, bringing their knowledge and concerns more actively into our classes. In a related vein, I think of Belenky et al. proposing the following approach: "In considering how to design an education appropriate for women, suppose we were to begin by simply asking: What does a woman know? Traditional courses do not begin there. They begin not with the student's knowledge, but with the teacher's knowledge" (198). To pose that challenge more generally, how might we begin in ways that strive to bring our students' knowledges into our classrooms in ways that serve their learning? As Nam wrote in his final essay for Basic Writing, "Thou Shall Not Judge":

> To seek understanding is wiser than to judge our neighbors. . . .
> And sometimes we misjudge the person from his appearance.
> Whereas, by seeking knowledge about the individual, we can
> understand why he is acting as he is.

This seems a good maxim for all teachers.

It has now been some years since I last saw Nam, although we exchanged Christmas cards and letters the first two years after he left the University. When we last corresponded, he was completing his third year of seminary. I wrote to see if we could arrange a meeting, but that proved impossible because he was going to California to continue his studies for priesthood.

Our last exchange helps put this chapter—so absorbed in his past—in perspective. In my letter, I told him that I had been thinking a lot about him because I had been rereading all his writings and our interviews. I went on to mention his College Writing essay, "The Lord Is My Shepherd":

> To me, the essay is a beautiful and moving meditation on being
> torn between a need and desire to be in the world and a need
> and desire to step away from the world and to God. I realize
> that you were reflecting on your own intentions of becoming a
> priest. Still, reading that essay also makes me think about how
> easy it is for me to focus too much on worldly affairs and not
> enough on spiritual ones and serving others. I wanted to tell
> you that since we never talked about it in interview.

His response:

> Hi Anne,
>   I am very glad that you write to me. I have forgotten all
> about you since your last letter. Forgive me for not responding
> earlier.

I am touched and honor that you still have my writings. I thought they were history by now. And more important, you have found something I wrote which was once a highlight of my life, and it becomes beneficial to you. Thanks for telling me that.

For Nam, his first year at UMass, his writings, and I are "history." But they are part of his history, a history that he created, and, in the creating, he helped himself create his future.

Notes

1. Having left Vietnam as a child, Nam did not learn to read and write in his native language. In an interview, he told me that he could speak Vietnamese and that his family spoke it at home. Wanting to learn to read and write in his native language, he took a Vietnamese language course his first semester at UMass.

2. At the end of the semester, when I asked Nam how he felt about his essays not being included, he said, "For me, it doesn't matter much whether or not people would read it." But then he went on to say, "But if it's helpful for other people . . . I guess it would be helpful too if I had my writing there. They would see a different style, a different style of writing . . . because this is my writing, my style." This comment again reflects Nam's strong sense of himself—that he can maintain his own sense of worth and affirm, "This is my style." He is also right. Just as Nam felt he had been helped by reading a range of styles in the Basic Writing publications, he felt others would have been helped if they read his writing, implicitly a different style from others in College Writing.

3. Nam's statement "the book was not brainwashing me" could be read as his response to a poststructuralist interpretation that the discourse of religion was constructing his subjectivity with Nam passively taking it in—being spoken by it. I do not mean to deny the force of this discourse. Certainly, many of his writing course essays could be read as a sort of confession, with Nam positioned as confessing to God, the authority who demands the confession. But that is only part of what is happening in these essays. While the discourse's shaping force—which, for Nam, is its attraction—is evident, so too is his active role in working through whether and how to make that discourse his own, in other words, what to believe and how to live his life. Indeed, the successive drafts for "The Lord Is My Shepherd" are the means for this thinking. A more persuasive poststructuralist interpretation, then, is that this es-

say evidences what Bronwyn Davies terms the "tension [inherent in the process of subjectification] between simultaneously becoming a speaking, agentic subject and the co-requisite for this, being subjected to the meanings inherent in the discourse through which one becomes a subject" (22).

CHAPTER THREE

Composing a Self He Can Live With: Lawrence/Steven

When I think of Lawrence Beatty, I think of Tobias Wolff's "An Episode in the Life of Professor Brooke": of the professor's chance encounter—and one-night affair—at an MLA conference with a recovering cancer patient, and of the recovering patient's equally chance—and equally life-inspiring—encounter with a popular writer's poetry, which, she says admiringly, doesn't make you "feel like killing yourself after you've read it" (36). To Professor Brooke, the popular writer's lyrics are New Age doggerel; for the woman, they are literally the stuff of her new life. "When I got to the end," she recalls of one piece, "I read it again and again and I just knew I was going to live. And here I am." Once saved from death, there is no looking back:

> "Life," Brooke said, "is not always uplifting."
> "I know all about it," Ruth said, "believe me. But why should I rub my nose in it? I like to read about lovers. I like to read about how beautiful the mountains are, and the stars and so on. I like to read about people taking care of injured animals and setting them free again." (37)

It is not because Lawrence read New Age verse that I am reminded of him, nor because he wrote about injured animals and their deliverance. It is because Lawrence, more than any other student of our study, would likely antagonize the faculty folk who populate Wolff's MLA. For Lawrence wrote unfailingly for and about himself, with a purpose that many would no doubt criticize as "expressivist," "Romantic," and "confessional." Like Wolff's death-defying cancer patient, he proclaimed himself a "survivor." But even more enlivened and active than she, he determined early on to be his own author. His project was to recuperate a self he could live with, to compose a viable self and world by every means of signification available to him: dress, sex, his curriculum vitae, the words he wrote, his name. Lawrence was his own composition, and the product of all his composing efforts was Steven.

Written in a survivor's defiance of death, both essential and actual, Lawrence's story challenges the notions held by those of us who, for professional reasons, intend for students a course of increasing separation from private into public expression and who, for whatever other reasons, distrust all talk of "recovery" and writing for therapeutic ends. While most students come eventually to reflect, in writing and in writing about their writing, the course that teachers conventionally want for them, from self-discovery, through self-expression, to other-directed—at the extreme even intentionally selfless, I-less—prose, Lawrence's academic history is a steady restorying, a continual reauthoring of himself and revising of the dominant narrative into which he was born. He occasionally worried about this—worried about his almost obsessive preoccupation with personal themes, particularly his early suicidal impulses and his later, salutary "coming out"—but even in his fourth year clearly stated he was not yet ready to stop writing about himself. And more than occasionally, we ourselves may worry that as we see Lawrence extricating himself from one culturally, socially, or familially determined narrative, we are watching him immerse himself in another. But even his movements from one dominant narrative into the next demonstrate that, for some, writing is more than "academic": it is a statement of personal agency, an act of survival, the performance of a lifetime.

Background

Lawrence attended his last two years of high school in a Boston suburb among classmates who predominantly were, like Lawrence, white and middle-class. Before that, as he says, he "lived just about everywhere." His mother was twice divorced, the second time from Lawrence's stepfather, a military man, which accounts for the constant moving. Lawrence's own father is deeply

religious; as Lawrence will come to reveal in writings and interviews, he also physically and sexually abused Lawrence,
Lawrence's mother, and a second son. So Lawrence has since located in this father the source of a persistent need to construct
his own identity in a new image. Toward the end of his third
year, he wrote:

> When I was growing up my father used to beat and sexually
> abuse my mother, brother and me. As my father was the only
> role model I had, I thought that if that is what a man is sup-
> posed to be . . . then I don't want to be a man. This being so, I
> thought my only alternative was to be a woman. At a very
> early age I got the message that it wasn't okay to be me. . . .

Lawrence attributed problems with writing to both the constant
moving and the sexual abuse. He recalled in our final interview:

> My writing has changed because I've changed and I'm starting
> to have more confidence in myself. But when I was growing
> up, as a child, I moved so much that . . . I missed out on a lot.
> So I feel like I'm still in stages that other people were in maybe
> five years ago. I'm still growing and developing as a writer. I'm
> not saying no one else is, too. True, everyone else is developing
> as a writer, but I feel like I missed out on a lot growing up as
> far as school is concerned because I moved so much, and also
> being an incest survivor, having very low self-esteem. I still re-
> member how I just really had no self-esteem coming into your
> writing class. How much I hated writing! I didn't want to be
> there, I didn't want to. I really just did not like writing.

Lawrence had his first homosexual peer experience—or at
least awakening—at ten. When he told his mother and stepfather
about it, they fought, and the family never discussed it again
until Lawrence was seventeen. The intervening seven years con-
stituted a slow and lonesome "coming out" process in what he
clearly perceived to be a hostile environment. Then, while living
near Boston, Lawrence began to attend teenage gay support
groups in the city, and simultaneously began to come out in writings for his high school English class. The writings were read,
with apparent acceptance, by the teacher and a couple of close
friends, but no others. Throughout Basic Writing and College

Writing, coming out remained a recurrent purpose and theme. As a senior, Lawrence successfully petitioned to graduate with a cross-disciplinary major in gender studies, and the study of homosexuality (through a wide variety of related courses taken across the five campuses of Amherst, Hampshire, Mt. Holyoke, and Smith colleges as well as the University) informs his curriculum vitae.

Lawrence's comments in our original questionnaire, completed when he was an eighteen-year-old entering first-year student, reflect the intimate connection between experience and expression:

> I'm most confident writing about my personal experience due to the fact that . . . my attitude on life has changed. . . . I am much more optimistic than ever before and for once I can say I am the happiest I have ever been and that I finally love "me."

Two years later, in personal conversation, he reiterated that observation. Commenting on an advisor's surprise that, given his current writing skill, he had been placed in Basic Writing, he attributed the change primarily to his own personal growth and deepening self-confidence. And again, in his final formal interview for this project, he credited not only his comfort with writing but the very quality of his writing itself to his sense of self-worth and happiness. He also credited his still-growing self-esteem to his increasing success as a writer. When asked in the spring of 1993 to characterize his writerly journey since the fall of 1989, he answered:

> LAWRENCE: I know my self-esteem has grown. I still feel like I'm not a great writer, but I know that I am a heck of a lot better than I was. . . .
>
> MARCIA: Do you see points of development or growth, or does it seem to be a steady progress over four years?
>
> LAWRENCE: I think it's steady. I mean, there are still things I need to improve on, but I think that's true for anyone.
>
> MARCIA: What do you attribute the growth to?
>
> LAWRENCE: Hard work . . . asking for help from professors . . . and I think just having a greater self-esteem to do it. Before I

didn't have that, before [Basic Writing] I felt like I hated, I hated writing . . . and now I try to write on a regular basis. I have a journal I write in, and I write as often as I possibly can. That's more free style . . . but last semester I wrote my first big research paper, and I got an A. It was excellent.

Crossing borders of departmental disciplines, institutional settings, gender identity, and even dress, Lawrence created for himself a web of relationships, a context, in which to define, organize, and structure—really to author—himself. As we will see, the new context enabled Lawrence to give life and language to his felt experience in a way that his pre-college world had failed to enable. In the new life-text, homosexuality was not to be the counterculture, but the dominant one.

MARCIA: That's terrific! What was it on?

LAWRENCE: Homosexuality.

MARCIA: What course was it?

LAWRENCE: The History of Homosexuality at Amherst College . . .

MARCIA: Who was the teacher for this one?

LAWRENCE: [A lesbian professor.]

In the new life-text, Lawrence could—in and through writing—compose another "me." In his fourth year, he would change his name to Steven.

Essays for English 111, Basic Writing (with Occasional Reference to Others)

The function of writing as a mediator between self and other—as a way of being in the world as well as a way of communicating with and presenting oneself to the world—and as a mediator among selves is evident in nearly all of Lawrence's essays and comments on the writing process. The majority of his essays for both Basic and College Writing issue from his coming out process; personal honesty and public acceptance are the theme, the tenor, of his essays, whatever the apparent vehicle. Of the six essays composed for Basic Writing, two deal explicitly with the issues of coming out, and three do so implicitly. As we explore these essays, and the early drafts out of which the final papers arise, and as we listen to Lawrence explain his intentions—and interpret the final, presented pieces for us—we see that they are, individually, metaphors. Only as we move across the individual essays, through the writing course and over time, does Lawrence's intentional narrative take form.

The first illustrative example is Lawrence's second full essay from Basic Writing, a short piece modeled, more or less, on a one-page excerpt (anthologized as "The Iguana") from Isak Dinesen's *Out of Africa*. Her reflection on three occasions in which beauty, once possessed, and dispossessed of its native setting, loses its hue prompted Lawrence to make similarly public meaning from private events, and he produced a reflection on a friend's suicide that is similarly hortative. It is also a simultaneous reflection on and act of coming out to me, his teacher. It may well have been a rehearsal for coming out to the class; for the moment, he chose to go outside, to friends, for his two peer reviews.

A SIGNIFICANT EVENT

When I was a sophomore in high school one of my friends committed suicide. I will never forget the day after it happened. My math class was in shock, I remember running out of the room crying when I saw his empty chair. It was as if we had just had an earthquake, the room was desolate. I couldn't understand why he could have done it.

On Saturday of that week, the funeral came around. I dreaded going to it, but I knew I had to go to pay my respects to his family.

This unfortunate experience has made me realize that committing suicide is not worth all the hype that teenagers make it out to be. I think his suicide made me stop and think why I wanted to kill myself. I just wish it didn't have to happen this way. After the procession of cars and seeing the casket being lowered into it's grave, I said to myself, I could never do this to me or my family.

From first to final draft, these introductory paragraphs change little, if at all. But what follows changes significantly. In Lawrence's final draft, the next paragraph reads thus:

From the time that I was ten to sixteen years old I thought about killing myself everyday because I felt guilty for being gay. I thought it was wrong since society says that it was and still is and I thought no one would ever except me for who I was. Therefore, I couldn't accept myself either. I remember times when I spent hours in my room thinking about the ways I could kill myself. But after Michael killed himself I knew that that wasn't the answer and I didn't want to be a quitter.

The felt connection to Michael is clear; the motive behind Lawrence's own suicidal impulses—"because I felt guilty for being gay"—is equally clear but not dominant, expressed instead in its dependent clause. In fact, these relatively general remarks are all we are shown of Lawrence's own torment. The course of remembrance turns on them, toward the release and recovery that began with words to a counselor and culminate here in the writing:

Approximately two years later I went to my high school guidance counselor and explained to her all of the guilt and hatred I had in myself. *She was the first person I ever told that I was gay. From that moment on things began to get easier for me* [emphasis mine]. I started to see a psychologist to see if this was right for me.

In March, I went . . . to a Boston Alliance of Gay and Lesbian Youth meeting. I was so scared and nervous at the same time. It was the first time I had ever encountered . . . people like me. This group helped me to come out and to finally accept who I was. After coming out I didn't feel as much pressure as before. I even grew out of my asthma, which is caused by stress and anxiety. I felt a great deal of relief and I was the happiest I had ever been. After coming out, I can truly say now that I love myself for who I am and I am not ashamed of it.

Lawrence's earlier drafts are all without the pivotal motivational passage. Instead, they move directly from Michael's funeral to Lawrence's encounter with his guidance counselor, and from there through a catalogue of recriminations and rejections by family members as well as friends—including his mother's attempts to make dates for him with girls, his former friends' threatening harassment, and his younger brother's hateful anger—that reveals his initial coming out experience to be the disappointing anticlimax it undoubtedly was.

However, this catalogue of the alienation caused by public and familial censure is not the "truth" that Lawrence wanted for his essay, and those of us reading the essay (i.e., Lawrence's chosen peer reviewers and I) felt that the catalogue created a jarring rupture in the established narrative. The two peer reviewers urged Lawrence to include "more details about how your friends turned on you" and "how your mother reacted," but Lawrence chose to delete all mention of such particulars, to add the brief but pivotal description of his private moments of guilt, and to lead us in smooth transition to exhortative denouement:

> My advice is that if you are thinking about committing suicide talk to someone about it. Don't give up! It's not the end of the world. Look what I went through and look at me now!

To reinvoke Tobias Wolff's short story, "Life is not always uplifting," and Lawrence knows all about that. But he was not willing to rub his own nose in it, or his reader's. That is not what he wanted, nor is it what his peer reviewers wanted. These reviewers (both of whom are heterosexual) may have asked for "more details" about life's real rejections, but in completing the sentence "For me, the most interesting part of your essay is . . . ," both of them wrote to the effect of "when you 'came out' and how happy you were."

Questioned about the specific changes he had made—deletions as well as additions—Lawrence spoke of formal considerations:

> ANNE: I notice in the draft you've got a lot about telling your
> mother . . . telling your best friend and then your brother
> finding out. And that doesn't [appear in the final]. . . .
>
> LAWRENCE: I didn't think it was the right place for it, because . . .
> it wasn't the same focus as the suicide and why I was
> triggered to come out. . . . [I]t had a lot to do with coming
> out, but it didn't have anything to do with suicide. So it
> didn't belong in the paper.

In terms of the "reality" his essay represents, we may think his observations in certain respects odd: as here Lawrence attributes his suicidal thoughts to guilt, we may well attribute that guilt precisely to the attitudes instilled in him by his family and, later, expressed by mother and brother. But already, Lawrence as the writer has relinquished that discourse, that narrative, in order to be true to his own. Those familial expressions of shame did come *later*, after Lawrence had seen Michael's corpse, and, against such a durable image of death, they apparently lost, along with their power, their place in the narrative now taking form.

The act of writing, too, helped displace the family's narrative from Lawrence's new one.

> ANNE: [Y]ou chose to write on this, though . . . you didn't like [the experience of writing it].
>
> LAWRENCE: Right. . . . [I]t was depressing, . . . but I think it helps, too, to realize it, helps, you know, just to think about it, and to write about it—helps to see it on paper . . . helps deal with the problems.

Writing helps. It helps to see problems there in the early drafts, but once writing has helped to dissipate the anguish, what sense does it make to reinscribe it in the final draft? To many students, writing is just this magical, and their use of the magic is absolutely sensible. Problems solved in the narratives of first drafts are absent from the last; anguish relieved through mere utterance is replaced by images and expressions of hope. So Lawrence's final draft inscribes the narrative of one who has been mightily helped—saved from death and ready to lead others away from it, too.

The next essay is also on suicide, but it is "more positive," because in living Lawrence can do for others—and urge others to do for others still—what Michael in death did for him.

> ANNE: Now, the second writing, what did you think the assignment was for that one? . . .
>
> LAWRENCE: . . . Oh, I didn't like writing that. I hated it so much . . . . [I]t wasn't the actual assignment I hated. I just didn't like talking about suicide because it gets so depressing.
>
> ANNE: Uh huh.
>
> LAWRENCE: And the third paper I wrote was about suicide, too, but it was more positive, because I was telling people how to help other people if they notice the symptoms.

ANNE: How do you think, then, you got into writing about suicide?

LAWRENCE: Because I think that triggered me into coming out . . . because since I was ten till I was about seventeen—yeah, till December '88—I wanted to commit suicide. When I was fifteen years old, I had a friend that committed suicide, and I knew I could never do it. I went to the funeral. It was a mess. . . . I just couldn't put my family through that. And then I think that just got me to thinking, you know: "Your life has to get better, it can't get worse, and you're not going to kill yourself. That's stupid." I think that had a lot to do with me coming out.

In fact, the class assignment for this third writing offered a natural occasion for Lawrence's second essay on suicide: it was to be an interpretive piece derived from Sophronia Liu's published memoir "So Tsi-fai," in which she recalls a young schoolmate who, like Michael, had committed suicide:

"I don't need any supper. I have drunk enough insecticide." So Tsi-fai. My fourteen-year-old classmate. Daredevil; good-for-nothing lazybones (according to Mung Gu-liang). Bright black eyes, disheveled hair, defiant sneer, creased and greasy uniform, dirty hands, careless walk, shuffling feet. Standing in the corner for being late, for forgetting his homework, for talking in class, for using foul language. (Liu 127–28)

Used here to provide the students with either a foreground object of interpretation or a background support for their own discussions of educational and/or class issues, and thus to introduce them to the use of other texts in their own writing, Liu's narrative provided Lawrence with what was really a pretext for continuing his own exhortation begun in his second writing. The piece begins with a very brief reference to Liu's narrative, then moves—actually, viewed across essays, *returns*—quickly by analogy to Michael's death:

THE SYMPTOMS OF SUICIDE
In the story, So Tsi-Fai, the main character was a hopeless case. His teacher only saw the bad in him. She couldn't help him because of her pessimistic views. His parents couldn't help him either. They didn't care enough about him. What is sad is

that they didn't know him because they didn't spend any time with him.

Twenty three years later the students in his class realized that they weren't seeing him for who he was. Their teacher made him out to be bad, therefore the students were led to believe that he was bad. If only the students could have helped him before it was too late. He died a tragic death at the age of fourteen.

When I was a sophomore in high school I had a friend that committed suicide. The day after it happened it was as if we had just had an earthquake. I remember running out of my class crying when I saw his empty chair. We were in a total state of shock.

But from here, the writing moves in a new direction or, perhaps, still farther along the previously begun narrative path away from victimhood. Lawrence does project his own sense of parental abandonment onto So Tsi-fai: Liu makes it clear that ignorance and poverty—not the carelessness of son or parents, as Lawrence implies—determined the family's course. But aside from that projection, it is now not with the suicide but with the classmates that Lawrence explicitly identifies.

Thinking about the days when he was alive and kicking, I don't remember ever seeing any signs of depression. The only characteristics about him were that his moods always changed quickly. One minute he was happy and the next minute he was depressed. . . .

The day of the funeral was the worst. . . . After the procession of cars had left the cemetery and after we saw the casket being lowered into its grave I wondered how come I had never noticed that he had thought about killing himself. At first I blamed myself. I said to myself that I would never let this happen again.

In this restorying, Lawrence's contemplation of Michael inspires a different resolve: to prevent this from happening not to Lawrence himself but to another. And life as well as essay affords opportunity to keep his promise.

Two years later in the second week of my freshman year at UMASS, one of my friends . . . tried to kill herself. . . . She and

I had been drinking heavily that night to forget our problems. She was depressed about some personal problems and she didn't want to face them. I was depressed because I had had a one night stand the weekend before.

. . . I spoke to her resident assistant about her problems to make sure she would keep her eye out for her, since I can't always be there for her. . . .

As before, a peer reviewer urged Lawrence to "relate more to the story"; as before, he refused to revisit publicly his private depression and suicidal thoughts. In an interview he observed:

I realize I should have talked more about me, but at the time I didn't want to. It's a personal thing. . . . I didn't want to talk about . . . why I wanted to commit suicide and failed. I didn't want to express it for some reason.

Instead, Lawrence composed the narrative as a storied map for others to follow, exhorting not those contemplating suicide but rather their friends to follow his lead and break the secret's silence:

I guess what I am trying to tell you is that if you suspect someone is thinking about committing suicide tell someone about it or get them some help. Don't give up! You are their only hope! And if you feel guilty about telling someone think of it this way would you rather have a dead friend or a living one. If you really care about him/her get them help. Don't let it go or pass it off. Life is a gift that shouldn't be taken for granted. Live life to its fullest and you will be the happiest!

Still, something tricky is happening here in these closing lines.

"Live life to the fullest and you will be happiest!" Is it really their associates or is it potential suicides themselves being addressed? If we had only this single, final draft to go on, only these pages from which all mention of Lawrence's own gayness and own flirtation with death have been expunged, then we might be tempted to say that his conclusion really languishes in platitude; he has let his essay drift into cliché until we can no longer identify with certainty the intended audience. But knowing this piece is the second element in a developing narrative sequence, we know that the two audiences conflated here are truly one, and they are Lawrence. It is not so much a sliding into commonplace that we are witnessing as it is a yielding to that narrative, as the writing process draws him compulsively, almost obsessively, back to himself and his originating depression, and forward to self-directed exhortation and near-ritual incantation: "Live life to the fullest and you will be happiest!" roughly translates, I think, as, "To be, I must be me; to be me, I must be," and, like all his writing, it serves to deepen Lawrence's own conviction that gay is good even as he tries to persuade others.

The gay underlife of Lawrence's narrative, though expunged from the final version of "The Symptoms of Suicide," is evident in earlier drafts, where his peer reviewer—this time a member of the class—read,

> She was depressed about some personal problems and she didn't want to face them. I was depressed because I had had a one night stand the weekend before *with a guy* [emphasis mine].

Asked why the telling prepositional phrase was afterwards deleted, he explained his fears surrounding both telling and not telling his own secret:

> See, that's one thing that bothers me. I keep thinking that that's all I'm thinking about. But it's so hard because I just, you know, came out, and . . . I asked Marcia if it was okay because it seems like everything is geared towards that. But I don't know, I think that's helping me come out more, but I still feel bad about it, writing about it. . . . I just feel like I'm obsessed with it or something.

So this time, Lawrence fought the obsession and struck out that signal gay reference: "I just didn't think it was appropriate."

Appropriate or not, I believe it is as much to the point that that three-word prepositional phrase had already done its job, representing Lawrence's sexual preference to a single classmate. By the closing weeks of the semester, he was fully "out" to the class. He put "The Symptoms of Suicide" up for publication in that unit's class magazine without its tell-tale phrase, but around the time of its composing he volunteered to read aloud a brief class exercise in which the students, having read Langston Hughes's "Theme for English B," composed a verse "theme" of their own: Lawrence's depicted his academic experience as a young gay man. And two essays later, he created a pamphlet for gay and lesbian teenagers that was published with the rest of the class's work.

The pamphlet was written in response to a course assignment instructing the students to revise one of their earlier writings. Though it appears to a reader as quite unlike "A Significant Event," which Lawrence identified as the object of revision, to him it represented a real re-seeing of and continued progression beyond that earlier one. In an end-of-term interview, he described his intentions:

> ["A Significant Event"] was about suicide. . . . I think I wanted to talk about that because that's what had triggered the whole coming out process in me. I didn't want a negative thing in there, but at the time that was the right thing for me to write, because it made me understand better about what was going on. But [the pamphlet] was more positive. That's why I wanted to do it. . . . [I]t shows [readers] they're not the only one . . . that they're not the only one in this.

This "revision" may be drawn from personal experience, but it is hardly a "confessional" or even "personal" essay: in composing it, Lawrence showed himself to be composing in a fully public medium and with political concern, without giving up the affective dimension of gayness.

> LAWRENCE: [I was] reading through different pamphlets . . . thinking of what's missing. . . .
>
> ANNE: . . . What did you feel was missing that you put in here?
>
> LAWRENCE: . . . [T]he feelings that you have, like at the very beginning. . . . They have commonly used terms about what a homosexual is, what a bisexual is, or a lesbian. But they don't talk about what the feelings are. . . . And that's what it explains, what homosexual feelings are. . . . And just having information about AIDS, and coming out stories, and things . . . helps.

ANNE: Why does that help?

LAWRENCE: Because it shows that they're not the only one. . . . Because everyone thinks that they are when they're in the process. . . .

ANNE: So this becomes a piece of a bigger context, this story.

LAWRENCE: Yes. And it makes people stop and think about their coming out, or their wanting to come out.

ANNE: I was struck, too, when I read this very political definition of homophobia: . . . "The irrational fear, disgust and hatred of gays, lesbians, bisexuals and homosexual feelings."

Lawrence went directly on in this interview to offer a highly personal example of the political phenomenon under question:

LAWRENCE: [My mother] was saying, "Why do homosexuals have to flaunt it so much?" I told her, "We're not flaunting it. We're just making people more aware that we do exist, so that we can prevent homophobia, you know." I didn't want to say anything like that, but she is going through homophobia. She has internalized it. . . . As much as she says she still loves me.

ANNE: Mmm. Hmm.

LAWRENCE: The sooner she accepts it, the better she'll be. I'm not going to change. And I feel bad because I told her that's the reason that I'm not going to live there [at home] this summer. But I can't live there this summer—somewhere where I'm not even accepted in my own home. I can't and I won't. I'm not going back to that.

Lawrence's pamphlet certainly contains a good deal of common "politically correct" language and even draws upon the language of popular psychology—ironically, Elizabeth Kubler-Ross's five stages of reaction to terminal illness—to describe the "Five Steps of Coming Out": "Denial, Anger, Bargaining, Depression, Acceptance." And structurally, it resembles a collage more than an essay: a collection of signals, terms, and stories of gay life marking the gaps, "what's missing," in other pamphlets designed for gay youth. It also stands, however, as Lawrence's favorite work in Basic Writing: he enjoyed its production and published it with confidence in the class magazine.

The pamphlet, I believe, marks not only the lack that Lawrence identified in "self-help" literature for gay youngsters who are coming out or thinking about doing so: it also marks for him an important forward step in coming into his own. Clearly, Lawrence himself associated it with a sort of sexual, familial, and social Rubicon: a refusal to accept as "home" the home that refused to accept him. It seems in some ways, then, to represent, too, Lawrence's first attempt to people his new home with a truer kin, with an audience of peers ready to join him in growing up gay:

HAVE YOU EVER LOOKED AT ANOTHER
MAN/WOMAN THE SAME WAY YOU LOOK
AT SOMEONE OF THE OPPOSITE SEX?

Well you picked it up, I thought it would catch your eye! If you have ever fallen in love with someone of the same sex as you, don't panic. You aren't the only one! And there isn't anything wrong with it. If you think you might be gay or bisexual just ask yourself these questions:

1. How do you feel when you see a man/woman or both?
2. Have you ever fallen in love with your best friend?
3. Have you ever dreamed about having a sexual experience with someone of the same sex?
4. How long have you felt this way?

In answering these questions did you come up with what you thought you would? If so, don't be afraid! There are many groups that can help you, and I will tell you about them a little later.

I believe Lawrence managed, over the course of the semester in Basic Writing, to use his preoccupation with sexual identity to healthful and productive ends, progressing toward a sort of subjective coherence both within the narrative that his writings form and in the forms of his various writings. If in his earliest writings Lawrence's intention had been to intervene before suicide could be committed, in his last writing of the fall term it was to intervene before suicide could be contemplated. And as his purpose and intended audience shifted, his identification with both audience and subject shifted, too: from potential victims of suicide—

and, by implication, potential victims of a gay identity—to gay youths embarking on a life course pursued with zest, humor, and political savvy. Thus the writer we sense behind this last composition, the writer Lawrence composed within it, appears to have fulfilled those earlier optimistic promises. And this is the writer who presented himself with confidence and authority in Lawrence's first essay of the spring semester.

Essays for English 112, College Writing (with Occasional Reference to Others)

By the time he left Basic Writing, Lawrence appears to have been sufficiently comfortable with writing and with his fellow students' acceptance of him as a clearly gay writer to open his College Writing career with an explicit autobiographical essay entitled "Free to Be You and Me" that begins with a reconstruction of his homosexual awakening:

> What is homosexuality? One day in 1981, I looked up this word in the dictionary because I had heard someone talking about it in school. When I read the definition I was astonished because I knew then that I was gay. I had a few sexual encounters with boys my own age. At that time I was confused and I told my mother that I was a homosexual. She didn't know what to say so we never talked about it again until January of 89. However, I think she suspected it over the years because I never went out with many girls and she knew about the boys that I experimented with.

What follows from this is largely what appeared in the early drafts of "A Significant Event" and was afterward expunged: his coming out to a school counselor and a female friend, and their supportive acceptance; his coming out to male friends, and their hostile rejection; and his trip to the Boston Gay and Lesbian Youth Alliance. Added are two new pieces of information: Lawrence's being fired from two summer jobs when bosses learned he was gay, actions which, he writes, might have been prevented by the recently passed Massachusetts Gay Rights Bill; and his coming out to his father, who "is very much into religion and thinks that homosexuality is wrong," but who "said that he understood and it didn't matter because I was still his son."

Both new pieces of information figure in Lawrence's conclusion:

> Even if some people had the opportunity to take advantage of the many programs that there are to help prevent homophobia, many wouldn't bother because some people just will never understand. There are many reasons why this is true because of religion, plain ignorance or the way one is brought up so that they have internalized homophobia as well as prejudice. However, one must not give up hope because the fact that Massachusetts has passed "The Gay Rights Bill" is only one of the many incredible things to come as we become educated about different facets of life.

As experiences from earlier essays reappear in this latest one, so do earlier exhortations echo through these closing lines: "My advice is that if you are thinking about committing suicide . . . Don't give up!" ("A Significant Event"); "If you suspect that someone is thinking about suicide tell someone about it or get them help. Don't give up!" ("The Symptoms of Suicide"); and now, "One must not give up hope because the fact that Massachusetts has passed 'The Gay Rights Bill' is only one of the many incredible things to come . . ." ("Free to Be You and Me").

Yet "Free to Be You and Me" is different from Lawrence's first writings. At three pages, it is a full page longer than most of his basic writings. Within its last draft, he was able to integrate the problems as well as the delights of coming out: that is, he was able to contain within the finished, published piece (as, we might hope, within himself) the darker moments of experience elided in the final version of "A Significant Event" while still maintaining the forward momentum of optimism. And finally, though still essentially a narrative and, as an autobiographical narrative, essentially incorporating information found in "A Significant Event," in "The Symptoms of Suicide," and in Lawrence's final pamphlet, this essay begins to situate Lawrence's private gay experience within larger social and political contexts. Correspondingly, Lawrence's relationship with his audience is formalized as he pulls back a bit from the earlier "you" (which I take to have been the equivalent of the more intimate form of second-person address in Spanish, i.e., *tu*) to "one," and, overall, he gives this essay more than the mere rudiments of—more than an excuse for—a rhetorical and expository frame.

I would attribute these contextual and relational shifts, at least in part, to new techniques Lawrence was learning in College Writing and also, in large part, to the new socio-political discourse he was learning at the time, both from the Social Diversity in Education course (Education 290A) he enrolled in that spring, and from his participation in the Speakers' Bureau, a University group of gay, lesbian, and bisexual faculty and students who, on invitation, speak to campus and community organizations on matters of gay life. In a real way, his life at the University was following the course established by his writings, just as much as his writings reflected his campus experience. And a précis of that narrative line appears at the center of "Free to Be You and Me":

> Since coming to UMASS, I feel more confident in myself and I don't have to hide my sexuality like I do when I am living at home. Here at school people are much more understanding and accepting. I think of UMASS as my home before I think of my home in [hometown]. In Amherst I don't feel threatened to be myself but in [hometown] I was almost killed.

With Lawrence's closing disclaimer, we have reached a point requiring a shift in my own narrative, in my restorying of Lawrence. To this point, I have intentionally dwelt only on the positive aspects of his carefully wrought narrative in order to mirror what I believe to have been his intentions and his achievements. The hope he repeatedly urged his readers to maintain was precisely the sense of determined optimism by which he maintained his immediate integrity and forward momentum not just as a writer but as *a person writing*. It was also, I believe, the hope by which he had, until now, successfully warded off, not recollections of suicidal impulses perhaps, but at least the impulses themselves. This would not remain true through his term in College Writing, and so I will now admit into my own narrative other discordant interpretations, not in accordance with some objective "Truth" but in accordance with Lawrence's earlier request that, under extreme circumstances, we break a secret's silence:

> . . . if you suspect someone is thinking about committing suicide tell someone about it or get them help. Don't give up! You are their only hope! . . . Don't let it go or pass it off. ("The Symptoms of Suicide")

The secret is, of course, something of which both Lawrence and I have been aware throughout my reading of his narrative, just as I am sure you have been throughout your reading of my narrative: There *is* something disturbing in his persistent echoing of earlier writings; in Lawrence's insistent optimism, there *is* something of the manic person's incessant flight from depression; there *is* something desperate about these expressions of hopefulness; and there *is* something obsessive about Lawrence's preoccupation with himself.

In establishing a narrative course guided by hope, Lawrence was all along running against a powerful current. For in fact, I doubt that any of us today escape the notion of narrative left to us by Freud, and with it Freud's grand interpretive narrative itself, which would have us see Lawrence's recurrent themes as manifestations of "the repetition compulsion," even the "death wish," whether we phrase them thus or not. Even those most suspicious of my "psychologizing" Lawrence here and indulging his continuous self-exploration throughout Basic Writing will find their readings determined by psychoanalytic notions so commonplace today, so absorbed into Western patterns of thought, as to go largely unheard, unnoticed and, as a result, unchecked. It seems to me critical, however, that as teacher I do notice and check those impulses, for, as Salman Rushdie so succinctly puts it in *Shame*, "Every story one chooses to tell is a kind of censorship: it prevents the telling of other tales" (qtd. in Sawatsky and Parry 405, 406). And to impose another story on Lawrence (for that is what any contrary interpretation of his story is) would have been to censor, silence, or quite possibly shatter him. That is why I have delayed such alter-interpretations—such interpretations of hopelessness—until now: to be true to Lawrence's intentions here as I write about him, just as I tried to do in the classroom when I taught him, and to give priority to his narrative over any other, even the most apparently "objective" and "true."

Certainly Lawrence is clear that he, too, is constrained by other narratives. But he is equally clear about the need to press on with his own. We have seen how he explained to Anne in the fall his dilemma and decision to excise reference to his own gayness from "The Symptoms of Suicide." A semester later, he explained his perplexity to me:

> LAWRENCE: The only thing that I sometimes feel . . . is that in [Basic Writing] I always talked about homosexuality, and in [College Writing] it sort of comes up again. And I feel like, should I be writing about this, because it's the same topic? But when I write the paper . . . it's totally a different view of it. So . . . I asked Anne if it was okay, and she said it was fine. But you know, I just feel weird writing about the same thing. But in a way it's not the same thing.
>
> MARCIA: Why do you feel "weird" about that?
>
> LAWRENCE: Because it's . . . repetitive. I mean just the thought, the first thought that comes to my mind is "Oh, let's talk about me." But when the paper is done, the final draft, it's not the same perspective as it was before. It's something maybe further, like going on further, or a different view of it. . . .
>
> MARCIA: Do you learn anything from writing it again?
>
> LAWRENCE: Yes, because you just learn more about yourself, and how other people look at it.

All of Lawrence's observations in this interview section are, I think, interesting. On the one hand, his consistent need for permission—first from me, then from Anne—is intriguing, a dependence, it seems, on one authority to release him from the strictures of another, to tell him it is "okay to be me" over and again in writing. On the other hand, his view of revision—as a mode of reseeing and rethinking, not just through drafts but across sets of papers—is perhaps surprisingly sophisticated for a "basic writer," a surprisingly sophisticated defense of his chosen narrative course within writing's own terms. Yet it is the last line I find particularly suggestive—"because you just learn more about *yourself*, and how other people look at *it*." The referent of "it" may well be homosexuality, but it is difficult to read that line without expecting to hear "because you just learn more about *yourself*, and how other people look at *you*." Set against that alternate reading, Lawrence's words suggest, I think, the extent to which "you" are "it," not just an agent but also a construction of writing, and one contingent on an audience's reading of "it."

This is Lawrence's real sophistication: the sense of contingency we get from his writing and his descriptions of writing. For all his self-scrutiny, his is no naive search for an authentic self once present but now lost. The "self" inscribed takes form in expression and is discovered in its own words, in a language system in which author and audience are intimately involved; it is a self open to constant re-vision and re-presentation. Taken together and over time, therefore, Lawrence's writings constitute a narrative that carries with it both the intentions he meant to convey and the original narrative of loss he meant to overwrite and thus escape. Reading, we see that escape is impossible or at least declined in these writings: early drafts show through each revision; early devastations show through later claims to hope; and each repeated act of self-assertion is compromised by its very repetition. And with each showing-through, each compromise, there is susceptibility to a questioning capable of more than challenging Lawrence's meaning, capable of utterly disorganizing his narrative and, certainly more critically for him, the self it constitutes. By telling his story, Lawrence little by little entrusted the power of such questioning to us, his readers.

So we come to yet another reason for my admitting only now the darker elements of Lawrence's narrative into my own: fairness. It would be both deeply disturbing and radically unfair to impose on Lawrence an interpretation he at once opened to us and simultaneously struggled so hard to overcome. For if his narrative contains the fissures of its own disorganization, then neither Freud nor "Truth" nor our keen insight, but Lawrence's story itself, holds the power to expose those chinks as well. We may have been chafing since the start of this chapter with thoughts of obsessive or destructive behavior, but not because those interpretations are in themselves "right." Rather it is because Freud, perhaps more than any other modernist writer, persuaded both future psychologists and readers of literature that any narrative's real meaning is closed to the teller and open to us, its close listeners. Yet more rightly, the privilege of meaning belongs to Lawrence. He made those chafing alter-interpretations available to me, and I made them available to you when, in constructing my narrative, I disrupted the sequence of his and brought to light, in the opening pages of my story, a knowledge he kept hidden—deleted from the present story—even until now:

> When I was growing up my father used to beat and sexually abuse my mother, brother and me. As my father was the only role model I had, I thought that if that is what a man is supposed to be . . . then I don't want to be a man. This being so, I thought my only alternative was to be a woman. At a very early age I got the message that it wasn't okay to be me. . . .

We can now trace back to this original betrayal Lawrence's compulsive determination to prove that it is, in fact, "okay to be me," however that "me" may be constructed between man and woman—two impossible alternatives. Set against this hidden passage, we can also see all of Lawrence's calls for silence-breaking and secret-telling—for coming out, for divulging suicidal impulses, whether one's own or another's—as instead a kind of secret-sharing, a simultaneous telling and keeping of secrets, here a deeper secret of trauma and abuse. We can even go as far as to suggest that Lawrence's incessant coming out is more self-destructive than salutary, less an effort to gain back the "me" lost to an abusive father than a compulsive repetition of that first act of shame, betrayal, and destruction of a son's prior felt self.

We might indeed read Lawrence's story any of these ways (other ways, too, I am sure), but all the while we must keep in mind that it is just that, Lawrence's *story*. It will be another two years after completing College Writing, and three years since beginning Basic Writing, before Lawrence himself commits these "memories" of paternal betrayal to writing, admits them into his story. The revelatory yet still-hidden passage quoted above does not come until later—until the spring of 1992—so it may not contain accurate or original material after all. It may instead be a late metaphor for and compilation of other betrayals related in or omitted from writing. This would seem unlikely, even far-fetched, if Lawrence had not provided the following account in an essay written for his Social Diversity in Education class during the spring term of 1990, the semester he took College Writing:

> What is a male identity? While I was growing up the first time I realized that I was a male was when I was eight years old. I was molested by my baby-sitter. The first time this occurred she was only fourteen. The nightmare continued for about three months.

This revelation may be construed as a report of actual retraumatization. Or it may be another instance of what I have called "secret-sharing," a simultaneous telling and keeping of that still-secret paternal abuse, with this "nightmare," as Lawrence calls it, serving as a storied metaphor for that prior assault on Lawrence's sense of self. Or, like the later revelation, this one too may be a literal as well as figurative nightmare—Lawrence's way of concretizing a generally felt sense of exposure and violation. We cannot know.

What we can know, again, is the contingency of Lawrence's self, a self he represents to us as fragmenting and reforming against the felt assaults of a once-trusted audience. Thus, whether we take these figures as actual persons or as symbolizations of betrayal, we can, in both father and baby-sitter, read a lesson: The sort of destructive questioning I spoke of before issues from storied figures like these. Such questioning has the power that Lawrence ascribes to these figures, that is, the power to discompose, possibly even to silence him. And as his writing works to contain them, it does precisely that: it continues to contain them and, with them, their power. In short, Lawrence's authorship, like his felt self, is equally contingent on the narrative he authors and on the audience sustaining it. That is why the hope he extracts from others propels his every revision. That is why his unflagging desire to show others "they are not alone," "they're not the only one," measures his own need to feel in the company of kindred selves. That is why, in writing about Lawrence now as in teaching him before, my aim has been away from a questioning that challenges his intentions, toward an understanding that helps preserve his core self and its coherent expression. And that is why Lawrence's success in Basic Writing—the successful construction and maintenance of his personal narrative—depended in no small measure on the receptive student audience it found there, a student audience different from the one that comprised Lawrence's College Writing class. Without that propping audience of fellow "others" whom he had found in Basic Writing, his sense of himself, it seems, was deeply shaken, and his sustaining narrative shifted perceptibly, not to change its course but, as we will see, to travel underground and reform itself in metaphor.

Some two months after he wrote "Free to Be You and Me" and published it in the class magazine, I asked Lawrence how he would rank himself among the other class members in College Writing. His answer was an interesting mix of formal and affective considerations:

> I think I'm above average. . . . When I came to class with the midprocess draft [of "Free to Be You and Me"], and people were reading mine, they were like, "Wow, this is incredible." And that just totally pumped me up and made me realize that I am better than average. I read some of their things and . . . I could see a total difference in my style and theirs. My punctuation and my grammar were much better, and the context of the information was better. . . . I'm just so happy that I took [Basic Writing] because . . . if I had gone into [College Writing] . . . without taking [Basic] I would have had the confidence level that some of them [in the College Writing class] have, and it would be awful.

By now we are hardly surprised to find Lawrence connecting self-confidence with writing performance, but his concern for the class's general "confidence level" is intriguing. He develops the notion more fully later in the same interview:

> I don't know, just from my [Basic Writing] class I felt more comfortable than my [College Writing] because, I don't know, I just did. . . . [Basic Writing] was very comfortable and cozy, and [College Writing] is like—I mean, the people are nice, some of them, but then there's some that . . . ever since I came out in that class, it seems that that class is just like, not close-minded, not intentionally, but they are in a way. Like some of the men in there . . . it's kind of scary because they'll look at me, and then they'll start talking and laughing. . . . Not that in [Basic Writing] we were all in the same state of mind, but it seemed

> like everyone was much more accepting because they were dif-
> ferent just like I was. . . . I don't know. I just don't feel as
> comfortable. . . . It's not what they say—or sometimes it is
> what they say—but it's just their hostility, or their anger, or
> something that I have inside, you know. It shows. It's so there.
> It's amazing. . . . Maybe it would be different if they were more
> positive about writing. Maybe they need something like a con-
> fidence booster like I did. I don't know.

I find Lawrence's comment interesting, principally because it is so consistent with the inseparable involvement of writing and being that Lawrence depicts for himself. The primary distinction he draws between his classmates in College Writing and his fellow members of the Basic Writing class, among whom he felt acceptance and kinship, is "in the writing, and even in the . . . state of mind." It is a kinship, a likeness, not of similarity but of *difference*: "[T]hey were different just like I was."

Lawrence's perception of Basic Writing as a "cozy" community of "others" is one, I believe, that many of us share. In a class where 20 to 60 percent of the students may be second-language (or third- or fourth-language) English speakers, some 30 percent of the native English speakers may be black Americans, and some 10 to 30 percent may come with diagnosed learning disabilities, there is room for "otherness" of all sorts. We might call it a phenomenon of local demographics that heightens one's sense of personal difference and, with it, one's empathy for others in all their differentness. The situation in which Lawrence found himself in College Writing is also a matter of local demographics. Against current social, economic, and educational forces, and against the predominantly white and English-speaking college populations that these forces produce, no single teacher can shelter a student like Lawrence. It was against such a bloc that he experienced his difference as alienating, and their sameness as threatening.

As Lawrence proposes it, however, a route out of alienation does lie open; that route is writing. Writing, if engaged in fully, can heighten one's sense of both personal difference and empathy for others. In his final interview with me during his fourth year, he will express both his belief that "if people looked inside themselves then they might know . . . they might be able to understand other people" and his reliance on writing as "one of the greatest tools I have" for such self/other understanding. At the moment, he renders with less clarity this complex notion of a kind of enlightened narcissism. But the notion is nonetheless apparent, as, in describing it here, he demonstrates it as well—his words composing, it seems to me, an astounding act of charity toward his aggressors: "Their hostility, or their anger . . . shows. . . . Maybe it would be different if they were more positive about writing. Maybe they need something like a confidence booster like I did."

Writing offered Lawrence a secondary escape from his classmates' hostility as well, a way to continue his own self-exploration as well as his enlightenment of others, but within the shelter of metaphor, and highly self-conscious metaphor at that. For their second College Writing essay, Anne asked the class to assess a particular social or familial tradition and introduced the assignment with a heuristic that Lawrence described in this manner:

> A lot of people didn't know exactly what they were going to write about . . . so we did a little brainstorming. . . . [Anne] would say, "Well, what happened between this time and that time?" And people would yell out things, and . . . we would tell her some important things that happened in our life. And that's what kind of got my mind moving . . . about animal rights and why it's not good to eat animals. . . .

Following this lead, Lawrence composed a piece entitled "Breaking Traditions." In it he recalled the Thanksgiving he declared himself a vegetarian and the impact his declaration had on the family gathering. His move away from "coming out" stories is significant: other traditions—weddings, funerals, senior proms— might have served him well as pretexts for his more customary explorations. But his introduction is no less characteristic: its tone, its voice, even the narrative rhythm in which the scene is set are all recognizably Lawrence's.

> Well, its November 21st and its Thanksgiving Day. As we sit down to eat, my grandfather says grace and then my mother cuts the bird. When I heard the electrical knife cutting the turkey, I shrunk in my chair. I wanted to be excused from the

table right at that moment. Then my uncle passed me the turkey dish and I said, "No thank you." At that point he asked me how come I didn't want any turkey, and I told him that I didn't believe in eating turkey or other kinds of animals. All of a sudden all heads turned toward me and then there was a family discussion on the fact that I wasn't eating meat or poultry any longer.

So what I am a vegetarian. What's the big deal? They just thought it was weird or crazy because I am going against the norm. When you think about this, it's kind of silly because the reason why they feel this way is because it's different from the way they eat. After they discussed my vegetarianism, they started asking questions like: Isn't it dangerous not to eat red meat or poultry because you won't get enough protein or iron? Don't you miss eating meat or poultry? How can one survive eating vegetables alone? Well these questions are the typical misconceptions of vegetarianism.

To help them understand these misconceptions, I explained to them that one can get enough protein, vitamins and iron in vegetables as well as by taking multi-vitamins if needed . . . .

Through the succeeding three paragraphs, Lawrence moves quite deftly in and out of personal experience in order to present the health and ethical benefits of vegetarianism, finally arriving at this conclusion:

After my spiel on animal rights, they said that it is your prerogative and if that's what you believe then that's okay as long as you eat safely. Well, they think I'm crazy but at least they won't bring up the subject again because they know that their opinions won't affect me. I'm thinking to myself, what's the big deal? So what I am not eating turkey? Then I thought maybe its because I am going against the norm. Additionally, it seems that I broke a family tradition because until this Thanksgiving everyone ate turkey. I think the reason why they made such a fuss over my vegetarianism is because they didn't think that I would stand up for what I believed in. Furthermore, by not eating the turkey I was making a statement that I'm growing up and making my own decisions. Also, since I am going against the norm, as well as the tradition, this shocked them because they had never thought about breaking this tradition until I did. Hopefully, my family will be able to accept my differences because I'm not going to change to please them.

Knowing Lawrence as by now we do, we can hardly read "Breaking Traditions" as anything but the metaphor he himself recognized it to be. Certainly the last sentence alone bespeaks an intensity of emotion beyond one we would expect to find invested in eating habits. In his end-of-the-term portfolio review, Lawrence focused on this line:

> When writing throughout this essay I learned that breaking this [Thanksgiving] tradition also symbolizes the other traditions that I am going to break since I'm gay. In addition, if my family doesn't accept my differences then I am going to have to go out on my own and accept this.

And in our spring interview, he discussed his metaphoric ruse with a revisionist sense of history and a Wildean delight in self-plagiarism:

> [T]he introduction I thought was awesome. And the ending was great. I ended it with, um, it had something to do with the first [essay]. I wrote, "Well, I am growing up and making my own decisions now, and I am free to be me"! So I kind of like ended it in the last one but . . . told my spiel about animal rights, and told my parents how I wasn't going to back down to their beliefs. Because it's . . . the same thing as being gay. It's different, so it's wrong. So it's sort of the same thing: coming out as being a vegetarian instead of being gay.

That the telling clause—"and I am free to be me"—does not actually appear in "Breaking Traditions" matters little: it is there unspoken, and the point is made. "Breaking Traditions" is, as Lawrence implies, a sort of continuation of his first essay, or, perhaps more accurately, a repetition of its theme sung in a different key.

Taken on its own and judged against the first-year essays we typically receive, "Breaking Traditions" is an acceptable College Writing piece, one that would not necessarily have marked its author as a "basic writer." It is clearly a "personal essay" but could not be characterized as solipsistic. It carries social implications and an intentionally more public appeal. The introductory paragraphs are recognizably Lawrence—echoes of the early "Significant Event" run throughout—yet suggestive of something new.

Whereas, before, external events served largely as pretexts for self-directed ruminations, now personal experience sets a context for discussing social issues and serves a conscious rhetorical purpose: "I wanted to pull the reader in," he observed in our interview, and, according to his peer responses, he did. The scene he narrates gives his readers a sense of dramatic immediacy while affording Lawrence himself opportunity, by way of dialogue, to turn away from the familial audience he renders and toward the audience of readers he intends to address. Personal experience, in terms of his act of "breaking traditions" and his situation outside the family norm, also affords him the perspective from which to develop his argument, to critique the holiday and its dietary "requirements" as the social constructs they are and his behavior as the extended "statement"—the discourse—it was: "[B]y not eating turkey I was making a statement that I'm growing up and making my own decisions. Also, since I am going against the norm, as well as the tradition, this shocked them because they had never thought about breaking this tradition until I did."

All in all, "Breaking Traditions" embodies a good measure of quite sophisticated rhetorical and social insight, along with the usual deal of awkward rebelliousness found in first-year themes. As an essay, it can certainly stand on its own. But it could not have come into being on its own. It is part of Lawrence's developing narrative, and contains within it parts that have gone before. Much of Lawrence's delight in it clearly derived from his extended metaphor, from this three-page pun. Here he was able to contrive, but in a different form, a successful coming out for himself, and to realize, if only imaginatively, the power he believed would come to one truly "free to be." Moreover, as his process notes reveal, he was able to arrive at a hard "truth" within its relative safety, acknowledging, as he reflected, "if my family doesn't accept my differences then I am going to have to go out on my own and accept this."

Much of the pleasure I take in reading it, too, derives from the power I hear behind Lawrence's voice, coupled with my own knowledge of those earlier essays and their resonance in its lines: "Isn't it dangerous . . . ? Don't you miss . . . ? [I]t is your prerogative and if that's what you believe then that's okay as long as you . . . safely." The entire essay reads like a parlor game that I am in on and enjoy, a trick played on relatives then and classmates now, on people who, as we know from Lawrence's narrative, deserve to be so gently but fully duped.

Finally, I do not believe it would be too much to say that "Breaking Traditions," even taken as an entity unto itself, benefits from its position in Lawrence's ongoing narrative and the resonance it draws from its predecessors. It focuses on Thanksgiving but has the feel of Mardi Gras. Within its metaphor, Lawrence has dressed himself up, assumed the guise of a vegetarian in order to hide and simultaneously come out as a gay man. For once, he is his own secret, and he revels in the play. Secrecy gives him the courage to speak and act—perhaps before his family that Thanksgiving, certainly in the retelling here—but the hidden truth gives his speech act its force. Secrecy gives him control over himself, his family, and the essay in which he renders them both, but the truth impelling him gives timbre to the voice we hear. That his voice breaks occasionally in somewhat squeaky petulance, as in the closing line, serves but to show the delicate balance of containment he managed until then. In fact, it may be just this delicate and risky balancing act that gave Lawrence obvious pleasure in writing this essay, and me, another gay writer, pleasure in reading it: it may be the signal satisfaction of writing we shared, of translating into distant forms thoughts too dangerous and deeply felt to be rendered bare in prose. But if the particular tenor of "Breaking Traditions" gave both Lawrence and me a particular satisfaction as gay writers, the discovery of writing's metaphoric possibilities intimates, I think, a more universal writerly delight—and progression. For is the pleasure of "academic discourse" not at least in part the opportunity it affords to infuse personally distinct, if not distant, objects with the most deeply felt, personal care? And does that care not come, in turn, from our object of study's often undefined capacity to reflect, mirror, or in some way re-image our own core habits and concerns? If so, then Lawrence's achievement in this essay lies in his ability here to maintain harmonious resonance between manifest and secret subjects, between subject and subjectivity; to maintain the poise; and, as he himself might well suggest, to maintain confidence in his disguise.

A subsequent essay Lawrence composed, however, demonstrates just how easily such a delicate poise can be upset and pleasure lost. "Fur is Dead," representing an argument for animal rights that Lawrence consciously and wisely left to the background of "Breaking Traditions," developed quite literally out of the earlier piece. Like "Breaking Traditions," it remains, as we will see, largely metaphoric, the tenor simply less evident and *temporarily* more deeply suppressed; unlike "Breaking Traditions," on the other hand, this metaphor contains the dark elisions rather than the hopeful, delight-filled inclusions of his earlier pieces, and—or perhaps, *so*—cannot contain them for long.

As his "persuasive" essay, Lawrence considered "Fur is Dead" his "strongest." Though his explanation of its strength focused on its form and its formal comprehension of its argument's bleak, impelling "truths," it may also have signaled to him that he was effectively fighting the worrisome urge to write about himself and was writing the way one *should* write. "Fur is Dead" does indeed move out of narrative and into a fully expository mode. Yet I cannot see this as Lawrence's strongest essay, nor do I see its form as successfully containing his intended—or more important, as we will see, his unintended—message. To the contrary, while demonstrating *some* advancement in his composing skills, "Fur is Dead" in the main exemplifies for me the sorts of formal distortions that can appear when a student like Lawrence tries to retreat too deep into metaphor, to contain the uncontainable, and essentially to express and simultaneously suppress himself in composing. I might even go so far as to say that Lawrence's dilemma in this essay suggests to me that metaphor is a privilege unavailable to some students, perhaps to all students at some moments in their writing careers—that metaphoric disguise has the look of Mardi Gras but can take on the feel of the closet, too.

Lawrence's assessment of its strength not withstanding, as the title would suggest, "Fur is Dead" is no pleasure to read. Having been made conscious by a peer during the revision process of his tendency to "jump too quickly" to optimistic conclusions, he opens the essay with an almost suffocating catalogue of killing methods. And beginning with distance enough, it soon envelops us in Lawrence's own "truths," becoming less pleasurable by degrees as echoes of other writings intrude.

Fur is Dead

In every fur coat there is the suffering of up to 120 animals killed by a very ugly business. "Every year in the U.S. alone, at least seventy million animals suffer and die to produce luxury fur garments. Whether they are trapped in the wild or raised on the intensive confinement fur 'ranches,' the animals suffer incredible torment and are often killed by primitive and barbaric means." In other words, many animals are killed every year by many different cruel ways.

There are many methods commonly used to kill minks including poison, strychnine, which causes the animals to suffocate; electrocution causes acute suffering before death and the use of uncooled and unfiltered carbon monoxide gas can cause severe burning and distress in the lungs. Trappers are also an important part of the killing of animals . . . .

An equally torturous catalogue of trapping methods then follows before the essay turns to a discussion of some of the recent legislative acts and lobbying activities aimed at restricting or, in some cases, altogether preventing the slaughter of animals for the fur trade.

Through these initial three pages, Lawrence handles the normally difficult task of integrating facts from outside sources into his own argument with competence if not flair. And according to his own assessment, "Every sentence, every paragraph went together. . . . They flowed really clearly with linking sentences." Toward the close of his essay, however, Lawrence introduces an extended quotation from the Isak Dinesen piece he read in Basic Writing and, along with it, reminders of his own first writings.

During the years of 1971–1986, fur sales in the U.S. climbed steadily to a record high of two billion dollars. . . . Furs, once symbols of fashion, are actually the end products of misery, suffering, pain, and death.

When an animal dies, it loses its color and its life. Dinesen's "The Iguana" explains this:

The big lizards . . . . are not pretty in shape, [but] nothing can be imagined more beautiful than their coloring . . . . Once I shot an Iguana. I thought that I should be able to

make some pretty things from his skin. A strange thing
happened then, that I have never afterwards forgotten. As
I went up to him, where he was lying dead upon his stone,
and actually while I was walking the few steps, he faded
and grew pale, all color died out of him as in one long
sigh, and by the time that I touched him he was gray, and
dull like a lump of cement. [53]
This explains that when one kills an animal its beauty disap-
pears when it dies. Therefore, don't take life for granted because one only has one chance to make something of themselves
and when they die then there is nothing left but memories of
their existence.

Dinesen's passage might be made to fit Lawrence's argument, in
sentiment if not in tone. But against his interpretation of it and
the prior narratives his interpretation recalls, it is nearly impossible to envisage Dinesen's iguana "lying dead upon his stone"
without envisaging Michael, perhaps even Lawrence, lying dead
there, too. As we move to the conclusion, these human and animal images become inextricably mixed:

> Someday hopefully we won't have to worry about [such] cru-
> elty if people become more aware of what they are doing to
> innocent animals. They are living animals just like you and me.
> There are many ways that you can help. . . . A single individual
> might not be able to change the world, but with the help of
> others, we can end the exploitation of animals once and for all.

It is not only my reading, I believe, and not only my knowledge
of Lawrence's previous pieces, that find disturbance here. Despite his own emphasis on "linking" sentences and the coherence
they effect, Lawrence included the Dinesen passage in order to
give his readers "something else to think about." And I would
venture that Lawrence's discussion of "The Iguana," including
his interpretive simile equating "innocent animals" with "you
and me," is no throw-away set of lines. I would venture to the
contrary that its very ill fit correlates with his need to assimilate
it: the Dinesen passage and Lawrence's rather idiosyncratic interpretation of it at some level are just what "Fur is Dead" is all
about. For, like "Breaking Traditions," "Fur is Dead" is a metaphor, a set of images and ideas driven by a wholly other set of

messages and motivations. Unlike "Breaking Traditions," this metaphor is not sustained; this vehicle, so attenuated, cannot fully contain the tenor, and Lawrence's own private plea for acceptance erupts in anthropomorphism—"Don't take life for granted because one only has one chance to make something of themselves and when they die then there is nothing left but memories of their existence." With this eruption, "Fur is Dead" rounds back upon his earliest writings, becoming once again a hortative piece in the tradition of "A Significant Event" and "The Symptoms of Suicide" rather than a step forward into disinterested persuasion.

Metaphor, even one as deeply imbedded as this, was not new to Lawrence. It is a conscious—perhaps more rightly, self-conscious—form of secret-sharing, and for him, as for most gay people, a way of life, an habitual form of discourse in which one continually changes pronouns, speaks of something but means another, or does not speak at all. Even his first essay for Basic Writing ("Life on the Streets") was, in fact, metaphoric, though I did not know that then. And in many respects, "Fur is Dead" resembles that earliest essay more than any other. Like "Fur is Dead," "Life on the Streets" was composed in response to an assignment asking for something other than narrative, it suppresses all mention of Lawrence's gay identity, and it represents an act of suppression, a metaphoric ruse, that Lawrence would not or could not maintain. I return to that very first essay now for the lesson it holds for teachers.

For their initial assignment, students in Basic Writing were asked to observe and interpret a single photograph from the then-current *Newsweek* series "A Day in the Life of America." Lawrence chose the photograph of a city alley and the homeless people populating it, and his essay begins with a catalogue of observed and imagined horrors that savors of the opening passages of "Fur is Dead":

LIFE ON THE STREETS

This picture shows two men assault a drunk in an alley off Winston Street, part of the city is skid row in Los Angeles, California according to Sarah Leen.

When I think of poverty, in America, I think about the hungry and the homeless. How hard it must be to survive? The

American society thinks that being poor could never happen to them. That's not true! All it takes is for someone to get hooked on drugs or become an alcoholic. Also, someone could get laid off or lose their job and they have nowhere else to turn but the streets. That person may rely on welfare and before they know it, they can't get back on their feet. Therefore, they become attached to this lifestyle.

Unfortunately, where there is poverty there is crime. The crime rate appears to be higher. Cocaine is sold more readily than candy. Beggars harass people walking down the street. The aroma of alcohol and marijuana greets visitors to the slums. The streets reeking of sewage . . . rats, rodents, and cockroaches rummaging through old trash. Ominous, black clouds hover over the city like someone is watching. The smog gets thicker as the day moves on. The stale, raunchy air sticks to your lungs . . . .

The essay ends with Lawrence's signature conclusion:

However, there is hope. I believe the attitude of the average American person toward the hungry and homeless has changed. . . . Although the attitude is changing, there is still so much to do. We can make a difference if we all work together as one and give our time to those who are in need. We can do it, just believe in yourself and never give up hope!

When in responding to Lawrence's essay I suggested he spend more time observing and translating for his readers the horrors of the street that Leen records for her viewers before moving to his own interpretations of them, I did not know Lawrence or how deeply his own visions of abandonment and alienation ran. And when I tentatively suggested a different interpretation of Leen's photograph and, with it, a different, less optimistic conclusion another reader might reach, I did not know the intimate matter on which I was commenting or the deeply felt need he had to maintain his hopeful vision. I did not know, in short, how inextricably Lawrence's felt self—his private, abiding theme—was tied even to this apparently distant subject. It was a full semester later, in College Writing, that he composed the following letter with which he introduced himself to Anne and raised to the surface the hidden tenor of that introductory metaphor of street life:

Dear Anne,
While I was visiting Boston one afternoon and I saw the bums
as well as beggars on the street, I felt depressed and I wanted to
give them the money that I had in my pocket. It was then that
I realized that I wanted . . . to help adolescent children deal
with their homosexuality and not to be ashamed of it.

However oblique the connection between homelessness and homosexuality may be to us (and I think for some of us the imagined connections are not all that oblique), the presence of both
images in this letter means that we cannot deny the meaning Leen's
photograph held for Lawrence. Nor should we deny it. For it is
often, I believe, when students have done what Lawrence did in
both "Life on the Streets" and "Fur is Dead"—when they have
composed what seem to be safer, less self-expressive, and more
analytic or argumentative pieces—that their writing is most apt
to reflect in its form the attenuation of metaphor it constitutes as
well as the subjective division and conflict they are struggling, in
that delicate metaphoric balance, to manage. Unfortunately, it is
also pieces like these that we teachers feel safest in meeting with
the sort of destructive questioning I spoke of before, with the
sorts of challenges—to Lawrence's happy conclusion in "Life on
the Streets," for instance, or to his ill-fitting inclusion of Dinesen
in "Fur is Dead," or to the merit of the very argument undertaken itself—that can drive these students still deeper into metaphor, disorganization, and, at the extreme, silence.

Ruth said that she had been just lying there, waiting for it
to happen, when a friend of hers came for a visit and left a
book of poems by Francis X. Dillon. "Do you know 'Sunrise
near Monterey'?" she asked.
"Vaguely," Brooke said. He remembered that it ended with
the command "Embrace!" He had thought it silly.
"That was the first poem I read," Ruth said. "When I got
to the end I read it again and again and I just knew I was going
to live. And here I am." ("An Episode in the Life of Professor
Brooke" 40)

If in Basic Writing, Lawrence had begun his self-narrative in
metaphor, the class's unified acceptance of him had, in large mea-

sure, emboldened his writing and allowed him to "come out" of his metaphoric disguise. By midsemester, not only was he writing, and publishing in class booklets, overtly gay pieces but also he had assumed an increasingly "gay" appearance, in the cut and color of his hair as well as in jewelry and dress; his book bag was adorned with gay symbols; and, by the start of the second semester, he had become an increasingly outspoken advocate of gay rights, both in the Speakers' Bureau and in informal debates. All this made Lawrence a conspicuous target for homophobic groups and individuals, including editorialists in a right-wing campus newspaper. Toward the close of the spring term, while participating in a Speakers' Bureau presentation at the local high school, he was harassed and physically assaulted by the president of another far-right student organization. The situation was sufficiently threatening that police were called upon to intervene.

Expressions of hostility from classmates in College Writing, and presumably other courses as well, no doubt conspired to expose the sad lie of "Free to Be You and Me" and its image of the University as safe haven, and they may well have initiated Lawrence's retreat into metaphor with "Breaking Traditions." To the degree that "Breaking Traditions" had been successful, its success was attributable to its position in Lawrence's larger narrative, as the secret repository of his coming out stories and, even more, as a moment suspended in narrative time when he could still maintain the illusion that his retreat was out of choice rather than fear, and that he could participate in the power that sent him there. But, as the semester progressed and the threats Lawrence felt both inside and outside the classroom intensified, that illusion became increasingly difficult to maintain. "Truths" very different from those he had sought so diligently to compose, "truths" he had fought first to elide in narrative and then to suppress in metaphoric form, began to erupt, initially in "Fur is Dead" and then more ferociously in Lawrence's last essays composed for College Writing.

The first of these final pieces, entitled "The State of the World Today," opens with this paragraph:

> In today's society everyone is so concerned with being politically correct that they are made to believe that prejudice doesn't exist. For example, many of today's music has many

sexist, racist and homophobic remarks written in their songs. And this promotes the many prejudices that do exist. However, society says that they won't tolerate prejudice but if that were true then why are groups like Guns and Roses and Public Enemy so popular? Also, when prejudice incidents do happen they are taken lightly because they never happen. But in reality that isn't true. People are harassed everyday. There are many people who take going to school for granted. Some of us have to worry about walking from the campus center to our dorm, walking across campus without being harassed, or being beaten up or killed. This is because people haven't conformed to society's social norms of being "the all-American" men and women.

To most readers, I think, this passage is barely comprehensible— at best. And while we might try to explain it away as a hastily written, unrevised draft, we cannot: in fact, it went through a number of revisions and, what is more, even the first jottings of "Free to Be You and Me" as well as "Breaking Traditions" are without the syntactical and logical flaws of this piece.

As Lawrence later admitted, "The State of the World Today" was written in angry response to the ridicule to which he had recently been subjected. It exemplifies, I believe, just the sort of "decomposition" such anger can produce, the confused fragmentation we see in it better explained by the motivation behind its writing, the audience it was intended for, and the topic Lawrence undertook in it: the blend of institutionalized discrimination and denial that is at once contradictory and insoluble, at once incomprehensible and, for all too many students, inescapable. For them, as for Lawrence, their position outside "the all-American" pale leaves them square in the middle of these complexities, and to narrate or describe them, much less to analyze or argue them, is daunting. I have seen any number of students brought to silence by a knowledge like Lawrence's: gay students, black students, Asian students, women; students whose perspective from the "margin" is equally clear and, at the same time, perplexing; students who face an audience of uncomprehending "all-Americans," an audience with whom they share no assumptions, no common ground from which to speak, and so they give up speaking—or writing—altogether because they would "just have to explain too much." Lawrence, however, would not give up expressing the Gordian contradictions endemic to a reality—to his reality—that is not what it seems to be and whose occupants are not truly free to be. Their expression was his project. Here, in "The State of the World Today," he faced them head-on, only to become mired in their complexity.

Previously Lawrence had used various forms of narrative sequencing to manage these same sorts of contradictions and conflicts with varying success. Often, as we have seen, he separated them, loosened their strands in his characteristically linear narrative: "once I was unhappy, but now I'm better, and soon, with hope and help, I'll be better still." At times, however, with a sort of re-visionary power, he barred darker images from his final drafts altogether or buried them deep beneath more tolerable scenes of suffering. Now, having struck back full force at his perceived offenders, at his narrative's disruptive naysayers, he apparently at least contemplated not just metaphoric retreat but full surrender. His final works of the semester are companion pieces of a sort: one is a suicide note; the other, an essay about the occasion of its composition. With them Lawrence provides us with both a sample of and a commentary on writing that is at once enormously personal and enormously valuable—lifesaving, in fact. Ironically, set against "The State of the World Today" and taken together, they reveal the essential role a trusted audience plays for a student like Lawrence and, alternately, the destructive impact a hostile audience can have on a writer's self as well as on his or her writing.

Late in Lawrence's process journal, this passage appears:

> What's on my mind? Mmm. Well, this past Friday night I wrote a suicide note. I was with some of my closest friends and we talked until the wee hours of the morning about my cry for help. That was the best talk I ever had because I realized that I can make it! I can make it on my own!

The note reminds those of us who teach writing for a living that some students use writing to live. The essay Lawrence wrote about that note—an essay then unpublished, shown only to Anne and one trusted classmate, though granted to us for publication now—demonstrates the internal coherence *and* integrity writing can have.

Dead or Alive

A cry for help! This was what I was thinking when I wrote a suicide note last Friday night. I was thinking about how I really don't have a home because my family is distant with me now that they know that I'm gay. My grandfather no longer speaks to me. My aunt says, "It's your own fault that you're being harassed since you are openly gay. Your being gay should be your business and nobody has to know." In other words, she thinks that no one else should know me, like she is ashamed of me or something. Actually, I was just feeling that if I killed myself I wouldn't have to suffer anymore. Although if I killed myself I wouldn't feel anything, I would be dead to the world.

This suicide note made me realize how much I really do want to keep on living. After I wrote the note I showed it to some friends and we talked about how much I do have to live for. They made me realize that I can make it as an openly gay man with the support of my friends. . . . In the long run, this cry for help was the best thing I could have done.

By writing this note it was like a new beginning because I reached out and told my friends I was considering suicide. Fortunately, with this experience I became aware that I really want to live. I just have to learn to deal with my problems and I have to be patient about how long it may take until they are resolved. Also, I need to find a way to stop thinking that suicide is the answer to my problems because it isn't.

Suicide is the result of a person's giving up because he/she doesn't want to deal with anything anymore. I think this is one of the reasons why it is so prevalent in teenagers. For instance, today in our society suicide is the third leading cause of death in teenagers. Suicide may seem to be the only way out while going through a rough time. I can identify with this thought. I have thought about suicide since I was ten. Most recently, because of the homophobia that exists in today's society. Furthermore, I feel I will never be accepted as a human being in our society because I am gay.

During the teenage years acceptance is the most important aspect of one's life. Without acceptance one's self image is blown because of what others think. It is very important to fit in. One's self esteem is greatly hindered as well as the chances of having a positive outlook on life. Many suicides occur because of people's fears of not being accepted for who they are.

As we grow up we are socialized to believe what is "right" and what is "wrong" by the norm of that time period. For example, in the sixties high waters were in but now in the nineties they are not. If one goes against the norm then they are . . . rejected by their friends and family. Then they may feel that they are alone and something is wrong with them. Depending on the person, suicidal feelings may exist. These feelings may also stem from whether or not the person is strong enough to see that they are okay to be who they are. In other words, insecurities can play a major role in deciding whether you or the world is right.

Believe what's in your heart and don't let anyone tell you different just because they might not agree with you. Fight for what you believe in and make sure whoever knows you that you won't tolerate their ignorance. Remember the serenity prayer:

> God grant me the serenity to accept the
> things I cannot change. To change the things
> I can. And the wisdom to know the
> difference.

Keep up the fight! In the end you'll know what you did was right and it will mean more than anything to you because you didn't give up. You can do it. You can survive! It's your choice whether to be happy or sad!

In our interview, Lawrence talked of the history and context of "Dead or Alive":

> LAWRENCE: The last essay I wrote [for College Writing] was about suicide. Just talking about suicide. Just talking about how I am. One night I wrote a suicide note . . . and I just talked about how the suicide note affected me, how, after writing it, I started to think about what I was actually saying . . . and it was like a new beginning.
>
> MARCIA: What was it like for you to write the note?
>
> LAWRENCE: It was a release of all my frustrations and fears, and it was like a new beginning. I know that it sounds weird, but it was like all my friends reached out to me, and it was really important. . . . Like this one man I didn't even really know sat down and started talking to me about it. He really cared about me, and I didn't even know this man. He was so nice, and so caring, and he gave me a hug. And it just made me feel so great.

And Lawrence talked of the way "Dead or Alive," like "Fur is Dead" before it, demonstrated his progress as a writer. But this time, it was not a progress in form that showed in the writing; it was a progress of person: "It demonstrates the progress that I have made as a person," he said, "and it also lets me know that it's okay to make mistakes, and that I can move on from them and learn from them, instead of feeling like a failure. . . . I can learn from that." Yet as personal as the suicide note was for Lawrence, the essay about that note—the essay sprung from and containing that note—is not all self-directed. As so often before, he has here once again set himself before his audience—like an iguana on the rock or Michael in his coffin—as an object lesson in hope:

> Marcia: So at this point were you writing more for someone else, or were you writing for yourself?
>
> Lawrence: For me, but also for other people, because then I went on to talk about the serenity prayer, and how that's helped me to deal with things, and also helped other people deal with things. So it's more out in the open, so it's more clear to them how they can go on. . . .
>
> Marcia: The prayer functions in some ways like your suicide note.
>
> Lawrence: Right. I tried to give them some hope. I said, "Just keep up the fight. In the end you'll know that what you did was right, and it'll mean more to you than anything because you didn't give up. You can do it; you can survive. It's your choice." I don't know. I just think the serenity prayer is just so wonderful because it shows that you can do it. Just don't give up.

In suicide note and serenity prayer, Lawrence reads all the recurrent exhortations that went before: "You can do it; you can survive." And his reading rings right, for "Dead or Alive" is all those prior essays, as is the suicide note at its center. It is the hopelessness embedded in all his dogged claims of hopefulness, the death wish we read beneath his compulsive revisits to the same fatal scene, his retellings of the same defiant tale. But while a statement of intended suicide, the note was intended—in the act of writing, or later in Lawrence's interpretive reading—to be "a cry for help!" that could successfully move readers to "reach out for me," and by their reaching release Lawrence from "all my frustrations and fears." Condensing all Lawrence's iterations, all the sequential linearity of his "once I was unhappy, but now I'm better, and soon, with hope and help, I'll be better still" narratives into a single plea, it is what it is not. At once, it both evidences the dark undercurrent of all Lawrence's narratives and simultaneously confirms his faith in writing as that which keeps him alive. For us, this slippery equation is also a palindrome of sorts. If the suicide note is all Lawrence's prior essays condensed, then all Lawrence's prior essays are suicide notes, and we who read them are—whether we choose to be or not—inextricably involved in, perhaps even responsible for, his narrative life.

"Do you know 'Sunrise near Monterey'?" she asked.

"Vaguely," Brooke said. He remembered that it ended with the command "Embrace!" He had thought it silly.

"That was the first poem I read," Ruth said. "When I got to the end I read it again and again and I just knew I was going to live. . . . Isn't that why you write books? . . . To bring people together and help them live their lives?"

Brooke did not know exactly why he had written his books. He was not sure that his motives could stand that kind of scrutiny. ("An Episode in the Life of Professor Brooke" 40–41)

I wonder why so many of us shrink from, run from, the sort of texts that Wolff's heroine reads and that Lawrence writes; why so many of us doubt, that is, the value of writing to live, as though something else were more important, as though something else would better justify what we teach and do—as though writing that calls life into question is somehow more worthwhile than writing that calls us into life? What is the source of our own embarrassment that makes us turn from the command "Embrace" and call it "silly"?

Compositions and Decompositions: Writing After College Writing

When three years later Lawrence walked into my office for our final interview, he was transformed. Gone were the pink triangles

from his face and peace earrings from his ears, the exotic haircut
and colors, the bright yellow halter top of before. He was tall
and lean; his hair, its natural dark brown, was fashionably cropped
and brushed casually to the side; he wore horn-rimmed glasses,
khaki trousers, and a polo shirt. He looked, in short, like my
image of the Amherst College students he was studying among;
he laughed and said he was in drag.

Having availed himself of our Five-College Consortium offerings as well as the University's Bachelor's Degree in Individual
Concentration Program, Lawrence had designed his own major
in gender studies and mapped his own curriculum vitae, which
took him through such courses as, at UMass, "The Sociology of
Sex Roles" and "The Psychology of Women"; at Mount Holyoke,
"The Psychology of Motherhood" and "Race, Class, Culture and
Gender in the Classroom"; and, at Amherst College, "Women
and Gender Studies: Cross Dressing," "Topics in Feminist Theories: Identifying Bodies," "Political Science: Authority and Sexuality," "The Cross Cultural Construction of Gender," and "The
History of Homosexuality." He had spent two years in intensive
therapy with a gay therapist and in an Alcoholics Anonymous
(AA) group for gay men and lesbians in the "Valley," as our
Northampton/Amherst area is known. He had changed his name
to Steven.

Lawrence sat down talking: "My name is Steven. I took your
class four years ago, a long time ago. Time goes by so fast. I just
got all this writing collected for you in the last few days, and I
can't believe how many papers are here. It's amazing." The stack
was truly daunting: essays on "Social Diversity in Education";
"How Has Culture Constructed Gender and How Is That Reflected in the Law?"; "Claude Hartland and His Homosexuality"; "Everybody's Free"; "Madonna: The Queer Queen"; and
"Is It Compulsory Heterosexuality or Compulsory Patriarchy?"
The titles and the stack went on . . . as did Steven: "I guess looking back, the ones I don't particularly like so much are the ones
from English 112 [College Writing]. I didn't look at English 111
[Basic Writing] because I didn't think to, because you know what
that writing was like. But looking back at 112 now, I don't like
them as much because they're not as focused, I think, as, for

instance, these papers that I have to write now, because they're on a specific topic or it's my own topic, but they're within a context." I asked him to elaborate, and he went on: "One thing I liked about 111 was the reading of the books, because that gave us more of a way to look at ourselves . . . another external way to look in at ourselves, and it was easier to write. That might be why in the classes now I like writing papers better, because there's a focus around the writing as far as what we already read." That readings provide a context in which students can situate themselves and out of which they can generate ideas for writing makes sense to me; indeed, it has been a major factor in my decision to include readings in a composition curriculum. But all this seemed in direct opposition to something I remembered Steven had written at the close of his term in College Writing: that he "thought it was most helpful when we were allowed to write most of our papers freely without a specific topic" because then, as he said, he "took pride in what I was writing." So I wondered whether the readings did not provide something else as well, and I asked Steven whether he sensed any effect of shared readings on the class as a community:

> I guess, in a way, I might have felt more of a community in 112 than I do now. But still, now I know what people are working on in their papers. I knew what they were working on in 112, too, but it was a little different because of the context, because they could write about anything in their life, whereas in these other classes it's writing about a specific topic of the class. And that feels a little bit more comfortable because there's more of a general idea of what people are writing about.

The example he then offered was, I think, significant:

> For instance, this semester I wrote about RuPaul, the black drag queen, and the class was about cross-dressing. The context was cross-dressing, whereas in a writing class, the context is writing. It's not a specific topic; it's whatever you want. So it's a different dynamic totally.

My own sense is that more important than the fact of a context was the particularity of the contexts in which Steven found himself or, more rightly, located himself: that the freedom he experienced in College Writing to say what he wanted to say to—and in the face of—an overwhelmingly heterosexual group had been replaced by the more profound sense of freedom to say what he wanted among his own. Those contexts in which he described finding comfort were his milieu, specifically, classrooms in which the shared topics and expected talk were of cross-dressing, homosexuality, and the like; classrooms in which Steven's respondent classmates—largely gay men, lesbians, and their "allies" —were truly peer readers; classrooms within whose confines, at least, the answer to the question he had posed in English 112— "Is homosexuality normal?"—was "yes." Having constructed a curriculum vitae that was truly a *curriculum vitae mei*, he had refined the comfort he took in Basic Writing, where "they were different just like I was," and found a place where he could say, "They are gay just as I am."

In his last two years at the University—or, more accurately, among the five Valley colleges—Steven had also found a selection of instructors, a group of mentors, who both challenged and applauded his abilities, who both met and mirrored his needs. During our final interview, Steven talked at length about two women in particular who had played such important, "supportive" roles in the past two years of his academic life. Then suddenly he changed our conversation's direction:

> I was just thinking about not getting so much support from Professor [Murray] who taught a comparative literature class. The papers I did not like so much. You know, I think that makes a big difference . . . not really feeling comfortable with him because of his opinions about things. . . . I just didn't feel comfortable with him as a person, as a professor. . . . It's interesting to look back now because I didn't really know why I didn't like the class. I didn't like writing those papers. I hated them, and I hated the class.

Now he could offer a number of reasons for his discomfort: the instructor's pro-life position, oddly and unexpectedly expressed as he encouraged women in the class who might have had abortions to write about the experience in their assigned "reflective papers"; remarks in the class regarding incest that "triggered a lot of my anger"; and comments by the instructor's teaching assistant on Steven's own reflective paper, a paper recounting his decision not to sing in his Christian Church choir, "to the effect" of, as Steven expressed it, "I can't believe you go to a Christian church . . . or something in that way." In characteristic fashion, he struggled for graciousness: "Maybe age has something to do with it," he wondered aloud. "As people get older they have less patience." But he stumbled often in the effort: "Like he was a really, actually he was a really, you could see that he had a heart and he was really caring but sort of for the outside, in a way. He had a caring side, but he also had this other side. He tried to be supportive, but I just couldn't feel it." The result: utter confusion . . . and anger.

> He was open in a sense, and, in another sense, he wasn't. Now looking back where I was and thinking about where I am today, I almost want to be more direct and say, "Well, what the hell do you want? What do you want? You know, you're being this way, but you're also being this way. I feel like you're giving me mixed messages. So who are you, and what do you want from me?"

Finally Steven arrived at the real catalyst of his anger in this course he remembered as "Good and Evil: East Meets West Something Ethics—I hated it." The class had read, discussed, and been assigned a comparative paper on the book of Job, the *Bhagavad-Gita*, and *The Way of Chuang Tzu*—no simple task for anyone. Steven's essay, entitled "The Conceptions of the Absolute," begins thus:

> In each of the three books that we have read there seems to be three distinct conceptions of what the absolute is. For example, God is fear, Krishna is love and Tao is selfless. In the *Book of Job*, God is fire and brimstone. As follows are the passages and my interpretations of the passages themselves.

> > And the Lord said to Satan, "Have you noticed my servant Job, and that there is no one on earth like him, blameless and upright, fearing God and avoiding evil?" But Satan answered the Lord and said, "Is it for nothing that Job is God-fearing? Have you not surrounded him and his family and all that he has with your protection?

You have blessed the work of his hands, and his livestock are spread over the land. But now put forth your hand and touch anything that he has, and surely he will blaspheme you to your face." And the Lord said to Satan, "Behold, all that he has in your power, only do not lay a hand on this person." So Satan went forth from the presence of the Lord. (*Job* 1:8–12)

This passage shows the concept of the absolute as being a condemning God. For example, it says that Job fears God instead of having faith in God, assuming that the absolute is all powerful and wants one to be afraid of it. Therefore it seems that Job only is good because he is afraid of being evil. In turn, this concept of evil only perpetuates the fear of God and makes the absolute seem like the devil.

Furthermore, the concept of evil I believe is a human construction because as I understand the absolute, it doesn't believe in evil. It seems by using the term evil this only scares people into being "good" and it makes them feel ashamed of themselves if they do make mistakes. In verse 8 it seems that their God expects them to be perfect. This only creates failure because nobody's perfect. And as they fail this causes them to feel ashamed and as far as I understand the absolute he expects people to make mistakes because their human. So by having the idea that they are bad explains why their conception of the absolute is one of a condemning nature.

Throughout these passages, question marks are scattered, the phrase "as I understand the absolute" is lined out each time it appears, and in the gap between paragraphs is written in the teacher's hand, "This sounds more like a private war than an analysis."

Indeed "The Conceptions of the Absolute" *is* more private war than analysis. Steven's dialogue with the book of Job is immediate and personal; at its center lies an issue far more of faith than of aesthetics. Job's verses speak to the heart of Steven's conception of God and his self-conception, too, and it is clear from Steven's words that, in his view, they speak offensively. His later remarks to me indicate that his intention had been from the start to meet that offense. "The book of Job really triggered me," he explained, "because it sounded a lot like they're condemning God, and I wrote about that—how much I hated reading or getting that type of an interpretation. I don't see God in that way." He *could not* see God that way, I suspect, for at the center of his faith—as at the center of this vision of Job the dutiful son, shamed and made to suffer arbitrarily at the hands of God the Father— lay something more deeply personal. And, according to Steven's reading, the demand to uncover the personal within them all unites the three disparate books of Krishna, Tao, and Job: "And for the similarities," his essay's last line reads, "it seems the general knowledge from spirituality is supposed to be to find one self through the deities." So, in this section, he continues:

> The absolute they speak of sounds scary to me because I thought that God was supposed to be this great power that loved you. However this doesn't sound like a very likable deity. Their view of the absolute is a conditional God meaning that if they do as they are told then they will be granted happiness but if they don't then they will go to hell. It seems that their God is shame based and it's out to get them. Therefore, they believe that if they make mistakes then they have to make as little as possible in order for them to get to heaven. Again the message is that one should be afraid of the absolute if they aren't good so you better be careful.
>
> Then the absolute bets Satan that Job won't blaspheme him under any condition. Once again this reveals their God to be all powerful and scary. And it seems like he's out to get Job by letting him suffer until he gets too desperate. They make it sound like the absolute wants him to suffer however I don't think that is the case.
>
> Job's life is in their hands and it's all because of a bet to see how long he would last under such circumstances. I can't see this happening because the absolute as I understand it wants one to be happy and the last thing it wants is for one to suffer. Could this really be of the divine, I doubt it.
>
> This knowledge of their absolute seems to have come from human origin. I mean what kind of a God would expect one to be perfect and what kind of a God is going to love them conditionally which means that if they don't do as they are told then they won't be considered good and that means that they are on their way to hell. I also believe whoever wrote this book of Job used this knowledge as a way to control people. And the people who wrote this book only knew of their own experience so that anyone else's experience in life is not taken into account therefore what others do with their lives is wrong, that's the logic that they used when writing such biblical stories.

These, as well as the four pages following, largely devoted to less-impassioned discussion of the *Bhagavad-Gita* and *The Way of Chuang Tzu*, are, as is easy to recognize by now, characteristically Steven. The style is his: the syntax of sentences, paragraphs, and overall essay is at once loose and redundant, more cumulative and additive than truly coordinated, suggesting a mind still sorting out discordant elements, not yet having achieved steady understanding of their relative dominance and subordination. The style is, in short, syntactically reminiscent of the almost-compulsive reiterations of theme and content throughout all his narratives, as here Steven attempts, over and over again, to articulate what "I thought that God was," what "I understand the absolute to be," with and against the alter-interpretations the book of Job presents—with and against, that is, a nearly unassailable image of paternal hurt, abandonment, and shame.

It is with good reason that Professor Murray writes across the passage's opening sentence, with a black pen darker than Steven's original type, "'I thought' is rhetorical, doesn't persuade the reader. Either means you were wrong, or absolute isn't absolute," continuing on to cross out each succeeding "I thought" and "I believe." "The Conceptions of the Absolute" does not persuade the reader, not wholly at any rate, perhaps because Steven's argument lacks the logical objectivity Professor Murray wants or perhaps because, from the start, it is an argument that pits Steven against not just Professor Murray but Yahweh, too, in a contest that makes David's assault on Goliath appear a fairly even match. Yet, if "The Conceptions of the Absolute" is not wholly persuasive, it *is* partially persuasive, in the same way that it may well be "more private war than analysis" yet (contrary to the implications of Professor Murray's tone) is not wholly without its analytical elements. And it seems to me that the persuasive parts and analytical elements contain commendable—though uncommended—insights.

It seems that Job only is good because he is afraid of doing evil. In turn, this concept of evil only perpetuates the fear of God and makes the absolute seem like the devil.

Furthermore, the concept of evil I believe is a human construction because as I understand the absolute, it doesn't believe in evil. It seems by using the term evil this only scares people into being 'good' and it makes them feel ashamed of themselves if they do make mistakes . . . . So by having the idea that they are bad explains why their conception of the absolute is one of a condemning nature. . . .

This knowledge of the absolute seems to have come from human origin . . . . I also believe whoever wrote this book of Job used this knowledge as a way to control people. . . .

The people who wrote this book only knew of their own experience so that anyone else's experience in life is not taken into account therefore what others do with their lives is wrong, that's the logic they used when writing such biblical stories.

Awkward as the phrasing may be, rushed as I suspect the drafting was, nonetheless keen insights inhere in these observations, waiting to be teased out. These are signs of a readiness to martial the vocabulary and politics of social construction that Steven was then just beginning to assimilate in the service of literary analysis and, paradoxically, of faith—a faith in Steven's own freedom to be, a faith originally shattered by a father who, like the God of Job, "was supposed to be this great power that loved you," a faith only recently begun to re-form in the unstable media of suicide notes and serenity prayers.

Thus Professor Murray identifies precisely what is at stake in the essay when he comments in the margin that either Steven is wrong in his notion that "God was supposed to be this great power that loved you" or "the absolute isn't absolute." In fact, however, Professor Murray is right on both counts and thus mistaken in framing them as an either/or proposition: that is, Steven's original notion that "the absolute was supposed to be this great power that loved you" did prove wrong, *and* it was replaced by an "absolute [that] isn't absolute," an absolute who would sacrifice neither servant nor son, who is absolute only insofar as he is absolutely tolerant, absolutely forgiving, absolutely relative—an absolute reflection of Steven's wishes and an image of his unyielding optimism. Otherwise the paradox of Steven's efforts in this essay would be an intentional—and irreconcilable—oxymoron: otherwise he could hardly dispute one absolute on the tenets of another and could hardly deconstruct "the knowledge of the absolute" and expose its attendant concept of evil as a "human construction" on the grounds that "as I understand the absolute, it doesn't believe in evil."

"The Conceptions of the Absolute" *is* "a private war" between the factions embroiled throughout Steven's narrative: the force of "once I was unhappy" pitted against the force of "now I'm better, and soon, with hope and help, I'll be better still"; and the power of a "deeply religious," fundamentalist father whose incestuous assaults gave birth to Lawrence's homosexual identity against the vital gay identity Steven was struggling to construct for himself. Professor Murray had the intellectual acumen to detect all of this. But Steven was right, too, about Professor Murray. Though not known among students for callousness, he seems here to have lacked the empathy necessary to express his insights in a way Steven could hear. His final comment on "The Conceptions of the Absolute" opens thus:

> CD Lots of energy & strong <u>feelings</u>, but little analysis. It seems you are over reacting to <u>Job</u>, as though some prior scar-tissue prohibits objective reading. You like "pleasant" absolutes. Isn't that a little silly?

Perhaps Steven is right again to suggest it is a matter of age that I have no patience with these remarks. Therefore, I will simply wonder what so embarrassed Professor Murray that he felt compelled to shame Steven for his "silly" desires; how a man who had witnessed a boy's "scar-tissue" as surely as Professor Brooke witnessed his lover's bald head could commit to paper the kinds of thoughts that Brooke had grace enough to keep to himself.

At the close of his note, Professor Murray commanded, "See me, then do a rewrite," and Steven did. Murray later commented on it as "much improved": Steven had "cut irrelevant & redundant passages, & seen texts more fully . . . [to] better, balanced results. Good for you." And good, apparently, for Professor Murray, who felt satisfied enough to grant Steven a B for the paper, and a BC for the course. Steven himself, however, shared little in the satisfaction. "I have a lot of shame still about who I am when I write," he said, summarizing his experience in "Good and Evil: East Meets West Something Ethics":

I have a lot of fear about what people are going to think when they read it. What are they going to think? Who are they going to think I am when they read this paper? Why are they reading this? What is their motive? Are they going to shame me? How are they going to treat me? Are they going to abuse me because I don't write a specific way that they want? You know, I don't like this but professors have a power over students. I think it sucks, personally, but they do have a power because they are our teachers.

I told Steven I understood, that "it feels very exposing to hand someone your naked paper." "Exactly," he replied and then related his fears to our study: "When you were suggesting me leaving these all here," he said, referring to the stack of essays in front of us, "I trust you, but I also don't know if I could do that, leave them here over night. These are me."

Steven then stopped. "I was just thinking," he said a few moments later,

about some papers I forgot to bring in, which are incredible, too. Actually, it's amazing that I forgot to bring them. . . . The class was called "Spiritual Autobiography," and those papers, every one of them, I got an A or AB on. There were four of them. One in particular is incredible, absolutely incredible. It was the discovery of my incest that I wrote about. And that was the most powerful paper I ever wrote, because I was asked if the class could read it, and it was read in class. They talked about being abused and, of course, the first thing that came out of the mouth of one man, who was very homophobic and scary, was, "It sounds like she went through a lot." He automatically assumed that the victim was a girl. The TA said, "Well, he was a boy." And the next comment from another student was, "I can't believe he made it through that." You know, the incredible validation of that. It was just incredible for this teacher to be reading this in front of thirty students with me in the room. It's called "Live to Tell," from the Madonna song. I'm surprised I forgot to bring them up. But I guess I know why: I don't keep them with all my other papers outside in storage. I keep them in my room, because they're sort of my prized possession.

The course Steven refers to, called Spiritual Autobiography, was Comparative Literature 132, in which he enrolled for the fall of

1990, the semester following his term in College Writing. The course instructor was Professor Evelyn Peterson; the discussion leader, teaching assistant Robert Southwood. Steven described them both as "very, very, very supportive" and "just great, just great." The curriculum consisted of the students reading eleven full-length autobiographical writings and writings about autobiography—a range of texts including Maya Angelou's *I Know Why the Caged Bird Sings*, Alex Haley and Malcolm X's *The Autobiography of Malcolm X*, Carl Jung's *Memories, Dreams, Reflections*, Carlo Levi's *Christ Stopped at Eboli*, and Homer's *Odyssey*—and writing four short autobiographical papers of their own, along with a reading journal. In her initial course description, Professor Peterson provided the students with this definition: "Spiritual Autobiography is self writing that focuses on the soul's journey, that looks inward as much as outward. Spiritual autobiography in this sense has little to do with institutionalized religion, but it often deals with the big religious questions, such as 'Why Am I Here?' and 'Does God Exist?'" She also provided students with a list of eight suggested paper topics from which they could choose, or they could substitute one of their own design in consultation with the instructor. The assignments required that students neither talk about the texts nor talk about themselves through the texts, but rather that they create their own spiritual autobiographies alongside the others, centering their discussions on such phenomena as "memorable dreams," "early memories," "journeys taken," "paranormal experiences," and encounters "with death or near death."

Reviewing these essays now, I find little surprise that Steven "forgot" to bring them with him to our interview or that he kept these "prized possessions" in his room, separated from other academic writings that he kept "outside in storage." Taken together, they form a true series, the members of which—bound to one another in theme, imagery, and phrasing—are as self-consciously referential as the earlier "Free to Be You and Me" and "Breaking Traditions." Separately as well as collectively, they constitute Steven's narrative laid bare, and I suspect he was initially hesitant to entrust them to us. The first in the series, "A Re-Genesis," revisits Steven's suicide wish but from the perspective, and with the vocabulary, of one who has been in therapy and in AA:

> In the beginning, I was in therapy because I was extremely suicidal. My whole world was falling apart. I couldn't function physically or emotionally because I was living in fear. I wasn't eating properly because I spent most of my time drinking. I felt like I was alone in this world and that it was my fault that I was being victimized because I thought I was a bad person. I blamed myself for other people's ignorance and I chose to be the victim. It was easier to believe the bad than the good about myself since I had always had low self-esteem.

From this start, Steven goes on to relate a vision that came to him as he sat, meditating, in his therapist's waiting room. Beckoned toward "a man sitting in the center of a room on a throne . . . I was seeing," he testifies, "a vision of my God."

> After I stepped inside the room I asked him a few questions concerning my life. First I asked him why I was gay. He said, "Because I sent you here as a missionary to help other people." Next I asked, "Why did you pick me?" and he said, "Because you are strong and have the power to help others." Finally, I asked him if suicide was an answer to my problems. He replied, "No you can make it—just keep trying." This was my first experience with a higher power. After having this spiritual awakening I felt somewhat relieved because I found out that it was okay to be myself.

Having received from God's mouth the liberating imperatives of his own previous narratives, Steven moves on, through what seems a brief revisionary history, to recount his subsequent introduction to AA and, through AA, his introduction to God, the "higher power" not of "religion" but of "spirituality." The circularity of this narrative notwithstanding, "A Re-Genesis" remains a testament to faith in a newfound God, in whom, Steven tells us, he has entrusted his life:

> With God's help I began to work on my recovery and I started to understand more about myself and my feelings. As my faith grows and God keeps sending me signs of his presence in my life, I become more motivated to stay clean and sober. I have a lot of gratitude towards God, and I am grateful to have received the chance to begin to start my life over again and to be a part of his life. I also have realized that he has always been there—I just never chose to let him in because I was afraid of putting my life in someone else's hands.

Furthermore, I was ready to turn my will and my life over to the care of God. This action has helped me to get rid of the self so that I can live for God's will and not my own. I am no longer alone because I know that he is looking out for me today and all that I have to do is ask for his help and he will be there for me.

Difficult as it is to read these passages without being reminded of William James's remark that the only radical cure for dipsomania is religiomania, we have to remember that Steven's alcoholism is not the primary wound in need of healing. Therefore, while "re-genesis" intimates the discovery of a new God, its more crucial revelation is a new God the Father. The next essay, to which Steven referred in our interview, provides that gloss.

"Live to Tell," actually the third in Steven's four-part series, begins thus:

While I was growing up there was always violence in my house. My father was mostly the abusive one. My mother and I were always in fear of being beaten or killed because he used to beat and rape us. During this time of my life I chose to close myself up in my room in order to get away from all the commotion as much as I possibly could because it wouldn't be long before it was my turn to get hit. There really wasn't a safe place in my house for me, but my bedroom was where I could live in my own little world. I used to eat, sleep, listen to music and study in my room for as long as I can remember because this was how I survived. I lived in my own little world that I felt safe and at home with. To this day I don't know how I made this little world possible with all the abuse that I grew up with.

With the next paragraph, Steven begins to answer the question implicit in that closing line and, at the same time, to deliver out of scenes of paternal abuse a singularly homosexual, as well as paternal, vision of God. First, however, he conjures up an intermediary image, locating the creative force—and, in a sense, the personification—of his fantastic sanctuary in dreams of a man:

As a child when times got progressively worse I started to dream about how I was in love with some man. This dream gave me some sort of hope that someone would love me. I never felt like I existed. I felt like I was dead to the world because I had no control over my body or myself. I felt out of touch with people because I couldn't even talk to people because I was afraid of what might come out of my mouth.

Steven takes no time to explicate further the dream or his own protective silence, turning abruptly instead to abundant evidence of his childhood quest for attention—at school, among grandparents, and most especially with his parents, whose failure to attend to his pleas nears black comedy. ("At one point of this nightmare," he writes, "I asked my parents if I could move into an orphanage. . . . They responded by saying, 'Let's go to dinner first and then if you still want to go we will take you.'") And so we are left to share in the teaching assistant Robert Southwood's question, written in the paragraph's margin and linked to Steven's stated sense that "I had no control over my body or myself": "Why," Southwood asks, "because you dreamed about a man and not, as you were 'supposed to,' about a woman?" "Or," we might add, "because you were being abused?"

I suspect, however, that, whatever his intention, Steven's words overflow in ambiguity because both conjectures are equally implied and equally true, linked together in the shame of paternal incest. As abruptly as he moved away from it, he returns to what is revealed to be a recurrent dream:

> By and by the dream kept coming up in my sleep about some man that I loved and felt safe with. I was able to be with this man truly and I could be myself and I didn't have to worry about him hurting me. I never really could see him, I could just feel that it was safe and comfortable and that he really loved me.

Then, mirroring the pattern of the periodic dream experience he describes, Steven once again seems to leave it behind:

> Finally, my parents got divorced and my brother and I went to see our father every other weekend. I felt torn between two people I loved. I felt like it was my fault that they were getting divorced. I always thought I had done something wrong and it

was all my fault since my father used to beat me if my brother did something wrong. He always blamed me for everything. In his eyes my brother was the perfect child because he was just like him. I was always favored by my mother and my brother was always favored by my father. He never let me get close to him because I wasn't the child he wanted. He never told me he loved me and he never gave me a hug. He never shared his feelings with me so I always thought I couldn't be loved because I thought I wasn't good enough.

And again, Southwood is prompted to proffer his own interpretive junction between the two apparently diverse paragraphs: "At the risk of sounding like a stupid, homophobic shrink," his marginal note reads, "Does this absence have anything to do with the presence (in your imagination) of the male lover mentioned above?" Southwood's question seems to me neither stupid nor homophobic. But it is asked too soon, for immediately this time Steven provides his own interpretation:

Today, I still have this dream and I am starting to understand what it means. I feel that by having this dream it was one of the keys to my survival as an abused child. I also think that this dream was in my life because I was always yearning to be loved by my father. This image of someone loving me gave me hope that maybe someday it would be possible for someone to actually love me for me. Subsequently, I believe that this dream was also put there for a purpose and that the man in that dream was God. I feel this way because he put this powerful message in my life so that I knew that there was a way out and by my having this reoccurring dream I felt like there was hope and somebody really did love me and that was what kept me alive.

Out of the "nightmare" of abuse and abandonment arises a dream of safety and love; out of an abuser's presence appear visions of a lover, a savior, and ultimately an embracing God. With the help of therapy, AA, and his own intuitions, Steven renders his interpretation. Stripping away layers of "prior scar-tissue"—or, it may be more accurate to say, letting us watch them build—he reveals not only the dark undercurrent running beneath his early optimistic narratives but also, in the dream's recurrence, the salutary force of their reiterative patterns, of the longing to repeat, in writing as in life, both nightmare and dream over and again without end.

The other two entries in Steven's "spiritual autobiography," like the serenity prayer and the suicide note composed a semester before, are essentially companion pieces. Entitled "Letting Go" and constructed as a letter to his mother, the first proposes emancipation not from his natural father but from his mother as the first step toward re-genesis. Here rebirth constitutes redefinition and reinvention of self: "time taken away from you . . . in order for me to grow up as a person instead of as your son." A succession of painful memories, made all the more painful for his mother's refusal to hear or soothe them, follows Steven's vow of independence. Closure comes, however, in a return to pain's source and the unpunctuated, unrelenting lyrics of Madonna's "Oh Father," which tell of escape from paternal abuse and which Steven quotes in their entirety.

The companion piece, actually last in the series of four, looks back to these closing lyrics of "Letting Go" for its title; it looks eighteen months ahead to "The Conceptions of the Absolute" in its sentiments and forms as well as its motivating force. Steven's own "Oh Father" begins as follows:

> The way I see this person that they call my father is different from what most people would describe as their father. I always grew up thinking that he was supposed to be this perfect person that would love me and take care of me. Unfortunately, this conception of what a father is supposed to be crashed after he left me and moved away.
>
> As a young boy growing up without a father figure I don't remember too many times that he spent with me. He never had time for me. He was too busy fighting with my mother. I tried anything I could to get his attention but I didn't matter as much as his marriage did. Throughout my parents' marriage it was a struggle to keep it alive. I got lost somewhere in the shuffle of all their problems. I loved him so much because he was my father and he was supposed to love me.
>
> The time that he was there was during the times when he could get out his anger by beating me and then molesting me as a young boy at the age of eight. After awhile I got used to the pain and I thought it was a part of life and this was just his way of saying that he loved me. During this period of my life a

part of me felt loved because at least someone was paying some attention to me. I truly believe that this is the only time that I ever felt like he loved me.

"I always grew up thinking that he was supposed to be this perfect person that would love me . . . this conception of what a father is supposed to be. . . . I loved him so much because he was my father and he was supposed to love me": For us, who've already read the paper Steven is yet to write for Professor Murray, these opening passages of "Oh Father" recall the "private war" waged in "Conceptions of the Absolute." Now for Steven, though, they look forward to the replacement figure—to the "pleasant absolute"—who will be asserted there, along with the belief that if not one's natural father then certainly one's God "was supposed to be this great power that loved you." And they reaffirm the beneficial as well as beneficent nature of the dream image of his "Live to Tell," the invoking of which undoes the most critical knot of Steven's self-narrative, the complex of pain and love that molestation elicits. But "Oh Father" achieves something new also. Returning to the scenes of absence and abandonment that Southwood remarked upon in "Live to Tell," Steven fills the lack this time not with a dream image but with understanding, empathy, and, eventually, himself:

> As I look back now on his life I realize that when he married my mother he was still searching for himself and he thought that he could have everything he ever wanted if he was married and had children. He never found out who he was before he got married. Therefore the marriage ended up being his whole life. In addition, he put so much into finding someone else to love him, he never learned to love himself.
> Furthermore, it's scary to say this but I feel as if we, my father and I are one in the same in that we never got what we needed as children therefore we went looking for it somewhere else. For example, I turned to alcohol and he got into a relationship thinking that could solve all of his problems.
> When my father married my mother he was still living under his parents' wings so to speak. In other words, he never broke the umbilical cord with them. Furthermore, he never dealt with his feelings because he never expressed his ideas because he thought that his parents were perfect and if he didn't agree with what they said then they wouldn't love him anymore.

I have no doubt Steven did find it "scary to say . . . my father and I are one": This is, after all, the same person about whom he would also say, "If that is what a man is supposed to be . . . my only alternative was to be a woman." Therefore, his move to separate is swift:

> Coincidentally, I am in rather the same position as my father was except I am doing something about it. I am cutting the umbilical cord with my mother. For instance, I'm making the choice today to grow up and change by questioning who I am. Fortunately, this is where my father and I differ because I am being honest with myself and I am breaking the chain of dysfunction in my family today through my belief in God.

The God of his dreams not only replaces an abusive father but ensures Steven's own actual as well as internal separation from him. However, as the image of God depicted in "Live to Tell" grew out of a father's absence—grew out, that is, of an absent father—here Steven's God runs the risk of duplicating his father's God, his father's conception of the Absolute. And Steven runs the risk of duplicating his father, except for a crucial difference:

> Unfortunately, my father believes in a religious God and he is a God that is very limiting in that if one doesn't believe what he believes then one will go to hell. For some people religion can be a good thing, but my father uses it as a way to escape reality.
>
> Today, I see a father as someone who has always been there for their children. And as far as my father is concerned, I don't consider him a father. The only thing that he ever did was to take part in my conception. I hope that someday I will be able to forgive this man whom they call my father.

The conception of this earthly absolute is Steven himself, but this absolute is not Steven's "father," nor is the God of "this man whom they call my father" Steven's God. He cannot be. For Steven's father engendered more than two sons: out of his abusive acts was born an image in his own likeness, Steven's dream-vision of "some man that I loved"—the object and manifestation of Steven's homosexuality. To break "the chain of dysfunction" in his family and, with it, the more profound cycle of replication that this dream-vision might otherwise comprise, Steven could not allow the likeness to remain intact. Difference had to distinguish father from Father: what love the latter offered had to be unmixed with the pain Steven had gotten "used to . . . and . . . thought . . . was a part of life" and of love. A trauma victim's dissociation? A survivor's denial? Perhaps. But faith, it seems to me, carries Steven beyond both, into a narrative cycle of his own making and back to "Re-Genesis," where God Himself pronounces homosexuality a product of His divine will, rather than of a father's sexual assault.

The spiritual changes recounted in these four autobiographies reflect changes in Steven's social life, too, changes that also helped determine his course of study by giving him the ambition and confidence to construct his own bachelor's degree in gender studies out of the Valley schools' Five-College offerings. While students from the other four colleges are more likely to enroll in our University courses each year than are University students likely to venture out into the four private, "elite" domains, the exigencies of gay life both prepared and impelled Steven. The vast majority of University undergraduates seem to move between two circumscribed worlds, remaining on campus during the week to take classes, and returning to their hometown friends and families on the weekends. Steven, on the other hand, determined early on to return home as seldom as possible and had begun as early as the fall of 1990 to seek gay companionship, counseling, and support services throughout the Amherst–Northampton–South Hadley area. No foreigner to these places or the other gay students populating them, he appears to have found the step into their classrooms a relatively small one.

By the fall of 1991, Steven was taking Women and Gender Studies at Amherst College, and by the fall of 1992 he was traveling beyond the University for most of his course work, nearly all of it focused on issues of gender and (homo)sexuality. In these particular contexts, where Steven wrote about the history of homosexuality or the social construction of gender for lesbian teachers and gay classmates, and where books and other discussion materials provided "another external way to look in at ourselves," the divide between external and internal, between vehicle and tenor of Steven's habitually metaphoric self-narratives, measurably narrowed. The books he read, the lectures he attended, and the discussions he heard were all, in some way, spiritual autobiographies reflecting his own. In the spring of 1993, self-involvement still worried him:

> I feel some shame talking about this, because I feel it's been a criticism that I don't know how to get out of me to write things that aren't about me. That's where I've been focusing for so long, the last three years, on me. I never was focused on me before, so it's hard now for me to get out of that place and talk about something without being part of me. Actually, I don't know if that's even possible. Maybe it is, but I really have a hard time setting myself aside.

And even those teachers among whom he met greatest success had gently criticized him, he said, for focusing his writing more on himself than on the texts or other subjects at hand. Yet it seems to me unquestionable that, in these contexts, Steven could talk about himself through the experiences of other homosexuals, drag queens, and those generally outside the heterosexual mainstream with far less attenuation of external and internal worlds than in other academic contexts, and therefore with far less conspicuousness or criticism. For the most part, the papers he did for these courses were, in form if not in content, traditional academic research papers rather than "personal" essays. Yet, as the split between the vehicle of subject matter and the tenor of Steven's own abiding theme of homosexual development lessened, so, too, did the split between "private war" and "analysis" that had so peeved Professor Murray. With it was gone the need to assert continually "I believe" or "I thought" against a text's alien argument—and world. Steven's own experiences matched his subjects'; his concerns, too, matched theirs. And so Steven could move between his own words and others' more easily, if not seamlessly. In these essays, he was able, for the first time he claimed, to insert quotations from other texts into his own in order to "enhance what I had written already . . . to sort of back up what I was talking about. . . . It was perfect."

The sort of integration I am describing is demonstrated in passages from Steven's fall 1992 essay on Claude Hartland's *The Story of a Life*. (This essay, written for a course on The History of Homosexuality at Amherst College, is the one that earned him that A on his "first big research paper.") Here, for instance, he writes of Hartland's battle with the concept of sin, his homosexual inclinations, and his longing for suicide:

> Not only was Hartland a victim of the medical establishment but he was also a victim of the church because he also internalized the idea that his homosexuality might be a sin. For example, he felt that unless he became a Christian he would be lost forever. He prayed to God everyday asking for his help so he could get through the day without sinning. This sinning that he talked about was that he felt lust or sexual feelings towards men. The following quote is an example of his struggle with sin.
>
> > I struggled to be pure and good, and day after day would fall down on my knees and in my agony of grief and despair, beg God to help me; to give me strength; to save me from the awful gulf that yawned to receive me (Hartland, 49).
>
> The awful gulf that was going to receive him was his sin of his homosexuality. There was nothing he could do to get away from his sin of his homosexuality because this was who he was. Therefore, he felt doomed and he often spoke of his wanting to be put out of his misery because he felt like there was no other way out but to die.

The instructor, according to Steven, had worked with him between drafts, pointing out places where he had been either more or less clear, asking questions to prompt further clarity, and helping him, sometimes with specific suggested phrasings, to distinguish between "Hartland's beliefs about himself" and Steven's beliefs about Hartland, or about himself—between, that is, Hartland's "I" and Steven's. Her comments on the final draft acknowledge success: "I really like the way this turned out, " she writes. "Your hard work shows. Also your writing style is definitely improving. If it's the reading aloud, keep doing it! A-." Yet to those of us familiar with Steven's ongoing narrative, the affinity, "kinship," or "twinship," we might even say, between him and his subject remains evident.

If with Hartland Steven explored the dark side of homosexual guilt, with "Madonna: The Queer Queen" he returned to the singer and to the fulcrum of "Letting Go" to illuminate the delights of gay camp. Composed for another Amherst College course, The Cross Cultural Construction of Gender, during the spring of 1994, it opens thus:

> Madonna has been an object of the media's gaze since her debut album *Holiday* was released in 1983. Eleven years later, after eight albums, five bombshell movies (including a documentary of her life on the road), five concert tours and many appearances on television and in the news, she has millions of fans, including a large number of gay men. This essay explores the construction of the gay male identity in our society and why gay males identify strongly with the feminine and come to rely so heavily on female stars, in particular their fascination with pop culture's sex icon, Madonna. In order to illustrate the importance of gay men's interpretation of camp, camp and gay male camp will be distinguished from one another. Thus, Madonna's alias the "Queer Queen" (Doty 10) will be presented as resulting from the combination of gay men's identification with women and camp.

Steven goes on to identify camp's uses for gay men and, in doing so, suggests that camp is for them both a retreat from the everyday world and an exaggeration of their experience in it. If camp is the gay world's playground, it is built of social construction, and this new wave of thinking is, his observations imply, but the late straight consciousness of what gays have known—have had to know—all along:

> Camp is used to make light of the serious. According to Susan Sontag, "the whole point of Camp is to dethrone the serious. Camp is playful, anti-serious. More precisely, Camp involves a new more complex relation to 'the serious.' One can be serious about the frivolous, frivolous about the serious" (288). The reversal of being serious about the frivolous emphasizes the necessity of having fun and being relaxed in a stressful world. Furthermore, camp is employed to take a break from the monotony of everyday life. It is expressed through "life as theater" which means everyone has a part to play in life just as actors have parts to play in movies. In other words, life is the stage. Theater provides a place for individuals to play a wide variety of roles because "life itself is role and theatre, appearance and impersonation" (Babuscio 44). Everyone takes on an identity given to them from society whether they realize it or

not. Thus, people aren't being their authentic selves because of
who they have been taught to be. As a result, people are imper-
sonating the qualities that society wants them to be composed
of. Although many gay men often impersonate the accepted
male personality they are well aware of their doing this. In the
"straight world order" gays are often forced to pass for straight
in order to survive. The act of passing for straight is also part
of the theatricality involved in camp. "The experience of passing would appear to explain the enthusiasm of so many in our
community for certain stars whose performances are highly
exaggerated (usually sexual) role-playing" (Babuscio 45). . . .
Thus, gay men are excited because they see the absurdity of
"natural" gender roles. There is nothing natural about any role
since anyone, man or woman, can simulate whoever they wish
to be.

"Camp," Steven summarizes, "is a powerful instrument used in
deconstructing the ever-pervasive polarized male and female archetypes." And this, he goes on to say, "is central to the appeal
of female stars to which gay men are drawn." For decades the
brightest star in the constellation of camp icons was, of course,
Judy Garland. But she has now been replaced, Steven writes, by
the icon of the ACT UP generation—Madonna, whose "in-your-
face politics strike a chord with the gay community's expression
'Visibility equals life.'"

Like the Hartland piece, "Madonna: The Queer Queen" was
well-received. The instructor's comments, nearly a full handwritten page, are not without critique—a good deal, indeed—but they
are encouraging, too, and, just as important, I'm sure, an AB
stands circled at the top of them:

> Steven,
>
> AB
>
>   This is an ambitious paper! You are really trying to grapple
> with some difficult theoretical issues and you do more or less a
> good job of it. On the organizational side, I had the feeling at
> points in the first half of the paper that you were repeating
> yourself (or piling quote upon quote)—I know you cut a lot
> from the original paper but I think the points about gays, camp,
> and identity could have been made more tightly than you make
> them. Stylistically, the paper jumps around a lot. Beautifully

written clear sentences are followed by confusing ones. (Some of the confusion comes, I think, from the difficult theoretical language, but some of it is just awkward writing.)

At this juncture, the instructor's comment turns to matters of content and rhetorical faults similar to those Murray had noted two years before. But in her voice we hear a different tone, and Steven could listen to it, too:

> Now to content: Your thesis statement does not give the reader a sense of the really complex way Madonna foregrounds gender construction. (I'm referring to your whole uneasiness about the business of appropriation you go into toward the end.) As a reader, I got the feeling that you're still not sure how you come down on this issue—is she or is she not appropriating? You close with the quote from Crimp, but your summary paragraph seems unconvincing after the wealth of evidence (that she <u>does</u> appropriate black, Hispanic, and gay culture) you present on pages 14–16.

The comment is then signed with the instructor's full name and dated.

The reception of the Madonna paper, like that of the Hartland piece before it, pleased Steven, the more, it seems, because they came from Amherst College faculty and, as he said, "I feel like Amherst is an Ivy League school." Hence it was a special academic legitimacy given to his development as a writer and as a *gay* writer. He had other reasons, too, I think, to be pleased with the Madonna paper and with the Hartland piece as well. The occasional confusions, awkwardnesses, and questionable conclusions notwithstanding, Steven seems for the most part to have contained successfully in these late essays that "once I was unhappy, but now I'm better, and soon, with hope and help, I'll be better still" linearity characterizing his earlier narratives, along with the contradictory forces its sequencing continually displaced, condensing them both in the language of social constructivism and in the ironic perspective it shares with drag.

All of Steven's early narratives, in fact, are in both the Madonna and the Hartland pieces. It is difficult, nearly impossible, for me to read "Madonna: The Queer Queen" without hearing echoes of "Breaking Traditions," with its Mardi Gras exuberance and "in-your-face" self-assertion spoken from behind disguise; or to read "Claude Hartland and His Homosexuality" without hearing "Fur is Dead" and "Dead or Alive," along with the anxious sadness they all share, a sadness that lay beneath the flamboyant gaiety of Steven's happiest writings. Now and then, the new language learned in gender studies does erupt, as did the old language of those previous narratives, causing faults in logic at both the paragraph and sentence levels, as well as the global level, and producing sentences like "Although they are empowered by this awareness it is very challenging being a minority of the greater population who is still under the guise of what is universally or naturally male and female" or "[Camp's resistance to institutionalized power] is illustrated by making fun of the traditional sex roles by exaggerating what the appearance of these roles look like through the performance of them." In other sentences, however, like "Thus, camp is a powerful instrument used in deconstructing the ever-pervasive polarized male and female archetypes," which the instructor characterized as "well put," Steven assimilates the new language of his studies successfully enough to frame new conceptualizations and construct new nonnarrative, analytical pieces within which both to express and contain them—and to earn himself an AB for "Madonna: The Queer Queen" as well as an A- for "Claude Hartland and His Homosexuality."

But again we have arrived at the sort of palindrome reached in his suicide note. If Steven's early narratives are contained in "Madonna: The Queer Queen" and "Claude Hartland and His Homosexuality," then conversely these two essays are to be found in the early narratives and even as far back as "The Symptoms of Suicide." There Steven had written, "I felt guilty for being gay. I thought it was wrong since society says that it was and still is and I thought no one would ever except me for who I was"; in writing this, Steven had expressed the felt sense he would later assimilate in the language of social constructivism, in visions of drag, and, just as much, I believe, in his new and liberal use of the term "queer," which holds the same ironic place in the vocabulary of sexual identification that "nigger" holds in the vocabulary of race.

Conclusion

> She slid a book from the shelf, opened it and cleared her throat. "'Sunrise near Monterey,'" she said, "by Francis X. Dillon." She glanced up at Brooke. "Oh," she said, "I love how you look at me."
> "Read," Brooke said. He forced himself to smile and shake his head in the right places. After a time he began to enjoy it, and even allowed himself to believe what it was saying. . . . ("An Episode in the Life of Professor Brooke" 41)

When Anne and I presented our initial observations of Nam and Steven to the MLA/ADE gathering in Waterloo, the chair of our panel introduced us with a disquieting ice breaker. "We all enter this profession because we love the world's greatest literature," he said, "and then some of us end up reading the worst—freshman essays." His comments met appreciative nods and chuckles from a good portion of the audience. But they set me to thinking. Why the distinction? I would be a fool to claim there's no perceptible difference between the "world's greatest literature" and most first-year student prose, but does that necessarily mean we must utterly polarize our approaches to the two—and make ourselves sorry victims of our jobs in the process? I had spent years in graduate school reading some wonderful Wordsworth, and some dreadful Wordsworth as well. As delighted as I am even now, in my life as a composition instructor, to return to "Tintern Abbey," I was delighted then to reach the end of "The Idiot Boy." And I have never managed yet to read in "The Thorn" of the cruel, cruel fire that dried poor Martha Ray's "body like a cinder, /And almost turn'd her brain to tinder" without laughing. Still, I learned to read the full span of Wordsworth's oeuvre with an eye for images, rhyme schemes, and leitmotifs signaling his development from sometimes-less-than-successful experimenter to grand lyricist, and the pleasure of my reading came as much from the critical methods I was trained to apply to poetry as from the poetry itself. In fact, to be fully honest, I would have to say that my pleasure in the latter derived wholly from the former. I was trained to find pleasure in Wordsworth's great lyrics, every bit as much as to distinguish the "great" from the far less than great: I had to learn Wordsworth in order to learn from him and to find any real pleasure in reading him at all. Like Professor Brooke on first hearing Francis X. Dillon, I had initially to force myself to smile and nod in the right places, until eventually I discovered I truly did enjoy this great Romantic, and even believed what he was saying.

I am not insisting, nor about to insist, that "Madonna: The Queer Queen" approaches "Tintern Abbey" in achievement or that "The Concept of the Absolute" matches "The Thorn" in promise (though neither could I wholeheartedly insist that lines like "The owlets hoot, the owlets curr, /And Johnny's lips they burr, burr, burr" are *inherently* more promising than, for instance, "[The book of Job's] concept of evil only perpetuates the fear of God and makes the absolute seem like the devil"). But I would insist that it matters a great deal to our students whether we use the critical methods we were taught to apply to the "world's greatest literature" in order to appreciate their potential or, as our ADE chairman seemed to do, to accentuate their failings. And I would insist that, as chief conveyors of our students' image of the audience for whom they are writing, we are fully implicated in what they write. I would even suggest that the sort of audience we represent to students matters as much to them and to what they write as does the sort of curriculum we devise or the instruction we conduct. Perhaps it matters more.

In "How to Recognize a Poem When You See One," Stanley Fish describes the effect a reader's training has on the "ongoing accomplishment" of poetry: "It is not that the presence of poetic qualities compels a certain kind of attention," he notes, "but that the paying of a certain kind of attention results in the emergence of poetic qualities" (143). Without dwelling on all of Fish's ideas, I would suggest that we apply this principle to the attention we teacher-readers pay to our students' "writerly" qualities and that we extend it. Fish's "attention" informs written objects with a certain kind of subjective life, with what we recognize as the object's own "poetic qualities"; the attention teachers pay to student writing informs the intersubjective life of writer-and-audience. As a result, it helps constitute not just our impression of what we read but also the actual text and its writer. In other words, it is not simply that by recognizing the nascent coherence of a student's as-yet-unshaped ideas we can *see* more coherent forms emerge. It is that by presenting ourselves to students as an audience able to comprehend their writing we help them express themselves more coherently, both over time and in the present moments of their writing for us. By attuning ourselves to the Steven within the Lawrence, to the writer within the basic writer *in statu nascendi*, to the "Claude Hartland and His Homosexuality" within "The Symptoms of Suicide," we not only instruct our students in the development of their writing skills but also aid them in the "ongoing accomplishment" of the writers we see them to be.

To recognize this is not, as some will still worry, to "psychologize" our students. It is simply to acknowledge the real impact of audience on both composer and composition, in the same way social and physical scientists have come to acknowledge the role their own subjectivities play in determining not just the interpretive outcome of the research undertaken but also the lived experiences of their research subjects and even the physical configurations of the molecular structures observed. Nor does recognizing our full implication as audience to our students' writing vitiate the efforts of those who, steeped in the "process" ethos, have gone to great lengths to diffuse their presence as sole intended audience of student writing among peer groups, community members, and so on. But it does intimate the power we hold to provide a receptive—and recuperative—audience, especially for students who have not felt understood, or capable of making themselves understood, before.

Certainly Steven's own commentary bears witness to the impact student readers had on him and on his writing. But it testifies as well to the very real force teachers held for him as, in committing his subjective world to written form, he struggled simultaneously to construct a coherent self and to represent himself coherently in writing. Looking back over the writings Steven did produce, along with his commentary on them, and acknowledging the ways in which an understanding audience—teacher or student—contributed to his personal development as a writer might well require an act of faith. Of the opposite, however, of instances in which nonunderstanding or downright hostile audiences resulted in fragmented, nearly incoherent prose, we have evidence. Pieces like "The State of the World Today," "Fur is

Dead," and "Conceptions of the Absolute" all suggest that even as coherence in writing determines a reader's potential understanding, a reader's potential understanding determines coherence in writing.

What, then, might characterize truly helpful understanding and the sort of optimal responsiveness from teachers that is most likely to elicit from students coherent, comprehensible prose? To answer, I will borrow phrasings from psychoanalysts George Atwood, Bernard Brandchaft, and Robert Stolorow, who ask of their own reading of the human mind what might appropriately be asked of any reading: Does the mode of inquiry and interpretation "significantly enhance our capacity to gain empathic access to subjective worlds in all their richness and diversity?" (*Psychoanalytic Treatment* 8). Call this mode of inquiry what we will—the self- and intersubjective-psychologists' "empathy" or Peter Elbow's "believing game" or Blythe McVicker Clinchy's "connected knowing" or Nell Nodding's not-so-simple "caring" or, to return to my own narrative, Coleridge's "willing suspension of disbelief"—it is an act both of human and of poetic faith allowing us to hear the writer's voice within our students' work even before it has been given full throat. And the simple matter is, if we refuse to hear it, we constrict it; if, bent on playing instead "the doubting game," we refuse to nurture it as it comes to us, we cannot be part of calling it forth. Henry Miller somewhere described the process in which we and our students are inextricably entwined when he recalled that "in finding my way [as a writer], I found my voice." In finding our way as teachers of writers, we must find our ears. To do so requires, for some of us more than others, a reattunement of the inner ear and a change of perspective for the inner eye as we read our students' writings and listen *for*, as much as *to*, what they are trying to say. It requires, again for some of us more than others, a change of stance, a repositioning of ourselves not outside but, as much as possible, inside students' "subjective worlds," as they practice expressing themselves and their views in new registers—and as we practice listening for the ways they experience their difficulties both with the material they attempt to express and with expression itself, empathizing with them amid their difficulties, and recognizing as-yet-unshaped ideas beginning to form in order to guide them through difficult passages to more coherent expression. Finally, full attunement requires that we transmit an understanding audience-image to each individual student through our oral and written responses to them, responses that provide a mirror to their strengths, trusted mentoring through their weaknesses, and, perhaps above all else, confirmation that they are indeed, as Wordsworth said of the poet, "a man speaking to men" (48), or, as Heinz Kohut said a bit more comprehensively of the healthy self, "a human among humans" (*How Does Analysis Cure?* 200).

Such responsive listening takes time, but not so much time as we might think. Nor, I would emphasize, does it take more "psychologizing" of our students than most of us already do each time we sit down to read what they write. Professor Murray showed himself an astute reader and quick study of his students' minds as well as essays, but, with Steven at any rate, he used his acumen cruelly. Southwood was also an astute reader, and his kindness showed in all his comments on Steven's papers and in Steven's reactions to them. Southwood was, of course, privy to scars Professor Murray could only suppose. But Professor Murray did suppose them, did rightly interpret Steven's lack of "objective reading" and fondness for "pleasant absolutes" as protective "scar-tissue." And still he dismissed Steven's desires as "silly." Carelessly Murray "psychologized" Steven, though I doubt the professor would have called it that. But a dangerous dichotomy is deployed in insisting we "psychologize" students only when we are careful of them, and "teach" them when we are not.

There is, then, we might presume, the matter of contexts separating Murray from Southwood: the two courses they taught were altogether different. As I said to Steven quite spontaneously, when he first spoke to me of Southwood's class, "I can't imagine a more appropriate course for you than Spiritual Autobiography." And that may well account for the difference between Steven's experiences of the two teachers and for the difference between the two teachers' experiences of Steven: Steven's near-compulsive self-disclosure was appropriate to Spiritual Autobiography, far less so to "Good and Evil: East Meets West Something Ethics" and the more distanced academic style it required. Yet

Southwood's comments to Steven are not without critique, and the issues his critiques address are in many cases those addressed by Professor Murray. The difference is manifested in the tone; the similarity suggests that we should reflect a little longer before making easy distinctions between the two course contexts and the sorts of writing we presume them to require.

Like Professor Murray, Southwood questioned Steven's reliance on "pleasant absolutes": "I'm not quite convinced," he added to his closing comment on "Live to Tell," that God is "<u>always</u> quite as totally fulfilling as you imply." His words, however, carried for Steven no sense of dismissal or assault but instead, as with all of Southwood's comments, encouragement expressed in a request for further explanation, for "enough details" that the reader might become "involved in your account." More suggestive, though, is Southwood's attention to Steven's implication of himself and his beliefs in the observations he makes—to his insertion of self, of the "I," in his writing, which for Professor Murray signaled more "private war than analysis," a war Steven should not have fought (at least not so obviously) and could not have won. The instances are most suggestive in Southwood's editing of "Oh Father"—interestingly enough, Steven's prelude to "The Conceptions of the Absolute."

In one instance there—in regard to a sentence that reads, "I truly believe that this is the only time that I ever felt like he loved me"—Southwood does essentially what Professor Murray did throughout Steven's later essay, bracketing off with parentheses Steven's opening clause, capitalizing "This," and noting in the margin that the lead phrase is unnecessary. On the other hand, and more interesting, he alters another sentence in quite different fashion: "I loved him so much because he was my father and∧ ,I thought, he was supposed to love me." Southwood's insertion of ", I thought," subtly changes the sentence's meaning, ascribing the supposition to the speaker, making the requirements of fatherhood a matter of Steven's belief. But the really intriguing difference between Steven's "I truly believe" and Southwood's ", I thought," is in the form and in the tone that form conveys: that is, in Southwood's surrounding commas, which effect the simultaneous insertion and detachment of the speaker, his parenthesized presence in the sentence's declaration, into acceptable academic prose. It would have been so easy for Professor Murray to do the same for Steven's "The Conceptions of the Absolute": simply to alter a line like "I believe whoever wrote this book of Job used this knowledge as a way to control people" to read something like "Whoever wrote this book of Job, I believe, used this knowledge as a way to control people," instead of enforcing, by his black-lined erasures, complete eradication of Steven's self.

It would have been so easy to do but so difficult, perhaps impossible, for Professor Murray to explain. The conventional bracketing of the academic "I," affording compromise between naive subjectivism and wholly I-less positivism, is a subtle matter of coding, a metalanguage conveyed through punctuation more than words, and, in a way, a mark of privilege as much as sophistication—of a position earned as much as asserted within academic conversations. We who use it, I would in other words say, indicate that we know our place at the same time we take it. But, in the presence of those like Murray, our conventional bracketing of the "I" takes on a meaning more extreme than sophisticated or deferential compromise. A means for inserting ourselves within our own declarations parenthetically, locating ourselves at various positions within them willy-nilly without claiming our place as their syntactical subject, and thus dissociating ourselves from our own subjectivity, a bracketed "I" can imply a defensive posture protecting us from just the sort of shame to which Murray subjected Steven. Were we, like Steven, to (re)present ourselves bare and unbracketed, stripped of our conventionally protective gear, we might well expose our own fears and desires, those "keenly felt perspectives," as Murray called them, animating our writing in ways that thought alone cannot. Had Murray himself examined the discourse mode he was teaching, in all its subtle and complex codings, he might have acknowledged that all of us, "a little silly" ourselves, share writing's embarrassments. And, most important, he might have taught Steven to avoid the shame embarrassment can become, instead of imposing it upon him.

MARCIA: What use does writing have for you?

STEVEN: What writing does for me is help me work out a lot of

my stuff. A lot of what I write about pertains to me. A lot of
the things that don't pertain to me directly pertain to me
indirectly. It's just like therapy really. One of the things I did
in 112 was write in a journal every day. I still do that. Now I
belong to a twelve-step program that highlights writing, and
I write for that. . . . I don't even realize what I'm feeling or
thinking until I write. Once I write, I realize, Wow! I didn't
know I had all that stuff inside me—rage, anger, pain. You
know, it's very healing. But I feel some shame talking about
this, because I feel it's been a criticism that I don't know how
to get out of me to write things that aren't about me. . . .
Actually, I don't know if that's even possible. Maybe it is, but
I really have a hard time setting myself aside.

Steven rightly calls into question a criticism we so often level at
students. Is it indeed ever really possible to write things that are
not about ourselves? Do we have an easier time setting ourselves
aside? How many of us have not confessed, over drinks with
friends (and couching our confessions in academic wit), that everything we write is really about ourselves? Our disguises may be
more sophisticated. Our metaphors thicker. But we are not the
more honest for it. Nor are we less prone to shame.

At the ADE conference in Waterloo, Anne's and my introducer's
words implied that first-year student writing is an embarrassment. In truth, writing is embarrassing, or at least an occasion
for embarrassment. But it need not be shaming. Writing's embarrassment is the confusion and perplexity, the mixture of hope
and doubt, we feel when we attempt to put down in linear fashion our "subjective worlds in all their richness and diversity."
Shame comes when doubt is unmixed with hope, and it comes as
much from without as from within, from an audience, real or
imagined, who offers no felt sign of responsiveness but instead
turns a cold eye on the thoughts we have laid bare or turns away
from them in disgust. The product of writing's embarrassment is
writing; the product of writing's shame is often incoherent rant
or, more often, abject silence. Murray's critiques shamed Steven;
Southwood's did not. Nor did the critiques of the two lesbian-
feminist teachers about whom he spoke with such admiration
and at such length in our final interview. These women *did* critique Steven's writing, at times with observations he said were

"devastating" to hear. Yet their praise carried even greater weight and recuperative power. No doubt, as I have said, their positions in our area's private, prestigious colleges gave special validation to Steven's career as a developing writer, just as the courses and students they taught gave especially welcoming reception to his development as a *gay* writer. But more than that, both of these women seeded their critiques with suggestions for improvement and with promise that improvement would come: As we have seen, one had written of the Hartland paper, "Your hard work shows. Also your writing style is definitely improving." Of "Madonna: The Queer Queen," the instructor said, "This is an ambitious paper! You are really trying to grapple with some difficult theoretical issues. . . . Beautifully written sentences are followed by confusing ones. . . ." And a third woman, one of Steven's sponsors for his major, told him, if he wanted eventually to teach, "Your writing's got to improve at least five times." As "devastating" as that was to hear, Steven said, she gave him "incredible encouragement," too: "She said, 'Well, you know, I have never in twenty years seen another student work as hard as you and improve as quickly as you.'"

Lesbian instructors teaching a largely gay student population about issues of gender and sexual identity: this was Steven's audience and the milieu in which, during the last terms of college, he found himself a gay human among gay humans, "free to be me" shamelessly. Each of these three teachers provided that all-important context he mentioned at our interview's start, a context to which he could submit his self-narrative without yielding control. They were women, "liberal people," lesbians, among whom he felt "comfortable" and "supported": "I know where they're coming from, and I know what they're looking for," he explained. "I'm in that mind set, so I just kind of know. So I guess, in a sense, I don't really think about it. I just go out and write the paper; I just write the paper." What is more, he could do with them what he judged he would probably not have done were it "a white straight man": accept the stylistic suggestions he liked, accept the material "observations" with which he agreed, and retain ideas he maintained despite his instructors' disagreement. He was free to choose, with the result that "it's like I'm the writer here, and it's not up to them what I write." In a way, then, each woman, simply by her own presence, welcomed Steven, and the writings by which he composed himself as a writer, into her academic world. But in another way, each, by way of her comments on his writing, also entered Steven's world: in validating his promise as a writer, each validated his own early exhortations to hope as well, setting before him the sort of narrative he had all along set for himself, one in which hope lay not so much in the achievement as in the promise of achieving, not so much in the absence of obstacles as in obstacles being overcome. Perhaps unsurprisingly, the writings he offered them in return are filled with both promise and achievement. Freed from the need to shout out "what I thought God was supposed to be" to a condemning, uncomprehending readership, he produced just the sort of objective, analytic, seemingly I-less "academic" prose even Murray was after. Sometimes he did so with greater or lesser grace, to be sure. Yet throughout his late writings, Steven gives the sense of someone who has not simply matured but has finally found himself among kindred selves—in his audience and his subjects—to whom and for whom he can speak, not in disguise but in their guise.

Epilogue

> After a time he began to enjoy it, and even allowed himself to believe what it was saying. . . . ("An Episode in the Life of Professor Brooke" 41)

We can safely expect just some ten percent of our students to have experienced the dissonance between gender and sexuality that homosexuality affords, the fissure, between the imposed self and the felt self, out of which new selves are—indeed, must be—continually constructed. Of our students who are gay, most will appear in the person of Steven; few, in the person of Lawrence, festooned in the hot pink triangles and tube tops, nose rings and delicately wrought body chains that force us to see the dissonance they feel. Most will, that is, represent themselves to the world in metaphoric disguise. And they will recreate that disguise in the metaphors of their compositions, few of them writing for and about themselves as explicitly and insistently as Lawrence. And just a few of our students each semester will have suffered physical and sexual abuse; just a few will find reparation as well as solace in faith and the act of faith—the confessional act—that writing, however disguised, really is. Only a few will, like Steven, use writing to author a self they can live with, to restory their lives in meaningful and satisfying ways. Only as many, that is, as our own embarrassment will suffer.

For while Steven has an uncommon power to unsettle readers and teachers to the degree he does (judging at least by the reception he received from Professor Murray and the reception our story of him received from members of the ADE), he is by no means unique. At least ten percent of our students are gay men or lesbians, and those who least appear it are the ones most apt to be hurt, not by outright assault, but by the thoughtless comments of unaware teachers and peers. They present themselves to us as Steven; they receive us as Lawrence. They *are* the self-stories they write: veiled in metaphor, vulnerable both to our clumsy assaults and to assaults as astute as Murray's. And as many of our students have, like Steven, suffered untold abuse, so that, again as with Steven, faith is not just a comfort but a necessity, whether it comes from AA, organized religion, or their own dogged optimism. Often these students— prone to deep shame and self-doubt—have the greatest difficulty writing, the greatest difficulty expressing their thoughts and suppressing the feelings— as Steven put it in our final interview, "all that stuff . . . all that rage, anger, pain"—behind them. But just as often, such a student can come, like Steven, to depend most upon writing to find his or her "self," the felt core around which to structure and go on structuring his or her life—and, like the defiant cancer patient of "An Episode in the Life of Professor Brooke," to defend that fragile self against the living death of silence.

Therefore, Steven's story, however uncommon, holds a store of lessons for teachers and students alike. Throughout most all of his writings, Steven spoke, at times unintentionally, *of* himself, but he always spoke intentionally *for* others. And while he spoke so often of gay issues, he seldom meant to limit the group for whom he spoke to those precisely like himself in sexuality, gender, or background. Nor should we. He represented in his various writings gay youngsters and members of other minority groups, suicide victims and potential suicide victims, the homeless, vegetarians, even threatened animals—any and all who want a voice and need to be heard, who require narrative's organizing, composing thread in order to remain intact amid the contingencies of an increasingly disorganizing, de-composing world. In this regard, Steven speaks for all our students, and for all of us teachers, too, for all who need, and deserve, an empathic audience to elicit our stories, the tales of our "selves." For what we say of Steven's self-creating narratives, we might as easily say of all our students' prose: they are both self-expressions and expressions of the self. And what Fish says of poetry, we might as easily say of the self expressed: "The shape and meaning it appears immediately to have will be the 'ongoing accomplishment' of those who agree to produce it" (*Ways of Reading* 152), both in the reading and in the writing.

Steven's narrative—the narrative he created out of and for himself—is a powerful one both despite and (even more) because of his unshakable reluctance to bracket himself, to set himself off parenthetically from the story he spent his years at the University composing. Therapy, AA, the courses he took were all bound together in writing, and writing was Lawrence's means to an end that was Steven. He was the subject of his own narrative in the full sense of that word: its author, its topic, and its product. Hence the sense of contingency dogging his every act of authorship, as he continuously composed and revised himself—sometimes for, sometimes with, and sometimes against his audience. But hence too the sense of constancy pervading his narrative, the sense that every act of storying is an act of restoration, for, while Lawrence's narrative ended in Steven, Steven was present from the start in Lawrence's intentions. The week before graduation, he stopped by my office to tell me he would soon be leaving for a job in the counseling services of a small college north of us: he had been hired to create the sorts of pamphlets he had composed in Basic Writing and generally to do what he had told Anne he wanted to do some four years before, "to help adolescent children deal with their homosexuality and not be ashamed of it." He had also concluded at least this portion of his spiritual autobiography along with his curriculum vitae, and proven himself able "to grow up as a person instead of as [his parents'] son." Steven had changed his last name to Matthews. His oeuvre retitled, his re-genesis was symbolically—and legally—complete.

CHAPTER FOUR

Understanding Personal/ Academic Connections: Rachel

As I begin to compose this chapter, Rachel is finishing writing her senior honors thesis in psychology, "Intimacy Issues among Young Adults: A Study of Family Alcoholism and Its Effect upon Children," based on a study she designed and conducted on the "connection between intimacy and being an adult child of an alcoholic." It is a thesis of which she is very proud—proud of both her research and her writing. As she said in an interview, "I am really enjoying this writing. . . . I feel confident in writing now."

She did not feel at all confident about her writing when interviewed in January of her first year in college. Further, at that time, she recalled only one paper that she had "been happy writing," a story she wrote of a migraine headache:

> There's been only one paper in my entire life that I've been happy writing. It was a paper in my expository writing class in high school: "The Life of a Migraine Headache." I have them and I wanted to write about it. I wrote as me being the migraine attacking someone named Rachel. So, I wrote it from a different perspective. And I put in all these analogies so the reader could really know what it's like to have one of these headaches. You know, what happens to the migraine and how he goes away, and how he comes back. And that's the only paper I've ever gotten an A+ on and I guess I felt good about that.

I juxtapose these two ostensibly different writings because I see a thematic connection between them, a narrative thread connecting them, specifically, Rachel's ongoing efforts to move from victim to agent, from silence to speech. In the migraine story, Rachel metaphorically takes on a role that she would later assume directly in her honors thesis. That is, in the imaginative migraine story, Rachel attempts to shift from being the victim to being an agent, the migraine that victimizes someone. But, in this story, Rachel remains both the migraine and the named character having the migraine. Further, in this story, Rachel imaginatively takes on the role of the speaker, instead of the silenced one, and although speaking as the victimizer, she attempts to ventriloquize for herself, speaking for the victim as well, conveying, as she said, "what it's like to have one of these headaches." In her college honors thesis, she is the positive agent, conducting research under her own name with the ultimate aim of assisting those who are adult children of alcoholics. What remains veiled is her own, other lived position as an adult child of an alcoholic. While this positioning of herself in the honors thesis could perhaps be viewed as a further act of ventriloquizing, I believe the process of doing the thesis represented an achievement as Rachel came to realize that she could not split her psychological self from her intellectual self, even when following an objectivist research paradigm.

This chapter is framed around that realization and the greater achievement, of which her honors thesis plays a part, of her growth in self-understanding and confidence. Like Lawrence, throughout her College Writing and other courses, Rachel was using writing to try to reconcile painful past narratives with a more positive present and future narrative, in some instances reworking and reenvisioning her life imaginatively. Unlike Lawrence, Rachel in her final drafts would often veil her past trauma or even her involvement in the subject of the text in order "not to be pitied." The research paradigm of her chosen major, psychology, seemed to offer a way to pursue her interests while maintaining the veil. Still, while apprenticing herself to that epistemology, Rachel was also taking courses where a more personally involved empathic way of knowing was called for in course projects. The understanding she gained of herself through these projects and the associated writing helped work against the splitting of psychological and intellectual that she initially may have sought in clinical research.

Rachel completed college still working to compose an integrated self that could acknowledge her past as part of a healthy present self. Her achievement was in her growing self-understanding, specifically of the involvement of her personal experiences with her academic and research pursuits. Writing—whether in the form of personal essays, clinical research, or case studies of empathic identification—was an important vehicle for that self-understanding. She was using this writing for two intertwined purposes: to serve a private function as a therapeutic instrument, and to serve a public function of helping her position herself within a community and a discourse—those of clinical psychology— where she could speak to others about matters which were personally important. Rachel's experiences in her various courses also bring into relief questions about the purpose of a college education and the ways of understanding oneself in relation to and amongst others that we value introducing to students.

Background

I first met Rachel when she volunteered to participate in our study in January at the start of her second semester in college. At that time, she was beginning her College Writing course. In contrast to Nam, Lawrence, and Francois, she had been placed directly into College Writing. Although she entered the University as a regular admission student, she would enter the Honors Program in her junior year.

Rachel grew up in a suburb of a local city, in a middle class, Catholic family. Regarding her writing experiences she said, "I didn't do a lot of writing in high school." In addition to her migraine story, she recalled doing "a couple of term papers," a "fiction story" in one literature class, and a few writing assignments for a half-year "expository writing class." In an interview midway through College Writing, she said that the expository class "reminds me a little of the freshman writing, only it really stressed brainstorming techniques" and "he [the teacher] put a lot of emphasis on form." Although she felt she had not done "a lot of writing in high school," it appears to have been writing that prepared her in some ways for her initial writing experiences in college.

Still, despite this preparation and despite being placed directly into College Writing, Rachel was not confident of herself as a writer. In this respect she was like Nam and other ESL students and other young women who entered College Writing lacking confidence in themselves as writers. In the questionnaire she completed at the beginning of College Writing, she indicated that she "almost never" felt her writing was good in comparison to other college students and that she "often" felt that her writing did not match up to good writing that she saw. She felt this way despite her perception that teachers had often reacted to her writing in a positive way and often treated it with respect. These comments reflected Rachel's acute awareness of herself in relation to others and her tendency to diminish herself in comparison to those others. In a first interview after one month in College Writing, she said "I don't like my writing. . . . Maybe it's because I compare myself too much to other people. . . . I see what they do, and maybe I'm just jealous of the fact that I can't write like that."

Despite her own lack of confidence, Rachel's experience of College Writing, as a native speaker of English and a white, middle class, apparently heterosexual person, was considerably more positive than Nam's, Lawrence's, or Francois's. Simply put, she was part of the mainstream, looked and wrote that way, and did nothing to mark herself as going against that stream. Unlike Nam, she had no difficulty keeping up with the pace of assignments. For that reason alone, it was easier for her to participate as one among others in class activities. Further, given her self-identity at the time, she did not, unlike Lawrence, feel herself as having to write against an audience of peers that included ones who demeaned, even threatened, her very being. Nonetheless, being so self-conscious of how she was viewed by others, she was also much more guarded than Lawrence in what she disclosed to others in the class about herself. By the end of the semester, however, she felt more at ease with herself and with her writing in relation to others. As she said, she felt more "comfortable" and also more confident about herself as a writer. She also felt that she had learned about herself.

College Writing

> You're going to learn how to write. I think you learn about yourself, too. And I think this all goes into the whole idea of college to broaden your mind.

After having completed College Writing, Rachel used those words when asked how she would explain College Writing to students who were wondering why they should take the course. In saying this, Rachel seemed to be referring to having her mind broadened about issues in the world around her, referring, for example, to discussions of date rape and the role of advertising in shaping social values. College Writing also provided occasions for Rachel to write about painful experiences of her past and work toward a healthier stance toward them. Because Rachel was drawn to writing on these past experiences, College Writing brought to the fore a concern that would continue throughout Rachel's college years: the relation between intimate personal experiences and public writing. It also brought to the fore for Rachel a related concern for developing a writing style that would incorporate both what she called "my style"—a style she identified with writing from personal experience—and another style she identified with writing about "facts from a source such as a book or journal article," so that she would not feel like "a computer producing facts."

Like many sections of College Writing, the writing assignments in Rachel's section were structured so that some writings were open for students to decide the topic and purpose; others were framed to present a particular type of challenge (e.g., to observe and interpret a place, to explain why something is significant, or to research a subject and develop an explanatory or persuasive essay) with latitude for students to select the particular subject. The objective that Sharon (Rachel's teacher) set for the progression of writings was to move students from writing solely from their own experience to writing also from their observation and interpretation of others' experiences and of readings. As she explained, she wanted them to do so in a way that would keep "a more personal edge":

The other thing I hope to do in this class is to kind of work with their personal style, and into a more academic style, so that their personal isn't divorced from their academic style. So that when they start writing academic papers, they feel more comfortable talking about subjects with a more personal edge.

In this context, Rachel, like many other students, wrote about subjects to which she had strong personal and emotional attachments. As Rachel recalled the course in an interview her senior year, she termed it "a very positive experience," pointing to Sharon as "giving us freedom, but giving us structure as well."

For the first two writings, Rachel did not write on anything that would have made her feel personally vulnerable to an audience. The first writing was open for students to select the topic and, implicitly, the purpose and genre. After some brainstorming writing and talk in class, Rachel decided to write on her friend's grandmother who was undergoing quadruple bypass surgery that day. She wrote in her process notes after her midprocess draft, "If I had to write on anything else last Wednesday, I probably would not have had any progress because my mind couldn't think about anything else." In response to Sharon's request that they consider their purpose for writing, Rachel wrote, "This is almost a release of my worry."[1]

In her required cover letter to Sharon with the final draft, she again indicated her insecurity: "I am not very confident of my writing skills, therefore I do not feel like this is a great paper." Sharon's positive response to this writing and to the next provided Rachel with an important early validation. In both, Sharon conveyed that she was reading with Rachel, aiming to hear what Rachel was trying to convey and offer suggestions as to how to do so. For example, in her response to Rachel's first writing, she writes, in part,

> Rachel, I think you've got a good start here. . . . It's clear that you're very emotionally attached to these people. . . . It seems to me that you're exploring two, possibly even three different issues: your relationship to Al and his relationship to Nan, and the possibility of death in your life. . . . Think about which theme you want to focus on most. . . .

Responses such as these conveyed to Rachel a sense that Sharon perceived her role as that of a reader-coach, not an authoritative director. As Rachel said midway through the semester, "It's helpful to know how she feels about it. She's like, 'You don't have to follow my comments. It's just what I'm getting out of the paper.' . . . I find them [Sharon's comments] really helpful."

For the second writing, Rachel's perception of feedback from her peers is noteworthy. This essay was to be an interpretive description of a place on campus. Rachel chose to spend a few hours in a study area at the library and write on that. She devoted a good deal of time to this writing, taking pages of observation notes, writing an initial draft, reorganizing and changing focus for her second draft. In her final draft, she presents a humorous look at student life in the library. These final drafts were published in a class anthology. Rachel received positive feedback from at least two other students, feedback that was significant to her. In an interview, she said, "It was just nice to be complimented on it. Like, oh, I didn't do that bad. And when I read it over after that, I'm like, hey, it doesn't sound that bad. I kind of did like it." In her end-of-semester portfolio review, Rachel wrote: "The second discovery [about my writing] is one that I am unsure of, but I have come to this conclusion after reading my peer responses. My writing can be humorous at times. . . . If this is a part of my writing, then I am glad. A paper is much more interesting to read if humor is involved."

Rachel held apparently contradictory views about the peer responses to her midprocess draft and her final. Hearing mostly that her peer reviewer liked her midprocess draft, she wanted more "critique." That statement may reflect her insecurity about her writing and her desire to improve. But it is more likely that at the time—when she said she still felt "really intimidated"—what she wanted most, given that it is what she recalled from the final draft, was what Elbow calls "pointing," particularly, feedback about what readers liked (*Writing* 85–86). That feedback functioned as more than a validation; it also told Rachel something about herself as a writer: that her writing "can be humorous at times." Further, although she said that as a writer she wanted "critique," as a respondent she was aware, as she said in an interview, of how difficult it is "to be really open with someone when you don't know them that well." That feeling would change as the semester went on.

The third writing was to continue the focus on using detail to develop a focal point. For this writing, students were to write on a person, event, or object that was significant to them. This seems a variation on the assignment Nam received to write on a memorable object. As Rachel understood the assignment, it posed the challenge, "Can you prove to someone else how important one thing is to us?" Her initial brainstorming list included among other things her best friend Trish, parents, camp, mogul lessons, skis. She decided to write about Trish. While I do not believe the teacher invited it or Rachel intended it, memories of painful personal experiences came into her first draft. Yet, by the final draft, Rachel makes only a passing and veiled comment about these experiences. The changes she made were motivated by her strong intentions of presenting a positive, "optimistic" story—not only about Trish and their friendship, but also about her own life, and not only to her readers, but also, I believe, to herself.

In talking about her drafts, I will be disclosing sections that Rachel chose to edit out. I do so, with Rachel's agreement, because I feel it is the best way to make a point about respecting a writer's decisions to make such choices. Doing so is also consistent with Rachel's and Lawrence's belief—expressed in other writings—that it is important to break the silence about painful matters that are too often pushed away, hidden by a taboo against speaking of matters such as child abuse, teenage suicide, or homosexuality.

Rachel begins her first draft by telling that she and Trish met at a day camp when they were eleven. "Being silly little girls, we had much in common: trendy clothes, an interest in boys, and desire to gossip." She moves quickly into talking about experiences during adolescence, "one of the toughest stages of life." In this first draft, she talks about how they helped each other through problems: "Hers seemed to be her parents placing a strict restraint on her privileges and mine seemed to be the rocky, and sometimes painful relationship with my mother." In another passage, Rachel writes:

My senior year in high school was filled with dark moments and low feelings. I'm fat, I'm ugly, I'm stupid, I mess up everything. Nobody could pull me out of the hole except Trish. At one point I was on the verge of suicide, though I rarely talked about it. . . . All of the times I was in rude and almost heartless moods—Trish <u>NEVER</u> gave up on me.

The draft ends with the contrasting image of Rachel rising above her desperation because Trish stuck by her: "I would not be able to fly today if it wasn't for her, as Bette Midler sings, being the wind beneath my wings."

In her next draft, she edited the sections about the tough adolescent times, changing the specific details about her own life and her consideration of suicide to more general and veiled statements. In this draft, she refers to her "rocky relationship with my mother," omitting the phrase "and sometimes painful." Explaining her senior year, she writes, "In addition I have always been extremely hard on myself along with an inferiority complex. So I rarely went out of my house, and I laughed and smiled even less often." She keeps the closing sentences with the image of being "able to fly today."

Even though her first draft recounts painful memories, Rachel said she enjoyed writing that draft. In her cover note to Sharon about this draft, she wrote, "I enjoyed writing this paper. . . . When I wrote the first draft, I let the words pour out, saving the worry for later drafts. I discovered that I actually liked it and kept the basic structure throughout the mid-process draft." In her process note, Rachel went on to say, "I am a bit concerned about a few things. I am worried that some points are too broad or might provoke further thought by the reader. I am unsure about grammar in a few spots, too. Overall, I am pleased with this essay!" This comment represented a much more positive self-assessment than for her earlier essays.

Sharon's response to the midprocess began: "Rachel, I can see that your relationship with Trish is one of the most meaningful relationships you have." She went on to say, "I am surprised by your tone, which seems a little defensive—You keep challenging the reader to take back the thoughts of ordinariness that the reader has already assumed." Here, I think Sharon is referring to lines like the following that Rachel included due to her interpretation that the essay was supposed to "convince" readers: "Maybe you are thinking that Trish is like any other friend. I want to challenge that."

Rachel was very surprised by Sharon's reading of the essay: "I thought that I had a good paper, and then I got the thing back, and Sharon looked at it in a totally different way than I did." Since Rachel had interpreted the assignment as being to convince readers of someone's significance, it is understandable that she would have put in the "defensive"-sounding lines she did and that she would have been surprised by Sharon's response.

What is not apparent is how she would read Sharon's comment about a "defensive tone" as meaning a "pessimistic" or "dark tone." In a later interview that semester, identifying this essay as one of the more frustrating ones to write, Rachel explained:

> I didn't realize that the paper took on a really pessimistic tone. And, I was like wow. I couldn't believe it until she said something. And, that is the frustration, like, "How am I going to turn the paper around? How am I going to completely switch the tone around, but keep the ideas there and get my point across?" . . . I didn't realize it was so dark. I didn't want that, and I didn't realize that I had done that.

In her end-of-semester portfolio review, she makes a similar comment:

> Only after I received feedback did I realize just how pessimistic it was. I did not want the reader to be forced into throwing pity on me. . . . I did not want that tone to be carried across. Therefore, my final draft was much more optimistic and focused on the aspects of our friendship that hopefully brought smiles to the reader's face.

Although Sharon's comment about a "defensive tone" did not refer to the image of Rachel she inferred from the essay, her comment may have provided the pretext for Rachel to resee the narrative and reshape it, including the image of herself she projected. She did not want to be the object of pity, a victim.

So, for the final draft, she revised to make the essay more "optimistic" and more likely to bring, as she said, "smiles to the reader's face." She changed the references to troubles with her mother to a general sentence: "Whether it was talking through tears because our mothers made us angry or laughing hysterically about a 'cute guy', we always supported one another." She also added a paragraph-long anecdote about "one of these teenage crises" when they each "had a crush on boys that were out of our reach, due to age differences." In addition, she makes her senior year seem less traumatic by writing about it in a more distanced, general fashion:

> Trish was worrying about what she would do when I went to college, and I was having trouble with my boyfriend. . . . Trish, being the stronger of the two, helped me come out of my down moods. She taught me that life goes on. One terrific quality of Trish is that she has never given up on me no matter how bad a mood I have been in. I have returned all of her kindnesses when she was in times of need.

With her cover note to this final draft, Rachel writes, "I feel better about the final draft than about the first two—I believe it is much more optimistic—which is how I want my friendship with Trish viewed."

Recall that when Rachel wrote her first process note to Sharon she felt very positive about her first draft and "enjoyed writing it." Because her feeling about the overall story was "optimistic," she had not thought of her first draft as dark and had even experienced writing it as a kind of release ("I let the words pour out, saving the worry for later drafts").

However, when she reread the draft—after Sharon had read it as "defensive," instead of optimistic—it appears that the darker moments stood out more strongly to Rachel. In the final version, she pushed them back even more—wrote them out of her story— and highlighted the happy and light times they shared, in much the same way as Lawrence revised his Significant Event essay for Basic Writing. Rachel may have revised this way in order to repress the more difficult memories and distance herself from them. Or, perhaps, as with Lawrence, the act of writing about her pain in the first draft had already achieved its purpose, dissipating her remembered anguish, so that in her final draft she could focus on what was for her the point she wanted to keep in her own mind and leave in readers' minds: the specialness of Trish and how she helped Rachel rise to feeling more capable and positive about herself.

Rachel's successive drafts for this writing show how close an essay can be to intimate and difficult experiences and emotions—even an essay that appears not to be. Although to some readers, Rachel's final draft may seem to retell a familiar teenage narrative of two friends helping one another through bad times and good, a more complicated—painful and happy—narrative was veiled behind it in the first draft.

Rachel's teacher, Sharon, was aware that many students were writing about sensitive, sometimes still-unresolved, personal issues in their writings, whether directly or indirectly. Indeed, this understanding shaped her perception of the intimate nature of her relation to students when responding to their writing and to the vulnerability any writer can feel. As she said,

> I think being a writing teacher in this kind of program is really intimate. . . . I also think that each time someone writes something—I mean, I know it's true for me—that it's tender, you know. . . . So when I read their writing, I do feel like I'm looking in on something that's very personal. And I don't ever want to push them into feeling unhappy about it. I want them to feel as comfortable about the process as they can, without feeling, you know, uncomfortable about not moving any further—because not everybody wants to move.

While some may think Sharon is overly concerned that her students not feel uncomfortable or unhappy, her sense of the vulnerability her students may feel about what they have written is an important check on writing insensitive responses and a reminder that we are responding to people, not papers. Certainly, such sensitivity did not constrain Sharon from responding in ways that still instructed and challenged Rachel as a writer. With this essay and a subsequent one on child abuse, Sharon respected Rachel's decision to revise the narrative as she wished and did not push her to include the more emotionally intense sections deleted from her early draft—in the name of having her create a more dramatic and original essay, or pushing her to examine her "true" feelings. Rachel knew the fuller narrative. For Sharon, unsure about whether Rachel "wanted to move" and hyperconscious that she was "looking in on something that's very personal," it was appropriate for her to respect Rachel's decision to highlight the more positive narrative she wanted to recall about her friendship with Trish and the hopeful feeling that she wanted to compose both for herself and her readers. It was her life, her story, her "truth" to compose.

In *The Performance of Self in Student Writing*, Tom Newkirk comments on how such personal writing—whether in process or final drafts—may make some teachers feel uncomfortable because they feel they are being implicitly forced into the role of therapist. He questions the assumption that students want us "to assume a counseling role":

> In most cases, this represents a profound and presumptuous misreading of student intent. Paradoxically, these writing situations can be therapeutic precisely because we don't act as therapists. If the first response is "I can't respond to this as a piece of writing because it is so personal. Have you thought about talking to a counselor?" we are denying the student the "normal" role of writer. The experience is stigmatized, it is represented as outside the bounds of normal classroom discourse. . . .
>
> In fact, the therapeutic power of such writing may be the experience of having it treated as "normal"—that is, writing that can be responded to, critiqued, even graded. . . . By asking many of the most basic conferencing questions—those that encourage elaboration, reflection, and the exploration of other perspectives—I believe we can respond sympathetically and helpfully. Paradoxically, the writing can most effectively be therapeutic by not being *directly* therapeutic. (19–20)

The final and even the midprocess draft of this essay by Rachel might not make teachers uncomfortable or uncertain about how to respond, but her first draft might, and other essays by Rachel or Lawrence might—and that is partly the point: we cannot always know when students are writing about intimate matters about which they still feel pain or conflict. Whether the essay appears overtly "so personal" or not, Newkirk is counseling us to accept that in most cases students are writing to us in our capacity as writing teachers and that by drawing on basic response strategies and remembering that we *may* be looking in on something "really intimate"—to use Sharon's words—we can still offer empathic, in-process responses that can prompt further writing: writing to shape and reshape a narrative and to shape and reshape one's self-presentation, both constructive activities for developing writers.

The fourth essay assignment, like the second, asked Rachel and her fellow students to shift away from personal experience and knowledge and move toward observing and interpreting phenomena around them, in this instance, print advertising. Sharon saw this assignment as both another challenge of interpretation and an occasion for students to become more "aware of what's going on around them." She also saw this writing as moving toward the documented essay that would follow because, as she said, "they chose their ads and they chose what it was they wanted to write about. . . . And it was their own interpretation without there being a higher authority to rely on."

In her final interview for the semester, Rachel identified this essay, along with her essay on Trish, as one of the most frustrating ones to write. She said, "It was fun, but it was really, really challenging. I found it hard to stick to the point because it was such a broad topic." In her portfolio review, she elaborated: "I kept jumping from what the advertiser does to the reader's reactions." Interestingly, when Rachel looked at this writing at the end of her senior year, she said, "I think maybe that's when I first started becoming aware of all these things that are in the world. That's where I think college has definitely opened me up. And, I think maybe I was just angry at all these things that I saw." Given that she was just starting to "become aware of all these things," it is not surprising that she had difficulty fixing on a focus for her essay.

The next essay was the documented one, which, as we have indicated, was presented to students as a kind of hybrid research paper. It was to be like an academic research essay in that the writer was to explore a specific topic or issue by doing additional research (drawing on some published information) and use conventions of academic citation (either MLA or APA). It was unlike the way research papers are presented in many composition texts in that students were also encouraged to draw on their personal knowledge and experiences. Whatever they chose, they were encouraged to begin with something that interested them and that they wanted to investigate further. It was in writing this essay that Sharon's aim for her students to integrate their personal and academic styles became an issue for Rachel.

For her documented essay, Rachel returned to a subject about which she has personal knowledge and about which she wished to learn more. As she wrote in her proposal for the project, "I love kids. . . . It is a problem that I would like to see severely reduced. . . . Someday, I hope to work in a clinical setting with child abuse victims." By choosing this topic, she encountered again the question of disclosure that she encountered with her third essay on her best friend, where she deleted the reference to her "sometimes painful relationship with my mother." To research this topic, Rachel drew on the discourse of psychology, seeing it as a way to make the link between personal and academic. Through her successive drafts for this essay, Rachel was also able to position herself as the researcher: indeed, these drafts trace a path from being a silent/silenced victim to being a spokesperson for those who are victimized. Here, though, in contrast to "The Life of a Migraine," Rachel moved from the imaginative world to the lived world and took on the role of that spokesperson, ultimately veiling her direct experience as a victim. In trying to use the language of psychology, Rachel also confronted the question of how to write about psychological concepts and research in a way that felt like her "own style."

In her first draft, "The Psychological Effects of Child Abuse," she writes with a kind of double voice, as is evident from these excerpts from her first and third paragraphs:

> It may be a kick. It might be a punch. It could even be as extreme as a burn from a hot iron. It is called abuse. Unfortunately, the most common recipient of abuse is the child. This upsetting problem is worldwide and can cause psychological problems after in life. . . .

> In the development of a child (both physically and cognitively) there are critical stages. These critical periods are highly susceptible to outside influences. The child is highly

impressionable. He or she does not know much about life yet. An abused child only knows pain and suffering. . . . Starting with infancy, we discover that this can severely affect the remainder of the neonates life. A certain attachment between the infant and the primary caretaker is critical. . . .

The first paragraph presents concrete images that dramatically draw readers into the essay. Then the language becomes more distant and general as Rachel tries to use concepts and language from psychology books and articles. As Rachel indicated in a subsequent interview, the disjunction between these two styles would remain a problem for her throughout her drafts for this essay.

Later in the first draft, she moves from the research articles to her personal knowledge, writing that she has friends who were physically and verbally abused. Initially, she had added here that she herself was abused until she was fifteen. She crossed out this phrase in the draft, but left the passage that followed, with references to "we" and, finally, "me":

In none of our cases did we report our sufferings. We were scared, frighten, and petrified of our abusers. We were afraid that if we told we would not be helped, but only hurt more. Pushing our pain deep inside where no one can see it is a common defense mechanism. Why didn't any of us run for help? There are many reasons. The bottom line is that it hurts. It hurts unbelievably bad. No child should have to go through any form of abuse from their family, friends, or anyone. I think the part about being abused that hurts the most is that it came from people who said they loved me.

Having crossed out the narrative of her abuse in the first draft, thereby silencing herself again, Rachel broke the silence in her second draft and *added* a full paragraph referring to her own abuse. This draft was retitled "How Much Do They Really Hurt?" In an interview, I asked her about including herself, and she said "I don't know why I did that. That's what made me want to write about it." She said another reason she included the passage was that "it helped prove my point": "I thought maybe if I put it in there, it would be like, bam, that would pull them in."

Although she may have wanted to "pull them in," she didn't feel comfortable sharing her experience with others in class. In fact, she said that she thought that for this writing they would not be doing peer review and that her teacher would be the only reader. They did have a peer review session, however, and she participated—feeling hesitant but not asking not to participate. She said in her final interview that by that time, in contrast to the beginning of the semester, she knew her peer reviewers and felt comfortable with them:

> Toward the end, the last couple of writings we did, we were comfortable with the writings. And, we got comfortable with the class. You get comfortable with going in there and seeing people and knowing how they respond. It made it easier to be like, you know, "Maybe you shouldn't do that. . . .Maybe you should do this." I really felt more comfortable with peer editing—both giving it and receiving it.

She said that her peer read it, and "it was strange because he thought it was good. He's like, 'Wow, it really hits you at the end. It really makes you stop and think. Wow, leave it in there.'" Rachel said that when she talked with Sharon in conference about the paper, Sharon suggested she might not want to leave it in, conscious that these essays would also be published for the class to read. Sharon's suggestion may have reflected her own feeling of discomfort knowing such intimate things as well as her acute sense of not wanting students to feel "uncomfortable."

Rachel said she thought seriously about still including the self-reference but ultimately decided not to and omitted it from the final draft. Seeing that omission, I recall a line from the omitted section: "pushing our pain deep inside where no one else can see it." Rachel still represents the pain, but in this final draft, only through the experiences of a close friend, who was also abused and to whom Rachel gave a pseudonym:

> One of my close friends I will call her Sandra Smith, had the unfortunate experience of psychological abuse. From the ages of thirteen to seventeen Sandra and her mother had a rough relationship. Although her father never contributed to the abuse, he never stopped it.
>
> Sandra's mother demonstrated terrorizing by calling her a "little bitch" and a "worthless lying thief" for no significant

reasons (Smith). Isolation was a significant part of Sandra's torture too. Many afternoons she was confined to her room until it was unrealistically immaculate. . . .

In this passage, Rachel positions herself as the reporter of her friend's abuse, not one abused herself, and as the knowledgeable researcher-writer. Also, by citing her friend with a parenthetical reference in the text and a listing in the Works Cited page, she elevates her to the status of an authoritative source along with the psychological sources.

In an interview, referring to her decision to omit any reference to her own experience, Rachel said, "I'm glad, I'm very glad that I didn't put that in the final one." She went on to explain her complex rhetorical and personal reasons for substituting her friend's story for her own. She had such strong feelings about child abuse that she wanted to get across to her classmates the seriousness of abuse and its closeness to all our lives. She wanted them to focus on the issue, not on her:

> I didn't want them going, "Oh my gosh, this poor person." I just didn't want them to be pulled away from the paper. It was still a true story I switched to, about one of my other friends. I just thought that sometimes with a topic such as child abuse— "not me, not anyone I know." I wanted to say, "Hey, it does happen, you know." I thought that might help.

Rachel would have been the "someone they know," but she was even more reluctant to be the "poor person" she was afraid her classmates would perceive. So, in the final version, she uses the story of her friend to try to achieve the sense of immediacy and presents herself as the knowledgeable spokesperson for victims of child abuse. In taking on this role, she found a place from which to speak publicly and authoritatively about a subject she has intimate knowledge of, keeping her focus on the subject, not on herself, and doing so without disclosing more of her personal involvement than she chose.

While Rachel was certainly more pleased with this final version than with the first draft, she was still not satisfied. In her portfolio review, she wrote,

> I noticed that the sections of this essay that I added my own thoughts or explanations flowed better and were easily understood. When the time came to be factual, I had trouble incorporating my style and the information on psychological abuse. . . . The facts seemed to overshadow the point I was attempting to make. Instead of making the information run along with my writing style, I appeared to be spitting out facts like a computer.

The difference she perceived is evident in the third paragraph, where she lists types of abuse, and in her final paragraph, where she speaks persuasively to readers:

> There are five types of psychological abuse. First, there is rejecting, which includes behaviors of abandonment. Next, terrorizing involves purposely threatening a child in order to produce fear. Ignoring is another form of abuse. The fourth form is isolating, which entails parents preventing their children from engaging in social interactions . . . (Garbarino et al. 25–28). . . .
>
> Psychological abuse: it is a sad, but real problem we are facing in the world today. Whether mistreatment occurs during infancy, childhood, or adolescence, it can have detrimental effects on the child's emotional and psychological well-being. No child should have to go through the humiliation and suffering that approximately one million children endure each year (LeFrancois 329). Hopefully, someday, through awareness, education, and group efforts we can erase this disturbing problem from our lives. It is the least we can do. Millions of abused children all have frightening memories of their torture, and they are scarred for life.

In an interview, Rachel said, "It was after that paper that I realized that I needed to change my style, and that I needed to learn how to incorporate the two. I think that's something that's going to have to come with time." In a parallel fashion, that statement could apply to a split between her position as victim and her position as spokesperson/survivor. Awareness of this parallel would come to Rachel as she researched and wrote her honors thesis during her junior and senior years.

I question whether Rachel would have come to the realization about language had she not been writing about something that was important to her and about which she had personal knowledge as well as "academic" knowledge. Trying to use the specialized language of psychology, while also using familiar language to present what she knew apart from her research, heightened her awareness of her lack of familiarity with the discourse of psychology and her difficulty in integrating what she experienced as two styles and two tracks of thinking. Further, and equally important, she felt a strong need to have a language and style adequate for making people aware of the "torture" that "millions of abused children" suffer. That motivating intention would come through in other writing situations, and integrating what she still experienced as two styles would be a project for Rachel throughout her college years, particularly in her psychology courses, so that she could use "facts"—research information—to make her point, not "overshadow" it.

Rachel still had one more essay to write for College Writing. As with the first, the students were free to choose what they would write. For this essay, Rachel returned to writing about a personal experience, an occasion of exuberant feelings, and, as in her fictional story "The Life of a Migraine Headache," it is an experience of being in control and conquering something that had previously controlled her, this time a challenging, mogul-filled ski trail called the Outer Limits.

She entitled the essay, "Win or Lose?" In it, she tells of her first attempt to ski the trail, an attempt that ended in failure. In what she described as the turning point of the essay, she tells of deciding to try again: "Because my philosophy of life is that you only live once, so go for it, I had decided to give the Outer Limits another chance." The essay ends with an exuberant description of her successful run:

> This time down, I did it right. The heavy snow from the morning had been packed down from the many skiers who had traveled over it. The quickness and sharpness of my turns carried me over the tops of the moguls with ease compared to the first time. Even though I fell a few times, it was nothing like the avalanche type of plunge I had taken earlier in the day. I smiled widely as I put the mountain in its place. Upon reaching the bottom of the trail, my feelings were not of relief and regret, but rather victory and rejoice. Although my knees were throbbing and I felt like I would collapse, I thrived on the great sense of accomplishment and satisfaction. Then, I hopped on

the chairlift and headed towards the wounded beast to rub in the loss a little more. I had finally attacked and defeated the Outer Limits.

In her end-of-semester interview, Rachel selected this essay as the one she had the most fun writing. "I really liked it. I had so much fun writing it. It was a free essay and I kind of went nuts on it. I was like, 'Wow, this is fun.'" She said much the same thing when recalling this essay four years later: "Wow, I really, really liked writing this. This is something I think about every time I'm at Killington [the ski area with the Outer Limits trail]. Writing this, I felt that I could paint a picture and it was easy to animate the story so this was a lot of fun to write."

Rachel's experience in writing this essay and her recollections of it show the power of writing and memory to evoke and even lead one to reexperience the emotion and physical sensations of a past moment. Now, when she returns to the Outer Limits, she remembers not only her first experience skiing it, but also her "Win or Lose?" essay, a writing by which she composed her meaning of the experience and, in a broader sense, reaffirmed her exuberant spirit and her will to persevere—even or especially when it is a real question whether she will win or lose.

Rachel finished College Writing feeling more confident and "comfortable with writing." In a final interview that year, she said that in her first semester, she was "scared about writing. Like last semester, I had to write a couple of papers, and I didn't really do that well. . . . I feel like I could write a paper now, and not be as anxious about it. I can stay focused on one topic instead of just going off and getting carried away from it." She also said, "I love writing, and though it's not anything I'd ever consider getting out in the open with, I just like doing it, you know, for my own. I love writing."

Writing after College Writing: Separate and Connected Knowing

During her sophomore year, Rachel entered a more varied world of academic writing, although one where what Belenky et al. term "separate procedural knowing" predominated, that is, an epistemology constructed as "disinterested reason" (110) and articulated in "a public, rational, analytic voice" (28). It was a way of knowing and using language—a discourse—that was called for in Rachel's psychology classes and that she, unlike Nam or Lawrence, seemed to seek. For her, the research paradigm of the distanced researcher provided a way of pursuing topics with which she had a personal connection—and about which, in some instances, she had unresolved and painful feelings—in a distanced way using the "procedures" of clinical psychological research. During her sophomore and junior years, she also had courses where writing projects called for connecting knowing, specifically through empathic identification. These courses invited Rachel to try on an epistemology quite distinct from that of psychology, an epistemology important for her developing understanding of herself in relation to others.

I use Belenky et al.'s categories here to refer to ways of knowing called for in particular courses, not, as Belenky et al. presented it in *Women's Ways of Knowing*, to describe stages of individual development. In a chapter in Goldberger et al.'s *Knowledge, Difference, and Power: Essays Inspired by Women's Ways of Knowing*, written a decade later, Nancy Goldberger, one of the original authors, argues that the categories are better thought of as identifying strategies than as developmental stages. According to Goldberger, focusing on strategies brings to the fore questions of how strategies may vary depending on "social position, cultural practice, situation, political objective, personal (even unconscious) motives" (362). In a comment relevant to higher education, she writes:

> Any individual's ways of knowing would be the constellation of various strategies in her repertoire, some perhaps more prominent or commonly used. . . . To the extent that a person's strategy for knowing adheres to a single strategy that is static or rigidly applied, then one can ask what are the contextual factors that limit or inhibit alternative strategies. (362–63)

The variety of strategies for knowing that Rachel experienced in her courses—even though limited—has underscored for me the importance of making room in students' studies for multiple ways of knowing, specifically for empathic as well as separate knowing, and for introspective as well as distanced knowing. It has also underscored the importance of naming these strategies to students and engaging them in reflection on the nature of the differences in strategies, as those are linked to specific contexts and discourses. This is work I have now begun to do in my first-year writing classes.

Sophomore Year

During her sophomore year, Rachel was to begin to learn the discourse of her chosen major, psychology. That year, she took two courses designed for majors, Psychology 241: Methods of Inquiry in Psychology—the same course taken by Nam, although they were in different sections—and Psychology 330H: Physiological Psychology (Honors). Like many other courses in the psychology curriculum, these two were designed to introduce students to the methods and materials of the field, and, like many others, writing was central to the courses. During first semester, Rachel took the Psychology Methods course simultaneously with a general education elective, Art History. In doing so, she experienced two quite different academic discourses. As a student aspiring to a profession in psychology, she found Psych Methods valuable:

> Writing the papers really helped me understand what was in the book because it was hands-on. It was firsthand experience, and that's what I think helped me learn as far as, "Okay, this is what this test does," and "This is how you do this type of research." . . . This is preparing us to do scholarly work.

Like Nam, Rachel was conscious that a different kind of writing was required for the laboratory report genre, one "unlike the style I was used to." As she said, "It was a very technical type of writing. . . . I'm sure I have my own style of writing within these papers, but it was hard to incorporate the style I was used to, as far as being creative." Using the same phrase she had used to describe her experience in writing some sections of her documented essay in College Writing, she said, "I felt like a computer spitting out facts." Yet, unlike Nam, Rachel seemed more adept initially at reading the expectations and performing as expected. One obvious reason is that it was easier since she was a native speaker of English and a native participant in U.S. school culture. Another significant reason, I believe, is that she did not feel the same resistance as Nam did to the style and way of knowing taught by the course. For Nam, it conflicted with his own beliefs about spiritual knowing, which seemed to offer him a better way to understand himself and those positioned like him in the world; for Rachel, in contrast, the procedures of psychology seemed to offer her a way to this same end, a way that would not require her to acknowledge her own position as victim. While Nam aspired to be a priest, she aspired to be a psychologist and was ready to apprentice herself to the discourse. So, while she experienced a gap between "my own style of writing" and the "technical" style of the report, she was disposed to want to try to bridge the gap, to "incorporate the style I was used to."

Figure 1 shows an excerpt from Rachel's first lab report, where she tries to take on the language and subject position of a researcher. She refers to "our team of investigators" and to "data" and "variables." Still, even as a native speaker of English, she, like Nam, has difficulty using the language, something the teaching assistant notes in her evaluation and corrections of the text. In her analytic evaluation of the introduction, the TA awards Rachel 3 of 4 possible points for content but only 1 of 4 for clarity. In this passage as in others, the TA comments on ambiguities in wording and on ways to cite statistics.

Rachel reported that students were also told not to use first person. (Although the TA did not correct Rachel's use of "we" in the Introduction, she did write "Use 3rd person" on the Abstract page.) Whether Rachel inferred that this comment applied to the whole report or heard it also in class, she made no first-person references in subsequent reports. When I asked Rachel the reason for this convention, she explained "I'm not sure. The only thing I can think of is that it's in the APA manual and I overlooked it." When I asked her if she thought there was a reason for using third person instead of first, she said, "I don't think so, because in most of the research articles I've read, they do say 'we.'" She went on to say that she thought as a writer it was easier to be clear if she wrote in the first person because she was

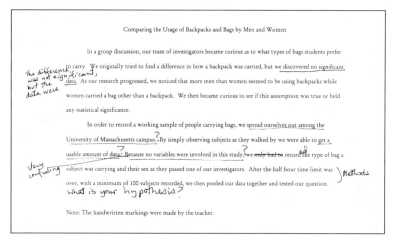

Figure 1. *Introduction to Rachel's first lab report for Psych Methods.*

the one who did the research: "It's easier to make inconsistencies if you use the third person because you're thinking in 'we' or 'I' instead of 'them.'" The viewpoint Rachel expressed is very close to that of the APA manual.

During that same semester, Rachel also took Art History, which presented a quite different intellectual task to her and a quite different style of writing. In an interview at the end of her sophomore year after having completed both courses, she explained her first Art History assignment in comparison to Methods Lab:

> They said you're going to have two papers to write and I figured I'm going to be analyzing a painting or comparing it to something else. I didn't expect to have someone say, "Pick anything and write it as if you were there." So, it was kind of neat because you did have to use your imagination. Then you also had to look at the piece of art and experience it as a person, yourself, and you had to spit out your feelings on it. It was neat to write about something personal, instead of something cold and technical. That's how we described it, my friends and I in the Methods Lab, it was cold writing.

As Rachel described this Art History assignment, it seemed to have been intended to invite the kind of imaginative, empathic knowing that Belenky and colleagues associate with connected knowing—a kind of knowing much different from that of the detached, observation of Methods Lab. Still, in her senior year, when Rachel recalled this assignment, instead of thinking the assignment was "neat," as she thought earlier, she remembered it as difficult to make that empathetic connection:

> RACHEL: That one I did not like writing. I had to put myself into the perspective of a person living in the time this painting was made. I knew nothing about it and found very little information.
>
> ANNE: So was it that you couldn't imagine yourself in that period?
>
> RACHEL: I think that's what it was.

What to make of this apparent change in attitude? Her later perspective may have been connected with what she had been learning over those three years in her psychology courses and what she was accepting: a notion that research information was essential and more imaginative knowing without that information was not as valued. Or, related to this possibility, the change may reflect a limitation of the assignment that Rachel could see in retrospect: it was difficult to identify imaginatively with someone in the Middle Ages when she had little information about that period. Still, when first commenting on the writing, she twice called it "neat," reflecting at least, I believe, that at the time she valued the different, more imaginative experience it offered in contrast to the more analytic experience of Psych Methods. At the least, having both writing experiences the same semester heightened Rachel's awareness that there were different strategies for knowing, although there appeared to be no forum in her courses for discussing these differences.

During second semester, Rachel took another course that furthered her procedural learning about research and writing in psychology: Physiological Psychology. She said she enjoyed the professor's manner of teaching and found him helpful: "He really got us thinking in a very empirical way. You had to question every type of research, as solid as it may be, and you had to question it and think of all the other possibilities." The method of topic selection for this class was similar to that in College

Writing: the teacher defined the type of task and gave students latitude to select the specific topic they would focus on. For this course, they were to review three research articles. According to Rachel, she chose "a physiological basis of addiction and he said it could be on anything on addiction and I've always been interested in the area of alcoholism and how it works. So, I just picked up on that." Later in interview, she indicated that she had a personal connection to the topic, one that she acknowledged in an oral presentation to the class.

> As I said in my oral presentation, alcoholism runs in my family, and I always wanted to understand it, and doing this paper really helped me understand it a little. At the same time, I realized "Wow, there's really nothing out there on it." So, I'm going towards that now.

She continued to pursue that topic, choosing an issue related to alcoholism for her senior thesis; however, the thesis topic was closer to her experience as a child of an alcoholic than was her project for this course, where she looked at something not directly focused on her childhood position. Still, in this course, she seemed to be beginning obliquely to work her way toward a study that would focus on the experiences of those in her own position.

For the paper she wrote in Physiological Psychology, the nature of the assignment did not lead Rachel to bring her personal connection explicitly into the written text itself. She reported that writing the paper was a challenge, particularly in deciding what articles to focus on. Once she had made her selections and worked out her interpretation of the articles, she said, the biggest challenge was trying to write condensed explanations of each article. She credited her experience in writing brief reviews of research for Methods Lab as helping her with this part of her task. Aside from this similarity, Rachel perceived the genres and styles of writing in these two courses as distinct, reflecting two types of articles done in the field of psychology. While Methods Lab would prepare her to write "an original research paper," Physiological Psych "would prepare me if I wanted to start learning how to write a review article." As far as the style, Rachel said that for her review article, "It was slightly more relaxed. . . . It's not an original research paper, so I'm not interpreting my own numbers. I'm interpreting someone else's numbers, so I think that there's more room for my saying, 'This is what I think that these numbers mean,' rather than, 'This is what these numbers mean.' You can't really stray from the numbers in a research paper."

Further, in contrast to all of her Methods Lab papers, she concludes her paper for Physiological Psychology not only with a call for future research but also with a statement stressing the importance of the issue:

> Even in the light of this developing research, no firm conclusions can be made from the results. The need for further research on these areas is great and will hopefully be fulfilled in the near future. As our society grows, the chances of alcoholism increasing seems more than likely. Through a commitment to science and society, some of the answers to nature's most puzzling problems will be found.

In an interview, asked about her reference to "science *and society*" (emphasis mine), Rachel talked of her beliefs about a researcher's responsibilities to society:

> ANNE: Why did you include "and to society"? Why not just "through a commitment to science some of the answers . . ."?
>
> RACHEL: Probably because alcoholism is such—is a disease that plagues society, and you can make as much of a commitment to science as you want, but I really think that you need to make that commitment to society. It's almost like you're the researchers and you're finding out the answers for those people so you can help them. And, I think in the long run you are helping those people, so it's a commitment to them also.

In this statement, she was articulating her conception of a role she would step into herself, that of a researcher aiming to help those who are affected by this "plague."

As her interview comments should make clear, Rachel was quite conscious of the different styles she was being asked to take on in her various courses. And, she took them on willingly, valuing particularly the procedural knowledge of research and writing that she was gaining in her psychology courses. Given this quite specialized writing—writing quite different from her College Writing styles—I asked her at the end of her sophomore year if she thought the writing she did in College Writing was useful in any way. She answered:

> RACHEL: It's funny because I was talking with somebody about that yesterday. I think that that was probably the best class I've had here at the University so far . . . as far as getting the most out of it. I use that almost every day, in just writing a letter to someone or writing a paper, or anything.
>
> ANNE: How so?
>
> RACHEL: Just because I feel I'm more confident about my writing. I can write a paper faster because I know that I can get all the gibberish and junk out of there. I know my grammar is still terrible, but I think even though freshman writing is more on the creative side, being able to organize my thoughts and being able to just put them out on paper helped in [Methods Lab]. It was definitely an adjustment, getting used to writing like this, but as far as being able to organize a paper and know what I have to say, it was helpful.

Junior Year

During her junior year, Rachel did a good deal more writing, in courses for her major and in ones to fulfill her general education requirements. In talking about these experiences, I aim to make three points: First, for Rachel—as, indeed, for many students—the character of the teacher as the dominant audience had a significant impact on what she would make of a writing assignment. Second, just as Rachel had chosen a topic for her Physiological Psychology paper with which she had a personal connection, during her junior year, she continued to seek out and create opportunities to make connections—and not all of them veiled—with her course work. While separate, distanced knowing predominated, two courses that invited personal, connected knowing were important for her, in learning about herself, and about herself among others. Third, through her experience in writing for her psychology courses and in finding a role model,

Rachel began to imagine and move into her own position within the discourse of psychology and to develop an image of a style that she aspired to, a style for writing psychology that would not be just "cold writing" but would also reflect "who I am as a person."

Rachel reported having quite different feelings about two of the general education courses she took. One was a course from a social sciences discipline that Rachel said "was not a learning environment at all"; the other was a women's studies course about which Rachel said, "I loved [it]." Her introductions to the papers she wrote for each course reflect these perceptions.

Here is her introduction to the paper for the social sciences course:

> The world has seen many changes. Some of these transitions have been smooth, while others have systematically dismantled an entire society of people. When considering the concepts of social change and mode of production, changes in groups of people can be viewed as both the causes and effects of these two terms.

And the introduction to her women's studies paper:

> The advent of the "Global Assembly Line" has brought many issues regarding the status of women to the surface. Companies that establish portions of their assembly lines in Third World countries are exploiting women for the sake of profit, and the men controlling these businesses seem to think that women are not only enjoying this grueling, near slave labor type of work, but that their lives are actually becoming better as a result. In reality, the lives of women in the United States and in the Global Assembly Lines are being destroyed, and the rein of patriarchy remains over their heads.

Consistent with the rest of the paper, the introduction to the social sciences paper is guarded. Rachel does not come forward to make claims or develop her views as fully as she does for the women's studies paper. For this paper, while she uses some abstract language unreflectively (e.g., "rein of patriarchy") just as she does in the social sciences paper, she is more direct and specific in putting her views into words, opening with a substantive position statement that she develops throughout the paper. She is using this paper to make claims and to try to support them, instead of backing off into more generalized and noncommittal language.

The difference in Rachel's intellectual engagement with these two writings is not, I think, attributable to the material; she said she was interested in the material for both. Rather, the difference seems to have more to do with her perception of the teachers' attitudes toward the students. In the social sciences course, Rachel felt that "there was a negative attitude toward students on behalf of the people who were teaching the course." She went on: "Sometimes people would ask a question and because it was 'something we were supposed to know'—I'll say this in quotes—the professor would snap back and almost degrade and embarrass that person . . . and not answer their question." Given that this was Rachel's image of her audience for her paper, it is not surprising that she was guarded, not leaving herself open for attack from an audience who was likely to be reading against her, not with her. That guarded stance included remaining general and avoiding taking the risk of developing an analytic position.

Further, Rachel felt she received little direction from the teacher or the teaching assistant. For the paper, she was to draw on three films and related readings, discussing the relationship between social change and modes of production in the three societies depicted in the films. She said, "I loved the movies and enjoyed the reading, but I just didn't want to write it." That is an unusual statement for Rachel, who approached most all of her writing positively, expecting that she would learn from doing it. Also unusual for Rachel, in contrast to her more detailed recall of writings for her other classes, in trying to recall her experience of writing this paper, she said, "I have blocked a lot of this out."

In contrast to her recollection of this paper, she had a much more positive memory of her paper for women's studies: "I enjoyed writing the paper. . . . I was very pleased with the way this one came out. . . . This one also seemed to flow very well as far as writing it." One of the reasons that the paper could "flow" very well was that Rachel perceived her teachers as respectful of the students, who could ask questions and explore their ideas without feeling that the teacher would "degrade and embarrass" them, as she felt for the social sciences course. It is not surprising, then, that Rachel would say of the course, "It really opened me up to a lot of new perspectives on life." It is noteworthy—and I think not coincidental with her perception of the course and her teachers—that Rachel also talked about her writing for the women's studies course in the language of connected knowing. In an interview during her senior year, she explained, "In writing about 'Global Assembly Line: Impact on Women around the World,' I was thinking, 'Wow, if I was the same person and I was just living in a different country, I would have a completely different life just because I'm a woman." In this comment, she conveys a strong empathic identification with these women who are more victimized than she. It is an identification that arose through her having done the research to learn of their situation. As Clinchy writes in an important comment on her conception of connected knowing, "To adopt the perspective of the other requires thinking (reasoning, inference) as well as empathy" ("Connected and Separate Knowing" 224). In writing her paper, Rachel draws on her knowledge, reasoning, and feeling to write what the teacher called "a prime example of critical analysis," working to develop a position in ways she did not for the paper in the other course.

During the first semester of her junior year, Rachel took another course which, like the women's studies course, invited her to learn more about herself and about herself among others. This team-taught course was an upper-level education course on multiculturalism and peer counseling, a required course for students who were working as resident assistants (RAs), as Rachel was that year. As for the women's studies course, Rachel also felt the teachers were respectful of the students and receptive to their ideas. Further, like the women's studies course, both the teachers' manners and the writing assignments invited her to learn about others through empathic, connected knowing—in this course, through direct interactions with others. For the first two writings, ones which Rachel found to be "great learning experiences," students were to pick a "targeted" group of which they were not a member and learn more about it. Rachel picked Jewish people. According to Rachel, for the first paper, students were "to go to an event that involved talking about that topic." She explained what she did:

I went to see Grace Paley speak and it was absolutely amazing. She read some of her work and it was a wonderful experience and I spoke to a few people there and [for the paper] I just had to write out what I did.

Toward the end of the paper, Rachel commented on the impact of this event on her:

This event was a major happening in my life. Not only did it provoke me to reevaluate my thoughts and ideas about Jewish people, but the mode of thinking it placed me in carries over into pondering how I view and perceive other oppressed and targeted social groups. Even after what I have just written, I feel as though words do not do any justice for what I experienced inside throughout this event. Hearing Grace, meeting Liz [a Jewish woman who happened to be sitting next to her], and discovering more about myself were all such fantastic experiences. I feel as though I am more capable of educating someone who may not possess an accepting view of Jewish people.

Interestingly, Rachel highlights the "mode of inquiry" this event placed her in, as well as what she "experienced inside."

For the second assignment, students were to learn more about their chosen group by interviewing two people and reading a relevant book. Rachel interviewed two Jewish people, a student and a psychology professor she knew (the one who would subsequently be her honors thesis director), and read Elie Wiesel's *Night*. In an interview during her senior year, she recalled that assignment as follows:

I learned so much; it was great. And, I had a lot of fun doing this. Oh, I also had to read a book. I read *Night* and that was an amazing book. It restructured the way I thought about things.

Here again, then, Rachel emphasized that the assignment changed her thinking: "It restructured the way I thought about things." It is interesting that both of these assignments that were transformative for Rachel called for an experiential and empathic mode of thinking—learning by trying to understand others' experiences from their own perspectives, and learning that calls on both feelings and intellect.

The third writing for the course was designed to have students reflect in a very specific way on themselves as RAs. The assignment was to prepare a case study of a meaningful event they had dealt with on their floor. According to Rachel, "the biggest thing I had dealt with that semester is a man on my floor who decided to 'come out' and he and I spoke almost every day over the course of a month." In the case study, she gives him the pseudonym Tim.

In an interview, Rachel said it was a difficult paper to write: "It was difficult to tell that story over again and make it clear and organized. . . . I had to relive some of those really awkward and uncomfortable moments that we had in talking." Part of the discomfort to which Rachel referred may have arisen because Rachel was one of the subjects of the case study, since it focused on her interactions with Tim as he talked through his decision to come out. Consequently, in presenting the case study, she felt she also needed to acknowledge her own identity as a bisexual woman as that related to her interactions with Tim. In acknowledging her identity, she acts on her conviction that the oppressive silence she speaks against in her paper needs to be broken. She was breaking the silence herself, obviously to Tim and also to the teachers of her RA course, an audience she trusted. The paper opens with a direct statement of Tim's identity as well as her own:

> A recent incident (an occurrence actually) that took place right here on my floor is one experience which has made me take a step back from my usual mode of thinking and learn a bit. . . . The people who were involved were a resident who lives on my floor and myself. The resident is a white, gay, 19-year-old man and I am a white, bisexual, 20-year-old, catholic woman.

Later in the paper, she shifts her focus from the experience on her floor to speak more generally about the oppression and willful denial that result from silence. It is a passage that echoes themes in her first-year documented essay about child abuse—the "not me, not anyone I know" attitude of many people and the oppressive silence surrounding child abuse and homosexuality and bisexuality:

> Because homosexuality, and bisexuality for that matter, are not able to be freely expressed without experiencing some form of

social pressure or fearing physical harm in this society today, it
is difficult to find the right opportunities to explore the issue.
Most people do not think about this everyday because the
majority believe that "It's not anyone I know." Thus homosexuality is pushed further into a dark, forbidden closet that
no one dare open. From this silence results the oppression and
lack of consideration of these individuals who are just as human as the next person.

Rachel knows the cost of silence from her talks with Tim and
from her own position as a child abuse victim and as a bisexual
person.

Toward the end of the paper, she reflects on what she gained
from her interactions with Tim:

> One of the most empowering aspects of watching someone come
> out is the additional reinforcement that you are not alone. Tim
> helped me install so much pride in myself that since we had
> our first talk I have come out to over a dozen people. I am less
> afraid of who I am and I have a stronger capacity to deal with
> pressure from others.

When we first talked about this paper, Rachel said that even
though her experiences with Tim were personally significant, the
writing itself was not as valuable to her as the first two assignments for the course, primarily because she did not feel she learned
anything new in doing it:

> It was reflective but I didn't feel as though anything I said in
> this paper made me realize something I didn't already know,
> which is what a lot of papers had done.

While she may not have learned anything new, it seems that writing this case study still did serve another personally important
function. In a subsequent interview, I asked Rachel how she felt
acknowledging her bisexuality in that paper and again in a final
paper, and also how she felt having come out to me by giving me
those papers. She said she had forgotten that the papers were
among those she had given me until we were going through them
together, and there they were. She said that she felt all right about
that: "It's not something I'm uncomfortable about." Not know-

ing whether she knew I was a lesbian, I told her—in order to be as forthcoming with her as she had been with me and to convey my own comfort with that identity.

Still, aware of the homophobia in the world around her, she was wary in the course. She said that before turning in the papers in her class, she had checked with the teachers to make sure that they would be the only ones who would be reading them. She felt safe and comfortable having them read the papers, but not others in the class: "I knew that other people in the class—I'm just glad they wouldn't have read it because there are definitely people who I didn't want to know because I didn't feel safe." She went on to say:

> It was kind of a neat thing: it was weird to see that on paper. But, I think it was—it was very progressive for my own development to write about it. It gives you a different perspective. I had never had to write it and it just reaffirmed—I should say, it affirmed—who I am.

While in writing the paper Rachel may not have learned anything new, she did affirm something about her identity by putting it in writing: "It was very progressive for my own development. . . . It affirmed who I am."

Rachel chose to prepare another case study of Tim for a second-semester course. Doing so presented quite a different challenge and also served quite a different purpose for learning. The course was Psychology 392: Human Sexuality, a writing-intensive course that focused in part on learning to prepare and write case studies.[2] This case study was to be of a person whom the writer would be able to interview about the person's sexual history. Since her experience with Tim from last semester was still strong in her mind, and because he was now a friend, Rachel asked him. Tim agreed. After the interview, students were to prepare an outline, showing they had covered all of the prescribed categories. As Rachel's extensive ten-page outline indicates, the focus of the study was exclusively on "the subject," that is, Tim: "background and early childhood" (e.g., "family background," "attitudes toward sex in the home"), "puberty and adolescence" (e.g., "sexual education," "dating behavior"), "current attitudes and beliefs," and "current behavior" (e.g., "extrarelationship coitus," "communication," "nature of sexual difficulty").

The difficulties Rachel articulated for this case study were different from those for the RA case study. For this case study, she was not one of the subjects as she had been for the RA case study. I think that is why she felt that, as she said in an interview, "For some reason, I was able to take that information and take that person and separate it." Separate it from herself, I infer. Here the focus was on Tim and on constructing a clinically detached report on his sexual history. While Rachel recalled some difficulty in interviewing him and writing the paper, "knowing I was writing about a friend," it was not the level of emotional difficulty she had experienced in writing the RA case study, where, as she said, "I had to relive some of those really awkward and uncomfortable moments that we had talking."

For this case history, the challenge was more methodological and compositional: making sense of the interview, structuring the paper, and representing the subject clearly to readers—difficulties she mentioned in an interview. As Rachel explained, "painting a clear picture of a person was difficult because you have to put yourself in the reader's perspective who knows nothing about this person or the situation you're writing about." For her the value of the assignment was that it presented her with the occasion to learn what she believed was valuable procedural knowledge:

> I think that definitely served a purpose because that's my field.
> I needed to know how to interview someone and how to take
> that information and paint a picture of someone even though,
> like I said, I knew this person and knew him well.

Although she could "separate" and still take on the role of a researcher presenting a case study of a subject, she did not distance herself totally from that subject: "I knew this person." She wanted to represent him fairly and in a way that she could share with him. Indeed, she said that she showed a copy of her paper to Tim.

During her junior year, Rachel had two other courses in her major for which she completed writing assignments. One of those, which she felt served no purpose, involved assignments exemplifying the kind of writing that another student I have interviewed calls "spit backs." Rachel told me about this course when I asked if she had had any courses that she felt were not "constructive for writing." She described this course, for which students were to write a two-page paper every week, answering questions on that week's reading. Rachel understood that such an assignment could help develop one's understanding of readings, but she felt that in this case the questions were too simple. As she explained:

> I don't think reading a few articles and spitting the information back out is—I think connecting two different articles is an important thing to do but for the most part the way the questions were formulated for the papers, I felt like I was reiterating what I just read and there didn't seem to be a point to it. . . . I found them to be repetitive, and boring, and nonprogressive.

That complaint sounds much like Nam's complaint about the assignments for his Introduction to Philosophy course: "When I have all these notes of what the teacher say, it's like I rewrote it again. . . . It seems like this is boring." Although Rachel kept the writings she did for all of her other courses, she did not keep the ones for this course.

In contrast, Rachel felt that the writing she did for Psych 370: Personality was more constructive. For this course, students surveyed a number of psychological perspectives and wrote three papers. Students were to pick a topic of their choice related to personality and, for each paper, write on it from a particular perspective (for example, psychodynamic, Rogerian). In the second and third papers, they were to compare and contrast the various perspectives. Thus, in contrast to the previously mentioned course where students were merely reiterating their reading, here they were asked to apply that reading by trying to see from the perspective of each theory and compare one to another. For Rachel, "it was a learning experience to do the three papers because it exemplified the true variety of the theories." For her papers, she chose antisocial personality disorders because the topic related to her interests in youth and abnormal psychology, although, she said, "it was less relevant to the class." Still, her professor, Dr. Vogel, approved her choice and, as Rachel reported to me, "I was thankful that I had that freedom to do that."

During her junior year, Rachel also worked as a research assistant for Dr. Vogel and another psychology professor, who were writing an abnormal psychology textbook. She said she learned much from that experience and noted two aspects of her job that she felt helped her develop as a writer: one was to take copyedited drafts that had been returned from the editors and enter the editorial changes into the word processor; the other was to critique and suggest revisions for the chapter summaries the editors had written.

Through the Personality course and her research assistantship, Rachel came to know and respect Dr. Vogel. In her, Rachel found a role model, a woman Rachel said she "looks up to a lot," both professionally and personally:

> She is an excellent role model. She's done a lot of work on intimacy and identity, and I read some of her publications. She is a very intelligent woman, and I look up to her as far as her pursuits about how much she puts into a day and how many things she gets involved in. Maybe it's because I can relate to her as a person.

In Vogel's writing, Rachel also found a writing style she wanted to emulate, a style that conveyed a sense of the person behind the words. As Rachel said,

> She's also a tremendous writer. I like her writing style. Whenever I read her work, I feel like I can see the energy in her writing that you see in her. I think it is very reflective of how she is and perhaps that's what—that's what I'm trying to attain, is to have my writing style reflect who I am as a person.

Rachel now had a vision of a professional writing style that bridged the disjunction she had felt between her "own style" and "writing about the facts."

Senior Honors Thesis: "an intellectualization of an issue that's painful"?

The culminating project of Rachel's college studies was her senior honors thesis in psychology, titled "Intimacy Issues among

Young Adults: A Study of Family Alcoholism and Its Effect upon Children." It was a marker of what she had learned in her psychology studies, signifying a further step toward her goal of graduate studies in clinical psychology. It was also a marker for her development as a writer, the thesis being a research report where—as with her imaginative story, "The Life of a Migraine Headache"—she felt happy with her writing. Commenting on writing the proposal, Rachel said, "It took weeks to do but it seemed to flow. And this was the first time I ever felt, 'Wow, this is me; this is my style of writing.' . . . I was happy with the way it came out." Rachel refers here to "My style of writing"—not a "computer spitting out facts" or a disjunction between "my natural style and the facts." Certainly, one of the reasons she was happy with the thesis is that she felt she had something important to say on the basis of her research. As she said in a final interview, "Now I feel like this is something I can share with people, and they'll be interested." Not only a marker, this project was an accomplishment.

Getting to this point of satisfaction with her study was not easy, however, and to do so Rachel had to address her own personal issues. As an adult child of an alcoholic, she was studying an issue directly connected with herself. Further, her hypothesis for the study was that adult children of alcoholics will have less intimate relationships than will adult children of nonalcoholics. As her research proceeded, Rachel's ongoing questions about her own childhood and intimate relationships led her to seek counseling on these issues.

When I try to write about this thesis, the phrase "approach-avoidance" comes to mind. Although I suspect I am not using the term in its formal psychological sense, it describes to me Rachel's stance toward her thesis research project. By choosing to do a clinical study of adult children of alcoholics, Rachel was able to approach a still painful and unresolved issue for herself as an adult child of an alcoholic; at the same time, the distanced research methodology seemed to offer her a way to avoid some of the pain by separating herself, that is, by taking the role of the researcher studying other "subjects," even though Rachel was a member of the group those subjects represented. As she worked on her study and worked with a counselor, she came to understand that she could not resolve her personal pain indirectly through her study of "others." By confronting her difficulties, she grew in both self-understanding and awareness of her approach to the research project. The following comment came in response to a broad question about the role of personal knowledge in research:

> ANNE: Here's sort of a big question to ask. What do you see for yourself as the role of personal knowledge and personal experience and choices for research and—
>
> RACHEL: Last August when I chose this topic, I hadn't come to terms with a lot of the alcoholism in my family, and I dealt with it last fall and this was very, very difficult. I did not want any part of this last fall. I spoke to someone about it all of last semester. Last semester was very, very difficult, and the person I spoke with said, "Well, you're intellectualizing a lot of your wanting to deal with this issue and find some resolution in it." And my professor, Dr. Vogel, also knows about the alcoholism in my family and she was very supportive through it all: "Look, I know you're going through a difficult time. If you want to pull out, that's fine." But this semester I'm taking a different perspective on it because even though I have a long way to go with dealing with things, I put a lot of the difficult part behind me. So, I have to admit this was definitely a personal endeavor but it's taken on more of an academic pursuit at this point because I'm getting into the data going, "Wow, it's contradicting current research, and some of the other current research is pulling together with it."
>
> So, I can only say from my perspective in some ways I think it's excellent to write about something that has personal relevance or you have personal knowledge about. You can really get into it, but at the same time if you get too close to it or you stop realizing the purpose of writing this paper or thinking in this way, it can really hold you back from doing your best.

Rachel's comments reflect some of the tension inherent in recognizing both stances and not tipping to either extreme—on the one hand, not "intellectualizing" and seeking personal resolution where it is unlikely to be found, and, on the other hand, not "getting too close" and seeing only her own pain and personal experience in the research. The balance is found on the continuum, where personal and academic are recognized as intermingled and one seeks, as Rachel did, to understand the nature of the connection.

Later in the interview, Rachel commented again on how recognizing one's personal connection can be a motivation:

> I know for me it motivates me. It says, "Okay, well, find out more about this because it affects you and you want to understand it, and you want to understand it so it doesn't happen to other people or it does happen to other people if it's something good."

For Rachel, as indeed for Lawrence, her personal connection motivates her to try to understand more about something both for herself and also for others. This dual motivation helps her enact a personal move from a passive, silent position to an active, speaking position as a professional committed to helping others.

As Rachel's comments show, she began to address her personal issues and also decided to proceed with her research. From her comments, it is evident that the support and understanding provided by Dr. Vogel were important to her. Here was a professor in her major, a mentor, to whom she could acknowledge the connection between her personal life and her research project and who clearly conveyed to Rachel that she accepted and respected the validity of Rachel's feelings. Thus Rachel proceeded, writing her proposal, beginning her research, and, in so doing, moving from personal involvement alone to a broader perspective of others who, like her, were adult children of alcoholics. Within her major of psychology—specifically, in clinical research—she had found an arena for acting in the world on an abuse she had suffered silently as a child.

Through first and second semester of her senior year, Rachel completed her research project and felt very good about it, in large part because she was obtaining results that seemed to contradict some existing research and seemed to challenge the notion that adult children of alcoholics will have less intimate relationships than adult children of nonalcoholics.

She carried her positive feelings into writing her proposal and thesis, writings that reflect her procedural knowledge—developed through the curricula and through writing she did in her many psychology courses—and her increased skills and confidence in writing. As she said, with her thesis she felt she had finally written in a style she wanted to claim as her own: "this is my style of writing." Yet in contrasting her style for the thesis with her style for the case study she wrote in Human Sexuality, she said, "Writing my thesis proposal, it felt like metal, it was just cold. With the case study, I had to be as clear and concise as I had to be in a scientific paper, but I could use some flourishy, flowery words."

In an interview, I pursued with Rachel what seemed to me like a contradiction between calling a style "cold" and "like metal" and saying with enthusiasm, "This is my style." Having talked with her, I think Rachel is saying that the documents as a whole—both the proposal and the thesis—felt like "her style" because through those documents she was using language to say something that she wanted to say. This sense of a guiding intention came through strongly as she talked about writing the proposal and the literature review section of the thesis. Rachel had a case *she* wanted to make. While not acknowledging her position amongst the population being studied, she was writing from the dual—not split—position of researcher and subject. Her personal agency as the one constructing an argument is evident in this comment:

> In the first part of it, I had to do a literature review and that I was more comfortable doing because I've written several papers where I had to do that. I had to take articles from the people who have done work along the same ideas but don't necessarily connect and I was trying to make a connection and I think because I knew what I wanted to do it wasn't that difficult to go to the library and say, "Okay, here's ten references, and I need to make a good argument about why what I want to do will be a valid study."

In a subsequent interview, I asked if she felt that these sections where she was making an "argument" were in a "cold style." In her response, Rachel talked about the multiple styles required for the thesis and the constraints imposed by the conventions of the APA manual and the psychology community to which she was writing:

ANNE: I was wondering about the comment you made about a "cold style." Do you think of this section as that?

RACHEL: I think the literature review is cold only in that I can't use certain words. I have to use a certain type of language and—maybe it's the "I" business because I have a hard time with—APA says I can't say, "I think that these two areas of research are connected because . . ." I have to say something like "it seems likely that these two areas . . ." And maybe that's why I think it seems cold. But the methods and the procedure are definitely—it's almost metallic. You just have to spit out sentences as far as what you did and you can't say anything more than that. Um . . . If I were sitting down telling you what I did I would definitely tell you in a different way. But with the literature review, it would be a little bit more similarity with if you said, "Okay, tell me what you're doing with the theoretical background behind your study."

The difference between the two styles—and between their purposes—is evident in the following excerpts from Rachel's proposal and, subsequently, her thesis, the first excerpt from the literature review section and the second from the methods section. In the first section reviewing other scholarship, Rachel is clearly trying to make a case for her study, making judgments about existing theoretical models, and drawing together research on intimacy and studies of adult children of alcoholics, and doing so in the style she understands from the APA manual (e.g., "There appears to be . . ."):

Erikson's model points out that only heterosexual couples can successfully master intimacy (Erikson, 1963). However, this view is outdated and in the present study same-sex couples will be considered for having the potential for achieving intimacy.
The manner that Erikson refers to intimacy excludes people who are in platonic, non-sexual relationships. Other research suggests that a sexual component is not necessary to achieve intimacy. Levinger (1977) describes . . .

Research on identity and intimacy is consistent in that results have shown identity is a crucial and necessary factor in achieving intimate relations with another. . . . Based on these two areas of research, there appears to be a solid basis for examining intimacy in people who may be or have the potential to be adult children of alcoholics.

In contrast, in the following excerpt from the methods section, Rachel is writing with the purpose she had learned from her Methods Lab and the APA manual: explaining her research methods to others who might want, as she said, to "replicate it without having to ask any more information than what is provided in that paper." A more "metallic" style comes through—clear, concise, and detached:

> Subjects will be interviewed in a private room. Upon arrival at the interview site, subjects will be given an informed consent form. Once informed consent is obtained, time for further questions will be provided. Interviews will be tape recorded for facilitating data analysis. Audio tapes will be kept in a locked file to ensure confidentiality.

This is the discourse of the neutral, objective researcher.

The style and tone of this section also contrast dramatically with the final paragraph of Rachel's proposal, which reads as follows:

> This is a sensitive area of study as it deals with issues that can be psychologically painful. Although most of the current research on adult children of alcoholics is consistent, the amount of information available is insufficient. It is the hope of the researcher that this study will shed light on some of the dark areas behind the dynamics of being an adult child of an alcoholic. Perhaps if more solid information were available on the nature of relationships and intimacy and identity conflicts of adult children of alcoholics, then more effective and applicable treatments could be provided, resulting in greater productivity and fulfillment in life.

In an interview, I told Rachel that I was struck by this final paragraph, with the first sentence particularly, because it was "a statement of the humanness of this research." Rachel replied:

> Yes, I get that sense too. I was almost debating whether or not to put that in there. I felt that when I wrote it, and then I sat there and I looked at this paragraph over and over and said, "Does this fit with all of this mechanical stuff that I've just written?" and I wasn't quite sure but then I felt—whenever I

write a conclusion, I feel as though, I almost feel compelled—
I think I did this in the paper I just gave you [for a cognitive
psychology course]—I just feel compelled to put in the human
component. . . . I also feel as though I need to leave the reader
with a direction. They need to be left, in my opinion, with
ideas of where they can go or where the research can go.

As her comment makes clear, Rachel debated whether to include
that final paragraph, that is, whether it fit with "mechanical stuff"
she had just written. In this statement, we hear her discomfort
with the "mechanical style" she uses elsewhere in the study, and
we hear her assertion of her will to say what is important, whether
it fits with learned conventions or not: "I just feel compelled. . . ." I
read that as Rachel's urge—from her personal knowledge—to
resist the splitting of psychological research from its lived "human component." In this statement, she conveys something of
the person behind the words: not a detached knower/researcher,
but one who conveys through her language and style her "commitment to science and society."

In her thesis, the emotional tone of the final paragraph of the
proposal is not as directly evident. Rachel speaks in the more
measured voice of the empirical researcher. Still, through her
writing, she conveys a sense of the importance of this line of
research for those who are affected. For example, in the introduction, in making a case for her study, she provides statistics
that show the magnitude of the problem of alcoholism for both
children and adults in the United States and the reason for the
dearth of research on adult children of alcoholics (ACoAs), until
recently:

> It was not until the 1970s that mental health professionals
> acknowledged alcoholism as a primary diagnosis (Brown,
> 1991). . . . Today, as the DSM-III-R indicates, Alcoholism is
> accepted by psychologists and psychiatrists as a disease (Ameri-
> can Psychiatric Association, 1987). However, ACoAs have had
> difficulty being legitimized (Brown, 1991), as the residue of
> the pre-recognition era of alcoholism clears. The lack of unani-
> mous recognition has spurred researchers to examine an issue
> which potentially affects millions of children and adults
> throughout the United States.

Rachel's study focused on the question of intimacy, specifically, testing the hypothesis that "ACoA subjects will have less intimate relationships than non-ACoAs." The primary finding of her study was that this hypothesis was *not* supported. She opens the "Discussion" section with an unadorned declarative statement of this striking finding: "The Adult Children of Alcoholics group did not show less intimate relationships than the non-ACoA group. On the contrary, the ACoAs displayed significantly more intimate relationships than non-ACoA subjects."

While this measured tone predominates in the "Discussion" section, as she discusses limitations of her study and considers her findings in light of other research, Rachel does not maintain it in all sections. Consider the following paragraph:

> Though there is a sufficient body of research which describes and confirms developmental difficulties in ACoAs, careful consideration for the extent of parental alcoholism is necessary. Perhaps the notion of Adult Children of Alcoholics is stereotyping millions of people (Goodman, 1987; Calder and Kostyniuk, 1989). Difficulties with trust, establishing intimate relationships, and identity are seen in several other disorders, and it does not seem appropriate to label all ACoAs as having difficulties in these areas of development. Alcoholism is often manifested with depression and/or anxiety disorders. It is possible that the more severe issues pertinent to ACoAs are a result of mental illness rather than alcoholism.

In this passage, Rachel seems to be speaking from her identity as an ACoA as well as a researcher, as one, that is, who could be a target of the stereotype. Although she uses the qualifying phrases ("perhaps") and indirect voice ("it does not seem") of the conventions she has learned, she moves from declarative statements to judgments and uses not only warrants based on accumulated research but also an ethical warrant based on the consequences of "stereotyping millions of people." By doing so, she conveys her strong awareness of the link between research and the people it affects.

In the final section of the discussion, returning to a more measured voice, Rachel suggests directions for future research that will move beyond the stereotypes. She concludes:

Currently available research questions the validity of the notion of Adult Children of Alcoholics, and the extent of the effects of any traumas they may have experienced during childhood. The present analysis of ACoAs demonstrates that the capacity for intimate, non-familial relationships is not necessarily damaged. Future studies should examine the quality of parental and sibling relationships, as well as the ability to achieve intimacy, so that there will be a more narrow focus on the problem areas for ACoAs. A reconsideration for the psychopathological system of alcoholism and its ramifications is necessary to clarify the level of functioning for Adult Children of Alcoholics.

The dual voices that speak throughout this thesis—and that Rachel was well aware of—reflect to me the subject positions that Rachel occupied as she alternately employed the research paradigm of objective, nonemotional "science" and also resisted it.

Looking Backward, Looking Forward

As we talked in final interviews, Rachel reflected not only on her style—as it connected to her strong sense of her emerging professional self and aims—but also on the role of personal knowledge and intimate experiences in inquiry and public writing in college classrooms. I will follow the course of her reflections at some length because, in taking us through the complex and often conflicting perspectives on these questions, Rachel helps us understand our relationships with our students in our capacity as the ones who decide what kinds of knowledge are authorized in our classes and the ones who help our students understand the functions of writing for themselves and for their negotiations with their audiences.

As Rachel leafed through the writings she had done in her first-year College Writing class, she came to the documented essay and initiated, without my bidding, a reflection on the role of intimate personal experience in writing for school. Here Rachel reflects on both the "appropriateness" of such writing in school and the possible function of it for the writers. She does so by considering two roles she has been in: that of an undergraduate teaching assistant for an Abnormal Psychology class and that of a student writer:

> RACHEL: I think that I remember writing this one [the documented essay on child abuse] only because I'm a teaching assistant for the Abnormal Psychology class. I had to grade about twenty papers and a lot of people put in, at the end, their personal views, but they also put in their personal experiences. And I was thinking, "Wow, this is really inappropriate, and I'm uncomfortable reading this about this person." I think a little amount of personal revealing part of your past that is painful to you is okay, but some of these people were really going into detail about what had happened to them over the course of their life and I was thinking that it made me uncomfortable to read and I thought it was inappropriate in regard to the assignment.
>
> ANNE: You say it's inappropriate in terms of the class?
>
> RACHEL: Well, um, I think the class definitely—Abnormal Psychology does warrant a lot of self-exploration. But I think—it's also a very personal view—maybe I should have added that I don't think that if you're supposed to be writing an assignment where you're taking at least eight scholarly references and doing a critical analysis of a current issue—for example, people did cults and David Koresh . . . or Jeffrey Dahmer and things like that—and we had people who did issues with [sexual abuse] . . . go into their own history with sexual abuse and it was really uncomfortable to me as the reader to have to see this person in class, to have a name and a face to connect and to know this part of this person's past.

Here, Rachel speaks first of it being inappropriate because it does not seem to fit the assignment. In saying that she seems to be accepting the separate knowing that Belenky, Clinchy, Goldberger, and Tarule found pervasive in the academy—where personal knowledge is kept separate from scholarly knowledge and is de-authorized as a possible contributor to the construction of knowledge in scholarly work and college classrooms. As I will show, when Rachel talks about her own knowing, she comes to a somewhat different view.

In this instance, it seems that an even stronger reason for Rachel's judgment of "inappropriateness" is her own discomfort as a reader. It may be that she was particularly uncomfortable because she was in many ways still a peer of the undergraduate students in the class. Still, other teachers—including experienced ones and ones with the title of Professor—feel similarly uncomfortable, and understandably so, when their students write of painful and scarring violations they have experienced, particularly when those writings trigger memories of a teacher's own feelings of pain or shame.

I asked Rachel what she would do were she a teacher. As she began her response, she did something that is instructive for other teachers: she looked to the students' positions as writers, considering the potential value of such writing for them:

> ANNE: Do you have—what would you as a teacher do? Have you any thoughts about what you would say to a person or even in general to a class?
>
> RACHEL: Okay, right, because you don't want to just shrug it off. If this is the first time someone is dealing with it, maybe this is the safest way. Honestly, I don't know. I think it's a catch-22. There's so many positive and negative aspects of going one way and saying, "Yes, feel free to do this" and "No, don't do this." Um, because I think by saying—even in my own thing—"I don't think it should be there," it's almost countereducational, by saying, "Don't write about this."

Rachel knows the catch-22 because she has experienced it and has in her mind both a teacher's feeling of discomfort and a student's feeling of wanting to use an occasion for writing to begin to deal with a personal issue that connects with the writing assignment.

As she worked through her thinking, she moved to a resolution that tries to honor what she feels is the possible educational value for students of stating their personal experience and connecting it with a classroom issue. As she talked, her focus shifted from the initial function of using writing to deal with a difficult issue to considerations of disclosing intimate subjects to others:

> Maybe I would say—and this is something I said to my discussion group because they had to do an oral report on a topic of interest and it could have personal relevance but it didn't have to. In my individual meetings with students they would come

to me with a whole section of their outline based on, "Well, my mother was abusive and she was this, that, and the other, and she's on medication for that. . . . "I told these students, I said, "You know, I think it's great that you want to be able to share this, and it would have a powerful impact. However, I think that a little bit of discretion is needed because you don't want to put yourself in an uncomfortable situation in front of these students." I think you're dealing with a sensitive area—that student's mother had attempted suicide.

This is also the professor's perspective as well. He didn't feel as though it was appropriate for these students to be blurting out some things they normally wouldn't say to a group of strangers, and maybe that's the key to it. And perhaps I would say something similar to what I said to my discussion groups, is that, "If this has personal relevance, fine, you can incorporate that into your conclusions. Just have some discretion as far as how revealing you are." I think that seems to be the best route as far as how revealing you are because when they think about it, they can still write about it, but not to the point where it's going to be—where they'll regret it. I would not want to have anyone regret what they wrote, and I know that if I had put more in this than I did and then everyone else got it, I would have been so uncomfortable.

In this last comment, Rachel returned to her feelings about her documented essay, and the regret she would have felt had she revealed more about her own story. And that is how she perceives relating a past trauma—including a parent's abusive actions: as "revealing" oneself and making oneself vulnerable. For another person—for instance, Lawrence—writing of a similar trauma can be perceived as a way of breaking an unhealthy silence and beginning to heal—even if the writing is more candid than some teachers would feel comfortable with. That discomfort should put such a teacher in the position of trying to understand, as Rachel would have us ask, "Why does reading these personal stories of pain and abuse make me feel uncomfortable, and how am I to understand my response to students? What might I be transferring to them?" Rachel's reflective comments model a willingness to engage in that self-reflection. While she carries her own feelings against "self-exposure" over to working out how she would act as a teacher, she still acknowledges the personal "educational" value that writing about one's own experiences can have.

As she continued her reflections, Rachel returned to the role her personal interests have played in selecting topics for her research and writing. As she did so, she also returned to the function that writing has played for her in helping her understand things she has wanted to understand about herself and her life:

> In retrospect, with this [the documented essay on child abuse] and with some other papers I know I've written, I think I've tended to surround my topic—they've all been topics that have had personal interest to me. I think with this it's more of an intellectualization of an issue that's painful. I think—just from my own experience and speaking with other students too—I think that's common where there's an issue that's painful and you're not sure how to deal with it. You don't know if you should talk to someone or if you can tell your best friend about it or whatever and so you write about it. And like you said, a safe way or socially acceptable way or academically acceptable way. And I'm not sure if it's good or bad or if it's just another step in the process of understanding something that you want to understand. But I know I have certainly done that a lot and part of me is happy I have. . . . I like some of the things I've written because of that. Maybe it's because it's that those are the things I understood about myself.

In our first interviews during College Writing, Rachel had spoken about the function of writing, especially private writing in her journal, as a "release." Here, she speaks of her recognition and her friends' recognition of how they have chosen repeatedly to write on topics of personal interest, especially things that are painful and that they do not know how to deal with. Here, writing seems to serve as a place of last resort when they do not know how to deal with something and do not feel they can talk to others. It is not simply using writing as a "release," but seeking some way to deal with the past and present that will allow them to go forward. As Rachel acknowledges, even undercover public writing, that is, writing without acknowledging one's personal tie—while it can mean "intellectualizing" unresolved emotional matters—can contribute to self-understanding: "Whether that's good or bad, . . . it's just another step in the process of understanding something you want to understand."

Later in that same interview, when speaking about the role

of personal knowledge as a resource for her inquiry about alcoholism, Rachel makes a comment that speaks to the power of putting things into writing, a power that she cannot quite articulate:

> For example, the alcohol stuff. Well, this is what my experience has been, but maybe it's not like that for someone else who has the opposite parent who is an alcoholic or who has an aunt who is an alcoholic who is close to the family and sometimes you probably—I think that I probably thought about things—after writing them down and looking at them, I think words look so strange. It looks so much different then—I don't know if that's helpful or not. It's such a difficult question to answer.

"I think words look so strange. It looks so much different then." Rachel's referent for "it" is, I think, not "the words" but the past experience itself. Here, Rachel is getting at one of the therapeutic values of writing: the sense of a different perspective we can get from seeing our thoughts and experiences as if they are out of ourselves and on paper.

In our final interview, just days before she defended her honors thesis and graduated, Rachel reflected as well on how she views herself now as a thinker and writer. Although she did not speak directly about herself as a maker of knowledge, it was clear from her comments about specific projects that she had moved into this position. Speaking about the RA course, she talked about how personal experience and the experience of others can constitute valid knowledge with which to question theory:

> Sometimes the way we experience things in the world isn't exactly how theories explain things or how something you learn in class explains things. I think because we experience life differently, writing it down and saying, "Look, this is what the majority of people say, but this is what I found and this is maybe what people I have spoken to have found." Even though that's not written down anywhere, you can certainly make some valid points about what's happened. For example, the things that happened on my floor, some of it contradicted theory, um—some of the ways that I tried to build community may have contradicted theory, but they were important. I felt it was im-

portant to make that point and to say it can be different and tie those two in, maybe, finding the similarities as well as the differences.

Later, talking further about the role of her own experiences as the adult child of an alcoholic in her honors thesis research, she said:

> It's helped me organize my thoughts and say, "Okay, this is what I know, but how do I know this is really true?" and even if it's not something documented, I think that thinking about something of personal relevance makes you think about the other points about it.

In these comments, I hear echoes of Belenky et al.'s discussion of women who were moving toward what they call "constructed knowing," where one believes that "all knowledge is constructed, and the knower is an intimate part of the known" (137). They say that for many of the women they studied, their path to this way of thinking "began as an effort to reclaim the self by attempting to *integrate* knowledge that they felt intuitively was personally important with knowledge they had learned from others" (134). In discussing these women's development toward "connected knowing," Belenky et al. go on to say that "during the transition into a new way of knowing, there is an impetus to allow the self back into the process of knowing, to confront the pieces of the self that may be experienced as fragmented and contradictory" (136). In all of Rachel's comments, I hear her recognizing and working to figure out how to honor the impetus "to allow the self into the process of knowing."

Furthermore, through her writing and her repeated returns to painful issues from her childhood, Rachel was working to compose—from what she may have experienced as fragmented pieces—a coherent self with some continuity across time, transmuting her past into a new narrative where she is a positive agent in the world. Striving to realize this identity, she is among those who, as Belenky and colleagues write of their group of constructed knowers, "want to develop a voice of their own to communicate to others their understanding of life's complexity" (137).

Rachel's impetus to present herself as the agent of her own research and in her own voice is evident in her resistance in one important instance to the convention she has learned from most of her psychology courses, that of avoiding first person pronouns. In a final interview, she explained:

> I was asked to apply for the senior honors director's award, and I had to write a six-page paper summarizing my thesis, and I was writing, "The researcher has done . . ." I was writing about myself in the third person, thinking, "This is nuts." And so, in the last paragraph, I said, "I did this . . ." and "This is what I want to do." And, it was so refreshing. [3]

Rachel resisted erasing herself and instead claimed her place as the agent of the study, the author of the thesis, and a future clinical psychologist. She was one of ten seniors campuswide to be honored with the Honors Director's Award for Excellent Honors Theses.

In refusing to follow the convention in that instance, Rachel was also reflecting her new confidence in herself as a writer, a confidence she did not have when she entered college. During our first interview, midway through College Writing, she indicated that she enjoyed writing—"the writing I did do [in high school] I enjoyed"—yet did not feel confident about the quality of that writing or about herself in relation to others: "I don't like my writing. I never have. Maybe it's because I compare myself too much to other people." In another exchange during that first interview—one in which she also acknowledged the magnetic draw of writing—I tried to suggest a way that she could acknowledge herself as a writer:

> RACHEL: I write a lot of poetry. . . . It's not anything like Robert Frost or, you know, all those people, but sometimes it's more of a release. Sometimes if I have something on my mind I'll just write. . . . And it's not like anything I want to do—well, I want to do it, but it kind of just happens on purpose.
>
> ANNE: So you *are* a writer.
>
> RACHEL: Not, I don't know, not in the sense that everybody else is in the class.

Even though she enjoyed writing and felt herself drawn to it for personal expression, she did not feel herself to be a writer in comparison to others, even—or most especially—her peers.

By the end of College Writing—having received positive responses from her peers and teacher and having seen her writing in relation to theirs in class publications—Rachel was more confident, or, as she said, "comfortable with writing." She went on to say, though, that she was still wary of making her writing or even her love of it public: "I love writing, and though it's not anything I'd ever consider getting out in the open with, I just like doing it, you know, for my own."

Now, as she talks about working with Dr. Vogel on a manuscript they hope to have published based on her honors thesis research, Rachel is ready to "get out in the open" with her writing, both for herself and for others:

> I feel confident in writing now. I'm interested in doing the research for the writing, and I'm really enjoying this [writing the honors thesis]. I'm even thinking of writing as a future career goal. Sometime, I'd even like to take on writing a book. I *never* would have thought that before. . . . Now, I'm feeling like this is something I can share with people and they'll be interested.

Notes

1. Rachel also spoke of keeping a journal and using it for writing about things that bothered her—again, as a release. Students were asked to keep journals for College Writing—ones they could keep confidential—and Rachel indicated she regularly kept one anyway, trying to write "at least once a week": "Sometimes if I'm feeling a certain way at a given moment, and I don't want to talk to anyone about it, I'll just write it down." She said she often wrote poems in the journal: "It's not anything like Robert Frost or, you know, all those people, but sometimes it's more of a release. Sometimes if I have something on my mind, I'll just write. And sometimes I'll whip out like just a huge poem in just ten or fifteen minutes. And it's not like anything I want to do—well, I want to do it, but it kind of just happens on purpose." Here she speaks to the function of the journal for her as a place to express something she may not want to say to others but needs to "release." Interestingly, also, she feels drawn to this writing in a way she cannot explain. In a final inter-

view during her senior year, she indicated that while she had not been writing as regularly in her journal, she still did so periodically, especially during the summer when she was not in school.

2. This course was designated as one of the Junior Year Writing Program courses available to psychology majors. As such, it satisfied the University's general education requirement that students take a writing-intensive course in their major during their junior year. In this course, attention was given to planning, outlining, and composing case studies. Students wrote four major papers for the course, in addition to preparing formal outlines for these papers. Because the professor kept all the papers and Rachel did not have copies, we did not have access to them.

3. In the summary of her thesis that she submitted for the award, Rachel consistently avoided direct reference to herself or called herself "the researcher"—until the third-to-last paragraph. There, when she writes about trying to publish her study, she refers directly to herself in the first person: "Through close contact with my advisor, who has several publications in related areas, I will work on submitting this thesis for publication in a scholarly journal." She then explains her career plans, again using first person pronouns.

In that interview, we discussed this convention further. Knowing that in Methods Lab Rachel had questioned the injunction not to use first person pronouns, I told her about one of the professional journals in psychology adopting a new policy of allowing first person references. She responded, "Oh wow," and went on to comment on the way that particular conventions can "depersonalize" subjects:

> I think sometimes, not saying "I" depersonalizes a lot of things
> and especially in my field, sometimes it's just talking around
> the situation; it's not getting to the point.

As she said, "It irks me." While she followed the convention in writing her honors proposal and thesis, I do not believe she was passively accommodating herself to it. She has developed her own view of some of the limitations of this convention and has challenged the convention in at least one instance. For these reasons, I think she is in a better position, as she grows into the profession, to negotiate her own style of writing within the psychological forums she will enter and, in so doing, perhaps join with others in changing those conventions.

CHAPTER FIVE

"A BILINGUAL AND SOCIAL STRUGGLE": *Francois*

Like most students I encounter, both Nam and Steven afforded me a functional, comforting, and consistent (though no doubt incomplete) vision. They presented—in their writings, conversations, and appearances—signposts to their identities, points of entry into their "subjective worlds." They shared with me the vantage points from which they thought and expressed their thoughts in writing. And from these shared perspectives I could empathize with them, imparting to them the reassurance that comes with at least a modicum of understanding, the sense that I would do my best to help them express their thoughts more clearly, while at the same time suggesting to them the perspectives that other readers might have and that therefore might need addressing. What happens, however, when a student resists being known? Defies his teacher's understanding and his own intelligibility? Evades identification by all the usual, seemingly innocent social, cultural, and linguistic markers? What happens if a student's subjective world appears to be almost too rich, too diverse? So disparate that he seems willfully to deny membership in any community, refusing to be read as simply a "man speaking to men," just another "human among humans"? What happens when, as a result, a teacher cannot with any confidence read the student or his writing? Cannot gain empathic access to his subjective world? Cannot find stable enough footing to hold a mirror up to his strengths or offer steady guidance through his apparent weaknesses? With Francois, I had to address all these questions. In his initial writings for my class, as in his early interviews with Elizabeth, he presented signposts pointing everywhere and nowhere at once—symbols simultaneously barren of and overflowing with meaning. Reading his essays and listening to his interview responses both reminded me of my childhood games of "follow the dots," but with the numbers missing: any one of a myriad of images might be traced.

I spent the fall term teaching Francois basic writing and conducted interviews with him for this project during his junior year. Throughout his five years at the University, I saw him more than occasionally, when he stopped by my office to seek advice on a paper, ask me for a summer employment recommendation, or just visit. Even after graduating, he called me a couple of times, once to tell me about a new job he had landed and once simply to "check in." Over that time, I came to like him and appreciate him enormously; I have to believe, given his attentiveness, that my appreciation was at least to some degree reciprocated. Yet in many ways, Francois remains for me a mystery—sometimes, I think, purposefully so. He attended my class regularly, participated eagerly, volunteered for our research project, and was good-humoredly respectful both to me and to fellow class members. Yet, as we will see, in his beginning writings he presented me with a nearly endless mix of early promise and later frustration as my quests and requests for greater clarity seemed inevitably to engender increasingly fragmented and disjointed prose. Other teachers reported or intimated similar experiences with him, some finding their frustration intensifying rather than subsiding as the semester progressed: Tim, Francois's College Writing instructor, first characterized him as "a super guy" and "sound writer" with "a neat sense of humor" but two months later reassessed his judgment, reluctantly admitting he did not know "how to respond to this kid" who now seemed to be "flippant and a little wise, a little standoffish," and not to be doing much work at all. Elizabeth, who conducted the bulk of our interviews with Francois as well as our two interviews with Tim, understood. Though Francois had been one of the first to volunteer for our study and remained absolutely faithful to our interview schedule (attending some impromptu group sessions that others did not), he comes across in a number of his interviews as at times sincerely thoughtful but at other times coyly evasive, toying with his questioners. Elizabeth ended up dubbing him, though with obvious fondness in her tone, the "cheerful resister."

Anybody who has taught basic writing, or any required writing course for that matter, has encountered resistant students: students who adamantly refuse to write "what you want to hear"; who insist any lack of clarity in their writing is really a lack of perspicacity in the teacher's reading; or who, in false compliance, make the single change explicitly suggested, but not very well and certainly no more. Sitting in my classroom during his first year, Francois typified these students, and, during his interviews with Elizabeth, he might have been their spokesman. When at the close of his semester in Basic Writing she asked him which papers had brought him most and least satisfaction, he answered:

> I should probably go by what I got on the paper grade-wise. You know, that was an A paper. Okay, then I guess it was the most satisfying. But then again . . . was it really? Was it that you wrote the paper the way that you know the teacher would like it, or the way that people would be a little more understanding? Or is it the fact that it's more readable, you know? And all these things come together and you get an A paper, while it wasn't really you writing the paper. You were just spitting back out what you know he or she wanted to hear. . . .

And when questioned about the teacher's role in the writing/reading process, he responded:

> Well, if you read a piece of literature, then you would just break it down. I want people to do that to my writing. I mean don't just read the writing, what it says, but go behind it. I mean, I might not say things, I might not say things purposely so that I can let the reader's mind work. . . . You might have to read a paper of mine more than once to understand it, not because it's not clear, but because you just need to do a little more than that.

While Francois's first remark echoes many I have heard from other students before and since, his second presses me up against the very wall of my own frustration—and principles. Asking that we read him like a book, not some easily accessible popular piece, but a "piece of literature," replete with what students so often call "hidden meanings," which they and their teachers together work to understand, he asks for neither more nor less than I have asked for Steven and others like him. In this chapter, then, I will try to accede to Francois's wishes, knowing that, as I do, I will make him more intelligible for myself and, in so doing, risk creating my "Francois." But at least I will respect his request and, to that extent, leave his own integrity intact. As his teacher, I sometimes tried to do otherwise, and that, I think, was my error and a source of my frustration as I tried to make Francois make himself intelligible to me. I will also try to show why I have finally come to see this frustration as a response I was experiencing *with* Francois in the full (i.e., contradictory *and* complementary) sense of that phrasing: that is, as a frustration that, at the time, I believed he was causing, intentionally or unintentionally, in me, only later to learn that it was as much *his* frustration I was feeling and, at least in part, causing as well. Finally, I will try to illustrate the ways in which our sharing of this response, even one of frustration, was salutary insofar as the combined emotions of admiration and frustration that I feel even now, as I review his writings some five years later, mark Francois's successful efforts to make me his ally. For despite all apparent evasions, acts of resistance, demands on readers, and distrust of what might make writing "more readable," I think what he wanted was an ally, someone to share, if not in the meanings he made, then in his struggle with meaning making itself.

Background

Francois is a handsome black man. He has the compact frame and wiry build of a gymnast or diver. At the University, he worked out with weights and played rugby. Though it seems he began speaking English more or less exclusively at age eleven, there is only the accent of Boston in his speech and, as our receptionist once remarked when he called on the phone, "He sounds very distinguished." The precise details of his linguistic background remain somewhat unclear to me, and that is not because we failed to ask. What follows is the opening exchange between Elizabeth and him in his first interview for our study:

ELIZABETH: Where were you born, Francois?

FRANCOIS: Oh, boy. I was born.

ELIZABETH: You don't remember where you were born?

FRANCOIS: It's kind of hard for me to say.

ELIZABETH: Do you know where you lived as a child?

Francois: Yes, I lived mostly with my grandparents.

Elizabeth: Uh huh. Were you here in Massachusetts?

FRANCOIS: Um, I was at a distance, a long way.

ELIZABETH: Until you moved here?

FRANCOIS: Yes.

ELIZABETH: When did you move here?

FRANCOIS: Uh, I think I moved with my mom until I was about maybe around twelve.

ELIZABETH: In this area of Massachusetts?

FRANCOIS: Yes. Boston.

ELIZABETH: Was English the only language spoken in your home? Did you speak any other languages?

FRANCOIS: Uh, yes, I speak, not I speak but I hear a combination of French and Spanish.

ELIZABETH: So do you understand when people speak?

FRANCOIS: Yes, I do.

ELIZABETH: But for you, you consider, is English really the language you consider to be your own language?

FRANCOIS: Yes, the only reason is because I'm Americanized, that's why. That's why I consider it, because that's the place that I'm at.

ELIZABETH: Did you ever study in French or Spanish?

FRANCOIS: Yes.

ELIZABETH: You did?

FRANCOIS: Yes.

ELIZABETH: Uh, several years? How many years?

FRANCOIS: A long time.

ELIZABETH: So were you writing in French or Spanish before you started writing in English? Or reading?

FRANCOIS: Yes.

ELIZABETH: So if someone were to ask you your first tongue, or your first mother tongue, which one would you choose? Would it be French or Spanish?

FRANCOIS: It's a combination of both.

ELIZABETH: Combination of both?

FRANCOIS: Yes. I speak equally as well French as I speak Spanish.

To read these lines, one might easily think Francois is being purposely evasive, almost sparring with Elizabeth; to listen to the tape of their discussion is to hear strange sincerity in his voice as he says, "It's kind of hard for me to say."

Only over months and years have I gathered more information about Francois's linguistic and family background. The pieces are difficult to fit—perhaps together, perhaps into the preconceived, undoubtedly race-based picture I have of this young man. In the interview I did with him in his third year, I learned he is the oldest of five children: two sisters are "a year or so younger" than he, and his two brothers are eight and seventeen years younger. The elder of the two brothers was attending school in a Boston suburb, and both sisters had attended college, one completing community college to become a grade school or kindergarten teacher, the other finishing two years of private college before leaving school "because personal things in her life have happened."

Francois himself attended a private junior high school in the Boston area, then attended a suburban public high school. In a paper written for an education course during his senior year, he is explicit about the quality of his early education:

> I began my schooling in a very rich community where the focus was on the quality of the education, rather than race related problems. As a student the issue was always class rather than race. I grew up where the schools were equipped with the best books that money can buy, the excess resources were allocated to the extra curricular activities such as music, theatre and dance classes. In the classrooms, the students behaved and the teachers taught. We never had delinquent behavior problems. If a child had a behavior problem he/she was attended to. If they were deficient in an area of study such as math, he/she was fortified with the resources needed. (Education Final, untitled interview with Jacob McCartny)

As clear as it appears from this passage that Francois began his schooling in a "very rich community," it remains unclear to me still whether he began his life in similar comfort, or whether the school he refers to here was in Boston or "at a distance, a long way." He did not say in the paper, nor did he ever divulge to us exactly where he began his schooling. As a result, I find it difficult to resist imposing my own vision on him, and it dims the image he expresses to me. It may be that, because he is black and I am white, I see him as poorer than he represents himself as being: in his writing difficulties, I see less rich educational experiences than he describes; in the location of his junior and senior high school education—"The outskirts of Dorchester," and later Brighton, towns on Boston's edges not known for their affluence—I see less community wealth and, therefore, less familial wealth.

However, it may also be that Francois purposely toys with my—our—biases. In his second interview with Elizabeth during his term in Basic Writing, he commented on a paper he had written for the course. The paper dealt with Richard Rodriguez's "Aria," a chapter from Rodriguez's *Hunger of Memory,* and Francois's comments were these:

> [Rodriguez] lived in a Spanish neighborhood, right? Pretty much everyone was Hispanic, and he would go home to his parents, and to me the biggest problem that was there was the fact that they couldn't speak English. And he wanted to get away from the parents. I mean not so much get away from the parents but be able to speak English and associate with the Americans, quote unquote, the other side of the street. And for me that's not really a struggle. . . . That's just things you live with. For me, I mean, it wasn't that I couldn't speak English; that didn't bother me, because I knew that would come in time. I mean that, that really wasn't a bother or problem for me. Instead of going home to a set of parents I would go home to my mom and then my stepdad, and have to watch out after my sisters. You know, I think that's a little more down to earth, and a little more realistic than the struggle to speak English.

While sharing Rodriguez's linguistic background, Francois could not or would not share in the "struggle" that writer defined: it was not "realistic." Elaborating, he implies that he speaks possibly from experience or possibly from empathy when he insists that language is not the primary concern of the disenfranchised:

ELIZABETH: When you were writing this [Rodriguez] paper, who did you see as your audience?

FRANCOIS: Who did I see? Not the minorities, because I think minorities could have written a better paper, not the same kind of paper, than I wrote and what Rodriguez wrote. So I wanted to get the audience that never had an experience like that, try to let them know that it's not easy. And at the same time I wanted to get to the people that agreed with [Rodriguez]. I wanted to tell them, "Hey, this guy said he had a rough time but that's not so true. You know, there's a lot of us around that things didn't go that way. A lot of us had to think if we were going to eat today or not. All of us didn't go home and say, 'I'm doing my homework, but damn, can't speak English. That really bothers me.' All of us didn't think of that. We thought of surviving."

ELIZABETH: Surviving?

FRANCOIS: Knowing that you're going to eat today, or tomorrow, and hopefully that you live the next day, you know. I mean he didn't talk . . . and that didn't seem much of a struggle. To me it seemed that his major problems were English. That's what he emphasized. Throughout the entire paper I thought that was really a bummer.

"As a student the issue was always class rather than race" for Francois, and here we may be witnessing his reach beyond class bounds to empathize imaginatively with those of his own linguistic and racial backgrounds for whom living, not speaking, is a struggle. We may be witnessing, too, a simultaneous disengagement from those Francois sees himself standing *among* but not *of*, from the "minorities [who] could have written a better paper . . . than I wrote." Or this may be the straight talk of experience from one who had to "think if we were going to eat today or not." Or it may be the very real confusion, and dislocation, of an individual who had just recently found himself defined—marked as "black minority"—by the color of his skin, who would write in a later essay that it was not until adolescence that "I realized that my skin color was starting to be a factor in my new society. This society unlike my last society takes notice of your skin." I still do not know which interpretation is closest to Francois's truth. But I do know that class as well as race would both remain defining issues for Francois throughout his five years at the University.

Essays for Basic Writing

When for their first essay in Basic Writing other class members chose a photograph from the *Newsweek* "Life in America" series, Francois selected instead as the basis of his essay a Victorian-era woodcut or pen-and-ink drawing reprinted in one of his textbooks. I had offered the students the *Newsweek* series to select from because it drew its images from the breadth of United States communities and cultures, and promised to reflect, in one instance or another, most class members' interests if not, indeed, their experiences. I had hoped, in short, to close the gap between "art" and life, between public expression and personal experience. Francois's choice seemed to widen it deliberately—even, according to Francois himself, to represent it. The reprint depicted in the foreground a man and woman sitting upon a stage, the two sipping from champagne glasses, the man gaily toasting his companion. The background of the piece was the stage backdrop, a countryside scene of a hilly glade and running brook. A third figure, a woman, stood behind the others. Here is Francois's initial rendition of the assignment that asked him first to describe and then to interpret the visual text.

[Untitled]

This picture is of a social gathering with a man drinking some form of alcohol. Around him there are two women which seem to be the center of his attention. The stage on which they are standing has a big black curtain, which opens to a view of a green grass land, trees and a stream.

This picture represents [the final *s* was added by hand] a problem that we face in our society today. Many people in society often consume to much alcohol and are enable to control themselves. The view in the background represents [again, the final *s* was added] the purity of nature depicted by the running stream of water.

It interests [*s* added] me that a picture created so long ago, can still have some meaning and is [*is* added by hand] relevant to the drinking problem we have today. However, nature is still pure unless of course man kind ruins it.

The idea of man <u>vs</u> nature is well illustrated in this picture. the younger of the women is not drinking she appears to be pure because she is dressed in white, nice combed hair. she

appears like an angel in the picture.(the rescuer) She came from
the painting to purify the drunks from the evil alcohol.

As I read this essay, I was baffled by it, and not with the same
confusion I often experience upon encountering student essays
but with a much more nagging perplexity. Within the context of
basic writing, nothing marks Francois's writing here as what might
be called, using Bizzell's term, "outlandish" ("What Happens"
164).To the contrary, I found it a highly suggestive and promising rough draft. And that was the starting place of my frustration.

Focusing on his selected artwork reprint, Francois had ush-
ered me into a world of pictorial and literary convention; describing that reprint, he had laid before me all the familiar elements
of an intriguing interpretive piece. Though wanting further development, some relatively minor reorganization, and more explicit connection among its various particulars, it signaled an
inescapable, albeit inchoate, message: the drawing represents
humanity's separation from nature both through the action depicted and by the setting in which the action takes place; alcohol
use and abuse is one instance of humanity's fall from a pure and
natural state; two of the characters pictured here are not *in* nature but rather are on a stage set *against* a background representing nature; and a third character crosses between the two worlds,
beckoning the drinkers out of the impure world at once created
and symbolized by alcohol, back to nature's purity. So far
Francois's writing had provided a sort of imagistic vocabulary;
my reading, the syntax of what I thought to be his tale. Through
questions and suggestions, written and spoken, I prodded him to
explicate the connections among ideas he intimated were linked,
to formulate for readers his own cognitive steps, which I believed
I now retraced. I did not respond to Francois's essay by demonstrating in any concrete fashion ways to construct those missing
stepping stones of thought. Today I might have even written out
a paragraph of my own, modeling ways to give coherence to his
fragmentary piece. But then I feared forcing Francois to echo my
notions or model himself on my forms, and so instead appealed
to the writerly image he presented to me, advising in what now
seems to me too-complicated language of my own that he sim-

plify his forms and pin his interpretations to a fuller, more solid foundation of observation. After noting what I read to be his two principal ideas—the evil of alcohol and "man versus nature"—and his suggestive metaphor of the "rescuer" as a mediating, potentially redemptive link between fallen humanity and pure nature, I concluded my comments, written late in the revising process, with this question:

> What would happen if you made that paragraph part of the first paragraph of your paper, describing the picture as fully as possible and then beginning to interpret the different parts of it for us? It would make everything easier for your reader to see, I think, and probably easier for you to explain. Try starting with your observations. Give as much information as you can about what you see, and then explain to your readers in very <u>simple</u> terms what meaning you want them to understand from the picture. You have extremely sophisticated ideas, Francois. We just need to organize your writing in a way that can contain them all. Keep up the good thinking!

"We *just* need to organize your writing in a way that can contain" all your disparate ideas! So easy to say, and yet helping students develop this type of organizational strategy—this essential technique of moving back and forth between summary or observation and interpretation, as required in traditional academic writing—is so difficult to do, especially when, for those like Francois, as I ultimately discovered, it is a matter not just of crossing cognitive bridges but of building them, and of decoding a vocabulary of conventional motifs so foreign to him, so familiar to me. We worked on revising this essay through a number of class hours; Francois, I presume, worked additional hours alone. This is his final draft:

MAN vs NATURE

This picture is a social with a man drinking some form of alcohl.Around him there two women which seem to be the center of attention(think of a beer commercial)., this picture represent a problem that we are facing today.alcohol drinkers in our society often consume to much alcohol and are enable to control themselves. The stage on which they are standing has a big black curting, which opens to a view of a green grass land, trees and a running stream. The view in the background represents the purity of nature depicted by the running stream of water.

It interests me that a picture created so long ago, can still have some meaning and relevant to the drinking problem we have today. However, nature is still pure unless of course man kind ruins it

The idea of man VS nature is well illustrated in this picture. The younger of the two women is not drinking she appear to be pure because she is dressed in white, nice combed hair. She appears like an angel in the picrure (the rescuer) She came to save them fom the devil (alcohol) her trail seem to have come from the painting to purify the drunks from the evilness of alcohol.

The different meaning of this picture is definitely not clear. The photographer have his readers, and viewers interpreting his picture in all direction, the posibilities are wild. The picture might as well be different, or difficult to explain because after all life is not easy to explain either The love and loyalty the two women show for the man is perhaps the virtue of this picture.

The spelling had deteriorated, the syntax had disintegrated, and despite—or perhaps because of—all my vain attempts to move Francois toward some explicit connection between his two principal themes of alcohol abuse and alienation from nature, he had broadcast even more fragmentary thoughts from a still-weaker center. My insinuations that his draft lacked clarity met firm agreement: "The different meaning of this picture is definitely not clear." A third possible theme, added for good measure, proved the case: "The photographer have his readers, and viewers interpreting his picture in all direction, the posibilities are wild. . . . The love and loyalty the two women show for the man is perhaps the virtue of this picture." Like some crazed cuckoo raised from the ashes of a phoenix, this was the truly outlandish essay I had helped him create out of a hopeful draft.

Four years later, in an interview with me in which we discussed his overall writing progress, Francois helped me understand that, in the fall of 1989, he was missing precisely the sort of mediator I urged him to provide for readers—even (as I know now) before he apprehended it himself. He described it as a missing "third piece to a triangle," using a metaphor much like the metaphoric angel he had posited in "MAN vs NATURE":

> In high school . . . I did book reports or summarizing, or something completely different such as [giving] my own personal opinion. So there were two different kinds of writing: I either summarized, regurgitated something that I read, or I talked about something completely different which may or may not have been abstract. So there was never the connection in how I was to write something to present it out to people. In a way, I was missing the third piece to a triangle. I could do that; I could do this. But I couldn't send them in the direction where they would eventually meet.

Unable to provide the "third piece to a triangle" linking summary and interpretation, Francois could neither concretize nor contextualize crucial abstract notions at the heart of his essay. Instead he condensed those abstract notions into their own concrete, metaphoric forms, into replicas of the original images he had set out to interpret, as in, for example, the "younger of the two women," who "appears like an angel in the picture": "her trail seem to have come from the painting to purify the drunks from the evilness of alcohol." His later explanation made it clear that the difficulties and disappointments we each experienced with "MAN vs NATURE" were matters not of Francois's resistance—or not of willful resistance alone, at any rate—but of his lack of training in writing or, perhaps, the ineluctable course of cognitive development. At the time, however, I could not—or would not—see them as such, perhaps because our discussions of his writings were then often as dizzying as the writings themselves. Elizabeth seems to have felt the impact when, during her initial interview with Francois, he offered this commentary:

> FRANCOIS: So I took a picture, an old picture from my history book. And I described that. And, uh, it didn't really have, I didn't really have like, I didn't go out and pick out that particular picture. I just opened the book and I picked the picture. And there was this picture with what seems to be a couple, and, from a distance, another woman that's dressed very differently. Or more conservatively than the other two.

And behind them was a painting of a landscape and a
stream, or a river, a stream I believe. That ran down, you
know, to the bottom of the picture. And, and you know there
was alcohol on a small round table on your right, you know,
on their right, uh, they were drinking and the background of
the landscape and the stream coming down was a painting,
'cause you can see the curtains on the sides of it. And I just
talked about that. I started out with the basics, said they
were drinking, they were dressed, they looked very dressed
for the time period that they were in. Uh, it could have been
a social gathering, I said that, uh, and I uh, I decided to talk
about the alcohol they were drinking. And I just said that uh,
the guy, I made up the idea that the guy was drunk, you
know, they had a lot of liquor on the table and they were
drinking it, and the woman that was standing with the guy
was . . . she seemed to be like pulling him back in, while the
guy's reaching out for the other woman that's dressed in a
long white dress, you know. And she had her hands together.
And I just went to the idea that some alcohol was what I was
narrowing down to. I don't know if she got that, but that's
what I doing. . . .

ELIZABETH: She?

FRANCOIS: Marcia.

ELIZABETH: Oh I see.

FRANCOIS: [I don't know] if Marcia got the idea that that's what I
was narrowing down to. And I just said that alcohol was the
killer, and the main frame of the picture, and the other
woman, that's dressed all in white, you know, taking something from the imagery, that white was pure and, you know.
And I just said that she was like an angel coming from the
background of the painting, coming to, to the rescue. So . . .

ELIZABETH: So, that was the point you were trying to get across. . . .

FRANCOIS: Alcohol is bad and this man versus society I believe I
said somewhere within the writing. And you know, nature
versus society. That's what I said. And uh, all I said is like,
the alcohol was killing them, while the other lady that's all in
white, you know, respectably dressed, very conservatively,
seems to be coming from the picture, from the picture that's
in the back, coming out, you know like an angel. And it all
seem to be telling them, "Don't drink, don't do this, don't do
that." And it's, I mean I say that, 'cause that's what the guy
did a little bit too much of.

ELIZABETH: Really? So nature versus society?

FRANCOIS: Nature being the painting, and the woman in the back, you know, that's all nature, and the beautiful picture of the landscape in the back. And society was the two, the drink, what goes on in everyday society, people drink at social gatherings, and both of them was coming together. Not like a battle but they were coming together.

ELIZABETH: In that one photo?

FRANCOIS: Yeah.

Later in the same interview, Elizabeth asked Francois which of the essays he had written for Basic Writing left him least satisfied. He answered "MAN vs NATURE": "I enjoyed working on it, but I guess it came out dissatisfied." And it was when Elizabeth pressed him for further comment that he moved into his distrust of the A grade and his suspicion that "all these things come together and you get an A paper, while it wasn't really you writing the paper. You were just spitting back out what you know he or she wanted to hear. . . ."

I find it quite remarkable that these particular statements were occasioned by this particular essay and discussion of Francois's dissatisfaction with it. I would not have considered it an A paper, nor could I have believed at the time that Francois had "spit out" what I wanted to hear. Yet again his remarks provide a key to our mutual frustration and to what I have since come to see as my own resistance. In the same way that in his attempts to interpret the original sketch behind "MAN vs NATURE" he had created metaphoric replicas of its various images, he had also created a similarly strange sort of replica of an "academic" essay. Beguiled by this promising and, at the same time, wildly skewed mimicry of literary analysis, I had failed to recognize the full significance of its distortions. As I look back now, I believe Francois was doing what he set out to do: By expressing himself in the discourse of literature as he had heard it to be, he was creating himself in the elusive image of literature that such discourse fashions. He was creating himself, that is, in the image of "a piece of literature," which, for most high school students, has little presence apart from the discourse surrounding it and which, according to that discourse, "you would just break down . . . and . . . have to read more than once," as I certainly had to read Francois now, "not because it's not clear, but because you just need to do a little more than that." I also believe, however, that in doing what he set out to do, Francois simultaneously did precisely what he set out *not* to do: echoing critical discourse, he was falsifying himself. It wasn't really him writing the paper. Francois was, in fact, "just spitting back" what he could of what I wanted to hear—even if I had not come to his first draft with the intention of listening for it myself. As I was retracing his untaken steps through the revising process, he was, in short, simultaneously tracing mine, as we both tracked—in our own clumsy ways—some obscure form of literary critique. Our shadow dance left at least two of the three—Francois, his essay, and me—deeply "dissatisfied."

As we moved through the term, my frustration with Francois surfaced and intensified. His drafts, my comments, and Elizabeth's interview transcripts all show how wide the divide can be between a teacher's and a student's understanding. And at times I believed Francois consciously widened that divide with my every attempt to cross it. He sat before me a mystery. I simply could not read him. In a further complication, I was no longer sure by midsemester whether the problem was mine or his. If it was his, I could not tell whether it was a problem of intention, unintention, or inattention. I could not tell, that is, whether he lacked all understanding of an essay's basic form and function, or whether he purposely played against all forms imposed upon—even suggested to—him. I could not tell whether he wrote with intentional obscurity, or whether—as a result of some learning disability, psychic disturbance, language interference, or educational failing—he was unable to transcribe his thoughts with any greater clarity.

I was failing and frustrating Francois, too. He wanted to be read like a book; I agreed he should be read like a book. I acknowledged the flashes of beauty and insight that his phrasings did indeed hold, while at the same time I encouraged him to abandon his own elusive, artful style for a more directly accessible prose. In matters of understanding, I took care to suggest that deficiencies and failures were faults of reception, belonging to Francois's audience, and that the power to overcome these deficiencies resided with him. Yet I was proving both a bad and a demanding reader. Despite my conscious efforts in conversation as well as in written comments to make us allies in the composing process, I think my questions said we were not: I was not understanding him; I was reading but making little or no effort to comprehend. I was another one of those people he described to Elizabeth, who

> don't find my writing comfortable because they look at it and go, "Why do you think that way?" There's nothing wrong with the way they think; it's just that they're so—they're just looking at things too straight. They can't look to the side, or look up or down, so they don't get to see things different, I guess. And when sometime, when I get that across in my paper, people say, "You know, that's just, that's just not what we want, that's just not what the writer's trying to say. Maybe you're going too far with that." . . . And people think that I'm totally crazy.

From his interview comments it is clear that Francois wanted to be understood, or, perhaps more to the point, to be shown he was worth the effort it took to understand him. As he and Elizabeth pondered my particular responses to his writing, he evinced genuine uncertainty, the same sort of uncertainty I heard when, earlier in the same interview, he declared it "kind of hard for me to say" where he was born:

> FRANCOIS: See, that's what sometime I don't know. I don't know how basic I should be. I mean, I can go as far as saying, "I'm this, I'm that," you know, and describing exactly step by step what I'm going to say, but I have to figure that the reader has some kind of common sense, that they understand. You know, I mean I can't assume, that's true, but I have to have some sense that some things that I'm going to say is going to strike off something to make them think.

> ELIZABETH: To make the reader think?

> FRANCOIS: Yeah, to make the reader think what exactly I'm trying to say. You know, I don't want, I don't want someone to just read something and just go, 'Blank, blank, blank.' You know, just because, you know, I don't know.

> ELIZABETH: Blank, blank, blank?

Even within uncertainty, however, there is another complication, another ambiguity, not so much of terms but within Francois's unfolding logic. He wants to say just enough to his readers to "make them think," but not, as it turns out, to make them think their own thoughts or entertain their own associations. He wants to say only enough "to make the reader think what exactly I'm trying to say." That, it seems to me, is a load of reader response he is asking for, but to Francois it is just a matter of "some kind of common sense"—and imaginative exertion.

> ELIZABETH: Blank, blank, blank? . . . [I]t sounds like for you you make that choice, you make a choice to not give it all.
>
> FRANCOIS: Yeah. I think, because I mean, if I write a note to my little baby brother, I can be really, I can just break things down, but I don't think I have to do that for people to read my papers. Even, I mean, if that what is required or necessary for me to get a grade, you know, I mean to get a good grade, I'll do that, I don't have a problem with that. But then again, I want to enjoy the course as I would if I didn't do that. I mean I can just go to the basics and go through the motions and stuff, I don't have a problem with that. But how much would I enjoy the class? You know, after the semester ends I'll just go, "It's just another class that I took." And you know what I mean? So, and I really don't want it to be that, because I think every class I take I should make the best out of it.

Francois seems to recuperate from doubt as readily as he slips into it, and so the failure of understanding shifts back again from the "flaws in my writing" to "people" who need meaning broken down, who need Francois to "go to the basics" the way his little baby brother might. Reading his interview now, I see Francois presenting himself as a writer working on his craft, refusing to "just go to the basics" or "go through the motions," and refusing just as adamantly to "go through the motions" as a student, to let my class become "just another class" he took. He is determined instead to "make the best out of" my course, and, as a teacher, I respect his intentions. I regret his need to apply these intentions to my course, a course he needed to transform and not simply "take." Yet along with regret, I cannot but admit a sense of frustration, too, even perhaps a sense of the ludicrous, and for that as a teacher I feel shame as well. The bald truth is that when I hold Francois's writings up against his reflections on them, I see a discrepancy between what is there and what is described, between what is communicated and what is represented as craft—a discrepancy approaching the absurd. And I see all my efforts to bolster Francois's confidence as my participation in—my promotion of—his absurdist fantasy. This is not the way I want to see my students or myself, and the reflected vision of both of us is deeply unsettling. That, I believe, was Francois's uncanny ability to induce in me an embarrassed honesty even by his own insistent denial. The simple fact was, I did see Francois as a "basic" writer, despite all my efforts to deny it.

Francois knew I saw him—the University saw him—as a "basic" writer, and, while he did not like that image, while he purposefully denied it, he would not let any of us forget it. He put it before us directly or obliquely fourteen times in his first interview. That is, fourteen times in his first one-hour interview, Francois used the term "basic," "basics," or "basically" in various phrasings: for example, "I started out with the basics, said they were drinking, they were dressed"; "I don't know how basic I should be"; "It just, it's just letting your mind go free, instead of just reading it, and just getting the basic things out of it"; and "I got really basic, because I didn't think people would understand what I'm, what they mean, what the words mean." Why? The answer may be . . . basic. Unfortunately, like many, many other students consigned to basic writing, Francois was, as I suspected, shamed by his consignment. Four years later, he looked differently on his enrollment in the course but, in doing so, offered at least a glimpse into his original disappointment:

> I'm happy I took 111 [Basic Writing]. I know looking back now that I needed to take 111. Entering 111, I was not happy. Entering 111, I don't think anyone is happy, because you're given the opportunity, the chance to take an exam. And the administration tells you that you're not qualified or you're not up to par or up to standards to enter the University writing level. So I was not happy.

During those early weeks of 111, I think he might well have interpreted my comments in the light of his placement in Basic Writing and so resisted them in particular in the same way he resisted his placement in general. As a result, we both paid the price of his placement. We can, however, also interpret the question "Why did Francois perseverate so on the term 'basic'?" another way. That is, why did he locate and condense his disappointment in a single word?

I have neither the insights nor the expertise to suggest an answer. I can, however, suggest a similarity between this sort of condensation of meaning and those earlier instances of his condensing all meaning in, for example, the concrete image of nature's maid in "MAN vs NATURE." In a way, these words and images seem to have been for him filled with their own opaque meaning but unavailable for any sort of communicable, expressible significance that might be abstracted from them. And he clung to them in all their materiality. "Interpret" provides as much an anchor to Francois's thought line in this first interview as "basic," though in almost every one of the fifteen occasions it appears the sense is positive, because, it seems, as much as "basic" connoted restriction, "interpret" conveyed a sense of freedom. It came, of course, from the central motif of the class itself—observation and interpretation—but apparently carried a personal meaning for Francois, as no other student interviewed used the term with any such frequency:

ELIZABETH: When Marcia talks about making meaning, or observation and interpretation—

FRANCOIS: Oh, I find that fascinating.

ELIZABETH: You do?

FRANCOIS: Yeah. 'Cause I always have a different, a different perspective on things.

ELIZABETH: A different perspective?

FRANCOIS: On how the thing, or the piece of writing should be interpreted. You know, I don't—that's why I guess I'm having a lot of fun with my writing, because I'm taking all these difficult routes, you know what I mean? I just, I just should look at what it is, but most of time I tend to look at it the other way. 'Cause it's, it's more fun to look at things the other way. It's more fascinating than to just read it and just say, "Okay, it meant this, it meant that," and nothing more, while you can take another way of looking at it. It's just, it's just letting your mind go free, instead of just reading it, and just getting the basic things out of it.

In many ways, a midsemester essay entitled "BLIND-INNO-CENT-PREJUDICE" became for me the opaque, unyielding image of Francois's will to interpret a piece of writing in just this way, and of his resistance to all things "basic" as well as his tendency to perseverate on certain terms. That essay became, too, the nadir of my frustration.

For this assignment, in responding to a written text (either of two short stories read in class), students were free to use the text as a prompt for an essay based on their own experiences or as the subject of a more directly interpretive piece. As we have seen, Steven elected to use Sophronia Liu's "So Tsi-fai" as a pretext for his own experiential reflections on suicide; Francois, on the other hand, chose to gloss "The Stolen Party," Liliana Heker's tale of a young working-class girl humiliated at the hands of her mother's employer. Although I watched him compose a series of drafts in class, I will include here, exactly as it appeared, only the one he finally submitted:

> SENORA: the misses, the owner or woman of the house.
> ACCORDING TO WEBSTERS DICTIONARY ONE WAY TO INTERPRETED THE WORD MONKEY IS : slang:a person who is mocked duped, or make to appear a fool.
> BLIND-INNOCENT-PREJUDICE
> THE "STOLEN PARTY" IS ABOUT THIS GIRL NAME ROSAURO. SHE GOT INVITED TO HER FRIEND PARTY LUCIANA. LUCIANA'S MOTHER SENORA INES IS THE EMPLOYER OF ROSAURO'S MOTHER. ROSAURO WANTED TO GO THE PARTY BECAUSE LUCIANA WAS HER BEST FRIEND ,AND ROSAURO WANTED TO SEE WHAT A REAL MONKEY LOOKS LIKE.
> DID THE MAGICIAN TURN ROSAURO INTO THE MONKEY(FOOL)? "YOU WITH THE SPANISH EYES" POINTING AT ROSAURO. THE MAGICIAN BEGINS WITHIN A FEW WORDS THAT HE UTTERED HIS TRICK HAD BEGIN AND HE MADE THE MONKEY DISAPPEAR AND REAPPEARED, SHE WASN'T EVEN AFFRAID OF WHAT WAS GOING TO HAPPEN.WHEN THE MAGIC WAS OVER THE MAGICIAN SAYS A FEWS WORDS OVER HER HEAD AND SAID THANK YOU MY COUNTESS. WHAT WERE THOSE FEW MAGIC WORDS THAT THE MAGICIAN UTTERED OVER ROSAURO'S HEAD. DID HE TURN HER INTO A MONKEY OR A COUNTESS

AT THE PARTY ROSAURO THOUGHT SHE FITED RIGHT IN ,EVEN AFTER SHE MET LUCIANA COUSIN. LUCIANA'S COUSIN ASKED HER "WHO ARE YOU?" "DO YOU GO TO THE SAME SCHOOL AS WE DO?" ROSAURO ANSWER "NO." LUCIANA COUSIN RESPONDED "THEN YOU'RE NOT OUR FRIEND" . AFTER SUCH A CON-FRONTATION SHE STAYED AT THE PARTY AND SERVED LIKE A SERVANT, meaning: SHE INHERITED THE SKILLS OF HER MOTHER A SERVANT BY BEING HELPFUL, LIKE WALKING FROM THE KITCHEN TO THE LIVING ROOM WITH OUT DROPPING A DROP OF ORANGE JUICE FROM A JUG, AND SERVING THE CAKE WITHOUT MAKING A MESS.
point 1
"I AM THE DAUGHTER OF AN EMPLOYEE" ROSAURO SAYS.AND "I AM PROUD OF IT." SHE FOOL HERSELF AGAIN. THE PARTY FOR THE RICHES WAS NOT FOR ROSAURO, SIMPLY BECAUSE SHE WASN'T RICH, BUT SHE GOES ON SAYING THINGS LIKE I AM THE DAUGHTER OF AN EMPLOYEE, BUT TO HERSELF SHE DARES NOT TO SAY SOMETHING OF THAT SORT.
point 2
THROUGHT OUT THE ENTIRE PARTY ROSAURO FOOLED HERSELF WITH ALL OF THE COMPLEMENT SENORA INES HAS BEEN MAKING TO HER. "HOW LOVELY YOU LOOK TODAY". SHE GRANTED ROSAURO WITH CERTAIN PRIVILEGES LIKE GOING INTO THE KITCHEN SO SHE CAN BRING OUT A JUG OF JUICE FOR THE GUESS AT THE PARTY. ROSAURA STILL DIDN'T GET THE HINT WHEN THE GIRL WITH THE BOW WANTED TO KNOW "WHAT KIND OF A EMPLOYEE'S DAUGH-TER WAS ARE YOU" SENORA INES CAME AND TOLD THE GIRL WITH THE BOW TO "shh shh" (meaning WE DON'T WANT EVERY ONE TO KNOW THAT THE DAUGHTER OF AN EMPLOYEE IS AT THE PARTY.) SHE ASK ROSAURO TO GO IN THE KITCHEN AND SERVE THE HOT DOGS, SHE ONCE AGAIN FEEL LIKE THAT IT'S AN OTHER PRIVELEGE THE KIDS DON'T HAVE.

THE PARTY CAME TO AN END, "THE GUESTS" ARE NOW LEAVING, BUT (the servant) ROSAURO DIDN'T LEAVE YET. SHE WAITED FOR HER MOTHER TO COME AND PICK HER UP.HER MOTHER FINALY CAME SE-NORA INES COMPLEMENTED HER ON HER DAUGH-TER "what a wonderful daughter you have" (meaning she is just like you a perfect servant)all THE OTHER CHILDREN RECEIVE A TOY TO THANK THEM FOR COMING TO

THE PARTY. ROSAURO ON THE OTHER HAND RECEIVE
"thanks for all your help my pet" and gave her two bills.

Within this shower of figures, insights maddeningly flash and just as maddeningly fade. To make them more visible, I will provide as a background the opening paragraphs from another student's essay, which I ultimately gave Francois to illustrate the sort of grounding summary his rendition lacked:

STEALING DREAMS
Liliana Heker's, The Stolen Party, is a portrayal of the class struggle. It has a young girl named Rosaura as the protagonist, she is the daughter of the maid to a very rich house. She is idealistic, showing the natural traits of her youth, bright, and intelligent. Against her are the forces of a very old tradition of class distinction, embodied in her mothers employer, who is also the mother of her friend, Luciana. Luciana is about to have a birthday party to which Rosaura has been invited. Before the party her mother tries to warn Rosaura, knowing, or maybe just sensing why Rosaura has been invited. "That one's not your friend. You know what you are to them? The maid's daughter, that's what." Her mother is trying to tell her that she has been invited because she is the maids daughter. . . . Rosaura in her infinite wisdom just yells back that her mother knows nothing.
The party eventually comes and Rosaura goes to it pristinely in her Sunday dress. At the party she plays the little helper assuming that she was elevated to this position because she was liked the best. She helps everyone including the magician, with his monkey. She has great fun in her important positions, and she carries herself like a princess. As the party winds down the children begin to leave with their mothers. Boys received a yo-yo on the way out, girls received a bracelet, and when Rosaura is on the way out she receives, money.

Francois's peer reviewers—Nam and Steven—knew Heker's story. In his review of an earlier but similarly obscure draft, Nam seems to have retreated from any helpful commentary. He completed his review sheet thus:

1. *As I read your essay, I hear you say* "Rosauro thought she was treated as a good little girl, but (later) she realized she was treated as a servant, a lower people."

2. *As I read your essay, I almost hear you say* "good enough: well explaination."
3. *In order to hear your message more clearly, I would need [you] to* "good."

Steven, on the other hand, goes directly to issues that, as we will see, I required many more words to describe:

1. *As I read your essay, I hear you say* "that Rosaura is made to be the fool."
2. *As I read your essay, I almost hear you say* "that it didn't really bother her that she was the maid and that maybe she was so happy about being at the party that she was blinded by her happiness."
3. *In order to hear your message more clearly, I would need [you] to* "explain more about the monkey and give more characteristics as to why the monkey may symbolize Rosaura's stupidity."

Like Steven, I found—and still find—myself intrigued by Francois's hints at the child's complicity in her own humiliation and by his reading of the monkey as a central motif. And, again like Steven, to achieve even the most tenuous grasp on Francois's meaning, I needed for him to explain his perception of the monkey's thematic role in Heker's narrative in terms of its symbolic association with the duped Rosaura. I needed, in other words, for him to integrate the crucial terms of his interpretation—"the word monkey" and apparently also "senora"—with his interpretation itself, literally to bring those terms down into the essay frame. Throughout the course of manifold revisions—really, various scramblings and rescramblings—I witnessed instead what appeared to be a deliberate and incremental disintegration of structure at every level: "senora" and "monkey" appeared defined variously at the top and bottom of the essay; paragraphs were separated by varying spaces; "points" were inserted at two paragraph breaks; and an early paragraph giving some sense of the plotline and Francois's reading of it was intentionally dropped. Yet ultimately he did manage to (de)construct an interpretive piece containing—perhaps less "containing" than intimating—nearly everything one could say about "The Stolen Party," though in what I have come to call "Francoisspeak" or simply "francois," that is, in a language resisting communication and a language lesson in which the vocabulary listed at the start offered essential terms removed from the subsequent text. I responded to his fifth draft in writing, as follows:

> Again I say to you, Francois: "You have so many insights, and the insights you have are so piercing and sharp." But still I also say to you: "I need your help understanding them. I try to grasp them, but the sentences they come in flash ideas at me, then fly away." I need you to stay with a single idea longer, to explain it slowly and carefully to me, as though you were a patient teacher and I were a student coming to you for help. When you write and I read, you are the teacher, and I am the student. Think of us that way.
>
> In one of your early drafts—the one on which you wrote "Summarize the entire story. The basics"—you do help us begin to understand your interpretation because you give us the meaning of the monkey right at the start: "As a child you can probably be fooled easily, especially if you want to be fooled." And on page 2 of that draft, you give us two points where Rosaura wanted to be fooled and was fooled.
>
> Now what we need is a careful explanation of just how the monkey and the magician help make the image of Rosaura's foolishness even clearer in the story. They are part of the story itself; they are also part of your meaning. Can you explain how they connect the two—story and meaning, i.e. that people can be fooled, especially when they want to be?
>
> If we look at your final essay itself, I think you'll see that I need help just where Lawrence said he needed help: understanding the monkey and why a monkey symbolizes Rosaura—or why Rosaura is a monkey. You've taken out the explanation at the beginning that helps us understand your meaning, instead of connecting your meaning to the monkey. We readers now get confused because this is a very complex idea, and it comes to us in separate pieces—the monkey appears in the first paragraph, then in the third, then disappears altogether. (Unless it reappears in another form, the form of "my pet," in your last line. But you need to help us make that connection—not leave us to make it on our own.) Please give us back the meaning—Rosaura is being made a fool when she thinks she's being a countess—and keep reminding us of the meaning until we fully understand.
>
> Why don't we talk about this on Friday after class, Francois, so we can really understand each other. I want those insights you flash in front of me.
>
> Marcia

Claim or Question (clear and significant)—2
Development (germane to claim and sufficient)—1
Organization (satisfying to established reader expectations)—1
Sentence Structure (effective as well as correct)—1

Total (out of possible 8 points)—5

In truth, I did and still do admire the bright moments of insight and style—"Did the magician turn Rosaura into the monkey (fool)? 'You with the Spanish eyes,' pointing at Rosaura"—that lighten Francois's writings in a manner I seldom see in more determinedly communicative prose from first-year students. And I hoped he might maintain them, though I also believed that even if Francois was not intentionally obscuring his thoughts, he was certainly making little attempt to clarify them for his readers. It seems too easy to me now to dismiss his obscurity as simple ideas dressed up in fancy language or as confusion masquerading as complexity. I believe Francois, like most of us, was struggling with something harder than that: with the really fundamental issue of what he would make of himself and what his readers would make of him—a monkey or a count?—through the few magic words of his writing. And so I believe his interpretation of Rosaura's struggle details his own struggle to compose that interpretation. I gave it these words in the fall of 1989: "[The monkey and magician] are part of the story itself; they are also part of your meaning. Can you explain how they connect the two—the story and meaning?" In the fall of 1993, Francois gave it these: "In high school . . . I did . . . summarizing or something completely different such as [giving] my own personal opinion. . . . So there was never the connection." It was a struggle, then, of skill and practice. But it was also a struggle of literal self-expression: the very same magical acts and words that might have transformed Rosaura into a countess exposed her as a monkey and fool, and Francois was not about to let that happen to him.

Words are slippery business. Sometimes the power over them stays with the speaker/writer. But sometimes, as we've seen Francois say over again in all sorts of ways, the power goes to the listener/reader, and, to the listener/reader, words do not always signify what the writer/speaker meant them to signify. So, as in the following excerpts, Francois meant to pin down crucial words without becoming pinned down by them:

> AFTER SUCH A CONFRONTATION SHE STAYED AT THE PARTY AND SERVED LIKE A SERVANT, meaning: SHE INHERITED THE SKILLS OF HER MOTHER A SERVANT BY BEING HELPFUL, LIKE WALKING FROM THE KITCHEN TO THE LIVING ROOM WITH OUT DROPPING A DROP OF ORANGE JUICE FROM A JUG, AND SERVING THE CAKE WITHOUT MAKING A MESS

> SENORA INES CAME AND TOLD THE GIRL WITH THE BOW TO "shh shh" (meaning WE DON'T WANT EVERY ONE TO KNOW THAT THE DAUGHTER OF AN EMPLOYEE IS AT THE PARTY)

> "what a wonderful daughter you have" (meaning she is just like you a perfect servant).

Or, as Francois explained afterwards:

> FRANCOIS: I got really basic, because I didn't think people would understand what I'm—what they mean, what the words mean, or another translation of what the word can mean. . . . I had the idea down. I knew exactly what I was going to say, what I was going to talk about. It's like, uh, this one I, I knew I was going to talk about her being tricked, or was the monkey at the party a fool, and the only hard thing for me was to read the story several times and pick out certain paragraphs or sentences or phrases that used the term, and interpret it to my way.
>
> ELIZABETH: Use the term?
>
> FRANCOIS: From the story, my way. The term "monkey" or "Senora," the way she did.
>
> ELIZABETH: I see. Okay. . . . At what point did you . . . realize that that was what you'd write about?
>
> FRANCOIS: After I really took a good look at the words "monkey" and "Senora" throughout the story.
>
> ELIZABETH: I see. . . . But part of the writing—so were you trying also in the writing to help me understand where you were coming from?

FRANCOIS: No, no, I wasn't, because that's why I had the meaning
of the words. . . . Once you understand that, and you think
of why they are in there, and once you start reading the
story, and noticing the same words appearing there, you'll
make the connection.

"No, no, I wasn't" trying to help the reader understand; or, as I
understand Francois to be saying: "Once you start reading the
story, observing the subject, through my linguistic lens, you'll
make the connection for yourself, you'll interpret things as I interpret them." Once again, I read Francois's expectations as part
of his ongoing struggle with the reader for dominance, part of
his insistence that readers immerse themselves entirely in his linguistic world, even as he makes no real attempt to reach out to
them. His words—spoken over and over, apparently meaning-
packed but practically impenetrable—have the ultimate effect, at
least on this reader, of some sort of chant, maddening in its effect
and autistic in its character. And in the struggle with me, if a
struggle it truly was, victory certainly went to Francois. These
are my notes, made in 1989 as I read over "BLIND-INNOCENT-
PREJUDICE" and his comments on it:

Writing3, "The Stolen Party" : Generally makes me go crazy
again just in the reading: Seems to me he perseverates on terms
"monkey" and "senora," never quite making apparent the connection between signifiers and meanings they hold for him. In
some spots, says consciously avoiding "breaking it all down
for reader," but I think he really doesn't see the need for a
bridge between tenor and vehicle. He's somehow content with
two parallel meaning systems, with no bridge between them.
We just rivet on those terms monkey and senora, monkey and
senora, monkey and senora, monkey and senora, monkey and
senora, monkey and senora, monkey and senora, monkey and
senora, monkey and senora, monkey and senora, monkey and
senora, monkey and senora, ahhhhhhhhhhhhhhhhhhhhhhhhh
hhh!!

And this is my one question as I read over Francois's essay and
his comments on it, in the dim light of those notes of mine: Who
is the monkey and who the "senora" now? Perhaps that is the
real question Francois meant for me—and all of us who had placed

him in Basic Writing—to ask all along. I was the instructor in
this Basic Writing class to which he had been consigned; it was
my house and my party. But he and I were now working within
his language system and quite literally under his terms, and I was
certainly beginning to feel the fool.

If "BLIND-INNOCENT-PREJUDICE" marked the nadir of
my frustration (and I assure you, it did), I believe it marked a
critical turning point for Francois. For while he did little in his
final revision to clarify his interpretation of Heker's short story,
his treatment of Richard Rodriguez's "Aria" and Sophronia Liu's
"So Tsi-fai," composed for his fourth essay, demonstrates an altogether new lucidity and an equally new positioning for the writer
himself. Alice's "Stealing Dreams" may have modeled for him
the missing "third piece of the triangle" crucial to communication. As it happened, she provided peer review for this next essay, and her opening line—"Lilian Heker's, The Stolen Party, is a
portrayal of the class struggle"—evidently gave Francois a key
term not only for its title and theme but also for so many of his
discussions to come.

A BILINGUAL AND SOCIAL STRUGGLE

THIS IS A COMPARISON OF SOME OF THE READ-
ING THAT I HAVE READ IN THIS ENGLISH CLASS. MY
THEME IS THE STRUGGLES. THE EXPERIENCES
PEOPLE OF DIFFERENT SOCIAL CLASSES AND ETH-
NIC GROUPS GO THROUGH.

IN TWO OF THE READINGS WE'VE READ AND
WE HAVE SEE TWO DIFFERENCES OF LOWER CLASS
MINORITIES. RICHARD RODRIGUEZ (ARIA: Aria: A
Memoir of a Bilingual Childhood) WAS BORN IN THE
UNITED STATES IN SAN FRANCISCO, THE SON OF
SPANISH-SPEAKING MEXICAN-AMERICAN. HIS
STORY IS ABOUT GROWING UP AND LEARNING EN-
GLISH AS A SECOND LANGUAGE. HE WAS SIX YEARS
OLD WHEN HE FIRST HEARD THE NUN PRONOUNCE
THE ENGLISH PRONUNCIATION OF HIS NAME
"RICH-HEARD ROAD-REE-GUESS." FROM THEN ON
HIS LIFE WAS TO BE DIFFERENT, BECAUSE HE WAS
ON THE PURSUIT OF LEARNING ENGLISH. "I
NEEDED TO SPEAK PUBLIC ENGLISH. . . ." AS
RICARDO'S ENGLISH FLOURISHED, THE SPECIAL
FEELING OF CLOSENESS AT HOME WAS GONE. HE

BECAME UNASSERTIVE OF THE PRONUNCIATION OF HIS SPANISH. "I WASN'T SURE OF PRONOUNCING THE SPANISH WORD gringo" OR "GRINGO IN ENGLISH." HE LOST INTIMACY BECAUSE HE FORGOT HIS OWN CULTURE.

I WAS ABOUT ELEVEN YEARS OLD, ABOUT FOUR FEET NINE INCHES, AND VERY SKINNY. I CAME INTO THIS NEW (WORLD) COUNTRY AND DID NOT SPEAK FLUENT ENGLISH. AS A FOREIGNER FROM MY FRENCH SPEAKING WORLD, I COULDN'T WAIT TO "parle engle", TO MY NEW AMERICAN FRIENDS, AND MY PARENTS. FORTUNATELY MY PARENTS ALREADY KNEW ENGLISH, ALREADY (BECAUSE THEY WERE ALREADY IN THE COUNTRY.)AND IT WAS ABOUT TIME BEFORE I SPEAK ENGLISH. UNLIKE RODRIGUEZ OUR FAMILY BOND GREW STRONGER BECAUSE WE WERE FINALLY UNITED.

I STRUGGLED WITH THE NEW COUNTRY, THE SCHOOLS, HAVING TO MAKE NEW FRIENDS,AND MOST IMPORTANT I ENCOUNTERED PREJUDICE, SOMETHING THAT I HAD NEVER FACED BEFORE. IN ADDITION TO EVERY THING I, NOW HAD TO BE AWARE OF MY SKIN COLOR. FACED ALL OF THESE EVENTS WITHIN A COUPLE OF MONTHS. RICHARD TALKS OF LANGUAGE DIFFICULTIES AND NOT FEELING COMFORTABLE AROUND THE "GRINGOS" AFTER ALL WHAT DO YOU EXPECT FROM A NEW COUNTRY (WINE COOLERS, CANDY AND WOMEN).

"THE SOUNDS WOULD GROW HARDER TO HEAR": AS rich-heard BRANCHES AWAY FROM HIS FAMILY, HE ALSO LOSES HIS CULTURE. "DIMINISHED BY THEN WAS THE SPECIAL FEELING OF CLOSENESS AT HOME." HE GREW LESS CONSCIOUS OF HIS PARENTS. "I NO LONGER KNEW WHAT WORDS TO USE IN ADDRESSING MY PARENTS" HE LOSES THE ABILITY TO TRULY SPEAK SPANISH. HE NO LONGER CAN ROLL THOSE PROUD SPANISH DRUMS ON HIS "R." RICHARD FINALLY AMERICANIZE HIMSELF, AND ONE GREAT CHANGE HAPPENS, HE LOSES THE CLOSENESS THAT HE ONCE HAD WITH HIS FAMILY.

RICARDO'S PARENTS HAD ENCOURAGED HIM TO LEARN, AND SPEAK ENGLISH. HIS PARENTS TOLD HIM, "RICARDO hable ingles". ONCE RICHARD NEW HOW TO SPEAK ENGLISH, THE BONDAGE THAT THERE WAS BETWEEN THE FAMILY GREW WEAKER. IT WAS TIME FOR THE PARENTS TO LET GO OF RICHARD. BEFORE

THEY LET GO OF THEIR SON IT WAS TIME FOR HIS PARENTS LET HIM KNOW THE DIFFERENCES BETWEEN GRINGO'S (AMERICANS) AND HIMSELF A MEXICAN-SPANISH SPEAKING.

RICHARD PROBLEMS CAN NOT NEARLY COMPARE TO MINE. UNLIKE THE NEW MR. RODRIGUEZ MY FAMILY WAS POOR, SO I REALLY DID NOT HAVE TO WORRY ABOUT LEARNING THE NEW LANGUAGE (BECAUSE I KNEW IT COME WITH TIME) I WAS WORRYING ABOUT LOOKING AFTER MY BROTHERS AND SISTERS FOR NOT TO GET INTO TROUBLE WHILE MY MOTHER AND STEP FATHER WENT TO WORK, AND I WAS WAITING FOR THE RIGHT AGE TO HIT THE "WORKING FORCE LABOR."

YES RICHARD WHY DID YOUR PARENTS HAD TO MAKE SURE YOU KNEW THE DIFFERENCES YOURSELF AND AMERICANS? UNLIKE RICHARD I KNEW EXACTLY WHAT MY CULTURE IS AND THERE IS NO WAY IN HELL OR HEAVEN THAT I WOULD FORGET WHAT MY CULTURE OR MY BACKGROUND (WHERE I'M COMING FROM) IS. "SUPPORTERS OF BILINGUAL EDUCATION IMPLY. . . . MISS A GREAT DEAL BY NOT BEING TAUGHT IN THEIR OWN LANGUAGE." THIS STATEMENT THAT RICHARD MADE (pg. 528) IS EXACTLY THAT WHY HE LOST HIS CULTURE, BECAUSE HE WAS NOT TAUGHT IN HIS OWN LANGUAGE HE LOST A GREAT DEAL OF HIS SELF IDENTITY.

THE SECOND PERSON THAT WENT THROUGH A STRUGGLE IS SO TSI-FAI. (SOPHRONIA LIU THE AUTHOR OF SO TSI-FAI WAS BORN IN HONG KONG, CAME TO THE U.S. IN 1953.) SO TSI-FAI IS THE STORY ABOUT A YOUNG CHINESE BOY WHO STARTED HIS STRUGGLE OF SURVIVAL IN THE SIX GRADE. SO TSI-FAI STRUGGLE WASN'T WITH THE DIFFICULTY OF LEARNING A NEW LANGUAGE. HIS STRUGGLE WAS WITH THE PREJUDICE THAT HE ENCOUNTERED IN SCHOOL. SO TSI-FAI IS PEER PRESSURED IN CLASS TO BE SOMETHING THAT HE IS NOT. SO TSI-FAI RELEASES HIS PRESSURE BY ACTING SILLY IN CLASS, BY DOING THINGS BEHIND THE TEACHERS BACK, "STICKING HIS TONGUE OUT BEHIND MUNG GU-LIANG'S BACK" AND OFTEN COMING IN LATE.

"FILTHY BOY!" "GRIME BEHIND THE EARS, BLACK RIMS ON THE FINGERNAILS, DIRTY COLLAR, CRUMPLED SHIRT." ONE OF SOCIAL DIFFERENCES BETWEEN SO TSI-FAI, AND THE CLASS WAS THAT HE

DID NOT DRESS LIKE THE REST OF THE KIDS. UNLIKE THE OTHER CHILDREN IN NUN MUNG LIANG'S CLASS THEIR FATHER'S WERE NOT FARMERS AND THEIR MOTHER'S FACTORY WORKERS. AT THE AGE OF FOURTEEN, HE DID HIS OWN LAUNDRY, MADE HIS OWN BREAKFAST, LOOKED AFTER HIS YOUNGER SIBLINGS AND STILL AFTER ALL OF THAT HAD ENOUGH STRENGTH TO GO TO SCHOOL. NUN MUNG LIANG NOT KNOWING ALL THESE FACTS SHOULD HAVE KNOWN BETTER THEN TO JUDGE SOMEONE FROM SO LITTLE THAT THEY SEE.

I SYMPATHIZE WITH SO TSI-FAI WITH THE STRUGGLES HE HAD TO LEAVE WITH AT SUCH A YOUNG AGE, BUT I CAN NOT TALK ABOUT THE STRUGGLES OF HIS SOCIETY BUT MINE ONLY. IN AMERICA MOSTLY ALL OF MINORITIES, AND THE LOWER CLASS STRUGGLES TO MAKE A LIVING EVERYDAY. BECAUSE WE ALL DON'T LIVE ON THE STREET DOES NOT MEAN WE ARE NOT POOR.

THE SOCIAL GAP IN THE WORLD TODAY IS GETTING WIDER THEN EVER. OUR SOCIETY HAS BECOME A PLACE WHERE YOU ARE EITHER GOING TO BE POOR OR RICH. IN SO TSI-FAI'S CASE HE IS POOR AND THEREFORE SUFFER. HIS PARENTS WERE POOR, AND NOT GIVEN AN EQUAL OPPORTUNITY THEREFORE HE MUST INHERIT THE MISERABLY LIVED LIFE. (IN SO TSI-FAI THAT IS EXACTLY WHAT HAPPENED.)

SO TSI FAIR WAS THE OLDEST IN THE FAMILY. HIS PARENTS WERE COUNTING IN HIM TO GET AN EDUCATION. HIS PARENTS WERE POOR, AND ILLITERATE. THEY WERE HOPING HE, BEING THE OLDEST WAS GOING TO GET THEM OUT OF THE SLUMS. SO TSI-FAI FATHER WAS A FARMER. HE WORKS IN THE FIELD ALL DAY IN TRYING TO PUT FOOD ON THE TABLE. HIS MOTHER WAS A FACTORY WORKER, SHE SAT IN A CHAIR FOR ABOUT EIGHT HOURS STRAIGHT WORKING HARD. THE RESPONSIBILITY ON SO TSI-FAI WITH SCHOOL ON AND THE BURDEN OF PASSING THE EXAM AND OF SOCIETY, HIS FAMILY EXPECTATION BROUGHT HIM TO HIS DEATH.

"LET US BOW OUR HEAD IN SILENT PRAYER FOR THE SOUL OF SO TSI-FAI." (YES, WHY NOT BOW YOUR HEADS FOR SO TSI-FAI, BECAUSE YOU (THE SOCIETY) YOU KILLED HIM) THE FOURTEEN YEAR OLD BOY HAD DRUNKEN ENOUGH INSECTICIDE TO KILL HIMSELF. "DAREDEVIL; GOOD-FOR-NOTHING LAZY

BONES" ACCORDING TO MUNG GU-LIANG. SO TSI-FAI
FACED THE STRUGGLE IN HIS SOCIETY AT AN EARLY
AGE, HE ALSO ENDED IT, AND FROM THEN ON HE
SHALL LIVE LIKE AN ANGEL.

With this essay, I was drawn into Francois's "bilingual struggle."
Evaluating it then, and still today, I wondered whether "A BI-
LINGUAL AND SOCIAL STRUGGLE" was truly more comprehensible in itself than were his previous three writings, or
whether it simply appeared more comprehensible to me. I had
spent the first three essays of the term suffering the disorienting
effects of being a stranger in a strange language. Perhaps I had
come by now to understand and even anticipate the structures of
his personal grammar: his idiosyncratic use of upper and lower
cases, as in "I COULDN'T WAIT TO 'parle engle'"; his use of
parentheses, as in "I CAME INTO THIS NEW (WORLD)
COUNTRY AND DID NOT SPEAK ENGLISH"; and his various nomenclatures, as in "rich-heard," "RICARDO," and "RI-
CHARD." Since I had come to know only with this, his fourth
essay, that THE YOUNG MAN, WITHOUT A TRACE OF
FRANCAIS (in francois) HAD ONLY COME (HERE) TO "parle
engle" IN HIS ELEVENTH YEAR, perhaps I had just begun to
see the sense of his highly accented writing in much the same
way that I normally come, some days or weeks into every semester, to hear the sense and un-hear the previously interfering (my
interference or theirs?) accents of other bilingual speakers.

On the other hand, with "A BILINGUAL AND SOCIAL
STRUGGLE," I believe I do see real change in Francois's manner
of exposition and with this change an attendant—maybe caus-
ative—shift in his own position vis-à-vis both subject and reader.
At four pages, this latest essay is substantially longer than any of
his previous writings, which suggests increased willingness on
Francois's part to stay within the writing and develop the ideas
expressed. He devotes more time and attention to both
Rodriguez's and Liu's narratives than he previously did to Heker's
or his own, thereby grounding in summary observations an interpretation which becomes, for that grounding, more accessible
to readers. In "A BILINGUAL AND SOCIAL STRUGGLE,"
Francois finally constructs that bridge of concrete particulars over

which readers can cross into Francois's meaning and motivation. Behind the contrast he established between his own linguistic concerns and Rodriguez's lay comparable experiences; behind the distance he established between himself and his subject lay identification. The following spring, in a paper for his Field Work in Anthropology course, he would write this:

> I did my field work in the United States during the early nineteen eighties. I was twelve years old. There was a lot of heart ache up ahead. In my new society, I spoke with an accent that no one would understand. Sometimes I could not even understand myself.

And toward the end of his term in Basic Writing, he admitted that clarity of expression remained a problem for him, not only as an act of communication but as an act of meaning making itself. For the first time, he named it "my struggle": "I think my writing is getting better, like Marcia said," he told Elizabeth,

> but I have difficulty writing down what I really want to say and actually making it readable to the readers. . . . Hopefully that's not a problem that I'll always have. But you know, that's probably my struggle. . . . Am I actually saying what I want to say, or am I just writing to make sense?

We were, it now seems, worrying our own versions of the same worry: he, whether he was "just writing to make sense", and I, whether I was just reading to make sense of him. In our shared struggle, it also seems now, we were making peace.

Indeed, with "A BILINGUAL AND SOCIAL STRUGGLE," Francois seems to have been ready to make peace with his readers generally, to establish a newfound trust in and alliance with them. The difficulty of "writing down what I really want to say and actually making it readable to the readers" seems to me fundamentally different from Francois's more-often-expressed worry about whether it was "really you writing the paper" or "you were just spitting back what you know [a teacher] wanted to hear." The difference is one of intention, as Francois struggles to write *toward* his readers rather than against them. And the redefining question of whether he is actually saying what he wants to say or "just writing to make sense" (like his childhood worry that "in my new society, I spoke with an accent that no one would understand. Sometimes I could not even understand myself.") paradoxically serves to narrow the reader-writer gap, as Francois admits of a sympathy with his audience in sharing, if not intelligibility, then confusion. Apparently, he was ready to share more as well.

With "A BILINGUAL AND SOCIAL STRUGGLE," Francois's rendering of personal experience became central to communication, a gift to the reader previously held in reserve. When Elizabeth asked him, "What was the hardest part about writing this essay," he explained:

> FRANCOIS: Adding my personal stuff was hard. Because the others I could always give my opinion and just put in what the book said. But my— if I write my personal experience, I don't know, it gives more to the paper. . . .
>
> ELIZABETH: What gave you the idea that you should add some personal experience?
>
> FRANCOIS: To make it a better paper. I mean, where are my opinions coming from, you know. It's like, if I state something . . . what's giving me the idea to think that way? . . . If I said that, I have to prove this, you know. So, I kind of have to work.

These comments come from mid-December, the end of Francois's term in Basic Writing and a month after he composed "A BILINGUAL AND SOCIAL STRUGGLE." In a way, then, the essay only hints at or promises the changes in attitude expressed here as germane to its inception. Nevertheless, there is change articulated here, fairly radical change, I believe, and the change registers in the writing. For once, Francois recognizes writing as "work"—and as his work, not just the reader's. And like all other work, it marks the worker as a mortal as well as a social creature. For the first time, that is, Francois seems to locate himself and the reader in a social context, one in which the reader has the acknowledged right to ask, "Where are my [Francois's] opinions coming from?" and the writer has the acknowledged obligation to work at proving the worth of his opinions by situating them in a social context—not by handing them down playfully like some act of God or Nature.

Writing has thus become for Francois an act of humility and, ironically, of faith:

> ELIZABETH: What did you find easiest about writing this essay on Rodriguez?
>
> FRANCOIS: Saying all this bad stuff about him.
>
> ELIZABETH: Oh that was—
>
> FRANCOIS: Yeah, yeah. That was easy . . . and that's why I think my personal experience kind of helped a bit, you know.
>
> ELIZABETH: Uh huh. It helped?
>
> FRANCOIS: My paper and helped me to put his points down, you know.
>
> ELIZABETH: Okay, your personal experience—
>
> FRANCOIS: So when you read my paper, you won't so much think of Richard Rodriguez, but you'll remember my section, my personal experience sections. If I can do that: "Who is Richard Rodriguez? Did you mention anybody? Oh I'm sorry, I didn't remember." If you can do that, if you can do that as a writer I think that's—personally I think that's great. If you can write a paper and compare someone else's and your paper, and have the reader come out remembering your section, you did a good job.

These words seem to me to inscribe a signal shift during Francois's term in Basic Writing. Here his struggle for survival seems not with the reader: he does not thrust and parry with his audience in a duel for power over meaning; nor does he, in fact, cast himself before the reader like some inscrutable object—some odd *objet d'art*—demanding to be animated by her response. He continues to struggle, but now with his subject rather than with his reader, and his aim is to survive in the reader's memory: a good paper is defined by the imprint of one's self it leaves on the reader's mind. And while a power over the writer's survival as writer still resides with the reader, power is not to be warded off but is to be courted in a relationship promising Francois a far less lonesome position than the oppositional one he assumed so often before and which, over the next four years, he would occasionally assume again.

A Postscript to Basic Writing

Like most basic writing teachers, I suspect, I worry about how my students leave my class and, just as much, how they enter their next writing course. To whatever degree I want them to proclaim themselves freely and confidently, I also want them to fit in, not to appear "outlandish," both for themselves and for the ways in which I believe their performance will reflect on me as well as on other teachers and students in the Basic Writing program. Francois was no exception, and so I worried that his signature use of uppercase and lowercase lettering would mark him immediately on entrance into College Writing or any other writing-based course he might take. Still, I felt we had enough else to negotiate: I intentionally let the typing go unremarked. To no small relief, I received as his final "reading project" essay a paper on Richard Wright's *Black Boy* and *Native Son*, typed in wholly conventional form. Linking the literal and figurative flights from oppression rendered in these books to the hopeless flights into fantasy of contemporary drug users in largely black, urban communities, the paper's argument was unconventional for a first-year essay, yet it was both clearly and cleverly presented. I was genuinely pleased by the progress that this essay, along with the previous "A BILINGUAL AND SOCIAL STRUGGLE," signaled, and I said so in my final note of the semester, at the same time taking the opportunity to remind Francois that in future writings, as in this one, the power of his imagination and his experience would show and be seen in direct proportion to the clarity of its expression. By the end of the term, I truly did appreciate Francois's many powers, and he apparently appreciated my consistency.

ELIZABETH: How could you describe Marcia as a teacher?

FRANCOIS: Well, she adds a sense of humor to the class, which is good. I mean, because our class was very quiet, and that I didn't like. Uh, she helped us a lot. She had a lot of patience, you know.

ELIZABETH: Patience?

FRANCOIS: From the beginning to the end of the semester. She was just overall really nice I think. . . . I mean, she's very positive, and, you know, it seems like she's really done a good job in keeping her personal life and class outside, you know what I mean? She comes in everyday the same way that she left. It's not like she went home and had a bad time and came back and was down, or just wasn't as active. She always has the same energy as she came in the last time with. Which is good. And it's not like, she came one day and gave us a lot of work and just started doing her own work. She was always with us, which is good. I like that.

As for my own clarity of expression, however, or, perhaps more to the point, my intentions:

> ELIZABETH: How about the way that she would respond to your papers? How did you find the manner of her responses, either spoken or written responses?

> FRANCOIS: Mmm. Fine, but there's one thing that I couldn't quite get. Uh, sometimes when she answered my papers I—not that I couldn't tell, but—I couldn't tell if she was judging the papers hard, you know, or was she just being all around easy, do you know what I mean. When she graded the papers—or not graded, but read the papers—was she being very easy and understanding in the comments, or was she being very difficult? Because all the comments that I got to me seemed to be really nice comments, and even though I do understand them, I don't know if she wanted improvement or not. . . .

Essays for College Writing

By all indications, Francois's fit into College Writing, English 112, should have been a good one. But something, as we will see, went awry. Tim had taught the course for seven semesters and so, if not a veteran, was not a novice either. A graduate student and instructor studying for his M.F.A, he had taught a creative writing course in fiction and poetry as well, and the College Writing course he offered, in both aim and design, reflected his thoughtful nature. In his initial interview with Elizabeth, he revealed his belief that he and his students shared an understanding of the "basics" of good writing: "The standard mechanics, structure and that kind of thing. It follows a good, logical order, there's a solid introduction, there's a body, there's a conclusion." But while reinforcing those notions, he aimed simultaneously to move his class toward more complex writings and understandings of writing: "I really stress content," he went on to say. "I'm interested in their engagement in the subject they're writing about, the sophistication of their thought, how they try to work to find something new, unique, and interesting and unusual to say about their subject." In short, he wanted his students to think of writing not just as a medium for reporting or even communicating but as "a tool of knowledge, of learning, of exploring ideas."

It seems precisely the sort of interpretive writing world Francois would have found "fascinating," where there would be little worry about a teacher "looking at things too straight" or himself "going too far," and where he could feel free to please himself and, by doing so, please the teacher, too. By all of Tim's accounts, what he wanted was for students to use their imaginations as well as their intellects to say what *they* wanted. Unfortunately, however, Francois entered College Writing prepared to submit himself fully to the teacher's desires—or at least to say he was so prepared. And that was clearly a mistake; that was clearly the one thing Tim did *not* want to hear. Early in the term, he gave students a brief questionnaire about their personal writing habits, interests, and concerns. The first question asked students to finish a sentence beginning, "When a teacher says, 'I want you to write. . . .'" Francois filled in the blanks this way:

> When a teacher says, "I want you to write. . . ." the very first thing that comes to mind is that I should write exactly about what they ask for. (I believe that one of the first rules of writing is to follow instructions.)

Even today as I read these lines, my initial reaction is to throw up my hands and ask, "Where in hell or heaven did this come from?" Tim, on the other hand, located the source at neither extreme but rather in the midground of Basic Writing. From peer reviews and comments made in class, Tim took Francois to be what he saw as the "111 type," and the impression of Francois as "mechanical," as rigidly adhering to the teacher's set task, stuck with him into the semester. This is one of his early-April observations to Elizabeth:

What I see [Francois] concentrating on and remarking on regarding other people is whether they know what the assignment is, whether they're doing the assignment—and whether it's really organized and very logical and reasonable. He'll say, "Well, they're not really doing the assignment," and I might not have a particular problem, I might think they're doing something very interesting. But he's interested in them understanding what the task is and then . . . almost methodically setting out to do that, clearly stating what is to be done in the paper, uh, clearly following through. I guess I said "mechanical," and I want to bring to his attention that those are good skills—I'd like him to become a little less mechanical . . . freed up a little bit more, at least so on the surface it doesn't look to a reader so mechanical in its approach: "This is my purpose. This is what I'm going to do."

By the semester's end, Tim saw Francois as going beyond just reflecting what the teacher wanted. He saw Francois as playing teacher. "He's pretty good at commenting on other students' writings," Tim told Elizabeth, "[but] he tended to be more critical than I like to see." Francois, it seems, would

get his pen in there . . . to circle all the grammatical errors that they had done, at an early stage, when we normally say you don't worry about that. But he was doing that with a red pen. . . . That was funny and probably says something about how he's been handled in the past: "This is how you do it, with your red pen."

But here we need to remember that Francois is one of those students who, in his struggle between giving his own interpretation and giving what the teacher "may be looking for," holds before us a strangely distorting mirror: a mirror containing images of what we truly do want beneath all our own rhetoric of denial. From my position now, reflecting on my own time with Francois, I see those images, which I did not see then: I see my own construction of an academic essay in "MAN vs NATURE" and my own vision of Francois as a "basic writer" in all his efforts to prove himself something else. In the same way, I suspect that, were Tim writing this chapter now, he would discover in himself the source of what was to become his mounting frustration with Francois. The second essay assignment of the semester is illustrative.

Tim designed the second writing for the course as an observation/interpretation project in the style of Ann Berthoff, a project meant to introduce students to the concept of "discovery in writing," in which they were to examine closely an object of their own choosing and then interpret that object for their audience. He did not want them simply to "stay on the object" but rather to "take off from that object to anything": to "try to know it physically, through all their senses, as much as they can. But beyond that . . . do metaphors for it . . . associations," and, in general, "make real leaps to see how that moves them to new knowledge." He demonstrated the composing process for this essay with a penny and followed up with a single-spaced, page-long written explanation, including three aims he hoped the assignment would meet; six suggested ways to examine "your object for the generating or first draft stage"; and two reminders for "planning and writing the mid-process draft," with the first offering six possible ways to capture the reader's attention, and the second reminding writers to "maintain the unity of the essay" by deciding "what the essential statement is you want to get across" and keeping it "in mind as you write."

With the route to imaginative freedom thus painstakingly mapped, Francois stuck close to home. For his first assignment in Basic Writing, he had struck out on his own, selecting a photograph from his history text rather than one of the dozen or so photographs I had set before him; now, with a near-infinite number of choices before him, he chose not Tim's penny but a nickel— albeit, as we will see, a special nickel—to inspire this:

A Meaningful Coin

The item's circular shape alone did not get my attention. Then suddenly, as I began to observe it more carefully, the object intrigued me. I glanced over; it looked like it was waiting there, just in case someone might see it and pick it up. I picked up the round object from the ground. It was heavier than usual because of the dirt and rock deposits resting on its back. When I got home, I washed it and then was able to regain the shine the item once had.

The sphere was clean now. I began to look at it more closely. On one side there was a picture of an Indian's head. His hair was braided in two—one on each side of his shoulder, and on the top of his hair was a feather. Above the Indian was the word L-i-b-e-r-t-y. The indian's face looked old and tired. The features of the indian's head was not erected like new. The edges were smooth and worn out. Now, holding the coin I could feel the smoothness, and the rounded off edges that made it distinguishable—like the indians who once occupied our land.

On the other side of there was a picture of a buffalo with his head down. The buffalo looked furious and unbeatable. Holding its head down with one hoof digging into the ground, it seemed like a raging bull who was getting ready to charge at whatever stood in its way. However, the buffalo also looked fatigued and tired of fighting. The buffalo appeared to have given up the battle, and was in need of rest. Above the picture of the buffalo read "United States of America." (and in very small writing—pluribus uniun—out of many, one) It was not until then that I realized what I was holding. I was holding a piece of American history. The Indian's head on the coin was not only a symbol of monetary value, but also a representation of the American Indians in the United States. Similarly to the indian and the buffalo, it was a rare and endangered coin.

The coin reminded me of the native Americans, especially the Cherokees. There were once hundreds of thousands of Cherokee Indians. They lived all across the Eastern side of the Mississippi river during the eighteen thirties. Later the Cherokees were forced to move west of the Mississippi, so the European could expand and explore the "new found land" thousands died during the forced long and cold journey west. Among other tribes of indians, the Cherokees suffered the most because of the number of members that died from their tribe. Like most indian tribes, the Cherokees were farmers. They cultivated the land so they can could eat. They killed wild animals to keep warm. They have lived that way for centuries. The journey to the west was a journey to their death. The western land was a forest full of trees, and wild animals, unknown to them. There they could not farm the forests to make a living.

The "trail of tears," so their journey was called, the cherokee Indians came to an end when they were forced to move west by the Europeans. Like the coin that represents a once living part of the U.S. history, its (coin) time has also come to an end. The only memories that are left of these two historical elements are the buffalo and the Indian/buffalo coin. They are both found in the historical books. It is a shame that the only way that these two elements (things) can come together is on the face of an old dirty, rusty nickel that I brought out the shine into for a moment of reminder. Don't forget our past.

With this particular assignment, Tim was apparently either un-aware of or unbothered by Francois's determination to "write exactly about"—or almost exactly about—"what [Tim] ask[ed] for," applauding instead his leaps of imaginative association, his "thoughtfulness." Speaking to Elizabeth during their first inter-view of the term, Tim described his perceptions of Francois and the ways in which "A Meaningful Coin" helped to form them:

> He's a super guy. I really like him. He has a neat sense of hu-mor that comes out occasionally. . . . He does write well. I guess I said "mechanical," but . . . there's no particular prob-lem or difficulty with his writing. . . . I think he's a pretty sound writer, and I think he puts a lot of work into it. . . . He's a very thoughtful person, and I think the last two or three essays have really shown me that, his concern with the Native Americans. That was a good example, the object essay. He did it on the buffalo nickel. And, boy, before long he talked about the fact that the buffalo nickel was kind of going extinct, but as well the Indians and the buffalo, and what that meant. Later, the white man came here, and almost made them extinct, and the suffering that they've had. And so there he started with this little nickel and zoom, off he goes, and he's talking about Na-tive American people, and all this important stuff. So he's thoughtful. He was thoughtful.

Tim expressed his appreciation directly to Francois as well, though a little less enthusiastically, his remarks tempered with some con-cern about Francois's ability to communicate his interpretations logically and clearly. Here is his written response:

> Francois,
> I remain impressed by the way you were able to use a small coin to retell history and relate the tragic plight of the Chero-kees to your readers. It is an unexpected jump, but it works well and shows your thoughtfulness. I learned from your quick history of the "trail of tears" and your knowledge of Cherokee life.
> There are stretches of good, clear writing in the essay (para-graphs 1 and 4, for instance). There are also places where the wording or the logic of the sentences breaks down. Look, for instance, at one sentence on this [last] page: "The only memo-ries that are left . . . are the buffalo and the Indian/buffalo

coin." The logic is questionable. A memory is not a thing. Countless memories of these things are possible. Also, what about the Cherokee Indian? There are still actual American Indians and memories of Indians alive today.

Like all writers, you need to pay close attention to see that your words convey your meaning in the clearest way. Beyond your own careful time, you can use classmates, friends, the tutoring center, or me during office hours to help you work at improving on this level.

BC

Tim

Francois, too, expressed satisfaction with his imaginative efforts, observing later to Elizabeth, that "the [essay about the] coin was being creative, because, you know, the memories that the coin kind of brought to mind," and then adding with a laugh that he had been "feeling kind of good about everything" he had been writing of late. But I suspect problems contained in that laughter. I suspect also that while both Tim and Francois expressed satisfaction with "A Meaningful Coin," it was something other than mutual satisfaction they felt, since the grade Tim awarded it, Francois would later complain, "just kind of puts everyone in the same pool, the BC pool." And there is more. I know. For while Tim and I seem so different in our emphases—he delighting in the precipitate "zoom" of Francois's imaginative leap and I stressing the need for a slow, careful closing of the gap between observation and interpretation—I see even here in Tim's comments—to Elizabeth, to Francois—tracks of my own frustrations.

I, too, was at first energized by Francois's apparent ability to make meaning of the elements he observed—to *read* the signs before him in intriguing ways—and to suggest, if not fully elucidate, those meanings through writing. And I, too, saw stretches—some short, some a bit longer—of "good, clear writing," enough to believe that with a little more care from Francois and a little help from his friends, his suggestive prose could become lucid prose. But if we look behind this essay's final draft, to its midprocess, we will see that Francois had already received help from "classmates, friends, the tutoring center," and Tim.

The midprocess draft, titled "out of many, one" and filling about one and two-thirds pages, contains over seventy-five separate emendations and suggestions in Tim's, Francois's, and an unidentified "friend's" (perhaps a tutor's) handwriting. In addition, this emended version was commented upon by two classmates during a peer review session. Finally, at the bottom of the draft, in Francois's hand, is written, "I have no question, but I am welcome to all suggestion," along with one question as an afterthought: "What is the location of the city of Boston globally (longitude & latitude)?" And in Tim's hand: "We'll talk in conference," indicating again that the draft was subject to discussion. In fact, the midprocess draft contains so many notations and proffered substitutions—the bulk involving word choices, pronoun referents, and spelling or grammatical corrections—that, soon after the last draft was completed, Francois could no longer distinguish others' marginal notations from his own. When asked by Elizabeth whether he remembered incorporating any of his readers' remarks or markings into his final draft, he scanned the draft and answered, "Let's see. I think I expanded on the Europeans. Yeah, because that was the comment—to expand on the explore of the new. . . ." What he was reading was actually his own handwritten insertion of a line appearing in the final draft as "Later the Cherokees were forced to move west of the Mississippi, *so the European could expand and explore the 'new found land'*" (emphasis added). It is hardly surprising then, when we look at the wash of jottings on Francois's midprocess draft, that he took a red pen to the drafts of his peers. Nor is it less surprising that in the final draft there remain, in Tim's words, "places where the wording or the logic of the sentences breaks down."

Tim's critique of that particular sentence's wording and logic—"The only memories that are left of these two historical elements are the buffalo and the Indian/buffalo coin"—puzzled Francois when, in their interview, Elizabeth questioned him about it:

> ELIZABETH: Tim here made some comments, and I was wondering. He says, "The logic is questionable." Do you remember reading—
>
> FRANCOIS: Yes.
>
> ELIZABETH: You've seen this one. And then he asks you to look back.

FRANCOIS: "The logic is questionable"?

ELIZABETH: Do you know what he means by that?

FRANCOIS: Paper's making sense, or not making sense. I don't know what he means by that.

ELIZABETH: Okay, so look, for instance, at one sentence on the page. "The only memories that are left—

FRANCOIS: Wait, where are we?

ELIZABETH: Okay. So, right here: ". . . that are left of these two historical elements are the buffalo and the Indian/buffalo coin." And then—

FRANCOIS: Yes, I was trying to say the buffalo, the buffalo itself and the buffalo coin.

ELIZABETH: Okay.

FRANCOIS: And then Indian/buffalo coin.

ELIZABETH: Okay. That's, um, not—let's see—he said, "The logic is questionable. A memory is not a thing."

FRANCOIS: A memory is not a thing? Hmm. So he's saying that I can't use memories and then . . . the Indians, then describe the same thing? See what I mean?

ELIZABETH: Okay, let's see. All right. One thing—well, I'm not sure what he means there. . . .

Bafflement ripples from Tim to Francois, ultimately leaving Elizabeth, the questioner, unable to answer the question of what Tim "means there." Even Anne, commenting on the interview, is prompted to note in the transcript's margin, "Seems like he doesn't understand Tim's comments. Same for a few of Marcia's. Wonder how much he tried to do so?" The whole project of understanding appears frustrated by what amounts to Francois's persistent interruption of a full and coherent question with increasingly isolated and therefore opaque words—nouns like "buffalo," "the buffalo itself," "the buffalo coin," and "then Indian/buffalo coin"—until other echoes—"senora, monkey, senora, monkey, senora, monkey"—begin in my mind. There is even a moment in his interview with Elizabeth that the very notion of words as something more than themselves, as conveyors of meaning, appears foreign to Francois:

ELIZABETH: In his mind, [Tim] is wanting you to pay close attention to see that your words convey your meaning in the
clearest way.

FRANCOIS: My words conv . . .

ELIZABETH: He says, "Like all writers, you need to pay close
attention to see that your words convey your meaning in the
clearest way."

FRANCOIS: Just on my two sentences, perhaps, you know, about
the buffalo, and then . . . But you know what I mean, if I
said the coin that wouldn't make sense, though. Even though
he might, he knows that I'm talking about the end of the
buffalo coin, but it just doesn't come off that way. Know
what I mean?

Still, I have come to believe that our shared frustration—
Elizabeth's, Anne's, Tim's (as he later came to experience it), and
my own—is born, in fact, not of Francois's resistance but rather
of *his frustration*. My sense is that he did try to understand Tim's
comments, but that Tim's focusing on that single sentence—that
single word in that sentence, i.e., "memories"—was as frustrating to Francois as Francois's fixating on "buffalo" and "buffalo
coins" was to Elizabeth and as frustrating as his use of "senora"
and "monkey" was to me. My sense is also that by fixing on
"memories," Tim diverted attention away from Francois's own
felt difficulty, a difficulty Francois may not have admitted but
indeed did articulate, again and again, with that oh-so-concrete
"thing" that would neither convey his meaning to Elizabeth nor
yield its own meaning to him: "Yes, I was trying to say the buffalo, the buffalo itself and the buffalo coin, and then the buffalo
coin."

Like his selection of the Victorian-era print as an object of
interpretation in "MAN vs NATURE," Francois's selection of
the five-cent coin confronted him with the problem of decoding
visual images already loaded with culturally determined significance. And looking back behind his drafts, to his prewriting notes,
we see him set out on that task:

Round Circular   Heritage
Faded - old   Old

Natives

5-cents
USA of A   Cherokees
                                Feather
Baffalo
                                Breaded hair
Rare
Smooth   Nickel/Silver

DIFFERRENT SHADES

---

1. One side is the Indian/A native of America
2. *Back of coin is a baffallo—an old Fashion source of clothes.*
   a. *Why not the supreme court?*
   b. *or the w/house?*

In reading Francois's problems as problems in "wording," Tim read Francois, quite accurately, as someone whose first language was not English. Yet the questions of "logic" this essay raised for Tim, I think, were not matters of literal vocabulary, of "wording," as his comment suggested. For "memories" poses a simple matter of word choice, easily remedied by a change to the more concrete sorts of "things" Tim was looking for, such as "reminders" or "remnants."

Francois's true dilemma seems to reside within the more complex vocabulary of cultural symbols. Arriving here in the early 1980s, he was not raised on American westerns, those myriad precursors of *Dances with Wolves*. His knowledge of North American Indian cultures, at least the knowledge he seems to have drawn on for this essay, came from a college history text and its discussion of the eastern Cherokees, who "cultivated the land so they can eat" and "killed wild animals to keep warm." Hence, for him the buffalo is neither integrally connected to nor immediately associated with the Indian—nor is its near-extermination at the hands of Anglo-European settlers. In short, he does not see them as two sides of the same symbolic coin. He sees them, instead, as just that: two diverse sides of the same literal coin. He asks himself a real question, not one whose answer is culturally preset: Why is "an old Fashion source of clothes" on the back of this coin, and "not the supreme court or the w/house"?

And as a result, his writing assumes a two-fold purpose: (1) as he himself noted, to use "the concept of how the nickel disappear like the Cherokee did before" to persuade readers to "treasure their present and hopefully remember their past," and (2) to discover how the buffalo fits meaningfully on the coin or how otherwise to assimilate this unruly symbol into his essay.

Francois had taken pains to achieve his first aim and convey his message clearly. "I read it over and over," he recalled to Elizabeth, "and it kept coming to my mind, would someone read it and go, 'What the hell is that? Why are we talking about coins, then all of a sudden jumping to Cherokees?' So I think I made that kind of clear. . . ." And still, what was clear to Francois was not clear to Tim. When Elizabeth focused their discussion on Tim's material question—"What about the Cherokee Indian? There are still actual American Indians and memories of Indians alive today."—Francois spoke not of survival but of loss and of forgetting and, intriguingly, of redefinition:

> Oh, I talked to [Tim] about that. I think I talked to him about that. When I said "the buffalo," I meant the animal itself is left, okay. But the Indian/buffalo coin, they aren't anymore. See? And the Indians, well, how many people do you find today talking about Indians? It's kind of a message, you know. Maybe I didn't get that clear then, but, I mean, people don't go around talking about Indians anymore. And, when they do talk about Indians, they're talking about the reservation. You know, when you really look at it, are they Indians, or are they just people?

In its way, Tim's "logic" composes a narrative of hope: for him the coin and its story both are individual acts of remembering among the "countless memories . . . possible," reminders that "there are still actual American Indians, and memories of Indians, alive today," despite a history of destruction. It is neither a logic nor a narrative that fits the story of warning and exhortation Francois intended to compose, the story of a culture's callous disregard for two once-vital elements from its own history—a people now segregated, forgotten, or redefined as "Indians," and a coin, like the figures on it, once of real value, now discarded in the dirt—and their shared moment of restoration in Francois's hands. In short, what Francois himself once said of a Victorian-era print might be said of this five-cent engraving:

> The different meaning of this picture is definitely not clear. The photographer have his readers and viewers interpreting his picture in all direction, the posibilities are wild. ("MAN vs NATURE")

I have dwelt longer on this essay than I will on other essays Francois wrote for College Writing for a number of reasons. First, if we set the stretches of relatively clear writing within this piece against its more problematic passages, I think we see, perhaps in something of a new light, the difficulties many students face when moving from largely narrative or descriptive writing into more interpretive or persuasive modes—when, in Francois's metaphor, they are faced with finding that third piece of the triangle which mediates between pure observation or summary and pure self-expression. Tim wanted his class to move—through their drafts and within the final drafts themselves—from "discovery" to "communication," keeping in mind, throughout the composing process, "what the essential statement is you want to get across" in order to maintain their essays' "unity." That movement in itself suggests an opening up of meaning—the sorts of imaginative leaps for which Tim applauded Francois—but then a subsequent closing down, i.e. a sifting through of various possibilities to discover one coherent, communicable interpretation. Francois's process of discovery was not yet complete—not complete enough, at least, either to eclipse or to contain Tim's interpretation (or, perhaps, his "friend's"). So all the well-intended notations, questions, emendations proffered to him—intended, that is, to help clarify meaning as those readers/writers saw it emerging from Francois's text—simultaneously served to disorganize the message toward which he himself was proceeding.

Now, by no means am I suggesting that Tim was culpable of something that I did not do as well. My own good intentions were often similarly disorganizing in their effects on Francois. Like Tim, I wanted Francois to start his interpretation from observation, to begin from the rhetorical point upon which his readers could agree, and to move on from there to his own views—or, as Francois put it for Elizabeth that first semester, "to write down how most people feel towards the subject instead of me just coming straight out and giving my opinions, which people might not understand, . . . to just write down what would be most common, you know, and then kind of like put mine in after that." But finding common ground upon which to begin is little easier than discovering a single, unified, communicable meaning upon which to close unless one is a member of that majority, unless one shares the majority perspective and its common symbolization or discourse base. As Francois's writing and Tim's reading of "A Meaningful Coin" demonstrate, Francois did not. Francois's difficulty, then, can be viewed as a cultural as well as a developmental matter, one that holds a lesson for teachers of basic—or, in Francois's system, not "basic"—writers for whom English is not a first language and for whom American culture is not a shared or shaping context.

I have dwelt on "A Meaningful Coin" for another reason, too: for both Francois and Tim, it marked a crucial juncture in Francois's career in College Writing, but, as divergent as were their readings of the buffalo coin, so too were their readings of his progress thereafter. Moreover, as those initial two readings set side by side cast each other in a different light, so do the various interpretations of Francois's experience through the remainder of the course.

Francois, in his end-of-the-year retrospective essay, identified "A Meaningful Coin" as a critical moment of recognition for him, for "at that point is when [he] knew this class is going to be okay." The assignment had challenged him, he noted, "because we had to write about an object in extreme detail" and because it required him to "capture" his audience with that "small, intriguing detail." A new sense of audience pervades his final interview of the year, a new willingness to accommodate readers' needs rather than struggle against them, to regard readers as persons to engage rather than challenge or dazzle with his performance. In fact, he suggested, he had begun to take pleasure in easing others' understanding of him: "I like my writing," he told Elizabeth.

I like my writing much better than at the beginning of the year.
I find myself writing much better in terms of it's easier for me
making transitions—easy, clear transitions. You don't want your
readers to guess; you want them to just read and understand . . .
the point that you're trying to make.

Adapting his writing to specific audience needs, Francois claimed,
was a primary lesson of Basic and College Writing both. Through
those courses, he had learned to employ "different ways of writing" and "different styles" when "writing to someone I know, or
someone who has a high status, or if I'm trying to capture a
particular audience." He had learned the virtues of multiple drafting, too, he said: "Before, I probably did, you know, maybe two,
three drafts," but by the close of spring semester, "I probably do
several drafts"—"*six*," to be precise. The result:

I like my writing much better than at the beginning of the year.
It's more understandable. It's more smooth. You know, I can
read through it and not have to stop to make corrections. I
think it's just much better. It's just really good.

How sincere was Francois in these sentiments he expressed to
Elizabeth? I will never know. He may well have meant what he
said, though saying it perhaps with a salting of exaggeration. Or
he may just as well have been playing his role as "cheerful resister" and doing what he had claimed to do so many times before: holding his mirror up to Elizabeth—his audience of the
moment—and allowing her to see in it everything (Francois believed) she was looking for, echoing all the key words of our
program and its teaching—multiple drafts, audience considerations, and varying styles for varying purposes. One fact is certain though: whatever readership Francois had found success in
writing for, Tim was not among them.

By semester's end, Tim, according to his own admission, could
no longer read Francois or his writing with the ease and certainty
of before. "I think it's going to be difficult to talk about Francois,"
he told Elizabeth as their last interview began. But he would try.
"At the beginning," he had "felt better about him and his work";
by the second half of the semester, he "really didn't feel good about"
it. In "A Meaningful Coin," Francois had shown "far more atten-

tion to language than he later showed," when there was "a reversion to a great deal of syntactical and grammatical error." In
addition, "he was starting to turn in one draft plus the final, and
not looking like he did much work at all," and Tim sensed that
"early on he was putting much more attention into his writing
than later on." It was really a matter of "effort," Tim told Elizabeth. At least he thought it was: "I'm not sure about if I'm right,"
he continued. "Well, I can say that I'm pretty sure I'm right in
that perception." Then, regaining balance, he once again posited
that a possible cause of Francois's backsliding was Basic Writing,
where perhaps "he didn't expect too much of himself": "Maybe
that's the problem. 'Oh, I'm a 111 student, so. . .'" Tim consigned Francois to the "bottom five" of a class of twenty-two
and reassessed him generally: what had been Francois's "neat
sense of humor" in February had by April become "flippant and
a little wise, a little standoffish," marking him as perhaps, Tim
reluctantly admitted, "just kind of a wise guy." He told Elizabeth this story to illustrate:

> Now you told me that Francois was talking to you this morn-
> ing before he came down for a conference with me. Well, that
> was weird. He came in a little late, and he said, "I was just at a
> board meeting." And I said, "A board meeting?" And he said,
> "What?" And I said, "A board meeting." And he said, "What
> are you talking about?" And I said, "What did you just say?"
> And he said, "I didn't say anything." This went on for a while.
> Then I said, "I thought you said 'a board meeting.'" He said,
> "No, I didn't say anything about a board meeting. Are you on
> something?" So I thought, "Okay. Are you being funny or not?"
> Meanwhile, he had a doughnut, and, a while later, he suddenly
> tells me he got it at the board meeting. I said, "Oh, so you were
> at a board meeting." And he kind of half-smiled and didn't say
> anything.

Tim apparently did not know "the location of the city of Boston
globally (longitude & latitude)," and, admitting he did not know
"how to respond to this kid," could not quite locate Francois
either.

A host of realities lie, no doubt, between the heaven of
Francois's rendition and the relative hell of Tim's. Anne and I,
too, were unable to collect from Francois early drafts of any es-

says after "A Meaningful Coin," it is true: if, indeed, he did *six*, we still have just one to show. His end-of-the-semester portfolio review stops with "A Meaningful Coin" as well, though we do have final drafts for two more essays, along with the brief retrospective essay accompanying his review. On the other hand, those three remaining essays seem less problematic to me than Tim describes—and far less problematic than "A Meaningful Coin." At the risk of running my metaphor too far, I would suggest that the world of Tim's vertigo is not hell at all but Francois's mirrored wonderland, where everything Tim asked for or wanted was presented back to him—in some distorted (or maybe a bit too-true) form.

I said before that tracks of my own frustration lay in "A Meaningful Coin" and Tim's comments on it. Tracks that would lead to Tim's frustration lay there as well. Despite a tendency to be too "mechanical," too "rigid," Francois's obvious capacity for imaginative association, coupled with his equally obvious willingness to "take risks with ideas," had appealed to Tim: Francois had started with just "this little nickel and zoom, off he" went. It seems, however, that a little zoom goes a long way; a lot of zoom, in this case Francois's third essay, entitled, appropriately enough, "ZooMass," went too far: Francois was "taking things too far," as Francois reported so many teachers had said. It was not what Tim "wanted to hear."

Even in his early interview, as he was praising "A Meaningful Coin" for its "thoughtfulness" and preparing to encourage Francois to be a little less concerned about "understanding what the task is and then almost methodically setting out to do it," Tim was simultaneously preparing to talk to him about his prospectus for "ZooMass," which, Tim said, "hits several different things that have to do with the topic, without clearly saying what he's proposing to do in the paper." The writing, he felt, was "confusing," too, so along with becoming a "little less mechanical," he would also have to encourage Francois to "pay maybe some closer attention to those mechanical, grammatical things." But by the end of the spring, when time had run out, Tim's hopefulness had, too. Looking back now on the finished product as well as the prospectus for "ZooMass," he recalled an essay marred by a general lack of the thoughtfulness shown before. Since this was to be his semester's "documented essay," Francois's job had been to ground his essay on his own experience and/or interests and then support and develop his argument by drawing upon three sources, either print sources or personal interviews. However, according to Tim, "he had simply, I think, grabbed a source that . . . had all the things that he basically used"—a source, it seems, that Tim had given him in the first place—and had otherwise shown no "real engagement of his own thoughts in it." Moreover, "there were plenty of errors" and "organizational problems," and Tim awarded it the same grade he had given "A Meaningful Coin," a BC. This is "ZooMass."

> The scene: the campus pond—I, Francois C_____,
> (a student at the University of Massachusetts)
> am approached by an unsuspecting outsider.
> "Hi, how are you?"
> "You look familiar, are you a student at U-Mass?"
> "Yeah I am."
> "Oh, do you know so and so?"

When I'm approached with this type of conversation I start thinking, "not another egotistical person who thinks that everyone knows everyone at U-Mass." After all, only about twenty thousand students are currently enrolled at our university.

The University of Massachusetts at Amherst had been known as "the zoo" for many years. The zoo. Our university is often referred to as "the zoo"—a place of mass production for partying and oh, education. If we are a zoo then the students are definitely the animals. The zoo is getting too crowded, and I feel like one of the many "chimpanzees" that get passed by unless I make a lot of noise.

The zoo's partying image is a thing of the past. This university used to be referred to as the zoo especially during the late seventy's. According to Marcia Curtis, who is a teacher at the English department, U-Mass is not the party place it once was. She can remember when the "college kids" would start drinking from Thursday night until Sunday morning. However, from what she hears and what she has seen, this university has definitely settled down. (Curtis) However, the current problem that we are facing is our financial crisis.

The University cannot afford to offer the quality education that it has been for the past several years. The university has been operating under a deficit of seventeen million dollars within the past three fiscal years (FY) (Team, published 1989). The results of such sharp cuts through our university has directly affected the quality of our education and the quality of our faculty members. The cut backs are causing the size of classes to increase in growing numbers. The teacher to student ratio is way above an environment that provides adequate individual attention between the professors and their students. Courses that were once offered are being canceled. The results of such cut backs reflect the quality of education especially of state schools. The number of years it takes for students to graduate is growing, and it becomes a more demanding struggle and burden financially for most students. Not only is the students' quality of education is being diminished, but also the availability of an education is suffering.

Tuition has continuously increased. Because of the rising costs of colleges in general, thousands of middle and lower class families are sending their children to one of the biggest factories of education on the east coast. That factory is the University of Massachusetts. It is where thousands graduate, and where thousands should come in each year but find themselves unable to because they cannot afford the high price of an education. Those who do come as first year students may not be aware of the crisis that the university is dealing with.

The financial status in the state of Massachusetts is at its worst. For example, half of the six hundred million dollars cut from state budget in the past six months of 1989 came out of public schools and higher education. That is not all. We at the university have suffered the direct impact of the cuts. Students are already paying over seven hundred dollars in tuition and curriculum support fees. Since most of these figures are from last fall, the figures are expected to become even more alarming. An unnamed source at the J. Duffey/public affairs office told me that she is expecting tuition to increase at a rate of fifteen percent for next semester (total costs now stand at $7,800), even though the state expects only a thirteen percent increase. Another source at the financial aid office told me that even though their particular department has not been damaged in the number of personnel that are currently employed, because of the hiring freeze, any new faculty that U-Mass wants to hire in order to maintain quality education will be denied. This source believes that they will soon be affected because he sees no relief ahead.

What are some of the impacts on the staff? The university has laid off fifty-two cooperative extension staff members. The university necessitates a further reduction of two hundred-fifty nine staff including sixty-two faculty members. For the past two years, the university has been on a hiring freeze: positions are available, but the money is not. (Team, published 1989) These consortium pose a very serious problem because as we stand right now more than half of our operating budget is not from the state.

In FY 1989 the university used more money from non-state sources than from the state appropriation. (U-Mass in Crisis, April 1990). According to the special report the state of Massachusetts is funding the University with only forty-eight percent of its total budget. The university is actively receiving fifty-two percent of the its total spending budget from students' tuition, federal government grants, research contracts, and industrial gifts.

It is time for us students of this university and all public places of higher learning to write our representatives in Congress and to demand affirmative action in dealing with cutting the budget for higher education in Massachusetts. At the same time, we want to tell them "enough is enough, no more cuts!" (The University of Massachusetts at Amherst budget crisis). As I continue striving along the road to fulfill my dream of graduating, my only hope is that the financial crisis here will not be a roadblock for me. Hopefully, this university will graduate their future students to be conscious of and to help repair the potholes and pave that same road of public higher education that they themselves once traveled

Bibliography

1) Interview: Curtis, March 1990.
2) Team, Budget cuts U-Mass Amherst fall 1989.
3) Marc Kenen, U-Mass in crisis! U-Mass Amherst April 1990.

Perhaps my own previous lessons in "francois" inured me to all evidence of Francois's "reversion" to syntactical and grammatical errors here. I can certainly identify the occasional mistake: a faulty word choice made (e.g., "these consortium") or not made ("fifty-two percent of *the its* total spending budget" or "Not only is the students' quality of education is being diminished"); a missing period to close the final sentence; and highly irregular documentation. But I do not see Francois's writing as error-riddled, certainly no more error-riddled than most first-year pieces our teachers receive—and accept. Having worked my way through "MAN vs NATURE," "BLIND-INNOCENT-PREJUDICE," and even "A Meaningful Coin," neither do I find "ZooMass" marred by "organizational problems." On the contrary, I would agree with Francois's self-assessment: I, too, find his writing "much better in terms of . . . easy, clear transitions" that take the guess work out of reading, and I, too, "can read through it and not have to stop to make corrections." The true awkwardnesses I do see I see as commendable attempts by Francois to give Tim precisely what he had asked for in the previous assignment and to make the present piece less "mechanical" and "rigid" in its approach to both reader and subject: that is, a dramatic opening scene with which to "capture the reader's interest" and a (somewhat awkward) extended metaphor with which to close. In fact, it might easily be said of "ZooMass" that Francois "started with this little interaction and zoom, off he goes, and he's talking about the image of ZooMass, the implications as well as the impact of budget cuts for state schools, and all this important stuff."

That Tim applauded the imaginative leaps of "A Meaningful Coin" but felt Francois was trying to cover too much in "ZooMass" may be understandable from a teacher's viewpoint but seems less understandable when we take a student's position. From this vantage point, Francois is not covering too much, that is, too many disparate ideas; he is trying, rather, to make real and symbolic connections among a variety of "elements," just as he did—just as he was supposed to do, and was praised for doing— in "A Meaningful Coin." The faulty (in Tim's view) prospectus that Francois did for "ZooMass," in fact, resembles the prewriting he did for "A Meaningful Coin":

[Typed]
"Hi, how are you?"
"You look familiar, are you a student at U-Mass?"
"yeah I am"
"Oh, who do you know so and so?"

Well I started thinking, not another egotistical person who thinks that just because he or she knows one person at UMass every one else does. After all, only about twenty thousand students that are currently at our University.
The zoo. Our University is often refered to as "the zoo"— a place of mass production for education.

> Thousands of the middle and lower class family are sending their children to the biggest factory of education on the east coast. That factory is the University of Massachusetts. It is where thousands graduates, and where thousands come in each year.
>
> The social problem and the financial status of our state and school has worsened the quality of our Education.

[Then handwritten]
U-Mass
ZooMass
Industrial Ed Place   Cut back the # of students
                                     at the zoo.
                                     Stats - on Budget cuts
Community
L[esbian] B[isexual] G[ay] A[lliance] _____
Soc. Prob. | Too much
                                        diversity
Budget Cost | is it really nec.
    Negative   _____ |

Tim noted in the margin of Francois's listing, "Random ideas at this point. I don't see your intentions clearly yet," and, as I said before, worried aloud to Elizabeth that the prospectus "hits several things that have to do with the topic, without clearly saying what he's proposing to do in the paper." Whatever Tim may have wanted, however, it is not a prospectus that Francois here produced: it is a brainstorming predraft, much like all the other brainstorming predrafts he had been taught to produce in Basic Writing and, until now, in College Writing. As such, it would not show his "intentions clearly yet." It would show, instead, his beginning efforts to read and interpret the social signs around him, just as he had previously read and interpreted the material signs of an object. And here he focused his interpretation on the semantic coin "ZooMass," which is every bit as intriguingly double-sided as any five-cent piece.

The "problem" of "ZooMass"—like the relative haze or clarity of "A Meaningful Coin"—lies not in the "organization" or disorganization of its too-disparate elements but in the fact that Tim did not read them as Francois did, did not see the connections Francois made finally in his essay and first in the observed world of which his essay was one interpretation. But those connections are nonetheless there to be made. I, of course, have an inherited investment in making them since, unbeknownst to me at the time, a conversation Francois and I had was to provide the critical segue from "ZooMass's" commonly accepted meaning as "a place for mass production of partying" to its redefinition as "a place of mass production for . . . oh, education" as well. At that time, I would not have read both meanings in the single term, yet when the two sides of this single coinage are placed before me at once, the reading is immediate: "ZooMass" denotes both the "party place" and the "working people's place," and, in this play on UMass, we are witnessing a latter-day "bread and circuses," the alcohol and entertainment intended to placate "thousands of the middle and lower class family" of our commonwealth; in the same instance, we are marking the distance— both geographical and socioeconomic—between UMass–Amherst and that private place of small classes and abundant funding in Francois's neighboring town of Cambridge, in whose shadow our public university stoops. Francois and I may render our interpretations differently, but I can nevertheless read his in its unified wholeness. Unlike Tim, I can also, with hindsight, recognize "real engagement of his own thoughts in it." For Francois worked throughout his time at UMass as a dormitory security guard and was to take what has become the average five years to graduate. He was, in short, one of those students for whom a university education had increasingly become, in his words, "a demanding struggle and burden financially," and, in everything he wrote and said, he showed himself to be personally interested in the rhetoric as well as the politics of class and race, especially as applied to education.

Essays for Courses Outside College Writing

For Courses in the Major

> The scene: a room in Bartlett Hall—Tim L_____
> (a graduate instructor in the UMass Writing Program)
> is being interviewed by Elizabeth for the final time.

"I was wondering. How do you feel Francois felt about the class?"

> "As he left, he thanked me for it, and said that it was a lot better than—it wasn't 111. He mentioned somebody's name: a lot better than so and so's class. And I didn't press him. That's about it."
>
> "Hmm."

Tim did not know "so and so's" name, but I do. Francois told me, once when he stopped by my office informally for a chat during that spring and again when I interviewed him formally during his fourth year; he also talked about "so and so's" class during his spring 1990 interview with Elizabeth, though there the professor remained unnamed. For the time being, I will leave the question of "so and so's" identity unanswered; I will also leave unraised the question of why Tim felt the need to say it "wasn't 111," that is, was not Basic Writing. I will ask instead: Why did it occur to Francois to contrast College Writing to "so and so's" class at all? And I will suggest that the beginnings of an answer lie here, in the start of another student's essay that directly followed Francois's "ZooMass" in the class publication Tim assembled for their "documented essays":

> Wherever you go in Boston you hear the same thing this gang did this that gang did that. You are constantly reminded of where you are at by the ringing of gunshots, when you go to "the black side of Boston"; Mattapan, Dorchester or Roxbury. . . .
>
> The one theory that I have heard and believe to be true is that there exists in the African-American community a very big identity crisis . . . plaguing the males of this race and . . . causing many of them to become very deviant.

There is no immediate relationship between Francois's essay and this one that followed it. Yet printed immediately after Francois's essay in the publication, the passage—whether composed by a black student or white—spreads across the final page of Francois's writing like a comment upon the sorts of assaultive notions African American students are subjected to daily by fellow undergraduates and faculty members alike.

It was, in fact, just the kind of theorizing in this second student's essay that Francois recoiled from in "so and so's" class. Professor Gates, an instructor central to the sociology department, was not someone a sociology major, which Francois was about to become, could avoid. Gates could, however, be resisted, and Francois did quite consciously and willfully resist him with all his might, at least through that first year. By his junior year, as we will see, Francois had learned to yield pragmatically to this particular faculty member's demands even as he held firm in his expressed opinion that this man is a "racist" and "should be reported."

As described by Professor Gates's teaching assistant Ichiro, a doctoral student in the department with a master's degree in sociology from a Japanese university, the course content centered on "contemporary American problems, social problems, like crime, inequality, racism." The class was large, serving some three hundred students and employing a number of graduate TAs. Professor Gates designed the course and conducted the weekly lectures; each TA was responsible for leading three individual discussion sections with twenty-five members each and for grading the exams as well as the paper assigned to students in those sections. Francois was composing that paper at about the same time he was composing "ZooMass."

According to Francois, his task for Professor Gates was to synthesize a number of theoretical readings pertaining to the "culture of poverty" and, by drawing from them, to argue both sides of the question, "Is it that your culture causes your poverty, or is it that your poverty causes your culture," in a three-page paper. Ichiro represented the task to Elizabeth in a somewhat less personalized form:

> The students are required to read quite a few articles. And for this assignment, they were required to refer to some of the articles and talk about, theoretically, the culture of poverty. They were expected to talk about and contrast some of the articles that differ from one another. There have been debates over causes of poverty: one theory says, "The poor are poor because they're lazy," and the other perspective says that's not true. So students are expected to discuss these theories. That was the assignment.

Francois wrote this:

Now! If I was to say that I was living in a housing project, not working, on welfare with two kids, living in the slums of Chicago. Would you immediately think that I was black (or a minority)? Why is that, why does America link their poverty to the minority? If I was to say that "culture is the cause poverty" I would be lying to you my audience.

Poverty is the cause of our culture. Take for example the !Kung society, their society was an egalitarian society. They believed in sharing everything (food, clothing etc.). However, all of that changed when the South African government decided to explore !Kungs' territory (during the nineteen fifties). Since then the !Kung society have gone through some drastic changes. They no longer share their food or clothing with their neighbors nor do they care for their friends and relatives like they once did. Instead they now fight over who might not be sharing their goods. The Kungs are now poorer then they were before the South African Government invade their land. They have adapted themselves to the new culture, and for that their poverty is the cause of their culture.

According to the poverty budget in the United States, a family of four earning a thousand dollars a month is considered poor (about twelve thousand dollars a year). Keeping all of that in mind they now must divide their earnings into— food, rent, utilities, clothing, medical bills, etc. What are the alternatives of someone who is living in what the U.S. considers being poverty level? For some family, the alternatives are going to the street and hustling so they can make "the ends meet." In the case of these family, they have cultivate their attitude of skepticism and let their poverty make their culture.

Some argue that culture is the cause of poverty. Take for example the same family that has to hustle the street to "make end's meat": their kids will grow up and see their parents (in most cases "a parent") hustling the street trying to make a living. Their young will grow up and follow into the streets environment of hustling or even crimes. They become "caught in the cycle of poverty." They become poor and trained in the way that their parent(s) have brought them into the world and let there culture be the cause of their poverty.

Culture is the cause poverty? If so, the poor are in their situation because they do not educate themselves. Whose fault is that? The idea that the poor have one culture and the rich have another is absolutely true. After all should not that be the way it is supposed to be? For example, if family (A) makes forty-thousand dollars a year and family (B) makes only one forth of that salary, family (A) eats steak and potatoes every evening, but family (B) probably eats steak and potatoes once a month. It is obvious that in such a simple analogy that they remain economically deficient because of their lazy attitude toward working.

After hearing both sides of "poverty is the cause of culture" which one do you think the government believe is true? Our government have fuel the matter of poverty by given the poor money instead of jobs. As the future generation we the people must educate our children. Education is the way out of poverty. Until then we can not look forward to a pluralism culture (society). The facts remain either way our you want to argue this point is that poverty is a problem our society must face, and the sooner we start the better.

At the bottom of Francois's essay, Ichiro made this comment:

> You are writing this too much on your own. This is not a free-composition. You have to refer to class materials (esp. readings). The central issue is the "culture of poverty" debate between Banfield and Ryan. And that is missing from your paper.

In addition to correcting a number of spelling mistakes, he also noted, in the margin next to Francois's opening paragraph, "too colloquially not appropriate," and, next to the closing line, "bad sentence." He awarded the composition "6" out of a possible fifteen points, which, he explained to Elizabeth, amounted to an alphabetical grade of "C."

In their interview, Ichiro also explained further his comments to Francois and the reasoning behind them. When assigned the essay, the students were given no "certain audience" to keep in mind, nor were they expected to make their own argument or interpretation: "They could, but, if they didn't, that was fine." They were simply to "compare and contrast the two kinds of viewpoints," and that, essentially, was what Francois did not do. Aside from committing "quite a few misspellings," he was writing, as Ichiro put it, "too much on his own"; the essay looked "more like a creative style of composition, rather than a term paper, or whatever." It was not "tightly based on the reading." Ichiro guessed that had Francois read the articles "in much more detail, probably he'd have been influenced by them. . . . Probably he'd have written in a different way." But, by the looks of the essay, Ichiro surmised that Francois had not read the articles "carefully enough" and so "ended up writing from his own." His introduction of the !Kung culture was a "good idea" but was carried on too long, and the direct audience address made Ichiro "uncomfortable" because it was "not consistent from beginning to end"; once more, however, the main fault lay in the fact that "his argument was not really based on those readings, and he was saying something on his own. Since he was not referring to the reading materials, the conclusion was not really persuasive."

Ichiro also expressed to Elizabeth a strength he recognized in Francois's writing, though he did not express it in his comment to Francois: while some students wrote "pretty superficially," he could say that Francois "was concerned about the problem of poverty" and demonstrated "his interest in this issue." Of himself, on the other hand, he observed that his own strength came from his position as "foreigner" to American society, a position that gave him occasional discomfort but more often a helpful sense of objectivity when "talking about American social problems." Ichiro presumed, however, that Francois's difficulties with the assignment arose, not out his experience with this particular social issue, but out of his inexperience with the particular discourse of sociology: "He is just a freshman," Ichiro concluded, "so maybe he's not used to the college kind of writing."

In a way we might say Ichiro's closing comment just narrowly misses the mark: Francois was just a freshman, so maybe he was *too* used to the *College Writing* kind of writing. Despite what seems a clear difference between Tim's abiding emphasis on finding "something new, unique, and interesting" to say about a subject, that is, on *interpretation*, and Ichiro's expectations— whether clearly established by the sociology assignment or not— that the writing would be "tightly based on the readings," that is, on *observation and summary*, and despite my own semester-long emphasis on the distinction between the two, when Francois was asked by Elizabeth whether his composing processes for these courses differed much, he answered emphatically, "No. Actually, no." And that may have been his mistake. Indeed, most everything of style or substance that Ichiro faulted reflected techniques learned in Basic as well as College Writing: an attention-capturing introduction, marked here as "not appropriate"; the imaginative inclusion of materials from other arenas, here his anthropology course, acceptable in itself but carried on too long; obvious attempts to address a recognized audience, unnecessary to this assignment; and, most of all, a persistent determination to say "something on his own." Tim, on the other hand, faulted Francois for having done in his "documented essay" what Ichiro wanted him to do in his "term paper": to paraphrase Tim, Francois had simply "grabbed a source" or two given him by the instructor, summarized materials from those sources, and otherwise showed no "real engagement of his own thoughts in it." "ZooMass" left Tim dissatisfied. And, Francois's untitled sociology paper left Ichiro equally so. As Ichiro himself phrased it, these three pages represented a "creative composition" instead of the required "term paper," or, as we might phrase it, a "personal" instead of an "academic" essay.

Taken together, however, the two teachers' complaints, as contradictory as they are, suggest that Francois's difficulties in sociology were not all a matter of inexperience in its discourse or methods. Tim's complaints indeed suggest that Francois might well have produced a "term paper" to satisfy Ichiro and, presumably, Professor Gates as well. And were he to set "ZooMass" and Francois's untitled sociology paper side by side, I believe Ichiro would see that Francois was indeed capable of producing a far more acceptable term paper than he did, except that he was more engaged in the former than Tim knew and more disengaged by the latter than Ichiro realized, both despite and because of "his interest in this issue."

In his midsemester interview, conducted shortly after the assignment for Ichiro and Professor Gates had been completed, Francois told Elizabeth he had just sat down and written it the night before it was due because it did not "really have any meaning" for him. He then went on:

> The question was, "Is it that your culture causes your poverty, or is it that your poverty causes your culture?" You had to

argue both sides. The one that I think is true is that your poverty causes your culture. And I argued that pretty effectively.
But when I got to the other side of the question—"or not"—I
found myself contradicting myself on what I said previously. It
was just not something that I really wanted to bring up.

I am inclined to trust students. When Francois says that he had
not spent much time on the assignment, I believe that this is the
case and that it accounts, at least in part, for his failure to synthesize the textual material more thoroughly—or at all, it appears—
and to compose a more coherently organized essay. But when I
see incoherence approaching fragmentation, as I do in this writing and as I did, for example, in Steven's "State of the World
Today," I suspect that the subject, which Francois claimed did
not "really have any meaning" for him, may in fact have had too
much. I suspect that, forced to take two positions, both of which
he found assaultive, Francois was left with no position from which
to speak as or for himself. Ichiro and Francois defined the "debate" into which Francois was to enter somewhat differently:
Ichiro rendered it as between theories that hold "the poor are
poor because they're lazy" and those that "say that's not true";
Francois set the question as asking, "Is it that your culture causes
your poverty, or is it that your poverty causes your culture?" But
however one phrases the two supposedly opposing perspectives,
both are equally offensive, and denigrating, to those outside the
white middle class or, more specifically, to poor and working-
class black Americans, to whom, as Francois's introductory passage points out, majority Americans erroneously yet inevitably
"link their poverty." Set against each other, they establish a cycle
of theorizing into which, as well as from which, perhaps not all
students but certainly a working-class black student like Francois
would be hard-pressed to deliver himself. For that reason, while
I am also inclined to trust the insights of teachers, I think in this
instance Ichiro's observations on Francois's "interest in the issue," as opposed to his own objectivity as a "foreigner" to American society and its social problems, again just miss the mark.
Objective as Ichiro may have been, his foreign vantage, and with
it his objectivity, derived in this case not from his position out-

side *American* society but from his position outside *black, working-class* American society, and alongside those majority students who, like Rachel, doubtless did have less interest in the issue than Francois did and may well have written "pretty superficially," but with acceptable "objectivity," about the debate as framed by the assignment.

Little wonder, then, that Francois felt he had represented the "your poverty causes your culture" view "pretty effectively" but, when representing its proposed alternative—"or not"—found himself mired in self-contradiction. "It was just not something that I really wanted to bring up"; it was, that is, the underside of a coin which, unlike the buffalo-head nickel, he resisted exploring. And I use the term "resisted" quite selectively here, for I do not believe this essay "came out dissatisfied" because of Francois's inexperience in the discourse of sociology, as Ichiro believed, or because the topic did not "really have any meaning" for him, as Francois himself initially claimed. Here I believe Francois, consciously or unconsciously but in either case quite understandably, resisted acquiring this particular discourse as it was presented to him and resisted engagement in a discussion that literally offered him no viable position from which to speak.

This is not to say that students of Francois's race and background cannot learn to participate in the sort of debate that Gates set before his students. In fact, as we will see, Francois himself came to participate in debates of precisely this nature in his Race Relations class, where he wrote "real papers that I'm deeply involved in" for another member of the sociology department whom he characterized as "devoted" to the subject and to students alike. But it is to raise again the simple—as Francois would say, the "basic"—question, How do you write an objective, academic essay about matters that are not, for lack of a better term, "academic" to you? In writing "A Meaningful Coin," Francois faced a similar dilemma: integrating the emblematic buffalo into his interpretive essay successfully required his knowing its predetermined, culturally set—and therefore shared—significance. Without such knowledge, he had to reinvent its symbolic content within his own narrative. In order for him to integrate "the other side of the question" into the culture/poverty debate, the task was the same but the stakes were higher. Either he had to accommodate a perspective that was foreign, if not antithetical, to his own, an option which would require inuring himself to its implicit assaults on his (still-forming) cultural and racial identity; or he had to redefine each and every term of the given narrative—literally to use the master's tools to tear down the master's house. The former, he would not do; the latter, he could not do—because the task was obviously overwhelming, and because, according to Francois, this particular master was not about to share his tools for any such purpose.

If in March Francois took his difficulties in Gates's class on himself, by May he located them squarely in the professor, "not the course," he would insist. "The course is a fine course. But the guy is biased, and I think in some circumstances he's racist." When pressed to explain further, he would say only that "he talked about minorities very, very, very downwise. I think he should be reported." Not the TA, he clarified, the professor. For Ichiro, Francois reserved a xenophobic critique of his own: "He just can't speak English. That's his problem." Three years later, having taken a number of required courses with Professor Gates, Francois was better able to explain in some detail what he saw to be the faculty member's technique. When discussion turned to the women's movement, for instance, Francois often found himself at odds with Professor Gates: "And when I would say it in class, he wouldn't laugh but have a sarcastic 'Ha, ha, ha! Well, come on now.'" On issues of race: "He didn't really want to touch too much." He talked about race "from an intellectual, a professor perspective," claiming "so and so had said it, so and so had written about it, so therefore I can say it." Students, it seems, did not have the same latitude: "He would pass out the pros and cons, and you would either take one side or the other." Usually agreeing with neither viewpoint and having a "completely different perspective," Francois could find "no place to fit in." When he did take a side, he "couldn't argue it convincingly because it just wasn't there for me"; when he took a position of his own, Professor Gates would "bat it down with the additional material" he had at his disposal.

A game of devil's advocacy? Perhaps. Clearly, however, when in class discussion Gates played by the same rules of objective debate he had set for his students' writing, arguing not "on his own" but from a position "tightly based on the reading," Francois and others perceived him as anything but objective: Francois felt Gates's remarks personally and felt them to be personally intended—as "biased" and at times "racist." Whether this assessment is accurate or not, Gates's tactics were, at the very least, unsportsmanlike, for this was a game that Francois, by his own admission, *could not* play as a first-year student. As a senior, he explained to me why he *would not* play it if he could. In our final interview of 1993, he spoke from a teacher's position:

MARCIA: Do you like to persuade people in your writing?

FRANCOIS: I like to persuade people, yeah, but I don't necessarily want to give them my perception or what they want to hear. No, I feel that I can take almost any perspective, whether I'm wrong or right or completely don't agree with it but argue and make it a persuasive argument either way.

MARCIA: Do you like to do that?

FRANCOIS: Ah, if I have to I'll do it.

MARCIA: Will you do that with every subject?

FRANCOIS: No.

MARCIA: What subjects won't you do that with?

FRANCOIS: Things that I teach and believe in.

MARCIA: Want to tell me some of those?

FRANCOIS: Oh, I don't know, you name it. Social injustice, things that will directly affect me or benefit me. I feel selfish when I keep saying "me."

MARCIA: It's an interview with you.

FRANCOIS: You know, stuff that I'll do it with is stuff that I probably don't care as much for or stuff that won't hurt me or anyone who is vulnerable to being hurt.

MARCIA: So if you were in a literature class and you were just arguing whether a poem was good or bad, and the poet has been dead for two hundred years so it's not going to hurt his feelings, you would take either side of that argument?

FRANCOIS: Oh yeah. I would argue my interpretation of what the author had written.

MARCIA: Would you be willing to take a different interpretation?

FRANCOIS: Oh, yeah.

MARCIA: In a social issues class?

FRANCOIS: Most likely not, because I think those are real facts and
they affect people more directly. . . . I mean, I can talk about
abstractions, but when we talk about things that are going to
affect other people . . . it seems to be common sense to me
that you just don't play around like that for the sake of an
intelligent argument. Make sense?

"Things that I teach and believe in" are honesty and clarity's
reserve; they are not to be played with, even for intelligence's
sake. I told Francois, "Yes, that made perfect sense" to me. I did
not tell him what else I thought: that to make a student who
considers himself a subject of discussion join in that discussion
objectively and, in doing so, voice opinions he considers assaultive is insensitive at best, sadistic at worst, and schizophrenic in
between.

Still, as I have said, by his junior year, Francois had learned
to play the devil's advocate, "to take almost any perspective,
whether I'm wrong or right or completely don't agree with it but
argue and make it a persuasive argument either way." Or perhaps it would be truer to say that he had found ways to make a
compact with the devil while keeping his fingers crossed behind
him. Here is a sample from a junior-year sociology course assignment entitled "Arguments: Pros & Cons of Affirmative Action,"
written, again, for Professor Gates:

The most controversial issues raise on affirmative action is that
"it" in itself is reverse discrimination due the special treatment
that is being given to blacks. The following authors G. C. Loury
and D. D'Souza are opposed to Affirmative Action because
they feel "it" shows "lack of honor" (Loury) and that it is
reverse discrimination (D'Souza). D'Souza in his article <u>Sins of
admission</u> attacks the unfair practice of affirmative action's
"meeting the target". He says that college administrators use
different indicators in accepting minority students. These indicators points out that even though minority students perform
at a lower academic entry level they yet have a better chance in
getting in certain universities because of their "quota" status:
minority.

Neither particularly graceful nor error-free, it was a style none-theless allowing for a synthesis of others' notions, however alien or repugnant. The word "it" allowed as well for a degree of manipulation that amounted, it would seem, to a forced collaborator's wink at the audience, a resister's code.

Francois's time spent as a sociology major was not all one of uncomfortable accommodation. At the same time his distaste for Professor Gates's manner was clarifying, he found a mentor in another figure central to that department, Professor Louis Marks, "a great guy." The courses he taught and the requirements for them differed little from Professor Gates's, at least according to Francois's descriptions of them. But the difference in effect was marked. During our final interview of spring 1993, I listened as Francois explained the sorts of writing he had done for Professor Marks's Race Relations class, which he was just then complet-ing. The assignments could have come from Professor Gates: "We wrote two papers in the class," Francois said, "all about social dynamics." The students were exposed to various "models," that is, various theories current in the field. "Model one, for example, would say, 'Your social class depends on your race or ethnicity, or doesn't depend on your race and ethnicity,'" and students then faced the task of determining "which one we thought was proper or which one we believed in . . . and we went out and did addi-tional research on whatever topic or side, whatever argument we wanted to make." Echoes of Professor Gates's poverty debate sound in my ears, even as I record our conversation here. Yet Francois appeared wholly unaware of the similarity, so different were the two experiences for him, so different perhaps was the effect of using research to make an argument of one's own choos-ing, and so different was the work he judged he produced—"real papers that I'm deeply involved in," papers "thirty, forty pages long."

I asked Francois pointedly about the two instructors:

MARCIA: What felt different about writing for Louis Marks and Professor Gates?

FRANCOIS: Well, he was devoted.

MARCIA: Did you feel differently about what you could say?

FRANCOIS: I didn't feel differently about what I could say, but when I would say something to him, when I would make a comment in class, he would give me an answer that may not always be satisfying but that makes sense, that is rational and has been thought about.

MARCIA: Did you feel he received your questions differently?

FRANCOIS: Yeah. Again, he was devoted. I mean, I've talked to him after class for hours. As a matter of fact, I went early this semester to sit down and talk to him. You know, we talked about different stuff, all kinds of stuff. He's into the material. It's always good when you can pick up on professors that are into their material.

I asked him specifically about the Race Relations course papers, too:

MARCIA: Would you bring in those papers? I would really like to see them.

FRANCOIS: Yeah sure, ah, sure, if you have time to read a couple of thirty pagers.

MARCIA: I do. I do. I have plenty of time.

I was anxious to see and to be able to show you now excerpts from those essays, anticipating how I might present extended passages of clear expression and coherent thought to demonstrate the difference in articulation that a difference in reception engenders. But Francois called me a few days after our interview to say he had been too slow to retrieve his graded papers from Professor Marks. They had been discarded. There might well be, he reassured me, copies somewhere among his dormitory belongings or at his family's home, printouts or perhaps original computer files. But subsequent calls to me, from the dorm and sometime later from Boston, told of fruitless searches. So I have no way of knowing the nature of these writings in which Francois found himself "deeply involved." Nor do I know Professor Marks's appraisal of them. Perhaps Francois does not know either; perhaps he does.

For Courses Outside the Major

Francois is not Steven. He kept no voluminous archive of his "spiritual autobiography." We have just a handful of papers written during his final two years, none accompanied by early drafts, only one with instructor comments, and most retrieved by me from the word processor he finally delivered at my door just days before his graduation. Still, I can say of the pieces he did preserve that the "stretches of good, clear writing" Tim noted in "A Meaningful Coin" are longer here, some quite extended indeed. An illustrative one is an untitled final examination paper composed for an education course in Francois's fifth year, the same paper from which I quoted earlier. It is his "chosen writing," the piece Francois would choose to represent him, if he were to choose just one. As in "ZooMass," he returned to issues of minority and working-class education and public support, and, as in "A BI-LINGUAL AND SOCIAL STRUGGLE," he set himself alongside another figure who spoke to the same issues. But this time, it was not to compete with that figure for dominance over the argument or survival in the reader's mind; it was to establish an alliance with his subject and to establish his subject as his mentor, with himself as a sort of amanuensis, who, ironically, manages from this position to inscribe the strongest essay of his career. To give a sense of Francois's ultimate choice, I will transcribe its opening two pages:

> The individual that I have chosen to interview is a professor of journalism at the University. His name is Jacob McCartny. I have known Professor Jacob McCartny for about two years. Although I have never taken any of his classes, I have made an effort to keep in contact with him. He is a native of America with an ethnicity of Puerto Rico. His educational experience took place in the city of Springfield, Massachusetts in the nineteen sixties. He considers himself one of the first beneficiaries of the nineteen fifty eight supreme court Brown decision, and of the civil rights movement in the nineteen sixties. The schools he attended in Springfield were predominantly black, the student body was black, and so were the teachers. During his early educational experience, schools were not de jure segregated, but rather by choice. For example, if your elementary school was black, that is because the students attending more or less

reflected your neighborhood. However, the schools were more integrated in the junior high schools and the high schools. He later entered an urban education program similar to the CCEBMS [Collegiate Committee for the Education of Black and other Minority Students] program here at UMass. He graduated from UMass in nineteen seventy six. His educational success continued, from the inner city schools in Springfield, Massachusetts, through college, graduate school and now as an educator.

In this essay, I am going to discuss **Dropouts and the Silencing of Critical Voices** in the American school system. However, since this essay is about the educational system, I am going to incorporate other material which is relevant to dropout rates. I am also going to offer a critical analysis of the system by Jacob McCartny.

Professor McCartny, as an educator, has articulated and speculated on some of the reasons why the national education system is structured the way that it is, and why it is quickly falling apart. In order to understand why and where the system has gone wrong, he said, one must be able to look at the system from a historical perspective. Historically, the system was not built to educate all members of society, it was designed to educate young white males. When women were allowed to obtain a formal education, it was assumed that since they were inferior to men and they were living in a white male society, they should be learning what the white males are learning. Issues such as women's future roles in this society and their contribution to the work force were not addressed.

The system became overwhelmed when other members of society (black, Chinese, etc.) were allowed to receive an education, without restructuring the system and preparing the system for the diversity and multiculturalism which was pouring into the system. Because the system never tried to accommodate all members of society, and did not offer the revolutionary changes which were necessary to the system's survival, it was bound to fail. . . .

Conclusion

If all a culture's institutions can be read like a language, then an educational system is a discourse system. And as Francois's concluding essay suggests, the question is not whether or to what degree the self has a place in that system, in that discourse, but whose self will find a place—and, with it, a voice—there. Francois struggled with this second question throughout his five years at the University; the various occasions of his struggle exposed the fallacy of the first question. Whether in a Victorian woodcut or a discarded coin or the predefined terms of a sociological debate, a "self" was already speaking. Implicit yet no less distinct, it was the representative voice of the "majority" for whom and by whom the culture and all its emblems, discourses, debates, and institutions had been designed. Occasionally in alliance with, but more often against, this voice, Francois struggled to insert himself into the discourse. To make himself heard. To make sense *to* himself. To make sense *of* himself. Simply to make himself. Try as he might at times to efface himself, he was not in a position to be implicit.

I have said that Francois is not Steven. And that is certainly true. Whereas Steven could not resist inserting his gayness into nearly everything he wrote, asserting its goodness through everything he wrote, Francois continued to struggle, throughout his tenure as an undergraduate, between his hesitation to tell too much and his desire to be fully known, between saying what he wanted to say and "spitting back" what others wanted to hear, between expressing himself as he intended and just plain making sense of himself at all. And whereas, through his self-created major in gender studies, Steven found entrance into an academic "discourse community" capable of embracing, both theoretically and linguistically, the contingency as well as the value of his gay identity, Francois found a less satisfying match. Navigating his way between criticism from his Social Problems TA that he had not been objective enough and from his College Writing TA that he had not made himself subject enough, he entered a social science "community" struggling with its own ambivalence regarding the self's epistemological and linguistic place in discourse.

Yet, like Steven, Francois too seems to have spent his five years at the University at once consciously constructing an identity out of the bits of race, class, and gender information given him and, at the same time, composing a curriculum vitae to inform that identity, to give it shape and to give Francois both vocabulary and occasion for its continued construction. The major he chose, the classes he selected to fulfill that major, and the electives he took to complement it, all point back to that moment he recorded in his first-year anthropology course—when he realized "this society unlike my last society takes notice of your skin color"—even as they build toward his authorizing credentials, toward, that is, his B.A. in sociology from UMass and the professional position that such a "simple piece of paper" would afterward afford him. The essays he wrote to meet the various major and nonmajor course requirements appear to have played their roles as well. Whether forced to stand outside his racial and linguistic contexts, as in Professor Gates's course, or encouraged to situate himself squarely within them both, as in Professor Marks's, Francois ended his time at UMass, it seems, with a wider vision of "understanding" and a wider vision of language's relationship to understanding than when he began. What early on had been cast always as a personal struggle with his reader and, occasionally, with his subject for power over meaning making and definition became a broader, social struggle shared with other minorities and women for the power of self-determination—the struggle to inscribe, over and over, their own stories on the ever-erasing cultural "palimpsest" that Francois himself once described as governing personal as well as public identity. In our final interview, I asked Francois directly about his apparent preoccupation with "struggle," and his answer was equally direct, as well as pragmatic:

> I do talk about struggles a lot. Maybe because I'm personally experiencing struggle in my life, in my everyday life, but I think everyone is experiencing struggles. I mean, struggles on the street: you turn on the TV, you see struggles. You go into a new family, you open up the door, you take a look, and you see struggle, whether it's between the parents or it's problems that the parents have with the kids, the fact that they can't interrelate. You see problems everywhere. So, it's not that I'm a sad or depressed person, but I like to look at struggle because it's a fact of reality. I mean, everyone is not living in La-La Land, you know?

I do.

As Anne and I noted in our introduction to this study, students beginning college are entering new discourse communities as part of their education. By definition, teachers play a role in the process, as principal interpreters, conveyors, and inhabitants of those new communities. Anne and I also proposed that students beginning college enter new discourses as part of their gradual effort to achieve self-definition. Whether they wish to or not, teachers therefore also play a role in encouraging or discouraging their students' attempts to achieve an enhanced sense of their identity within the world, of their humanness among other humans.

As individual persons, we all compose and revise our selves over time. Yet despite, or perhaps because of, this fact, we daily confront the urgency to express ourselves coherently, in our writings as in our lives. And, to repeat Heinz Kohut's words:

> Throughout his life a person will experience himself as a cohesive, harmonious, firm unit in time and space, connected with his past and pointing meaningfully into a creative-productive future, only as long as, at each stage in his life, he experiences certain representatives of his human surroundings as joyfully responding to him, as available to him as sources of idealized strength and calmness, as being silently present but in essence like him, and, at any rate, able to grasp his inner life more or less accurately so that their responses are attuned to his needs and allow him to grasp their inner life when his is in need of such sustenance. (*How Does Analysis Cure?* 52)

One of my hopes as a basic writing teacher has been to act, when possible, as one such responsive and available representative to students, one able to grasp their inner lives "more or less accurately," so that my responses are attuned to their needs and so that I can, at least to some degree, help them feel and display a greater sense of cohesiveness in their writing. Over the short term, Francois thwarted my ability to attune myself to him. As a student confronting what I termed for him the "university style," he seemed to resist writing in conventional syntax, essay form, or even standard typography. As an evolving young individual, he seemed to resist giving information by which other teachers and I might gain access to his "subjective world" and his own sense of identity: he left us unsure about his birthplace and native language. He gave confusing and sometimes even contradictory information about whether he came from a background of privileged schooling, economic struggle, or both; about whether race was an important issue in his own self-definition; and about whether he could or would profit from commentary praising some aspects of his writing and asking him to work on others. His statements implicitly raised questions about whether placement in Basic Writing was more hurtful to his sense of identity than helpful to his progress. And, as he seemingly resisted both revealing his past contexts clearly and entering new terrain in predictable ways, Francois raised doubts in me about whether I really could guide his passage into academically acceptable discourse forms, whether I ever would teach him to make himself intelligible to others at all.

Yet, as we also discussed in our introductory chapter, persons in new discourse and subjective realms may feel besieged and fragmented rather than enhanced—or may experience both sensations either successively or simultaneously. As Lisa Delpit has stressed, learning involves choice: consciously or unconsciously, students choose which discourses to participate in and which to resist. But that choice need not be simply an either/or decision: resistance can be coupled with efforts to acquire and reshape the dominant discourse. Teachers therefore must understand, Delpit advises, "that students who appear to be unable to learn are in some instances choosing to 'not-learn'" (*Other People's* 163). And to help them to learn successfully, teachers must assist in the reshaping process: "To do so, they must saturate the dominant discourse with new meanings, must wrest from it a place for the glorification of their students and their forbears" (164). In Francois's case, I now think that, while at some times his acts of apparent evasion and resistance belied a frustrated and frustrating effort to learn, at other times they signaled real attempts to exercise his own choice and retain some sense of autonomy. He did not want to be consigned to or confined by categories convenient for educational and social assessment—to be identified as "a minority" or "a basic writer," for instance—but wanted to be understood more fully, and to buy some time for carrying out his self-composition on his own schedule and, where possible, in his own terms. The reshaping process or, more forcefully, the wresting process described by Delpit defines

Francois's "struggle." What perhaps began as a personal struggle between saying what he wanted to say and saying what his audience wanted to hear gradually presented itself to me as a struggle having practical, moral, ethical, and political dimensions. What appeared first as insistence that his essential self be appreciated as one might appreciate the deeper, "hidden meanings" of some artifact became, most clearly in the light of his resistance to Professor Gates's demands and his embrace of Professor Marks's "devotion," an effort to protect his own integrity along with the integrity of others similarly "vulnerable to being hurt," either in the act of expression or in the experience of being read. But all along the way I now recognize Francois's "bilingual and social struggle" to have been the struggle literally to coin a new language which, like the buffalo nickel, might contain, restore, and glorify those whom the governing discourse has forgotten.

Over time Francois taught me that new language, as I learned to read, if not speak, what I have come to think of as *en francois*. And with that observation, I will return one final time to our introduction. There Anne and I explained our conviction that, without laying aside our responsibilities to provide students with instruction, we can best assist students not by overriding their voices or by withdrawing from them or by opposing ourselves to them, but by listening to them "afresh," attempting to sustain empathy with them and to find a place alongside them, learning from them as they learn from us. Francois both challenged and reinforced this conviction in me. For one of Francois's methods— call it a defense or a gift—was to reflect back upon teachers their own pedagogical styles and practices, in however fractured or incomplete a manner. The mirror image of myself that he presented to me often made me uncomfortable, frustrated, insecurely tethered to unfamiliar moorings. Eventually I had little choice but to suspend disbelief and put my faith in him as blindly, and as innocently, as we ask students to put their faith in us. It was through such an act of trust that I learned to work *with* Francois, rather than away from or against him, to yield to him—not to abdicate instructional responsibility, for I always offered some assessment of his writings and advice for improvement—but to surrender myself to unfamiliar possibilities for meaning, as one surrenders to the text of an unknown culture or idiom. Ultimately,

I think, Francois and I came to mirror each other. We became each other's teacher, each other's student, as I, too, entered a new, unfamiliar discourse. And that was Francois.

CHAPTER SIX

Persons in Process and Possibilities for Teaching

For many students, their years in college are a time of transi-tion and initial instability, moving from high school to col-lege and from a home environment to a new one away from most friends and family; thus the college years are a time for seeking stability, thinking toward their future, preparing for it, and figur-ing out its relation to their past. It is clearly a time when persons are in process, recomposing themselves toward their futures. In the preceding chapters, we have tried to show something of that process at work and how integral writing was to it for four stu-dents at a large state university. For them, writing and learning were both far from neutral activities, as they tried to make sense of what they were asked to learn in light of their personal histo-ries, perceived identities, values, and goals, and, equally impor-tant, as they tried to accomplish that learning in particular classrooms, in relation to—and in relationships with—particular teachers.

In these four young people, we see students striving to bridge the gap between private and public interests, between the per-sonal and the academic, a gap sometimes accentuated by genre conventions and teaching practices. We see also the significant role teachers have in students' ongoing self-definition—variously fostering and frustrating that project as student and teacher in-teract as writer and audience. Through their experiences and writing, we see a persistent personal impulse to construct coher-ent selves through writing, to make themselves understood through their writing to an audience capable of understanding them and for a kindred group capable of identifying with them. Finally, we see the resilience and accomplishment of students over their years of college and their sophistication in interpreting their learning and writing experiences.

In this closing chapter we aim to summarize what we saw of these four students' development as writers and persons and to reflect on possibilities for teaching and student development through course work. We focus on our roles as teachers and mentors, on the function of sponsoring discourse communities, on the linking of private with academic interests, and on specific classroom practices. The points we make reflect not only what we advise to others but also what we have learned regarding our own teaching practices and curriculum design.

As a preface, we want to respond to a thought some readers may have that these students are unusual or exceptional. We have not aimed to generalize that these students are representative types, but we do believe the backgrounds and experiences they bring represent something of the diversity amongst the students sitting in our classrooms and appropriately admitted to higher education in the United States: students of a range of national origins, ethnicities, classes, and religious convictions; females and males of various sexual orientations; students whose home languages are not all English and who possess varying ranges of facility with standard American English; and students with varied personal and family histories. As we have endeavored to show, these aspects of social and personal identity intermix in complex ways in particular students and are implicated in their learning.

Still, it may seem to some that these students are unusual for the complex and extreme personal issues they present in themselves and represent in their writings—absolute religious devotion, compulsive assertion of sexual identity, suicidal depression, confrontations with abuse and alcoholism, experiences of racism, confusion or subterfuge about national origins and native languages, and more. From our years of teaching, we believe this is not unusual: students, like the general population, confront such issues and hold a range of value-laden beliefs that enter into all of their thinking, including their thinking about subjects in school. Further, and not exceptionally, writing provides a venue for that thinking, indeed a venue where it is difficult to prevent the intersection—sometimes even collision—of personal and new knowledges. This dynamic is intensified when writers compose in new genres that ask them to take on new subjectivities.

What may be unusual, though, about these students is that they have been studied over a period of years, so that the complexities of their stories, as well as the body of course writings reflecting those stories, have had some opportunity to be represented. Our research was not only a set of tasks but a privilege, for, through the cooperative efforts of the students, we were able to learn rather deeply of their perspectives and experiences. The phenomenon of studying the writing they produced over a period of years has been similar to that encountered when one reads—not a single, discrete work—but the full works of an author who divulges patterns and changes in thinking and style within texts written over time. Our research also reminds us, however, that in our role as teachers rather than researchers the phenomenon is different: as teachers, we are deeply implicated in these long-term patterns and changes that we cannot, in the moment, see.

We undertook this project for the purpose of better understanding the long-term experience of writing for students and thereby better understanding our immediate roles and effects as teachers. Nam's, Steven's, Rachel's, and Francois's contributions are especially valuable because few longitudinal studies of undergraduate writers exist, and we did represent to the students that their participation would influence our own teaching, if not others'. Accordingly, we do extrapolate from their words and experiences, looking especially at issues more than one of them found important, at ideas and themes that have at once guided us and come through to us from the students' experiences: writing as a relational, self-constituting act, at once personal, social, and cultural; the desirability of reconciling personal with academic writing; and the roles of teachers as attuned and empathic audiences as well as guides to new knowledge, skills, and identities. Most important, we have seen how students come to use writing at once for self-reflection and self-fashioning—as a mediator between self and other selves—and for participation in the university world—as a mediator between self and other.

The Students' Development as Writers and Persons

When we began this study, we assumed that we would see some changes over time, and we have, particularly given the length of time spent with Steven, Rachel, and Francois. The word "development," of course, connotes positive change, and we believe we have seen that as well. We summarize that development briefly here and thread further observations as relevant throughout the following sections.

We do not claim that any of these students graduated from college as writers of flawless prose. Still, in their unique ways, all developed as writers, as is evident even from Nam's one year at the University. For all four, their writing became more fully developed, more coherent, and more surely articulated. Further, all were writing with more authority: their later writings conveyed more of a sense of personal assurance and of purpose in communicating with readers; those writings were also authorized by a sense of writers speaking from amongst a sponsoring group, for example a group of psychologists or gender studies scholars. Rachel's senior honors thesis, "Intimacy Issues among Young Adults: A Study of Family Alcoholism and Its Effect upon Children," is a persuasive study, evidencing her command of the discourse conventions of psychological research and her own developing sense of a style she could call her own. Steven's critical essay "Madonna: The Queer Queen" presents a persuasive reading of Madonna's position as gay icon, drawing on the scholarship of queer studies and the methods of cultural interpretation. Francois's untitled education paper, based on his interview with Jacob McCartny, is a persuasive argument for educational reform, as in it he positions himself squarely alongside his mentor in order to articulate more convincingly observations of his own. Even in Nam's later essays, especially in one like his penultimate essay for College Writing, "The Lord is My Shepherd," we see—despite the occasional unidiomatic expressions— an ease with language, a fullness of development, and a reflective quality we would hope to see in any first-year student's writing. And we hear a voice authorized by an assembly of past and present religious figures for whom and with whom he speaks.

These students' development as writers paralleled their personal development: in our interpretation, the two were interdependent. All four entered our classes and our study as newcomers, anxious about how they would measure up to others as writers and as citizens of this alien community of twenty-five thousand in the hills of western Massachusetts that is UMass. All left, no doubt, anxious about the next new world they would enter but also with a greater sense of personal agency and public purpose, prepared to help others with whom they identified, others, we might even say, who reflected their own prior selves—parishioners seeking spiritual guidance, gay and lesbian students adjusting to college life, children of alcoholic families, and minority youngsters struggling with the realities of life beyond the borders of "La-La Land." Again, this suggests to us *development*, positive change (though not, we would readily admit, radical transformation): it suggests change that carries with it into the future clear threads to the past, change not unlike the revisionary processes that over time moved these students' writings from private to more public voice, or our own reading processes that uncovered even in their most "academic" research an impelling personal interest. Some may well find this interpretation a matter of frustration or critique. From the perspective of strict social constructivists and adherents of critical pedagogy, all four students may be seen as neither products nor agents of change but as prisoners of cultural influence and background, each becoming little more than what they were: spokespersons of the subcultures that claimed them and thus paradoxically representatives of the dominant culture—the English-speaking, heterosexual, white culture—that rejected them. And looking back from this same perspective, their writings, too—Nam's essays about immigrant experiences and religion; Steven's suicide note, counseling pamphlets, and analyses of drag; Rachel's research into abuse and alcoholism from first-year documented essay to senior honors thesis; Francois's essays about cultural loss—all seem to be expressions of individuals who are themselves mere expressions of culture, tail-wags of the dogs of social forces.

On the other hand, if we choose, willfully perhaps, a more hopeful point of view, we can see clear traces of increased agency, initiative, and resourcefulness in the ways all four students moved beyond their prior experiences, even as they assimilated them. Admittedly such willful hopefulness calls Lawrence to mind and subjects us to our own brand of Laurentian "once I was unhappy, but now I'm better, and soon, with hope and help, I'll be better still" optimism. As Tom Newkirk recently pointed out, however, it is a both necessary and transformative optimism for young people. And the irritation with which we teachers sometimes meet such optimism is equally age-related, deriving from our own cultural positions and personal aesthetics (37). As Newkirk goes on:

> Students entering college have a psychological need to view their lives as progressive narratives. . . . The literature of self-direction suggests that this future is claimable if there is sufficient personal will. It protects against fatalism, helplessness, and determinism. It transforms that which is disagreeable and painful into strategically placed obstacles that both teach and strengthen. (51)

We suspect this same psychological need to believe in personal agency operates in all of us, in fact, and can operate as a positive force for structuring our futures without precluding recognition of ourselves as shaped also by our social and discursive worlds. As Rachel wisely pointed out time and again, when an abused child breaks the silence to admit her abuse, it may be victimization that motivates her expression, but in that expression itself she begins laying claim to power over it.

As Rachel also pointed out, for the abused child to speak, she must trust that she will be heard. And so we found among these four students: their self-development and ability to develop as writers in new contexts were inseparable from each other, and both were similarly codetermined by the felt responsiveness of their audiences, most notably the teachers and other representatives of their chosen social and discourse communities within the larger University milieu.

Teachers as Empathic Audiences and Mentors

Empathic Responsiveness, "Mirroring" Affirmation, and Self-Esteem

> Throughout his life a person will experience himself as a cohesive, harmonious, firm unit in time and space, connected with his past and pointing meaningfully into a creative-productive future, only as long as, at each stage in his life, he experiences

certain representatives of his human surroundings as joyfully responding to him. . . . (Kohut, *How Does Analysis Cure?* 52)

The first and most personal contact that most students have with their teachers is through writing, that is, through the essays students compose for their courses and the written comments they receive from their teachers in return. And as we have seen, Nam, Steven, Rachel, and Francois all saw writing as a highly personal matter, and all did indeed take their teachers' comments personally. However they may have approached a particular assignment or performed a particular writing task, the act of writing itself and the use of language generally remained something more for each one of them than a merely "academic" exercise. As second-language English speakers, Nam and Francois perhaps knew best the chafing limitations that limited language placed on their worlds, private as well as public. Recalling his elementary school years, Nam spoke not just of isolation from English-speaking peers but also of alienation from himself: "Emotion cannot be truly understood," he observed, "if there is no language to express it." And Francois remembered that not only did others often misunderstand him but also, as he said, "Sometimes I could not even understand myself." Memories of their earlier years reverberated in each young man's comments on writing for University courses. Feeling "stupid in English, intelligence in native language," Nam feared he would be linguistically marked and excluded—"If I write, I'm going to mess up"—and so was often late with his writing assignments, a fault for which he was just as often excluded from peer review in College Writing and penalized in Psychology Methods. Francois, whose writing, as we have seen, was often opaque, fragmented, and at times seemingly careless, worried that he would be (mis)taken alternately for "average" and for "crazy," if he gave his expression full rein. Yet, Steven and Rachel, too, though at home in their English, recognized the power of written language to reveal them to others and to themselves; it had the capacity both to contain and to express them. And that capacity both worried and pleased them. Steven said he "hated" writing in high school, and then, echoing Nam, added, "I still have a lot of shame about who I am when I write." But, like Nam, he sometimes did not know what he was thinking until he wrote. Steven wrote what mattered to him: he penned a suicide note as "a cry for help" and pamphlets to help others feel less alone; he saved his entire oeuvre, keeping his Spiritual Autobiography essays, his "prized possessions," next to his bed because "they are me." Rachel also used personal as well as more strictly "academic" writing to recall and move beyond prior self-definitions as an abused and self-contemptuous adolescent. In one first-year essay draft, she employed the present tense to relive her high school identity—"I'm fat, I'm ugly, I'm stupid, I mess everything up." And while, over the years, she increasingly segregated her confessional, private writing to a journal, adopting in her course work the more depersonalized voice required by her discipline, she continued to use both forms to explore issues about which she felt deeply.

It is not surprising, then, that what Nam, Steven, Rachel, and Francois experienced as writing students intertwined with how they were received as writing people. And an impression we had in their first year did not dissipate but instead clarified over time: Each student reported learning most from instructors who gave them positive recognition as thinking persons behind and within their prose; each reported learning far less—or nothing at all—from those who did not. Teachers who dismissed or demeaned the students' own felt presence within their writing—whether it was explicit there or not—were resisted, perhaps actively or passively, perhaps in the act of writing or in commentary on it afterwards, but always resisted. And that included instructors who turned writing into a simply "academic" matter. Steven, Rachel, and Francois all referred with distaste to professors who made belittling comments to students. Nam and Steven each recoiled at both well-meant critiques and gratuitous barbs aimed at their religious beliefs. And each of the four demonstrated that, without explicit or implicit invitation from teachers to let their voices be heard from within their written forms, they disengaged from task as well as text, writing less or less coherently and learning less in the process.

The combined attempts by Professor Gates and his graduate assistant Ichiro to make Francois participate "objectively" in a debate that he found, with good reason, personally and culturally demeaning—their attempts, that is, to make Francois renounce cultural and self-authorship and accept definition from academic authorities—inspired rage, as Francois later characterized Gates as a "racist" and Ichiro as a foreigner who "just can't speak English. That's his problem." His reaction was, indeed, highly personal—but no more personalized, in fact, than Gates's reported use of academic materials at his disposal "to bat down" and ridicule student arguments. Such was the case, too, in Steven's memorable encounter with Professor Murray and his "Good and Evil: East Meets West Something Ethics—I hated it." In heavy marker, Murray slashed out Steven's personal "I" references as inappropriate to an "academic" essay. Yet in his commentary on the paper, he lashed out at Steven in what was not just an abject failure of empathic responsiveness but a highly personal gloss on Steven's deficiencies, writing in effect: You seem to be in a private war. You have scar tissue. You like pleasant absolutes. Isn't that silly?

Gates and Murray provide extreme examples of the damage teachers can do to students when they fail, or refuse, to acknowledge the highly personal matters that are veiled, sometimes lightly, sometimes heavily, in the academic—fail or refuse to acknowledge, that is, their own highly personal matters as well as their students'. But they are only extreme examples of the hurt done to students, and to the quality of their learning, when teachers dislocate student writers from their own texts, demean the positions they take within them, or disregard the fundamental tenet of humane education articulated by Francois when he said, "I can talk about abstractions, but when we talk about things that are going to affect other people, it seems to me common sense that you just don't play around for the sake of an intelligent argument."

On the other hand, the teachers—and the readers they supervised, whether graduate instructors or classmates serving as peer reviewers—who listened with respect and evinced understanding spurred Nam, Steven, Rachel, and Francois to learn more, to write more thoughtfully, and to digest critiques of their papers more acceptingly. Peer understanding provided not only a "confidence boost" but also, as Rachel discovered, a wider self-understanding and, as Nam, Steven, and Rachel all expressed, an enhanced sense of agency based on the knowledge that not only

could they know and learn but also they could impart knowledge to others—about experiences such as immigrant life, homosexuality, and the effects of child abuse. Even greater seems the
knowledge-eliciting force of teacher understanding. Sociology
professor Louis Marks assigned Francois tasks discernibly similar to those assigned by Gates, but to Francois there was no similarity at all, so different were the two men's approaches, perhaps
to their subjects, and certainly to their students: Marks was "devoted"; he talked and he listened; and while he might not always
have responded to Francois's comments with a "satisfying" answer, nonetheless his answers were ones that Francois felt made
sense, ones that were "rational" and "thought about." Marks's
thoughtfulness elicited thoughtfulness in Francois. Whether the
"real papers that I'm deeply involved in," which Francois said he
wrote for Marks's course, were actually "thirty, forty pages long,"
we cannot know. But we can believe Francois was "deeply involved" in the learning process surrounding them. We can also
believe Rachel's descriptions of the importance that Dr. Vogel's
understanding—of the subject matter itself and also of Rachel's
own personal connection with her subject matter—held for Rachel
during the yearlong composing of her honors thesis.

Finally, in Steven's commentary on his work in gender studies, we can see that the image of themselves that students find
mirrored in their teachers' responses need not be flawless; receiving affirmation, they can receive constructive criticism. When one
of Steven's sponsors for his major told him that, if he wanted
eventually to teach, his writing would have to improve "at least
five times," he found that remark "devastating"; but, as we have
seen, in her concluding remark—"Well, you know, I have never
in twenty years seen another student work as hard as you and
improve as quickly as you"—he found "incredible encouragement," too. In his further commentary, we can also see the process by which the confidence accruing from a teacher's steady
affirmation of what one is and knows ultimately becomes the all-
important confidence to change and grow. As one of the "best"
compositions of his college career, Steven chose his research paper on Claude Hartland's *The Story of a Life*, a paper he wrote
for a lesbian instructor in an Amherst College course on the history of homosexuality. This instructor's methods and responses

emerge in Steven's interview, as do the successes as well as the difficulties Steven encountered while composing this essay. The difficulties are strikingly similar to the difficulties Steven met in treating the book of Job in his essay "Conceptions of the Absolute" for Murray's class; equally striking are the differences between Murray's and the Amherst College instructor's handling of these difficulties. With regard to his fifteen-page research piece on Hartland's work, the first Steven had written of such length, he recalled: "I put a lot of work into it, a lot of hard work. . . . We got to write one draft of it and then [she would] give it back to us with some ideas and corrections." The instructor marked confusing pronoun and point-of-view references, suggesting ways to clarify them and thus to distinguish Hartland's beliefs about himself from Steven's beliefs about Hartland or Steven's beliefs about Steven himself—ways that is, as we have seen, to distinguish between Hartland's "I" and Steven's. She helped him sort through contextual issues as well: "She sort of helped me look at [historical notions of homosexuality] in a broader aspect." And, to Steven's great satisfaction, she helped him integrate portions of Hartland's text, along with a range of other supporting materials, into his own: "The quotes really enhanced what I had written already," he recalled, "and backed up what I was talking about, so it was perfect." The teacher's short final comment—"I like the way this turned out. Your hard work shows. Also your writing style is definitely improving"—delighted but did not surprise him. Throughout the composing process, he felt she had been there with him, in the writing as well as the reading of his work: "I was best supported by her," Steven concluded, "That makes a big difference." We agree.

Idealizing, Mentoring, and the Capacity to Hold High Goals and Values

> Mirroring needs—affirmation, confirmation, guidance—blend with the need for merging with the idealized wisdom and competence of a broadening range of mentors. (Miriam Elson 92)

The "Scylla of non-interference" (to return to Freud's phrase)—whether it takes the form of entirely nondirective instruction or unabated approbation—is not sufficient for most of us teachers. Nor is it necessary for or desired by most students, if Nam, Steven, Rachel, and Francois provide any measure. The hand that holds the mirror of affirmation must be steady; the teacher, respected and admired. The infant not only finds himself in the "gleam in his mother's eye" but seeks calming reassurance there as well. As adults, we seem to seek something similar, if not the same, finding it in those we trust, idealize, and try to emulate. The four young people we studied found it variously in teachers, mentors, therapists, figures from literature and history, and God.

Committed to a clerical life from the start, Nam seems to have been least willing or able of the four to seek out a trusted faculty member for academic as well as personal advice and guidance. Or perhaps it was just a matter of time. As we have observed, the mentoring Nam did seek and receive seems to have come from Anne: Over the course of her interviews with him, he began to ask questions of her—"What is an essay?" and what books to read to better his writing skills—and he began occasionally attending her class in search of further answers. Linguistic differences may have become for him a barrier to other attachments: as so many of the comments he received from teachers and his own responses to them indicate, he was often faulted for his "style"—faults to which he was already deeply sensitive— and deprived of both peer-group and teacher attention because of the tardiness of his work or the teachers' failure to invite him explicitly into more extensive conversations about his work. Yet the nature of Nam's work—almost always grounded in his faith— in contrast to the nature of the work demanded of him at the University, which was almost always grounded in humanist/empiricist principles and discourse—also served to separate him from the community of others, including potential mentors. "Merge!": the irony with which that single command opens Nam's narrative of exclusion and isolation sets the tone of his less-sad-than-heroic year at UMass: psychology, the discipline he thought would best prepare him to serve God and counsel his parishioners, required he expunge everything Nam himself deemed human, let alone spiritual, from his texts; philosophy, in its turn, failed to evoke the sort of meditative and expansive thinking he valued, asking instead for a simple, unsatisfying, and largely "boring" recapitulation of others' ideas. Perhaps little wonder, then, that Nam found more honored figures to emulate in the persons of Thomas à Kempis and his own faithful childhood friend Joe, and that he sought more challenging yet appreciative audiences in himself and his God.

Steven, too, experienced alienation from a university culture sometimes more humanist than humane. At times the discrepancies he encountered were wholly matters of religious bias, as when Murray's teaching assistant expressed incredulity upon discovering Steven "went to a Christian church." At other times, as we have seen in Steven's writings for both the "hated" comparative literature course and his beloved Spiritual Autobiography, matters of spiritual devotion mixed with matters of sexuality (as they so often do), alienation born of religious faith in a culture of doubt mixed with the alienation of a gay student in a predominantly heterosexual world, and Steven's conception of the absolute blended both literally and figuratively with the man of his dreams. During his first two years at UMass, Steven sought to construct his own "role model," his own image of "what a man is supposed to be," out of childhood shards and fragments supplied by pop culture idols, as well as by respectful and respected teachers like Evelyn Peterson and her assistant Robert Southwood. During Steven's last three years of college, his desire to see himself as a gay person and as a gay writer coalesced, due in part to the help he received from mentors he discovered through his Five-College interdisciplinary major in gender studies. Three faculty members, "liberal people," lesbians, personified for Steven an academic community in which he could feel "comfortable," "supported," and, most important, "free to be me" shamelessly. They provided him freedom of authorship, too: freedom to choose, with independence and security, what advice to take and to leave, what opinion to accept and to reject, and thus ultimately freedom to feel "it's not up to them what I write," because "I'm the writer here." All three women had, it appears, through a careful mixture of affirmation, assistance, and critique, convinced Steven that he was worth their teaching and they were worth his learning. Under their tutelage, his writing gained greater coherence, the voice behind it greater clarity, and the person it represented publicly an enhanced sense of agency, assurance, and integrity of self.

To Rachel, mentorship may have come more readily than it did to Nam, Steven, or Francois. Both interested and comfortable in the field of psychology, and willing to apprentice herself to its discipline, Rachel soon began receiving affirmation from respected and admired teachers, including most especially her thesis advisor, Dr. Vogel, "a very intelligent woman" and "also a tremendous writer," in whose profession and position Rachel intended someday to place herself. When Rachel's own unresolved issues regarding intimacy as an adult child of an alcoholic nearly kept her from completing her honors thesis, Dr. Vogel listened and conveyed to Rachel that this intersection of her personal life with her research project was a valid issue to confront, not just something to suppress.

Mentorship seems to have come less easily to Francois than it did to Rachel, and that he did discover faculty members in whose guidance he could place his trust testifies less to his success as a student than to his resourcefulness as a person. This is not to say Francois did not want mentors. As Steven used writing to create his own "role models," prototypical images of the self he hoped to become, Francois used writing, it seems, to personify his own ideals, to embody abstract values in much the same way he concretized whole conceptualizations in single images and terms. And the course this process followed seems also to have coincided with his increasing willingness to come out from hiding behind his own words and to embody his own voice with locating, contextualizing references to personal experience in increasingly coherent, communicative prose. In "A BILINGUAL AND SOCIAL STRUGGLE," written midway through Basic Writing, Francois composed his first truly lucid essay, as well as his first self-referential essay, of the term, employing—recreating—Richard ("RICARDO") Rodriguez as a sort of counterimage to Francois himself, as a rival for authority regarding the "struggles" of working-class minorities and in Francois's own "struggle" to be "remembered" as an author. With his final Basic Writing essay, he again focused on figures from his readings, in this case Richard Wright's *Black Boy* and *Native Son*. This

time, however, Francois employed Richard and Bigger as allies
rather than antagonists, expressing through them as well as in
reference to them his own views on social justice and racism's
impact on minority culture.

As Francois pursued the themes he had begun to voice in
Basic Writing into his sociology major, he found little of the welcoming fit that Rachel found in her psychology studies. Whereas
she encountered affirming reflections of her childhood and adolescent experience, as well as reassuring guidelines delimiting its
exploration and expression, Francois met a body of scholarship,
much of it devoid or distortive of his own self- and cultural-im-
age, and an established discourse often without vocabulary to
express his truths. His relationship to its representative figures—
Professors Marks and Gates—largely recapitulated his relationships to Richard and Bigger, on the one hand, and to Rodriguez,
on the other: a mix of bolstering alliances and enraging antago-
nisms. Doubtless Marks and Gates, together in their stark contrast, contributed to the solidification of Francois's ethical
positioning, as it did to his articulation of that positioning, and
helped him formulate more clearly for himself the values he would
carry with him out of the University and into his work with
troubled youth: he would not play fast or loose with "things that
I teach and believe in"; with those things he would stay steady
and firm. But mentoring also came to him from sources outside
his chosen field, from figures like journalism professor McCartny.
Though Francois had not taken any classes from McCartny, he
had, as he wrote, "made an effort to keep contact with him"
throughout his last two years of school, and he had clearly accepted McCartny as a mentor, as do many black and Latino students on our campus. In his final paper on McCartny, Francois,
often happy to set himself apart from if not at odds with his
subject, stands respectfully within McCartny's shadow, transcrib-
ing his views faithfully, commenting on them sympathetically,
and describing with both clarity and precision McCartny's critique of the current public education system as it affects young
black men and women. Reading that paper gives one the sense
that borrowed authority becomes shared authority, which ultimately is the most authentic authority any of us can claim.

Discourse Communities and Twinship:
"To Be a Human among Humans"

> The third selfobject function, twinship, is related to the unre-
> solved need to experience the self as someone or something—
> "to be human among humans." Twinship needs, when grati-
> fied, facilitate the use of one's innate skills and potentials. Unmet
> twinship needs may lead to feelings of alienation, emptiness
> .... (Wagner 248)

> The drive
> To connect. The dream of a common language.
>
> ADRIENNE RICH (from "Origins
> and History of Consciousness")

Here we again weave together the psychological and the social,
the social and the discursive, to talk about how these students
sought, found, or created discourse communities that seemed to
offer social identities which enhanced their development. In so
doing, they found communities that could serve as sponsors for
their actions, including their actions through texts.

In a review of concepts of discourse community, Harriet
Malinowitz cites the above lines from Adrienne Rich to express
the human need that participation in a discourse or interpretive
community can serve: to provide connection with others through
a shared language, to be received, in Kohut's words, as "a human among humans." While Malinowitz writes as well of the
negative force discourse communities can exert to delimit identities, she returns to the basic human need to escape feelings of
dislocation and vertigo and to seek community, even to create
community when existing ones seem to offer no adequate or positive subjectivity, when they offer alienation, not identity. Writing
of the experience of students in her gay- and lesbian-themed writing course and of the community they formed, Malinowitz poses
these questions: "What about textual experience made community happen? What about community experience made textuality
happen?" (*Textual Orientations* 91).

Malinowitz's discussion of discourse community forecasts key
points that we have seen validated throughout our study: Com-

munity is created, maintained, and revised through both social and discursive relations, through people and texts. Texts—as they are read and circulated—can create a sense of connection and social identity, thereby creating a sense of community. That community, through the feeling of validation it offers, can in turn sponsor individuals in creating their own texts. Or, in Wagner's language, such a community can "facilitate the use of one's innate skills and potentials" (248).

Stressing the importance of feeling sponsorship from an institution (analogous to a discourse community), Eli Goldblatt observes that for students to write with authority, "they must feel a sense of identity with the sponsoring institution itself, so that to elaborate institutional categories is a satisfying and personal goal for writing" (45). Although Goldblatt's focus is on the social source of authority in a sponsoring institution, his language points as well to a need to feel self-validation and alignment of personal with institutional interests. Like Malinowitz, Goldblatt recognizes as well the oppressive force such institutions can exert when, experienced as inflexible and homogeneous, they fail to offer a sense of connection or identity for particular writers. Goldblatt argues that "the key for a writer who rejects dominant institutions is to embrace and elaborate alternative institutions that will help foster that position" (44). This is a tall order, one to be accomplished in connection with others, as the experiences of the students in Malinowitz's gay- and lesbian-themed writing course demonstrate.

Our study reinforces the importance both Malinowitz and Goldblatt place on finding a sponsoring ground from which to speak. Indeed, a primary project for Nam, Steven, Rachel, and Francois was to find discourses and groups with which to align themselves, ones that would offer them a sense of connection and seem to bring forth their potential. Each student's sponsoring discourse community would comprise areas of scholarship that corresponded with deeply felt personal interests, practices that seemed to offer them ways to pursue those interests, people with kindred interests to stand with, and a language and genres with which to shape a self to speak from. Viewed from the perspective of self psychology, such discourses function for these four students—as they do for others of us—as selfobjects, offering a feeling of twinship, an affirmation of one's own interests, and a way of realizing one's potential, specifically by helping connect personal with social projects and sponsoring pursuit of those projects in academic/public venues. Also important, as these students were developing the sense of a kindred group to speak *from*, they were simultaneously envisioning a group they spoke *for*, a group with whom they also shared an identity: they spoke, that is, not solely for themselves but also for others who, like themselves, had also experienced racial discrimination, abuse, alcoholism, or heterosexism and homophobic assaults—and for those who shared their values, whether articulated in terms of social justice, Christian charity, or respect for others.

Rachel was the only one of the four students to find a sponsoring discourse community within a traditionally configured academic area. For her, psychology offered a conceptual framework and methodology for pursuing her personal questions about alcoholism, including its effects on herself and on other children of alcoholics. From the start, the discipline of psychology provided Rachel with a source of sustenance, a *selfobject*. Unlike Nam, she found that it offered her a satisfying way to understand herself, and, significantly, a way to assimilate in adult life her own childhood experience, a way, that is, to speak of child abuse without having to acknowledge publicly her own victimization. Psychology's procedures set clear, reassuring limits within which Rachel worked for the most part comfortably to insert her own voice, her own knowledge, herself: psychology methods told her, "Okay, 'This is what this test does' and 'This is how you do this type of research.' . . . This is preparing us to do scholarly work." Over her years of study, as she gained more knowledge of the subject and more experience with research methodology, she felt more confidence in herself and more confidence to speak as a psychologist about issues that mattered to her. Further, in her mentor, Dr. Vogel, Rachel had a powerful image of the person she aspired to be; Dr. Vogel, in turn, in her role as gatekeeper of psychology's discourse community, clearly saw Rachel as a potential member and opened the way for her. Through Dr. Vogel and other faculty members, Rachel was able to internalize an abstract sense of a community that she could stand with and that could sponsor her work. In this way, psychology became a sponsoring discourse community for her. Significantly, she could imagine herself in a professional role, doing research and writing on issues of alcoholism and child abuse, speaking for others with whom she also shared an identity.

For Nam, on the other hand, a true sponsoring discourse community was not to be found at the University, and he had to seek an alternative, although clearly also a dominant one, that of Catholicism and a seminary. Evident in many of his essays is his feeling of twinship with God and priests. The discourse of Catholicism offered him connection with God and a means for understanding his own life and carrying on the work he wanted to do in the world. While at the University, through a number of his essays in College Writing, he was writing from the authority of this discourse, even writing in the genre of a religious meditation, and taking on the role of a religious counselor to others. Although he thought initially that the study of psychology might be compatible with his interests in counseling, he found that not to be so, at least not as he encountered it at our university. For him, leaving the University was not a sign of personal failure; rather, it was a sign of his recognition that a seminary was the appropriate place for him to pursue his interests. Neither was it a failure on the University's part that it was not a seminary. Still, the gatekeeping function exercised by the psychology teacher because of Nam's difficulties with English did represent a failure, one that is repeated by other teachers who judge the overall literacy skills and intellectual capacity of students for whom English is a second language on the basis of surface features of their use of the language. In this teacher's eyes, Nam was not a potential member of the discourse community, and she effectively barred the entrance before him. Fortunately for Nam, he did not wish to enter.

Neither Steven nor Francois, for different reasons, found a single academic department, as traditionally configured, that could serve as a sponsoring discourse community. During his first year, Steven was not sure what his major would be, although he too considered psychology. He sought acceptance along with an acceptable place for himself among numerous groups, inside and outside the University community, that combined various aspects of his life as a gay man: a gay-supportive church, the gay students' Speakers' Bureau, Alcoholics Anonymous, and other gay-friendly self-help associations in the area. Ultimately, through his own resourcefulness, he created his own major in gender studies. By doing so, he created his own coherence for his studies, one that was responsive to his interests. In essence, he created his own sponsoring discourse community, from courses and faculty available across the curriculum—indeed, across colleges in our area. Through his self-designed major, he was able to read and immerse himself in discourses of queer and gender studies that matched his interests and provided the self-validation that helped him evolve a stronger sense of his social identity. Equally important, it gave him a base of scholarship and methodology through which to locate his private interests in relation to others and pursue them in a public sphere. Further, in that scholarship and with the cross-disciplinary group of key faculty with whom he studied, he found a kindred group: a group he could imagine himself amongst and who conveyed to him that they could imagine him amongst themselves. It was in this community that he developed as a writer, writing for faculty and in classes where he felt some shared identity. Instead of writing to or against an audience that challenged his very being as a gay person, he was writing to ones who accepted, even shared, that identity while simultaneously demonstrating its multifacetedness and its overlap with other identities. Without the structural means to create his own major, without the resources of five area colleges, and without his personal initiative, Steven's options would have been much more limited and, we suspect, limiting.

It is difficult to say that Francois found or created a sponsoring discourse community. For him, any sense of a sponsoring group or discourse is more dispersed and perhaps even consists of disparate elements. Even though he majored in sociology, he did not appear to identify strongly with that area of scholarship or, more to the point, with that faculty as a group at our university. Certainly, his strong sense that a senior professor in the department—one with whom he had to take a number of courses—was racist was a factor in his less-than-strong identification with this department. In Francois's first sociology course, this professor and his graduate teaching assistant acted as gatekeepers in other ways as well, posing an assignment where

Francois felt, as he said, he "could find no place to fit in." Wisely, Francois sought other courses and other faculty who validated his existence in respectful ways and responded to his interests. The discourse he sought was that associated with studies of racism and social justice, as offered through courses in sociology, anthropology, education, and even both Basic and College Writing. Thus scholarship and opportunity that were spread across multiple disciplines offered him ways to pursue his concerns. Further, with Francois, the importance of having a kindred group is particularly striking. Rejecting the institution of sociology as it represented itself to him whole, he, like Steven, created his own community out of a dispersed collection of courses and faculty, acquiring his own essentially satisfying language of social justice and preparing himself sufficiently for his first job as counselor for families of troubled youth.

Linking Private with Academic Interests

> They told us that their current way of knowing and viewing the world—a way of knowing we call constructed knowledge—began as an effort to reclaim the self by attempting to integrate knowledge that they felt intuitively was personally important with knowledge they had learned from others. (Belenky et al. 135)

> The university curriculum encourages the separation of students' private and public selves. (Elizabeth Chiseri-Strater 164–65)

Chiseri-Strater reaches this grim conclusion after an ethnographic study based largely on case studies of two college students during their junior year at a public university. As we have shown, many of the experiences of Nam, Steven, Rachel, and Francois validate this claim regarding discourse conventions and teacher practices: examples include discourse conventions for a psychology course where the position of the researcher is effaced; writing assignments where students' own views and, in some instances, relevant personal, authoritative knowledge, are discounted, if not proscribed; teachers who "bat down" students' ideas, particularly when those ideas counter their own, or who shame students with gratuitous, hurtful comments. And, in many instances, these four students succeeded in making the connection, as Chiseri-Strater claims of the students she studied, "in spite of, not because of their contact with the academy" (143): Nam, by leaving the University; Francois, by seeking out specific faculty outside his chosen major; and Steven, by creating his own major. Still, as we write those lines regarding Francois and Steven, we are already acknowledging that the claim does not hold so categorically. These two students, and Nam and Rachel as well, did find teachers, discourse communities, individual classes, and writing assignments that helped them make this vital connection, bringing their selves into their learning by linking private with public interests, self with others, personal with social identities. It is a connection so important to personal development that undergraduate education—including our writing courses—should aim to foster, not frustrate, it.

We have already written of the central role teachers and discourse communities can serve in helping students make this connection. Discourse communities can function as sponsoring communities of people and discourses that help link a personal with a social identity and private with public projects. Teachers can help make that link between private and social identities by presenting students with an image of identity and possibility. Further, they can serve as sustaining, empathic audiences and mentors who affirm students and give them means to articulate and pursue their private interests in academic/public settings and texts.

Our framing of discourse community, however, focusing as it does on each student's formal or informal "major," does not account for the important function that specific classes, including ones outside of that cluster, played in helping these individuals make the link between private and social and between personal and academic. While we believe that their studies and interactions with teachers and, we presume, other students in their majors furthered their self-understanding, so, too, did courses outside of that discourse community, and in significant ways. These are courses with explicit aims of fostering self-understanding through reflection on self and on self in relation to others, aims that were furthered specifically through the writing assignments. For Steven, Spiritual Autobiography was such a course. Here, students read a number of spiritual autobiographies and composed their own. It was a writing experience so meaningful for Steven that he kept the sections of his autobiography with him, not "with all my other papers outside in storage. I keep them in my room, because they're sort of my prized possession." They represent Steven's extended self-storying in a genre at once private and public: at once reexamining the traumas in his life, breaking with them, and recomposing his faith in himself and in a spiritual source who affirms his homosexuality.

For Rachel, her women's studies and education classes were such courses. She said of her women's studies course, "It really opened me up to a lot of new perspectives on life." And specifically, she said of one of the writing assignments, "I was thinking, 'Wow, if I was the same person and I was just living in a different country, I would have a completely different life just because I'm a woman.'" For this course, students were writing a more traditional "critical analysis," although clearly the class context invited empathic identification, and the writing assignment—at least as evidenced by Rachel's well-received essay—allowed students to write in ways conveying identification with their subject, instead of enforcing their distance from it. For the education course, students were given less traditional assignments and were asked to write in a less traditional academic genre, composing essays that called for experiential and empathic modes of thinking, accompanied by explicit self-reflection on that thinking. As Rachel said of one assignment that asked students to learn about a group by both reading a book and interviewing people, "It restructured the way I thought about things." It did not simply confirm something she already knew, and it did not simply add to her knowledge; it *restructured* her thinking. Of another writing in that course—one where she chose to write about her experience of working with a student on her floor as he came out as a gay male and where she acknowledged her own bisexuality—she said, "It was very progressive for my own development. . . . It affirmed who I am."

Some of the essays these students composed for their Basic and College Writing courses served similar functions—by a teacher's and/or a student's design. These included essay assignments that invited reflection on a meaningful experience (e.g., Rachel's essay on her relationship with her best friend, Trish); prompts that encouraged students to make connections between readings and their own perspectives and lived experiences (e.g., Francois's essay "A BILINGUAL AND SOCIAL STRUGGLE," where he positions himself and his personal experiences in relation to his reading of Richard Rodriguez's "Aria" and Sophronia Liu's "So Tsi-fai", and Nam's essay, "The Lord Is My Shepherd," where he does similar work in relation to Thomas à Kempis's *The Imitation of Christ*); and assignments that gave students a heuristic for developing their perspective on a cultural form, such as a tradition (e.g., Steven's essay, "Breaking Traditions"). These assignments included, as well, readings in Basic Writing that provided a context and springboard for reflections on self in relation to others and on self in relation to institutions and social forces. We do not want to seem to be simplifying here: Clearly, as Nam, Steven, Rachel, and Francois's experiences have shown, the ways in which specific writing activities were presented and situated within a full course curriculum, the ways in which the teacher presented writing and worked with each student, and the ways students chose to define their projects mattered a good deal in determining their function. We do aim, though, to make a general point: In both courses, students' own lived experiences and their lived observations of others were treated as potentially valid, authoritative sources of knowledge—valid as sources for developing entire essays, and valid for developing essays that drew as well on other authorities. The combination of recognizing the validity of students' personal knowledge and showing them how to bring such knowledge into their academic worlds helps students bridge what may seem like a gaping chasm between themselves and readers, that is, between private and academic pursuits.

Just as we saw students using drafting and revising to fashion and revise their own self-presentations, they can use such writing to fashion and revise their self- and subject understandings. Having the occasion to do so during the transitional time of their first years in college seems particularly important as students attempt to locate themselves and what they know from their past in relation to new knowledge and new ways of thinking. For Nam, Steven, Rachel, and Francois, while the link between personal and academic was present even when veiled in their texts, in only a few courses could they bring personal knowledge into interaction with academic knowledge and view it through new perspectives: e.g., through self-reflection and autobiographical writing in Steven's comparative literature course, *Spiritual Autobiography*, and through experiential and empathic knowing in Rachel's education course for resident assistants. Often these courses were outside specific departments and on the academy's margins—in general education or residence hall programs. In other general education and departmental major courses, such occasions for reflexivity and bringing in relevant knowledge from personal experience appeared to be absent or at least not invited by the structure of the course. In his Introduction to Sociology class, Francois found no fit for himself. Not only did the racist tenor of the readings bar his entry, but also the writing assignment itself offered no opening for knowledge acquired from personal experience. The combination of those readings and that assignment not only made the writing task more difficult for Francois, it also precluded the possibility for productive understanding of the relationship between personal knowledge and the sanctioned knowledge presented in the class. As Rachel commented in her senior year:

> Sometimes the way we experience things in the world isn't exactly how the theories explain things or how something you learn in class explains things. I think because we experience life differently, writing it down and saying, "Look, this is what I found"—even though that's not written down anywhere— you can certainly make some valid points.

Francois could have made some valid points about the racism and classism inherent in the way the culture of poverty debate was formulated in the scholarship of sociology; he could have developed his own thinking further and contributed to others' thinking, including his teacher's.

Particularly in courses in the social sciences and humanities, it is our responsibility as teachers to create occasions for students to draw on their personal knowledge—if they feel it is relevant and if they choose to do so—not as privileged knowledge to be accepted as is, but as valid knowledge to be brought into their critical and reflective thinking along with other knowledge presented in and framed by the course. What are the obstacles to doing so? Certainly, two are the epistemological and textual conventions that privilege extreme constructions of objective knower and known. But something closer to home may be operating as well, that is, some teachers' resistance to experiences and ideas that challenge their own beliefs, as Francois felt was the case with Professor Gates, or that trigger their own feelings of vulnerability or pain. As an undergraduate teaching assistant in Abnormal Psychology classes, Rachel recognized the effect a reader's discomfort can have on student writing. In her final interview, she spoke of a number of students who included their personal experiences when writing about such topics as sexual abuse: "It was really uncomfortable for me as the reader," she said, but she quickly added, "I think by saying . . . 'I don't think it should be there,' it's almost countereducational. . . . Abnormal psychology does warrant a lot of self-exploration." As in her own writings, where the personal connection was either implicit or explicit, "It's just another step in the process of understanding," she observed, "something you want to understand. . . . I like some of the things I've written because of that. Maybe it's because those are the things I understand about myself."

What triggers our own discomfort will vary, as will the degree to which we are likely to feel discomfort. It remains important, however, to recognize such feelings as valid—not to displace them onto discourse conventions or, worse yet, onto students, but to work toward understanding ourselves and to learn through our own experiences the personal "educational" value that bringing one's experience into learning can have for the individuals we teach. Fortunately, in this study and in others, we find models of courses that can do so constructively and productively, e.g., Steven's Spiritual Autobiography and Rachel's education courses at UMass, and, further afield, in Steven Fishman's Introduction to Philosophy course at the University of North Carolina–Charlotte, where students learn philosophy by engaging in philosophic thinking about issues present in their own personal/social lives.

Grounding his pedagogy in the educational theories of John Dewey, Fishman uses both individual writing activities and class discussions as means for linking the "academic" knowledge of philosophy and the "personal" knowledge of his students in order to further their understanding of both themselves and others (Fishman and McCarthy). These models and others like them move us beyond the limited and flawed framing of a debate between personal and academic knowledge and toward considering how various sources of knowledge can come into our thinking and our students' thinking.

Classroom Practices

> Through . . . collaboration faculty have begun to understand that it is unrealistic and ultimately counterproductive to expect writing and ESL programs to be responsible for providing students with the language, discourse, and multiple ways of seeing required across courses. They are recognizing that the process of acquisition is slow-paced and continues to evolve with exposure, immersion, and involvement, that learning is responsive to situations in which students are invited to participate in the construction of meaning and knowledge. They have come to realize that every discipline, indeed, every classroom, may represent a distinct culture and thus needs to make it possible for those new to the context to practice and thus approximate its "ways with words." (Zamel 517)

Of the four students we have studied here, Steven was the most explicit about what had helped him progress as a writer. As a senior, in an interview with Marcia, he listed the main ingredients for his advances: hard work, help sought from teachers, and increased self-esteem. He also elaborated, saying that he benefited from clearly defined course and assignment expectations, his own interest in subjects, "supportive" classmates, and responsive teachers. With Steven's itemization as a starting point, we here propose our own list—based on the four students' words and our observations—of factors that assisted the students. It also reflects directions our own curricula and teaching approaches have taken in large part as a result of this study.

Time

Though time is absent from Steven's itemized list, we begin with it, for time essentially defines our study, and Steven himself was not unaware of its importance. Time applies its force variously: as limitation, encumbrance, assistance, and freedom. So, too, its measures: years, days, moments. As we wrote in our introduction, time—which always seemed against us because it was in too-short supply—also worked for us in that it both forced and allowed us to stay with Nam, Steven, Rachel, and Francois longer and to learn more from them as they developed as writers and as persons. Their years at the University make up our study, and in that span they felt the force of time in much the same way we did: with a sense of urgency—meeting deadlines, choosing majors, and generally increasing, if not, as Steven said of himself, catching up on, their writing and learning skills. But as time allowed us to follow the students' development, it allowed them to develop: to acquire the skills needed for increased confidence and the confidence needed for increased skills; to discover courses and disciplines broadening as well as reflecting the interests they brought with them to school; to gain trust in and the trust of teachers, peers, and themselves; and, in the main, to learn the ways of campus life and become full inhabitants of their various communities within the larger University polity, even as they prepared to move beyond it. Time gave them, in other words, opportunity to revise themselves in much the same way they revised their essays: opportunity to examine their own personal, formative experiences of spiritual devotion and doubt, of growing up gay, of suffering childhood abuse, of grappling with poverty and prejudice; to find ways of thinking and speaking about those private experiences within wider contexts and shared perspectives afforded by gender studies, psychology, and sociology; and ultimately to transform personally felt experience into publicly directed action as gay youth counselor, clinical psychologist, and adolescent case worker.

Time's smaller increments proved essential, too. While perhaps all students, and especially first-year students, need (even if they do not appreciate) the structure imposed by deadlines for meeting academic requirements, Nam, Steven, Rachel, and

Francois required and profited from certain kinds of latitude from the University, from teachers, and from themselves. Steven felt he needed extra time, along with understanding of the time he had lost in moving from school to school as a child. He spent five years completing his degree, as did Francois. Nam needed extra time to draft and revise written work for his classes, and to work on English language skills for various discourses. Without it, he suffered frustration and often alienation from quicker classmates. But all four students clearly benefited from time spent drafting and revising their essays, alone, in peer groups, or, especially, in consultation with teachers: they benefited, in short, from the time teachers both afforded and gave them.

As all of us who teach writing know too well, time may be infinite, but human time is terribly limited. And the time we spend with students or in responding to their papers often feels like time stolen from our families, our friends, and ourselves. In reviewing his Claude Hartland essay, Steven's description of the help he received from his Amherst College instructor underscores the tremendous time commitment that teaching requires and the value of small classes or reduced teaching loads. Yet the hurt he received from Professor Murray also serves as a reminder that the sometimes-lasting damage we do to students takes but a split second to prevent—the split second it would have taken Murray to suck in his breath, consider the implications of his observation, and imagine the impact his comment might have on any such "silly," scarred student.

Drafting and Revising

Steven indicated that hard work was essential to improved writing, and we observed all four students working hard—perhaps surprisingly hard—at achieving processes for drafting and revising. Nam, rather than seeking the tutors his instructors recommended, chose other measures, including taking his written work through several revisions. Steven repeatedly took opportunities first to get comments on his writing from classmates and teachers, and then to revise, redrafting even the hated paper for Professor Murray. Rachel already knew a careful process when she entered college and applied it diligently from the start of College

Writing. Francois, while sometimes turning in first drafts in his first-year course that showed more control over formal writing conventions than did his final "revisions," nevertheless claimed revising's value and did work on revisions for his own purposes of attaining a voice. In fact, what was striking to us was how frequently the students used revising processes to revise their own self-presentations in written work: Nam composing increasingly interiorized and complex personal meditations, Steven shaping and reshaping his own autobiography, Rachel editing her presence out of some essays and inserting it within others, and Francois trying varied cryptic, didactic, and authoritative voices as he guardedly began to delineate himself more clearly within his own texts. In general, the students seemed to use the drafting process as much to configure their identities in relation to their various subjects as to master the forms, genres, and language in which those subjects were conveyed. To look down through the drafts of a single first-year essay or across the essays composed in their first year is, therefore, to see a private sort of testing and rehearsing for the four-year-long academic and personal development process they were about to undertake. It is also to see the way in which students employ the "personal" essay for literal self-authorizing, as Steven so determinedly did, as a sort of groundwork for securing their position as subjects of experience speaking for others like them, and as a stepping-off place from which eventually to reposition themselves as subjects of the knowledge gained from experience speaking with others who hold kindred understanding and views.

Readings

Over the last decade or so, many writing programs have worked hard to maintain instructional focus on student writing itself, with some programs eliminating readings from their courses altogether in order to fight the pull of traditional model-based curricula as well as the drift toward literary critique, to which reading-based curricula may always be inclined. Yet our discussions with and observations of Nam, Steven, Rachel, and Francois revealed the importance that reading held for their development as writers. As we have seen over and again, Nam sought something more than a model for his own reflective essays in the inspirational meditations of Thomas à Kempis and other theologians; in their works he also found images of himself, as well as precursors to the struggle Eleanor detected in him between a fondness for "people and the social world in general" and a greater desire to "give them up for God." He found in them, too, a congenial audience for his own expressions, an audience that welcomed him, in Goldblatt's terms, as an "author-in-training" and thus, by their welcome, lent greater force, deeper timbre, to his voice. In surprising ways, Steven was not unlike Nam. In his own fashion, Steven sought calming reassurance in the idealized parent figure of a God who loved him absolutely, much as Nam sought, in his own words, a God "Who comforted [him] as a father to his son." And Steven took similar reassurance from his readings. Steven, however, did not have to go outside his course work to find readings reflective of himself and, later, reflective of his chosen authorizing group. He liked reading the stories, articles, and books for Basic Writing, because they "gave us a way to look at ourselves . . . another external way to look in at ourselves, and it was easier to write." The readings functioned as a selfobject for Steven, almost, as we have seen, irrespective of their actual, manifest content: whether it was Liu's story of a schoolboy's suicide or Dinesen's recollection in "The Iguana," Steven found a self-confirming presence of others whose experiences—along with the meanings ascribed to them—he could assimilate into his own. Later the selfobject relationship remained, though the precise nature of Steven's relationship to readings, especially as the readings made writing easier, changed. Maturing as a person, he made increasingly sophisticated use as a writer of materials he read. They came to serve him less as a pretext for talking directly about himself, and more as supporting structures or components of his discussions of gay culture at large: quotations from Claude Hartland's autobiography "backed up what I was talking about" and "enhanced" Steven's own argument, and the language of social constuctivists filtered into his sentences, sometimes awkwardly and sometimes with real finesse. This is not to say that Steven lost the need to find his own reflection affirmed in both reading and writing, but it is to say that the lens through which he read and wrote broadened in scope, producing more than a series of self-portraits. By his junior and senior years, he had found in gender studies a sponsoring discourse that had itself managed to integrate the gay subculture into its own sponsoring institution of academia, and Steven expressed the satisfaction that he derived from reading in terms of the cohesive force that the shared perspective, the "focus," and the language of gender studies held for his group: "That might be why in the classes now I like writing papers better," he went on to say, "because there's a focus around the writing as far as what we already read. . . . And that feels a little bit more comfortable because there's more of a general idea of what people are writing about."

During his final interview for this project, Steven recalled his childhood as a series of moves and misses that left him feeling as though, as a writer, he was still in a stage "that other people were in maybe five years ago." Perhaps he was right, for it does appear that Rachel began her college career where Steven left off insofar as she was able from the start to integrate academic sources into her own texts with a fluency and fluidity that Steven only later acquired. But while readier than he to submerge her own presence beneath a more apparently "public" surface text, Rachel, too, found that readings helped her set the course between the internal and the external influences through which all writers must constantly navigate, and she discovered that negotiating the right balance between them was part of an ongoing process of instruction and practice. Even as late as embarking on her senior honors thesis, she learned that to be both sustained and self-sustaining, research must involve something other than an "intellectualizing" of private pain. "I have to admit this was definitely a personal endeavor," Rachel said in her last interview, "but it's taken on more of an academic pursuit . . . because I'm getting into the data going, 'Wow, [my own experience with alcoholism in my family] is contradicting current research and some other current research is pulling together with it.'" Not so unlike Steven, then, as she first appears, Rachel began only over time to move personal experience from the foreground to the background of both her readings and her writings, employing it eventually as one measure against which to verify "current research," rather than employing "current research" to reflect and validate her own personal experience. Like Steven, she remained squarely within her writings and her readings but shifted positions there, finally assuming the voice and perspective of her fellow researchers not to silence but to authorize more fully the voice she had initially assumed as a representative subject of her research.

Reading coupled with writing activities also provided a means of furthering Rachel's understanding of others and of herself in relation to others: in the women's studies course, the readings and the writing assignment furthered her understanding of herself as both connected with and privileged in relation to most women in Third World countries; in her education course, reading Eli Wiesel's *Night* in conjunction with interviewing another person furthered her understanding of her own beliefs in relation to those of two Jewish people. As she spoke of these courses, it was clear that the reading and the accompanying writing activities provided occasion for the kind of reflexive thinking Donna Qualley advocates in *Turns of Thought: Teaching Composition as Reflexive Inquiry*:

> Reflexivity involves a commitment to both attending to what we believe and examining how we came to hold those beliefs *while we are engaged in trying to make sense of an other.* . . . The composition course can provide an excellent site for learning how to use reading and writing to engage in this kind of intellectual and ethical inquiry. (5–6)

Qualley stresses that such a course must allow time for students to think, rethink, and revise—that is, "time for inquiry, dialogue, and revision" (59).

Explicit Instruction and Critical Reflection on Discourse Conventions

In their own ways, Nam, Steven, and Rachel demonstrate the gratification that comes to students when they begin successfully integrating outside "authorities" into their own writing and first lay claim to the institutional authority that successful integration brings. Francois reminds us that such success seldom comes without explicit instruction. Missing the all-important "third piece to a triangle," that is, the piece connecting summarization with talking "about something completely different," he produced from his reading of Heker's "The Stolen Party" a maddeningly dis-jointed replica of literary critique. No amount of instructional prodding or questioning would have helped give "BLIND-IN-NOCENT-PREJUDICE" recognizable shape. But understanding did come to Francois and, in turn, change came to his subsequent essays, most likely, it seems, through reading, in this case Francois's reading of another student's more conventionally wrought essay on the same topic. That essay, which begins, "Lilian Heker's 'The Stolen Party' is a portrayal of the class struggle . . . ,'" provided Francois with a key term and theme for his next essay, "A BI-LINGUAL AND SOCIAL STRUGGLE," and undoubtedly a sense of essay structure as well.

Explicit instruction, however, involves more than requiring, explaining, or even modeling the *hows* of composing. It involves full explication of the *whys* as well. As Francois's confusion and Nam's question "What is an essay?" both imply, there is nothing "natural" about the essay, or about other written forms, most of which vary widely yet within limited parameters set by conven-tion or, more accurately, by various and varying conventions. All four students encountered, from their first semester to their last, a truly dizzying array of writing assignments and teacher expec-tations about them: depersonalized reports for psychology and sociology; similarly depersonalized literary analyses, on the one hand, and highly personalized pieces, on the other, for compara-tive literature; self-contextualizing social inquiries and critiques for anthropology and education; and "objective" summaries and arguments for philosophy as well as sociology. While most teach-ers described quite precisely what formal rules they expected stu-dents to follow in written assignments (sometimes with greater clarity in correcting product errors than in prompting the com-posing process), few if any explained so precisely why those rules existed, what purpose they served and what significance they held, or how they differed from other conventional demands outside or even inside their own disciplines. In "The Silenced Dialogue," Lisa Delpit cogently argues that the general failure among teach-ers to make explicit the essentially white, middle-class rules and assumptions implicitly governing most classrooms preclude many non-middle-class students of many ethnicities from full partici-pation in the classroom culture, resulting in the academic failure of some students and the "behavior problems" of others. Among Nam, Steven, Rachel, and Francois, we saw something similar occurring. Murray's failure to explicate his reasons and purposes for eradicating personal references from Steven's text, and for demanding the other changes he did, left Steven in angry confusion, wanting to ask, "What the hell do you want?" So, too, for Nam. Nothing, perhaps, would have prevented him from detaching so fully as he did from his Psychology Methods course. Yet Nam was curious about discourse forms, often even eager for structure, and, as we have suggested, an open classroom discussion about the place of one's own thinking in empirical research and the ways stylistic conventions reflect the researcher's self-positioning might well have given more meaning to the writing and to the course itself—for Nam and for other students, too.

Nam and Steven were caught—not in their own naive need to write personalized essays but in a much larger debate, within as much as among disciplines, regarding the self's epistemological and linguistic place in discourse. Their difficulties with and various "resistances" to instructional demands resulted in large part from the teachers' own failures to recognize these debates and contextualize their own teaching within them. If we shift our attention from failures to possibilities, the first move for us, as teachers, begins in recognizing that such debates are taking place within our disciplines and across them. Doing so requires giving credence to challenges to dominant practices and asking questions such as these: How are we ourselves positioned as knowers and as writers, and how are we positioning our students? What sources of knowledge are validated and what sources are not? Whose interests are being served by these practices and conventions? (Malinowitz, "Feminist Critique"; see also LeCourt).

The next move for teachers is to bring some of this debate into classrooms. Given the thoughtful reflection we have heard from the students in this study, it seems to us that we should trust our students enough to bring them into such debates regarding both disciplinary and classroom genres—in first-year writing courses and courses across the curriculum. We should also credit students enough to invite and listen to their questionings—even their challengings—of the conventions we valorize. And when they cannot articulate their questions, we should try to understand their difficulties. In Psychology Methods, listening to Rachel might have opened up a discussion of the variation in disciplinary practices that she herself observed. In Nam's section of that same course, fuller conversations with him might have helped him articulate his difficulties. Finally, we should present conventions as flexible, not static, thus giving students room to fashion their own ways of working within and against them. As Wall and Coles write in advocating what they call an interactionist pedagogy, "The relationship between a student's discourse and that of the academy is seen as dialectical, a two-way process of interaction that will, if it succeeds, necessarily involve teacher and student in the re-formation of both discourses" (235).

Within composition studies, the debates over disciplinary practices include questions about the genre that will be privileged in our classrooms (e.g., Spellmeyer "A Common Ground" and "Response"; Miller; Brodkey), how writing in the course is positioned in relation to conceptions of academic writing (Bartholomae; Elbow "Being a Writer"; Bialostosky; Bishop; Welsh [these last three in response to Bartholomae and Elbow]), and the subject position we ask our students to assume in their writing (Faigley). For our own teaching, we align ourselves most closely with the essay genre as presented by Spellmeyer, a genre for exploratory, reflective thinking with "I" as the knower, a genre that, as presented by Spellmeyer, "calls attention to the writer's situatedness" and calls on students to "use writing as a way of thinking dialogically" ("A Common Ground" 270–271), specifically as they engage in a dialogue with other texts. We have seen how important "essaying" was for Nam, Steven, Rachel, and Francois in constituting and reconstituting themselves as they wrote of past experiences, their ideas, and themselves in relation to other texts, including the texts of classmates, or some other framing context. We do not mean, nor do we encourage, unselfconscious, expressive emoting, but we find even less justifiable any approach that denies the possibility of composing a sense of oneself through language and that denies students the belief we hold for ourselves: that one can have thoughts one claims as her own. From what we have learned of these students' experiences in our own classrooms, we now take more care to create a curricular context that encourages students to consider how they shape and reshape their own identities and ideas in relation to other individuals and in relation to institutions, belief systems, languages, and larger historical forces (Curtis et al.; Malinowitz *Textual Orientations*; Fox). With Nam's question ringing in our ears, we now also consciously present the "essay" as a genre and explicitly discuss its conventions in relation to the conventions students may be encountering in other disciplines. And we engage our first-year students in considering not only the kinds of texts those conventions produce but also the kinds of assumptions they reflect about what counts as knowledge, whose knowledge counts, and where as writers they can position themselves in relation to the knowledge they express.

Reading some composition scholarship, it seems that positioning is all. And, indeed, it may be. In our positions as teachers, the dominant perspective is quite naturally our own—our own from our classrooms, our own from our disciplinary locations, and our own from our personal being. In this book, we have attempted to stand alongside these four students, to view their experiences of our writing classes and their education from their perspectives. It is from these multiple perspectives that we need to design curricula and decide on classroom practices. We believe that we learn not by cutting ourselves off totally from our past, from languages we know, from our own self-knowledge. We learn by extending from them, refashioning, or, by choice, moving away from them, and by feeling we have some ground on which to build our learning, rather than the vertigo of groundlessness. So, too, with our students. In our daily work as teachers, we should begin by respecting the positions of students as they enter our classrooms, trying to understand those positions, and helping support students as they work to reposition themselves as writers and as people.

Works Cited

Atwood, George E., Bernard Brandchaft, and Robert Stolorow. *Psychoanalytic Treatment: An Intersubjective Approach*. Hillsdale: Analytic, 1987.

Atwood, George E., and Robert D. Stolorow. *Structures of Subjectivity: Explorations in Psychoanalytic Phenomenology*. Hillsdale: Analytic, 1984.

Bacal, Howard A., and Kenneth M. Newman. *Theories of Object Relations: Bridges to Self Psychology*. New York: Columbia UP, 1990.

Bartholomae, David. "Writing with Teachers: A Conversation with Peter Elbow." *College Composition and Communication* 46 (1995): 62–71.

Bartholomae, David, and Anthony Petrosky. *Facts, Artifacts, and Counterfacts: Theory and Method for a Reading and Writing Course*. Upper Montclair: Boynton/Cook, 1986.

Bazerman, Charles. "Codifying the Social Scientific Style: The APA Publication Manual as a Behaviourist Rhetoric." *Shaping Written Knowledge: The Genre and Activity of the Experimental Article in Science*. Ed. Charles Bazerman. Madison: U of Wisconsin P, 1988. 257–77.

———. "What Written Knowledge Does: Three Examples of Academic Prose." *Philosophy of the Social Sciences* 2 (1981): 361–87.

Belenky, Mary Field, Blythe McVicker Clinchy, Nancy Rule Goldberger, and Jill Mattuck Tarule. *Women's Ways of Knowing: The Development of Self, Voice, and Mind*. New York: Basic, 1986.

Bialostosky, Don. "Romantic Resonances." *College Composition and Communication* 46 (1995): 92–96.

Bishop, Wendy. "If Winston Weathers Would Just Write to Me on E-Mail." *College Composition and Communication* 46 (1995): 97–103.

Bizzell, Patricia. *Academic Discourse and Critical Consciousness*. Pittsburgh: U Pittsburgh P, 1992.

———. "Cognition, Convention, and Certainty: What We Need to Know about Writing." *PRE/TEXT* 31 (1982): 213–43.

Briggs, Kaitlin. "Geography Lessons for Researchers." *Anthropology and Education Quarterly* 27 (1996): 5–19.

Britton, James. *Language and Learning*. Baltimore: Penguin, 1972.

Brodkey, Linda. *Writing Permitted in Designated Areas Only*. Minneapolis: U of Minnesota P, 1996.

Chiseri-Strater, Elizabeth. *Academic Literacies: The Public and Private Discourse of University Students*. Portsmouth: Boynton/Cook, 1991.

Clinchy, Blythe McVicker. "Connected and Separate Knowing: Toward a Marriage of Two Minds." Goldberger et al. 205–47.

———. "The Development of Thoughtfulness in College Women." *American Behavioral Scientist* 32.6 (1989). Rpt. in *The Composition of Our"selves."* Ed. Curtis et al. Dubuque: Kendall/Hunt, 1997. 149–157.

Curtis, Marcia S., and Anne J. Herrington. "Diversity in Required Writing Courses." *Promoting Diversity in College Classrooms: Innovative Responses for the Curriculum, Faculty, and Institutions*. New Directions for Teaching and Learning, no. 52. Ed. Maurianne Adams. San Francisco: Jossey, 1992. 71–84.

Curtis, Marcia, Sabine Groote, Emily Isaacs, Phoebe Jackson, Amy Lee, John Reed, Natasha Trethewey, and Julia Wagner. *The Composition of Our"selves."* Dubuque: Kendall/Hunt, 1994.

Davies, Bronwyn. *Shards of Glass: Children Reading and Writing beyond Gendered Identities*. Cresskill: Hampton, 1993.

"A Day in the Life of America." *Newsweek* 27 October 1986: 49–82.

Delpit, Lisa. *Other People's Children: Cultural Conflict in the Classroom*. New York: New, 1995.

———. "The Silenced Dialogue: Power and Pedagogy in Educating Other People's Children." *Harvard Educational Review* 58 (1988): 280–98.

Dinesen, Isak. "The Iguana." *The Practice of Writing*. Ed. Robert Scholes and Nancy R. Comley. New York: St. Martin's P, 1985. 53–54.

Elbow, Peter. "Being a Writer vs. Being an Academic: A Conflict in Goals." *College Composition and Communication* 46 (February 1995): 62–83.

———. *Writing Without Teachers*. London: Oxford UP, 1973.

Elson, Miriam. "Adolescents." *Using Self Psychology in Psychotherapy.* Ed. Helene Jackson. Northvale: Aronson, 1991. 91–116.

Emig, Janet. *The Composing Processes of Twelfth Graders*. NCTE Research Report No. 13. Urbana: NCTE, 1971.

———. "Writing as a Mode of Learning." *College Composition and Communication* 28 (1977): 122–28.

Faigley, Lester. "Judging Writing, Judging Selves." *College Composition and Communication* 40 (1989): 395–412.

Fairclough, Norman. *Critical Discourse Analysis: The Critical Study of Language*. New York: Longman, 1995.

Fish, Stanley. "How to Recognize a Poem When You See One." *Ways of Reading: An Anthology for Writers*. Ed. David Bartholomae and Anthony Petrosky. Boston: St. Martin's, 1992. 140–152.

Fishman, Stephen, and Lucille Parkinson McCarthy. "Teaching for Student Change: A Deweyan Alternative to Radical Pedagogy. *College Composition and Communication* 47 (1996): 342–66.

Fox, Thomas. *The Social Uses of Writing: Politics and Pedagogy*. Norwood: Ablex, 1990.

Freud, Sigmund. "Explanations, Applications, and Orientations." *The Complete Introductory Lectures on Psychoanalysis*. Trans. and ed. James Strachey. New York: Norton, 1966. 600–21.

Fu, Danling. *"My Trouble Is My English": Asian Students and the American Dream*. Portsmouth: Boynton/Cook, 1995.

Goldberger, Nancy Rule. "Cultural Imperatives and Diversity in Ways of Knowing." Goldberger et al. 335–71.

Goldberger, Nancy Rule, Jill Mattuck Tarule, Blythe McVicker Clinchy, and Mary Field Belenky, eds. *Knowledge, Difference, and Power: Essays Inspired by Women's Ways of Knowing*. New York: BasicBooks, 1996.

Goldblatt, Eli. *'Round My Way: Authority and Double-Consciousness in Three Urban High School Writers*. Pittsburgh: U of Pittsburgh P, 1995.

Halliday, M. A. K. *Language as Social Semiotic: The Social Interpretation of Language and Meaning*. Baltimore: University Park, 1978.

Hartsock, Nancy. "Foucault on Power: A Theory for Women?" *Feminism/Postmodernism*. Ed. Linda Nicholson. New York: Routledge, 1990. 157–75.

Haswell, Richard. *Gaining Ground in College: Tales of Development and Interpretation*. SMU Studies in Composition and Rhetoric. Dallas: Southern Methodist UP, 1991.

Heker, Liliana. "The Stolen Party." Verburg 132–37.

Herrington, Anne. "Composing One's Self in a Discipline: Students' and Teachers' Negotiations." *Constructing Rhetorical Education: From the Classroom to the Community*. Ed. Davida Charney and Marie Secor. Carbondale: Southern Illinois UP, 1992. 91–115.

———. "Reflections on Empirical Research: Examining Some Ties between Theory and Action." *Theory and Practice in the Teaching of Writing: Rethinking the Discipline*. Ed. Lee Odell. Carbondale: Southern Illinois UP, 1993. 40–70.

Herrington, Anne, and Deborah Cadman. "Peer Review and Revising in an Anthropology Course: Lessons for Learning." *College Composition and Communication* 42 (1991): 184–99.

Herrington, Anne, and Marcia Curtis. "Basic Writing: Moving the Voices on the Margin to the Center." *Harvard Educational Review* 60 (1990): 489–96.

Hughes, Langston. "Theme for English B." *Montage of a Dream Deferred*. New York: Holt, 1951.

Hymes, Dell. "Models of Interaction of Language and Social Life." *Directions in Sociolinguistics: The Ethnography of Communication*. Ed. J. J. Gumperz and D. Hymes. New York: Holt, 1972.

Kohut, Heinz. *How Does Analysis Cure?* Ed. Arnold I. Goldberg with Paul Stepansky. Chicago: U of Chicago P, 1984.

———. *The Restoration of the Self*. New York: International, 1977.

LeCourt, Donna. "WAC as Critical Pedagogy: The Third Stage?" *Journal of Advanced Composition* 16 (1996): 389–405.

Leki, Ilona. "Coping Strategies of ESL Students in Writing Tasks across the Curriculum." *TESOL Quarterly* 29 (1995): 235–60.

Liu, Sophronia. "So Tsi-fai." Verburg 127–30.

Luke, Allan. "Text and Discourse in Education: An Introduction to Critical Discourse Analysis." *Review of Research in Education* 21 (1995–96). Ed. Michael Apple. DC: American Educational Research Association. 1995. 3–48.

Malinowitz, Harriet. "A Feminist Critique of Writing-in-the-Disciplines. *Feminism and Composition Studies: In Other Words*. Ed. Susan Jarratt and Lynn Worsham. New York: MLA, 1998. 291–312.

———. *Textual Orientations: Lesbian and Gay Students and the Making of Discourse Communities*. Portsmouth: Boynton/Cook, 1995.

Miller, Susan. "Comment on 'A Common Ground: The Essay in Academe.'" *College English* 52 (1990): 330–34.

Newkirk, Thomas. *The Performance of Self in Student Writing*. Portsmouth: Boynton/Cook, 1997.

Noddings, Nell. *Caring*. Berkeley: U of California P, 1984.

North, Steve. "Writing in a Philosophy Class: Three Case Studies." *Research in the Teaching of English* 20 (1986): 225–62.

Odell, Lee. "The Process of Writing and the Process of Learning. *College Composition and Communication* 31 (1980): 42–50.

Odell, Lee, Dixie Goswami, and Anne Herrington. "The Discourse-based Interview: A Procedure for Eliciting the Tacit Knowledge of Writers in Non-academic Settings." *Research on Writing: Principles and Methods*. Ed. Peter Mosenthal, Lynne Tamor, and Sean Walmsley. New York: Longman, 1983. 220–336.

Phelan, Shane. *Getting Specific: Postmodern Lesbian Politics*. Minneapolis: U of Minnesota P, 1994.

Publication Manual of the American Psychological Association. 3rd ed. DC: American Psychological Association, 1983.

Qualley, Donna. *Turns of Thought: Teaching Composition as Reflexive Inquiry*. Portsmouth: Boynton/Cook, 1997.

Rich, Adrienne. "Origins and History of Consciousness." *The Dream of a Common Language: Poems 1974–1977*. New York: Norton, 1978. 7–9.

Rodriguez, Richard. *Hunger of Memory: The Education of Richard Rodriguez*. Boston: Godine, 1982.

Royster, Jacqueline Jones. "When the First Voice You Hear Is Not Your Own." *College Composition and Communication* 47 (1996): 29–40.

Sawatsky, D. Donald, and Thomas Alan Parry. "Silenced Voices Heard: A Tale of Family Survival." *The New Language of Change.* Ed. Steven Friedman. New York: Guilford P, 1993. 405–27.

Shaughnessy, Mina. "Diving In: An Introduction to Basic Writing." *College Composition and Communication* 27 (1976): 234–39.

———. *Errors & Expectations: A Guide for the Teacher of Basic Writing.* New York: Oxford UP, 1977.

Solsken, Judith W. *Literacy, Gender, and Work: In Families and in School.* Norwood: Ablex, 1993.

Sommers, Nancy. "Between the Drafts." *College Composition and Communication* 43 (1992): 23–31.

Spellmeyer, Kurt. "After Theory: From Textuality to Attunement with the World." *College English* 58 (1996): 893–913.

———. "Being Philosophical about Composition: Hermeneutics and the Teaching of Writing." *Into the Field: Sites of Composition Studies.* Ed. Anne Ruggles Gere. New York: MLA, 1993. 9–29.

———. "A Common Ground: The Essay in the Academy." *College English* 51 (1989): 262–76.

———. "Out of the Fashion Industry: From Cultural Studies to the Anthropology of Knowledge." *College Composition and Communication* 47 (1996): 424–436.

———. "Response to Two Comments on 'A Common Ground: The Essay in the Academy.'" *College English* 52 (1990): 334–38.

Sternglass, Marilyn. *Time to Know Them: A Longitudinal Study of Writing and Learning at the College Level.* Mahwah: Erlbaum, 1997.

Stolorow, Robert D., George E. Atwood, and Bernard Brandchaft. *The Intersubjective Perspective.* Northvale: Aronson, 1994.

Thesen, Lucia. "Voices, Discourse and Transition: In Search of New Categories in EAP." *TESOL Quarterly* 31 (1997): 487–511.

Thomas à Kempis. *The Imitation of Christ.* Trans. Richard Whitford. Ed. Edward J. Klein. New York: Harper, 1941.

Tobin, Lad. *Writing Relationships: What Really Happens in the Composition Class.* Portsmouth: Boynton/Cook, 1993.

Toulmin, Stephen. *The Uses of Argument*. Cambridge: Cambridge UP, 1958.

Verburg, Carol. J., ed. *Ourselves among Others: Cross-Cultural Readings for Writers*. New York: St. Martin's P, 1988.

Wagner, Gail. "When a Parent Is Abusive." *Using Self Psychology in Psychotherapy*. Ed. Helene Jackson. Northvale: Aronson, 1991. 243–260.

Wall, Susan, and Nicholas Coles. "Reading Basic Writing: Alternatives to a Pedagogy of Accommodation." *The Politics of Writing Instruction: Postsecondary*. Ed. Richard Bullock and John Trimbur. Portsmouth: Boynton/Cook, 1991. 227–46.

Welsh, Susan. "Writing: In and With the World." *College Composition and Communication* 46 (February 1995): 103–07.

Wolf, Ernest S. *Treating the Self: Elements of Clinical Self Psychology*. New York: Guilford, 1988.

Wolff, Tobias. "An Episode in the Life of Professor Brooke." *In the Garden of the North American Martyrs: A Collection of Short Stories*. New York: Ecco, 1981.

Wordsworth, William. "Preface to the Lyrical Ballads." *The Literary Criticism of William Wordsworth*. Ed. Paul M. Zall. Lincoln: U of Nebraska P, 1966. 38–62.

Young, Richard, Alton Becker, and Kenneth Pike. *Rhetoric: Discovery and Change*. New York: Harcourt, 1970.

Zamel, Vivian. "Strangers in Academia: The Experiences of Faculty and ESL Students across the Curriculum." *College Composition and Communication* 46 (1995): 506–21.

APPENDIX A: INTERVIEWING AND OTHER DETAILS OF THE STUDY

The interpretive stories of Nam, Lawrence, Rachel, and Francois are composed from the following sources: periodic interviews with each, a collection of their writings (all writings for Basic Writing and College Writing and selective writings as they gave them to us from other courses), interviews with their Basic Writing and College Writing teachers, selective interviews with other teachers, and classroom observations of Basic Writing and College Writing. The information collected for each student is listed at the end of this discussion.

Interviews with Students

As we look back on the transcripts and try to explain our approach, we realize that over the course of the study, interview relationships as well as the nature and substance of the interviews with the students changed. Initially, the interviewer/interviewee relationship was more distant, with the researcher posing questions and withholding her views, and the student answering. Toward the end, the relationship was less distant, with more mutual exchange of views.

During first semester of the study's first year, Anne and Elizabeth conducted all interviews with the students in Marcia's Basic Writing class. When we began interviewing during the first semester, we did not know the students, although we knew their names and they knew ours, and we had seen one another, because Elizabeth and Anne had been sitting in on the class (Anne approximately twice per week and Elizabeth once). In the class sessions, we sat taking notes, doing some of the writing activities, and chatting informally with students. With the students' permission, we also read their writings, and thus in that way we did know something more about them than they knew about us.

How each student viewed us when we interviewed him or her—and how the students viewed the interview and decided how they would present themselves—we cannot say. Obviously, we were not their teachers, nor did we perceive ourselves as distant and superior researchers. While not their teachers, we were teachers who were interested observers in their class and who wanted to learn from their vantage point. As we said before and as we tried to convey to the students: they were our expert witnesses, our primary "informants" about their experiences, about their writing, and about the class. In the interviews, our role was to listen empathically, accept the validity and value of their experiences and views, and prompt them to develop their self-understandings further. In retrospect, we believe we positioned ourselves as friendly yet reserved teacher-types—posing questions and nodding affirmatively, but not joining in an active give-and-take of conversation where we would offer our views in an exchange with students. We suspect they were equally reserved with us.

Our interviews included both open-ended questions and more focused, discourse-based questions (Odell et al., "Discourse-Based Interview"). In the first interview, we asked about students' prior experiences in learning English, their writing in school, and any instruction they had received in writing; about their perception of what they were doing in Basic Writing in relation to that prior experience; about writing they might have been doing in other courses; and about specific writings they were doing in Basic Writing. Our discussion of specific writings included discourse-based questions about changes from one draft to the next, aiming to elicit each writer's reflection on the reason for the change, his or her experience with this particular writing, and his or her interactions with the teacher and others. These questions elicited a variety of rich responses—including perceived writing rules, self-image in relation to classmates or the teacher, aims regarding meaning and particular intentions, and reflections on the personal import of a given writing.

In the second interview for the first semester, we asked again about specific writings and about specific aspects of the class (e.g., peer review, class publications, and the way specific essays were introduced and their purpose). We also asked students about their perceptions of Marcia as a teacher, what essay they were most and least satisfied with, what they felt they had learned, and what they were most and least confident of.

For second semester, the interview questions followed the same general format, asking students open-ended questions about aspects of each class, their perceptions of the teacher, their perceptions of themselves in relation to the class, and their reflections on what they had learned and on connections with other classes (including Basic Writing, College Writing, and writing they might be doing in any other University classes).

After the first year, Anne and Marcia conducted all interviews, with Anne interviewing Rachel and Marcia interviewing Francois and Lawrence. In part because these interviews were less frequent than the first-year interviews, they were more wide-ranging and less structured, focusing on what stood out as important for each student and on classes where the student had done or was doing writing that he or she wished to discuss with us. For these interviews, we asked the students to bring copies of any writing they had done for their classes. If they did not have copies available, we would proceed without them, still asking about their experiences in writing for specific courses. In either case, we discussed the nature of specific writing assignments, teachers' expectations and responses, possible connections with writing in other classes, how they felt about what they were asked to do, and the writing. For writings that they indicated were particularly frustrating or important, we inquired about reasons for these feelings. In the final, senior-year interview, we also asked them to reflect on writings they had done during their college years that they felt good about and their experience in College Writing.

For these subsequent interviews—particularly the final ones—our relationship was less reserved and distant. One reason was that all three had successfully completed our Basic and College Writing courses so were in a sense "graduates" of our program and no longer our students. Further, we were meeting because of a mutual choice to do so—an expressed interest on Marcia's and Anne's part to talk with the students and learn from their experiences, and a willingness—and, we would like to think, also an interest—on Rachel's, Francois's, and Lawrence's part to meet with us to talk about their writing and college experiences. That mutual choice to continue with the study and, over time, our growing knowledge of one another, led to a more coequal relation during the interviews. Marcia and Anne were still the interviewers, and we continued to pose some direct questions, but with more give and take—with Francois, Lawrence, and Rachel also asking some questions of us. We were also more forthcoming about our own viewpoints, identifying themes or issues that we felt were important and seeking their perspectives and sense of whether our views were valid. In this way, we were using the students more as inside consultants, that is, as authorities whose opinions we valued.

All interviews lasted approximately one hour. All were typed to produce numbered transcripts which became primary texts for us.

Interviews with Teachers

Marcia was interviewed twice by Elizabeth while she was teaching the section of Basic Writing that the participating students took. We also interviewed each teacher of College Writing twice while he or she was teaching a section with participating students, and in this capacity Anne was interviewed by Elizabeth. The first interviews occurred midway through the semester; the second were at the end. In these interviews, we asked the teachers about past experiences that they believed shaped their teaching, their vision of their course and aims for students as writers, their objectives for particular writings, their approach to responding to students' writings, and their aim for the classroom environment for their course. In regard to the participating students, we asked them to characterize each student, identify whatever stood out to them about the student (e.g., particular writings, critical moments of change, difficulty, or growth), and discuss specific writings, including responding to selected discourse-based interview questions asked of the writer as well.

In selected instances, we interviewed teachers whom the participating students had had for other courses: we did so when students had given us writings from other courses and agreed to our trying to contact the teachers, and when we could track down the teachers and they agreed to the interview. In all cases, we had only one interview with these teachers. We asked them about their purpose for assigning writing, how writing related to other course activities, their perception of the audience for student writings, and their approach to responding to students' writings. In regard to participating students in their classes and their writing, we would provide copies of final drafts of writings the student had done for the class, focusing usually on one writing, and ask them the purpose of each writing and their response to it. More particularly, we asked them to skim the writing and do an informal "read aloud" protocol of their thoughts and reactions as they read.

We used these interviews as secondary sources.

Classroom Observations

Elizabeth and Anne observed all sessions of Marcia's class, taking notes on the day's activities and the substance of spoken comments made by Marcia and the students. We also collected all class comments and did some of the in-class writing that students did.

During second semester, each of us visited the College Writing sections twice, each time for three successive classes—once early in the semester and once midway through. Our purpose for these observations was to get a sense of the class environment, particularly how the teacher interacted with students and how participating students interacted with other students. Over the six days of class we visited, we usually had occasion to observe an in-class writing activity, a peer review session, and a discussion of a class publication and/or other reading as selected by the teacher.

We used our observation notes—each to varying degrees—primarily as background information that we would draw on when it helped us understand something about each student's perceptions or actions—for instance, Nam's developing understanding of an essay, from his reading and the class discussion of a class publication in Basic Writing, and, later, his isolation in College English.

Materials Collected for Each Student: Interviews, Writings, and Class Observations

MATERIALS COLLECTED FOR NAM

Questionnaires at the beginning and end of Basic Writing (1989) and the beginning of College Writing (1990)

Observation notes: daily in Basic Writing, occasional in College Writing

Four interviews with Nam
Fall 1989 (I and II)—with Anne
Spring 1990 (I and II)—with Anne

Subsequent contacts
Summer 1990, exchange of letters with Anne
December 1990 and 1991, exchange of cards with Anne
Spring 1993, exchange of letters and brief phone conversation with Anne

Seven interviews with teachers
Fall 1989 (I and II)—Marcia with Elizabeth
Fall 1989 (I)—philosophy teacher with Anne
Spring 1990 (I and II)—College Writing teacher with Anne
Spring 1991 (I and II)—the teacher of Nam's section of
Methods of Inquiry in Psychology and the course supervisor, with Anne

Basic Writing essays (fall 1989), with drafts and process notes for all except the second essay
1. "Family Traditions Live!" (photograph interpretation)

2. "Love Your Neighbors As I Have Love[d] You"
3. "When Things Get Tough . . . " (interpretation of "So Tsi-fai" by Sophronia Liu)
4. "Family Solitary" (prompted by Richard Rodriguez's "Aria")
5. "Thou Shall Not Judge"

College Writing essays (spring 1990), with drafts and process notes for all except the second essay
1. "Self-Discipline" (plus initial notes)
2. "Memorable Object" (plus first draft)
3. "Money Is Not Everything" (plus two drafts)
4. "One of Those Days" (plus two drafts)
5. "A Fraud in GPA" (plus two drafts)
6. "The Lord Is My Shepherd" (plus five drafts)
7. "A Helping Hand" (plus two drafts)

Essays for other courses
Fall 1989—two papers for Introduction to Philosophy
Spring 1990—three of four laboratory reports for Methods of Inquiry in Psychology

MATERIALS COLLECTED FOR LAWRENCE/STEVEN

Original questionnaire (1989)

Observation notes: daily in English 111, occasional in English 112

Five interviews
Fall 1989 (I and II)—with Anne
Spring 1990 (I and II)—with Marcia
Spring 1993—with Marcia

Four interviews with teachers
Fall 1989 (I and II)—Marcia with Elizabeth
Spring 1990 (I and II)—Anne with Elizabeth

Basic Writing Essays
1. "Life on the Streets" (photograph interpretation)
2. "A Significant Event" (modeled on Isak Dinesen's "The Iguana")
3. "The Symptoms of Suicide" (interpretation of Sophronia Liu's "So Tsi-fai")
4. Pamphlet for gay teenagers (supposed revision of "A Significant Event")
5. "Sexism in China" (reading project essay)

College Writing Essays
1. "Free to Be You and Me"

    2. "Breaking Traditions"
    3. "Fur is Dead"
    4. "The State of the World Today"
    5. "Is Homosexuality Normal?"
    6. "Dead or Alive"

Essays for other courses

    Spring 1990—untitled final examination paper for Social Diversity in Education (UMass)

    Fall 1990—"A Re-Genesis," "Letting Go," "Live to Tell," and "Oh Father," all for Spiritual Autobiography (comparative literature, UMass); two short papers for Women's Studies 187 (UMass)

    Spring 1991—one paper for Comparative Literature 132 (UMass); one short paper for Health Services: Introduction to and Training in Alcohol and Drug Education (UMass)

    Fall 1991—two papers (including drafts) for Women and Gender Studies 11 (Amherst College); two papers for Sociology: Society and the Individual (UMass)

    Spring 1992—"The Conceptions of the Absolute" (two drafts) for course identified by Lawrence/Steven as "Good and Evil: East Meets West Something Ethics I Hated It" (Comparative Literature, UMass); "Gender Studies" (proposal for Bachelor's Degree in Individual Concentration)

    Fall 1992—"On Claude Hartland's *The Story of a Life*" for The History of Homosexuality (Amherst College)

    Spring 1993—"Men Acting for Change" for independent study project (UMass)

    Fall 1993—five short papers (two drafts each) for Education: Race, Class, Culture & Gender in the Classroom (Mount Holyoke); three papers for Black Studies 27 (Amherst College); three papers for Philosophy 381 (UMass)

    Spring 1994—"Madonna: The Queer Queen" for The Cross-Cultural Construction of Gender (Amherst College); two papers for Philosophy 392 (UMass); three papers for Political Science 32: Authority & Sexuality (Amherst College)

MATERIALS COLLECTED FOR RACHEL

Original questionnaire (1990)

Observation notes: occasional in English 112

Five interviews
    Spring 1990 (I and II)—with Anne
    Spring 1991—with Anne
    Spring 1993 (I and II)—with Anne

Interviews with Teachers

Spring 1990 (I and II)—College Writing teacher with Anne

Spring 1991 (I and II)—the teacher of Nam's section of Methods of Inquiry in Psychology (for purposes of comparison) and the course supervisor with Anne

College Writing essays (spring 1990), with drafts and process notes for all

1. "The Operation"
2. "It's a typical Sunday at UMass . . ." (an observation of people interacting)
3. "What is a best friend?"
4. "Famous Faces" (interpretation of advertising)
5. "How Much Do They Really Hurt?"
6. "Win or Lose?"

Essays for other courses

Spring 1990—"The Culture of Poverty" and "Arguments: Pro & Con on the Trend of More Women in the Work Force," both for Social Problems (sociology)

Fall 1990—"'Tony' Paper" (book review for Developmental Psychology); two papers for Art History; four laboratory reports for Methods of Inquiry in Psychology; review of research studying physiological bases of alcohol addiction for Physiological Psychology

Fall 1991—"Grace Paley: An Inspiration to Jewish People," "Jewish People: Struggles and Successes, Past and Present," "Learning About Homosexuality," and untitled final essay exam, all for Foundations in Human Services (education); "Social Change and Modes of Production" for Introduction to Anthropology

Spring 1992—"Antisocial Personality Disorder from the Psychodynamic Perspective," "Antisocial Personality Disorder from a Rogerian Perspective," and "Antisocial Personality Disorder: Radical and Psychodynamic Behaviorism Perspectives," all for Theories of Personality (psychology); personal statement for graduate studies in clinical psychology, for Clinical Psychology; extensive outline for presenting findings from an interview, extensive outline for a profile of rape offenders, and "Kyle: The Case Study of a Rape Offender," all for Human Sexuality (psychology); "Global Assembly Lines," for Introduction to Women's Studies

Fall 1992—"Prospectus for the Nature of Intimacy among Young Adults: A Senior Honors Thesis"

Spring 1993—"Cognitive Tasks with Korsakoff's Syndrome Patients," for Cognitive Psychology; "Intimacy Issues among Young Adults: A Study of Family Alcoholism and Its Effect upon Children" (senior honors thesis in psychology)

MATERIALS COLLECTED FOR FRANCOIS

Original Questionnaire (1989)

Observation notes: daily in English 111, occasional in English 112

Five interviews with Francois
Fall 1989 (I and II)—with Elizabeth
Spring 1990 (I and II)—with Elizabeth
Spring 1993—with Marcia

Five interviews with teachers
Fall 1989 (I and II)—Marcia with Elizabeth
Spring 1990 (I and II)—Tim with Elizabeth
Spring 1990 (I)—Social Problems TA with Elizabeth

Basic Writing Essays
1. "MAN vs NATURE" (photograph interpretation)
2. "You've Got to Have Faith"
3. "BLIND-INNOCENT-PREJUDICE" (interpretation of Liliana Heker's "The Stolen Party")
4. "A BILINGUAL AND SOCIAL STRUGGLE"
5. Untitled (on Richard Wright's *Black Boy*)

College Writing Essays
1. "My Joy" (with drafts and process notes)
2. "A Meaningful Coin" (with drafts and process notes)
3. "ZooMass"
4. "Formal Training Vs Experience"
5. Untitled letter to L.
6. End-of-year "Retrospective"

Essays for other courses
Spring 1990—"My Experience in Field Work," "When I say suppression . . . ," and "An American World View," all for Field Work in Anthropology (anthropology); "Now! If I was to say that I was living . . ." for Social Problems (sociology)
Fall 1990–spring 1991—"Gender Autobiography" for Sociology of Sex Roles (sociology)
Fall 1991–spring 1992—"Summary: Beyond Handouts" for Junior Year Writing in Sociology (sociology)
Fall 1992–spring 1993—"The Plan to Do Something" for Juvenile Delinquency (sociology); untitled final examination paper for Juvenile Delinquency (sociology); reflective paper for Culture through Film (anthropology)
Fall 1993–spring 1994—untitled (brief) final term project and untitled (longer) final examination research paper/interview, both for Education 391

APPENDIX B: SYLLABI FOR BASIC AND COLLEGE WRITING, 1989–90

WORK SCHEDULE

ENGLISH 111
WRITING ABOUT WRITING:
OBSERVATION AND INTERPRETATION

* * * * * * *

READING IMAGES:

Wed. 9/6
    1ˢᵗ Hour: Course Introduction
                    Brief Introduction to Writing 1
                    Observe "American Gothic" or other photo selected by instructor. Then set aside and jot down two categories: OBSERVATIONS (outer) and INTERPRETATIONS (inner).
    2ⁿᵈ Hour: Share jottings in pairs or small groups, paying particular attention to differing interpretations. Finish with short class discussion of relationship between "observation" and "interpretation."

Fri. 9/8
    Class: Complete previous hour's discussion, if necessary. Introduce writing topic: "Reading an Image," the presentation and interpretation of a photograph selected by the writer.
               Select photo from available collection or another of writer's own choosing.
    Outside: Using the two-category system developed for "American Gothic," brainstorm some notes on selected photo for next class hour.

Mon. 9/11
    1ˢᵗ Hour: Discuss briefly, in full group, work completed
                    outside. Expand brainstorm notes; share in pairs;
                    expand further.
    2ⁿᵈ Hour: Begin drafting.

Wed. 9/13
    1ˢᵗ Hour: Continue drafting.
                    Share drafts (in peer response groups).
    2ⁿᵈ Hour: Revise.

Fri. 9/15
    Class: Peer respond, revise, and/or edit as appropriate.
                    Final draft due 9/18.
                    Also, reading journal to be offered for response,
                    9/18

* * * * * * * *

READING EXPERIENCE:

Mon. 9/18
    1ˢᵗ Hour: Writing I due.
                    * * 1ˢᵗ Journal Response Session * *
                    Brief introduction to Writing II
                    Guided Reading of Isak Dinesen's "The Iguana."
    2ⁿᵈ Hour: "Observation" and "Interpretation"
                    I. *Summarize* Dinesen's story in your own words:
                    that is, write a brief, condensed version of the
                    story.
                    Discuss summaries in full group in effort to
                    define "summary" and prepare for interpretation
                    to follow.
                    II. *Interpret* Dinesen's story by completing the
                    message she begins when she writes, "For the
                    sake of your own eyes and heart . . . ."
                    Share interpretations or, if necessary,
    Outside: Complete the hour's work outside class, and
                    open next hour with sharing.

Wed. 9/20
    1ˢᵗ Hour: Having observed, summarized, and interpreted
                    Dinesen's experiences, brainstorm some of your
                    own. Simply recall some events/experiences from
                    your life and observations paying particular

attention to those you think contain a generaliz-
able lesson from which others might learn.
Expand upon a few perhaps related experiences
in rough note form.

2nd Hour: Share lists in brainstorm pairs and then in full
group.
Review materials collected thus far in order to
begin planning Writing II, "Significant Experiences." For this essay, you have a number of
choices: you may re-present and interpret
Dinesen's experiences to another person or group
of people; you may present and interpret your
own experiences to another person or group; you
may use both Dinesen's experiences and your
own to express a particular lesson for others. Just
remember: *significant* events say something to
other people, not just to you. They help reveal
the meaning of other events; they are events you
can help your readers interpret and take lessons
from *for themselves*. In the same way, significant
event essays reach beyond observing these events
to suggest a broader lesson we can learn from
them.

Outside: Begin drafting Writing II.

Fri. 9/22

Class: Continue drafting Writing II.

Outside: Complete rough draft for peer response group
next class hour.

Mon. 9/25

1st Hour: Share rough drafts in peer response groups and
complete peer response forms.

2nd Hour: Using peer response forms as a guide, begin
revising.

Outside: Continue revising Writing II.

Wed. 9/27

1st Hour: Share and respond to revised (mid-process) drafts
in full and small groups.

2nd Hour: Make any further revisions as necessary.

Outside: Complete Writing II and prepare for final editing
next class hour.

Fri. 9/29

Class: Edit final drafts individually and in small groups.

Outside: Complete final draft of Writing II and prepare to submit portfolio next class hour.

* *

READING "A WORLD IN A GRAIN OF SAND":

Mon. 10/2
    Class: Submit Writing II.
               Writing III introduced.
               Guided reading of Liliana Heker's "The Stolen Party."

Guided Reading

1. Read through the story once making quick checks in the margin to note anything that strikes you as important, familiar, or just plain puzzling.
2. Discuss initial reading in full group focusing on passages various readers marked. The first goal should be to understanding any puzzling passages. The second goal should be to understand why significant passages stood out as significant to the various readers and why different readers chose the different passages they did.
3. Re-read the story. This time, stop at your checkmarks and try to identify your own reasons for making them. Make fuller notes in the margin about your observations and interpretations.
4. Following the second reading, write out briefly your overall thoughts and feelings, describing the story's significance for you. Discuss the day's work in small groups and then in full group.

Wed. 10/4
    Class: Review "The Stolen Party" and notes prepared.
               Explore the story through guided writing.

Guided Writing

1. Imagine you are one of the main characters in "The Stolen Party" and express in your own words that character's understanding of the day's events.
2. Imagine you yourself were one of the invited guests, and express your own observations and interpretations.
3. Imagine Heker, the author, is a member of your peer response group. Say back to her what you believe she meant her readers to understand from her story.

Outside: Review "The Stolen Party" and your guided writing.

Fri. 10/6

Class: Read Sophronia Liu's "So Tsi-fai" following the Guided Reading procedure.

Outside: Complete Guided Writing of "So Tsi-fai" as outlined in class.

Mon. 10/9

1st Hour: Discuss "So Tsi-fai" in full group.
Writing III introduced.
Begin planning Writing III individually and in small groups. As you did with Dinesen's "The Iguana," you may again focus your essay on one or both of the stories we've read and offer your interpretation to readers, or you may use the stories to support and illustrate your own views on the social issues they raise, drawing on examples from your own personal experience and observations as well.

2nd Hour: Begin drafting.

Outside: Complete a rough draft of Writing III and prepare for peer response groups.

Wed. 10/11

1st Hour: Share rough drafts in peer response groups.
2nd Hour: Begin revising.
Outside: Continue revising paying particular attention to your own message and focus.

Fri. 10/13

Class: Share revised drafts with peer group paying attention to introduction, organization, and development.

Outside: Complete final draft of Writing III and prepare for small group edit next hour. Also prepare for Journal Response Session next class.

Mon. 10/16

1st Hour: Small group edit. Final draft and full portfolio submitted at end of class.

2nd Hour: Journal Response Session.

Wed. 10/18   OPEN SCHEDULE
Fri. 10/20   OPEN SCHEDULE

✳ ✳

READING POEMS, ESSAYS, AND OTHER MEDIA:

Mon. 10/23
1st Hour:	Writing IV introduced. Read Langston Hughes's "Theme for English B." Draft in rough form—poetry or prose—your own "Theme" beginning with Hughes's opening six lines.
2nd Hour:	Share themes in full group. Analyze Hughes's "Theme" through guided writing.

Guided Writing

1. Imagine Hughes is a member of your peer response group. Say back to him what you hear him describe as his principal problem or dilemma. Remember: you're not telling him what his problem is; *you're telling him what you hear him identify as his problem.*
2. Explain which feelings, ideas, or experiences he expresses seem similar to ones you've had and which seem different.
3. Imagine you are the teacher in Hughes's English class and comment on his "Theme."
4. Imagine you are the author or a character from one of your readings—including your journal books—and say something to Hughes. Or imagine you are Hughes and comment on one of these readings.

Wed. 10/25
1st Hour:	Share guided writings in full group.
2nd Hour:	Read Richard Rodriguez's "Aria" following Guided Reading procedures for a first reading.
Outside:	If necessary, complete first reading of "Aria."

Fri. 10/27
Class:	Do a second reading of "Aria" following Guided Reading procedures.
Outside:	Complete work begun in class if necessary.

Mon. 10/30
1st Hour:	Plan Writing IV individually and in small groups. Report plans to full group.
2nd Hour:	Begin drafting Writing IV.
Outside:	Continue drafting.

Wed. 11/1
>   1st Hour: Continue drafting.
>   2nd Hour: Discuss progress and, especially, difficulties
>   encountered first in small groups, then in full
>   group.
>   Outside: Complete rough draft of Writing IV.

Fri. 11/3
>   Class: OPEN SCHEDULE
>   Outside: Prepare rough draft for peer response session
>   next hour.

Mon. 11/6
>   1st Hour: Share drafts in peer response session.
>   2nd Hour: Revise.
>   Outside: Complete revised (mid-process) draft and prepare
>   for peer editing session.

Wed. 11/8
>   1st Hour: Peer edit Writing IV.
>   Full group discussion of most common editing
>   problems and errors.
>   2nd Hour: Complete final draft. Continue working outside
>   class, if necessary. Final draft and portfolio due
>   Monday, November 13.

Fri. 11/10
>   Class: OPEN SCHEDULE

** OUTSIDE: BRING FULL PORTFOLIO AS WELL AS
>   WRITING IV TO NEXT CLASS. ALSO BRING
>   JOURNAL FOR JOURNAL RESPONSE
>   SESSION.

* *

READING OURSELVES:

Mon. 11/13
>   1st Hour: Writing IV due.
>   Journal Response Session.
>   Review portfolio and select two (2) writings to be
>   revised for final grades.
>   Determine sorts of revisions needed and plan
>   revisions.

Wed 11/15–Wed. 11/22
    Class: OPEN SCHEDULE

Fri. 11/24—HOLIDAY

                     *

READING OURSELVES IN OTHERS:

Mon. 11/27
    1st Hour: Writing V introduced.
                   Final Journal Response Session.
                   Begin formulating possible topics based on
                   Reading Journals.
                   Share reading journals and reading project ideas
                   in small groups.
    2nd Hour: Report to full group.
                   Begin drafting one or two paragraph prospectus
                   (plan) for reading project.
    Outside: Finish prospectus.

Wed. 11/29
    1st Hour: Share prospectuses in small groups with a view to
                   developing both a framing interpretation and
                   supporting examples.
                   Report to full group for discussion.
    2nd Hour: Return to reading journal to begin gathering
                   support material in note form and drafting an
                   introduction that will frame it.
    Outside: Finish notes and introduction.

Fri. 12/1
    Class: Begin drafting full essay.
    Outside: Complete rough draft for peer response session
                   next hour.

Mon. 12/4
    1st Hour: Share rough drafts in peer groups.
    2nd Hour: Begin revising from group notes.

Wed. 12/6
    Class: Continue revising.
    Outside: Complete revised draft and prepare for group
                   edit next hour.
Fri. 12/8
    Class: Group edit of Writing V.

Full group discussion of particular editing problems.

Outside: Complete final revising and editing of Writing V, which is due next hour.

* *

THE READING PROJECT AND READING JOURNAL

For the coming weeks, along with your regular class assignments, you will be reading at least two books selected from the list below and keeping a journal in preparation for a last major essay, which you will develop as you read and reflect on your reading in your journal.

THE READING JOURNAL

While your reading will aim toward the essay you will write, you do not need to worry about developing a topic at the start. Instead, your topic will develop gradually from the journal you keep. For this to happen, it is important that you keep up with both the reading and the journal-keeping. THIS IMPORTANCE CANNOT BE STRESSED ENOUGH. Keep your journal notes in a specially designated notebook or folder.

In your reading and journal-keeping, follow this process:

1. As you read, mark in the book's margin next to any passages—descriptions, events, statements by the writer, dialogues between characters, etc.—that seem important to you for any reason.

2. When you stop reading—whether you've been reading for just a few minutes or a few hours—jot down the page numbers of the section you've just read and make some notes in your journal. These notes should include both a "summary" of this section—what was discussed; what happened; perhaps what new topic, idea, person, or scene was introduced—and an "interpretation" of its meaning for you—that is, a record of your thoughts and reactions as you read. Perhaps something reminded you of yourself or your own experience or someone you know. Perhaps something in this reading reminded you of an earlier event in the same book or in another class reading. Perhaps this section of the book puzzled you or angered you or excited you for some reason. Try to get at the reason in your notes.

3. When you've finished your notes, skim over one more time the section of the book you just read to see whether you've left any-

thing important out of your journal. If you discover new, "revised" thoughts, add them to your journal entry.

4. When you've finished reading an entire book, look over your journal and try to describe for yourself in writing the sorts of things you found significant. Skim over your journal and marginal notes and locate particularly striking points or passages in the book. Try to identify ways in which the various passages connect to other passages in this book or in other readings. Find the patterns among the various ideas or events that struck you as you read. Group them under larger headings or "themes." Try some of the Guided Writing techniques you've developed in class. Even compose for yourself a set of Guided Writing questions dealing with your particular book.

* *

READING PROJECT BOOK LIST

Letourneau's Used Auto Parts, Carolyn Chute
The Parish on the Hill, Mary D. Curran
Yellow Raft on Blue Water, Michael Dorris
China Men, Maxine Hong Kingston
Brown Girl, Brownstones, Paule Marshall
Hunger of Memory, Richard Rodriguez
Giants in the Earth, O. E. Rolvaag
Black Boy, Richard Wright

English 112: College Writing
SPRING 1990

Required Texts:
Diana Hacker, *A Writer's Reference*. New York: St. Martin's Press. A college edition of a standard desk dictionary.

Goal and Rationale
The goal of this course is to help you become better able to accomplish the writing you will be asked to do here at the University and in your life generally. Those of us in the Writing Program believe that writing is most usefully considered an activity, not a subject—that is, you are more likely to learn by doing, with some coaching, than by listening to lectures about good writing. This writing course is rather like a studio course in dance or music, or like the practice and performance schedule

for a varsity sport. It is therefore especially important that you attend class, where some of the writing and editing, and most of the coaching, takes place.

Writing is also an activity that involves discovering and making choices about what to say and how to say it in order to satisfy yourself and accomplish your purpose for an audience. The class will be your most immediate audience: peer response groups will provide an opportunity for you to receive response to early drafts; the class as a whole will be the audience for final drafts, which will be published in class regularly.

Required Amount of Writing

As the Writing Schedule indicates, you are to complete seven finished essays of approximately three to four pages, with preliminary notes, first drafts and mid-process drafts attached. In addition, you are to keep a regular journal and complete other shorter writing assignments and class work (e.g., peer review comments). You should plan to spend an average of five hours a week outside of class for your work for this class.

Essays

One of the aims of College Writing is to give you occasion to write a variety of types of essays—for various purposes and audiences, using various lines of development, and drawing on various sources of information (for example, your own experiences, observations, readings).

One of the essays will be a <u>documented essay</u>. The primary purpose of this essay is for you to extend your knowledge of some topic that interests you by doing some additional research and drawing on it to develop a point you want to make. A secondary aim is to gain more facility using a standard form of academic documentation. (You'll receive more information about this essay from your teacher.)

A major aim of the course is that you learn to manage the process of writing, working through multiple drafts of an essay to explore and develop your ideas and voice, and craft the essay for readers. Given this aim, we require multiple drafts for each essay. As you work from one draft to the next, you'll have the chance to assess it yourself and also receive some feedback from classmates and/or your teacher. The Writing Schedule lists the due dates for these drafts. All are due at the beginning of class. If you do not have a preliminary draft when it is due, it counts as an absence. If you do not have a final draft when due, it counts as a zero on your record. Late papers will not be accepted.

First Draft. Consider this draft an exploratory draft where you are getting down in some form all the information and ideas that come to mind and possibly trying out different approaches. Don't be too concerned with organization or how it will look to readers. Your aim is to explore possibilities and get a good bit down in writing to work with. Aim for three to four pages.

Mid-Process Draft(s). With this draft, you want to think more about readers and your intended purpose. Your first draft is your starting point although you may change it substantially. You are likely to re-organize, add and cut sections, rewrite to clarify your thinking, convey a particular tone of voice, and make passages more readable or striking.

Final Draft. This draft should be the version you are ready to present to readers as finished, as an essay that you have thought through and crafted as best you can, working with the feedback you received in process.

One of your responsibilities in preparing the final draft is to find and correct any mistakes in spelling, grammar, or usage. So, proofread carefully. Here is where Hacker, *A Writer's Reference*, and the dictionary come into play. Familiarize yourself with Hacker, and if you have any questions about using it, please ask. It's fine to admit you don't understand something; it's not fine to fail to proofread using the resources available to you.

All final drafts are to meet standard manuscript requirements. Refer to Hacker (160–62) for an explanation of these requirements.

When you submit your final draft, attach to it all preliminary work: all notes, drafts, peer-editing comments—everything. If you do not do so, your final draft will not be accepted and will count in your grade as a zero.

The Journal

The journal is for informal, personal writing and reflection. Use it as you wish. We ask you to keep it because we want you to be writing regularly, experimenting with your writing, and developing a writer's habit of observing and reflecting. Use it to play with language, too, if you want. Plan to write for at least one hour a week. It'll be more productive for you if you try to make entries three or four times during each week. That will translate into at least three or four pages per week. Your teacher will check the journal periodically, but will not read any passages that you mark as private.

Your Portfolio

As you move through the semester, you will be creating a portfolio of all your written work. The portfolio will include the major essays, all the drafts and preliminary work that accompany the final draft, the additional in-class and out-of-class writing exercises you do, and the written feedback you give to classmates about their writing.

Attendance

It is Writing Program policy that each of you is allowed one week's worth of class "absences" during the semester, no questions asked. These permitted absences are intended to cover the occasional emergency and illness. Save them. Except for exceptional circumstances, being sick does not entitle you to an extra absence. For each absence beyond the allowed week, you lose a half-grade for the semester.

If on a day when a draft is due you come without an adequate draft, you will be counted as absent. Missing one of the three regularly scheduled conferences counts as two absences.

Grading

Your end-of-semester grade will be based on attendance, completion of all assignments on time, the quality of your work, and your participation and improvement. So that you will know how you are doing in the course, you will receive a formal mid-semester evaluation at or before the second conference.

You should understand that the University's grading pattern is this: a grade of C indicates adequate or average work; A's and B's are reserved for above average work. They are honors grades. On the other end of the spectrum, a D indicates below-average work, and an F indicates failure without credit.

Conference and Office Hours

Twice during the semester, classes will be canceled for individual conferences with your teacher. These conferences will give you an opportunity to confer in more depth about your writing and your progress in the course. A third conference will be scheduled during final examination week.

Your teacher will also have regularly scheduled office hours. That's time set aside for you, so we encourage you to make use of it. For instance, you might want to stop by to discuss a draft you're working on or clarify questions you have about the course.

Sequence of Essay Units for Anne Herrington's Section of College Writing, Spring 1990

1. *Open Topic,* using structured guidelines for brainstorming possible topics, developing ideas, offering peer feedback, and deciding on a focus.

2. *Reflections on Tradition/Ceremony.* Here are my notes from Spring 1990 explanatory materials presented to graduate teaching assistants: "The aim of this unit was for students to reflect on themselves in a relation to a social group, tradition, or ceremony that they have participated in or observed. The aim for each writer was to try to come to understand something about the meaning or force of that tradition or their experience of it. I also assumed that the activity would provide an occasion for the class as a whole to become more aware of the diversity of family and ethnic traditions honored (or, at least, experienced) by members of the class and for reflecting on the nature of their participation in those activities."

   Prompts: (1) An episode of a television situation comedy, "The Wonder Years," where an adolescent non-Jewish male attends the Bar Mitzvah of his friend, feeling apart because he does not know the tradition and feels wistful that he is not a part of it. (2) An in-class brainstorming activity using Thanksgiving as the focal tradition. I introduced these heuristics: Try on alternative perspectives. For example, how would an outsider view x (the tradition)? An insider who believes in/follows x? An insider who does not? Consider x in relation to a larger context. Consider x as the context and how individuals within that context experience it. Consider how x may have changed over time. . . .

3. *Public Language.* I introduced it with public news reports and opinion essays regarding language that is used to stereotype and demean. The first was Gloria Naylor's "Hers" column (the *New York Times,* February 20, 1986) on how the meaning and force of the word "nigger" depends on who says it to whom. The second was a series of three articles from the campus newspaper on "Hate" graffiti on campus. The writing prompts asked students to consider instances where they may have been the subject of such language and, whether they had or not, its possible force.

4. *Persuasive Essay on a Public Issue,* written in the genre of an op-ed piece for a newspaper. In preparation, students were to read a major newspaper (e.g., the *New York Times* or *Boston Globe*) for a week and

make journal entries. I instructed them as follows: "Comment on anything that strikes you as interesting or that you react to in some way: makes you angry, makes you sad, makes you laugh, makes you think about something else. Use the journal to write out your reactions and thoughts."

In class, I presented persuasion as an attempt to gain cooperation, not to do combat or browbeat opponents. Consistent with this view, I introduced strategies for considering multiple perspectives, clarifying a particular aim for readers (e.g., to make them aware of a problem, to convince them of a particular perspective on something, or to persuade them to a particular course of action), and finding bridges of shared understanding with potential readers.

5. *Documented Essay.* Here is how I presented it to students in 1990: "The purpose of this essay is for you to extend your knowledge of some topic by doing some additional research and drawing upon it to develop your position. As with all essays you write, it should have a purpose and some point to make to readers and be interesting. A secondary purpose is for you to use a standard form of academic documentation accurately and with some finesse.

"I encourage you to begin with a previous essay for this course. It could be one that could be strengthened by incorporating additional information. It could be one that suggested a related issue to you that you want to investigate. Either way, choose something of interest to you."

The in-class work and writing schedule included brainstorming of possible topics from previous essays; a proposal for the essay; a short writing exercise requiring documentation using a newspaper article on an appeal to Canada's Supreme Court regarding Canada's "antihate laws," charging that they violate free speech guarantees of Canada's Charter of Rights and Freedoms; and three successive drafts and revisions.

6. *Open Topic.* When introducing it in class, I asked students to read through their journals and brainstorm two or three possible essay ideas that came to mind from their journal entries.

7. *Submission of Full Portfolio of Essays, along with a Portfolio Review Essay* reflecting on each essay written during the course, accomplishments for the semester, and perceptions of oneself as a writer.

INDEX

AUTHORS

Anne J. Herrington is professor of English and former director of the Writing Program at the University of Massachusetts Amherst. She regularly teaches first-year writing courses and other undergraduate and graduate courses on writing pedagogy and research. With Charles Moran, she co-edited *Writing, Teaching, and Learning in the Disciplines*, and, with Marcia Curtis, Moran, and Sara Stelzner, she co-edited the CD-ROM *Teaching in Process: Multimedia Resources for Writing Teachers*. She has conducted classroom-based research studies of writing and learning in various disciplines and published numerous articles on writing across the curriculum and, with Marcia Curtis, articles on basic writing curricula. Most recently, she has been working with a group of K–12 teachers on classroom-based "teacher-researcher" projects.

Marcia Curtis is deputy director of the Writing Program at the University of Massachusetts Amherst and director of its Basic Writing course. She regularly teaches both Basic Writing and an experimental grammar course. She contributed to and co-edited *The Composition of Our "selves"*, a textbook with readings for first-year writing courses. With Herrington, Moran, and Stelzner, she co-edited the CD-ROM *Teaching in Process: Multi-media Resources for Writing Teachers*. She has published on basic writing, computers and writing, and research issues for studying computer classroom pedagogy. Most recently, she has been developing a new approach to grammar instruction that links issues of grammar with issues of composing.

This book was set in Sabon by Electronic Imaging.
The typeface used on the cover was Berling.
The book was printed on 50-lb. Lynx Opaque by Versa Press, Inc.